Regulating Content on Social Media

Regulating Content on Social Media

Copyright, Terms of Service and Technological Features

Corinne Tan

UCLPRESS

First published in 2018 by
UCL Press
University College London
Gower Street
London WC1E 6BT

Available to download free: www.ucl.ac.uk/ucl-press

A CIP catalogue record for this book is available from The British Library.

ISBN: 978–1–78735–173–8 (Hbk.)
ISBN: 978–1–78735–172–1 (Pbk.)
ISBN: 978–1–78735–171–4 (PDF)
ISBN: 978–1–78735–174–5 (epub)
ISBN: 978–1–78735–175–2 (mobi)
ISBN: 978–1–78735–176–9 (html)
DOI: https://doi.org/10.14324/111.9781787351714

Prologue

In this book I analyse how the content-generative behaviours of social media users are regulated from a copyright perspective. My focus is on comparing copyright laws with other regulatory factors on social media. These factors, being the terms of service and the technological features of social media platforms, can alter the effectiveness of the regulation of content-generative behaviours by copyright laws. In making this assessment, I examine the regulation of such behaviours across five social media platforms, namely Facebook, Pinterest, YouTube, Twitter and Wikipedia. Together these popular platforms on which users generate content serve as a good sample for my purpose.

In particular, I consider the application of copyright laws to various uses on social media and the ways in which this application is aligned with the terms of service and the technological features of social media platforms. I have chosen to examine the terms of service and the technological features as they constitute the points of contact between users and social media platforms which can be readily surveyed.

I have two reasons for taking this approach. The primary reason relates to the dearth of in-depth discussions of how specific social media platforms affect the role that laws, including copyright laws, play in securing compliance from their users. The examination of the application of the terms of service and the influence of the technological features on users' content-generative behaviours is an attempt to address this. The second reason is to stimulate more critical reflections on how laws should develop to take into account the influence of social media platforms on user behaviours, through reform that gives users more leeway for the activities in which they engage. This is crucial as the platforms are becoming increasingly ubiquitous. With this book I will demonstrate how the regulation of users' content-generative behaviours by copyright laws, the terms of service and the technological features can be analysed in a structured way, even in a space as random as social media.

In this respect I will refer to the copyright laws of three jurisdictions – the United States, the United Kingdom and Australia – as well as to the terms of service and the technological features of the five social media platforms. I will also use a case study detailing the content-generative activities undertaken by a hypothetical user named Jane Doe and other users on the relevant social media platforms. This provides an anchor around which to conduct specific discussions on how copyright laws and the other two factors can regulate users' content-generative behaviours. Finally, I draw further from earlier empirical studies to support the arguments I will make in this book.

Acknowledgements

This book began life as a doctoral thesis undertaken at the Melbourne Law School. I owe a debt of gratitude in conceptualising my research to my supervisors, Megan Richardson, Sam Ricketson and Graeme Austin, who have patiently guided me throughout the various stages of my research. Without their incisive comments, unwavering dedication and encouragement, I would not have overcome the hurdles in completing my research, let alone this book.

Many others have contributed to this book along the way. I am thankful to have the support, resources and stimulating conversations I needed to complete the book as a visiting scholar at the Centre for Media and Communications Law at the Law School from April to June 2017. Thank you also to the colleagues and friends I met at the Law School, who supported me in various ways during this process. In particular, I would like to thank Adrienne Stone, Andrew Christie, Antje Missbach, Jason Bosland, Matthew Harding, Natalia Jevglevskaja and Rheny Pulungan. I am grateful for other friends outside the Law School such as Burton Ong, Candice Tan, Dorothy Ang, Mehmet Gurkan, Michelle Nai, Rena Tan, Yanni Tan and Wong Shiau Ching, who have kept me going with their advice, good humour and friendship throughout.

Finally, I would like to express my deepest appreciation to my family. To my dearest Kapilesh Taneja: Words cannot express my gratitude for having a partner like you. You are the most ‘leaned in’ partner any girl can dream of – you tirelessly took over more than your fair share of household duties. Thank you for fuelling my dream and for adopting it as your own. To my mother- and father-in-law: Thank you for your sacrifice in coming over to support me as a first-time mother while I worked on this book – I am forever in your debt. To my dearest son Keyan: Thank you for teaching me the value of time management, and for being an ongoing reminder to be present wherever I am.

Contents

List of tables

Introduction

I. Regulation on social media

In this book, I analyse how the content-generative behaviours of social media users are regulated from a copyright perspective. My focus is on comparing copyright laws with other regulatory factors on social media. These factors, being the terms of service and the technological features of social media platforms, can operate to alter the effectiveness of the regulation of content-generative behaviours by copyright laws. In leading up to this assessment, I examine the regulation of such behaviours across five social media platforms – namely Facebook, Pinterest, YouTube, Twitter and Wikipedia – by copyright laws, the terms of service and the technological features. Choosing to do so allows me to confine my analysis of a law's application to the diverse activities occurring on social media in a tangible way; it also accommodates a richer analysis of the application of a particular legal regime (ie, copyright laws) to these activities.

The sample of social media platforms I have selected for the book comprises popular platforms[1] on which users generate content. Each of these platforms falls under one of the four (out of a total of six) categories of social media under Kaplan and Haenlein's classification system – namely social networking sites, content communities, blogs and collaborative projects.[2] This gives me the opportunity to scrutinise, at a micro-level, how effectively copyright laws regulate users' content-generative behaviours on the chosen social media platforms.

The importance of studying how user behaviours are regulated on social media arises from the fact that the predominant experiences of users on the internet are increasingly those on social media platforms. Internet users are found to spend more time on social media than before.[3] In spite of the proliferative use of social media platforms, as well as social media's unique characteristics and business models, a lack of specific consideration has been given to how social media platforms affect the role played by laws – including copyright laws – in securing compliance from their users.

To date, research on the regulation of social media draws mainly from internet governance studies.[4] DeNardis and Hackl have highlighted the focus given in internet governance studies to governmental policies and global institutions.[5] They have further called for more consideration to be given to the direct policymaking role of private intermediaries and the accompanying phenomenon of the privatisation of human rights.[6] According to DeNardis and Hackl, existing scholarship has tended to focus on political transformation on social media, the use of social media for self-representation and the expansion of freedom of expression through social media.[7] On the other hand, there is a growing area of inquiry concerned with private information intermediaries such as social media platforms. The ways in which these platforms enact governance via their user policies and design choices[8] deserve more attention than they have received to date.

DeNardis and Hackl have also discussed the question of privatised governance *by* social media in their work. Their discussion on the extent to which social media platforms promote or constrain rights has been concerned mainly with three thematic areas relating to free expression. These areas pertain to: firstly, anonymous speech and individual privacy; secondly, the ability to express ideas; and thirdly, technical facilities, or 'affordances', of interoperability and permission-less innovation.[9] With this book, I intend to expand our understanding of how social media platforms can alter the effectiveness of the regulation of content-generative behaviours by copyright laws.

Recent controversies have brought the question of governance by social media to the fore.[10] In particular – and of topical interest to this book – are the filing of legal actions against Twitter in California for failing to respond to takedown requests in relation to professionally taken photographs,[11] Twitter's removal of plagiarised jokes in response to its receipt of takedown notices[12] and Richard Prince's sale of artworks incorporating images shared by other users on the Instagram platform.[13]

In this respect, DeNardis has argued that as content intermediaries such as social media platforms wield great power over the global flow of information, the challenges they pose to individual civil liberties through their privatised forms of governance are escalating.[14] She has also noted their direct manipulation of the distribution of content and their facilitation of transactions among users.[15] The acknowledgement of the incursion of human rights on social media and the need for user empowerment have spurred further research in these areas.[16] While we are increasingly aware that social media platforms influence our behaviours, we often fail to articulate exactly *how* we are so influenced, or 'nudged'.[17] In response to these concerns, this book pays attention to the processes by which social media platforms influence the behaviours of users through the specific means of their terms of service and technological features.

As a preliminary matter, it is worth noting that social media platforms have features that distinguish them from cyberspace in general. According to Mayfield, social media embodies five specific characteristics – namely participation, conversation, connectedness, community and openness.[18] In short, social media platforms allow users the opportunities to interact with others; enable two-way conversations; facilitate interactive dialogues among users;[19] encourage users to reach out to others, communicate with and develop communities; link users with others who share a certain commonality; and ensure that there are relatively few barriers to the accessing of information or the making of comments on social media. Social media platforms have been defined as providing three specific technological facilities, or 'affordances': the intermediation of user-generated content (UGC); the possibility of interactivity among users and direct engagement with content; and the ability for an individual to articulate network connections with other users.[20] Other definitions more generally characterise social media platforms by reference to their abilities to exchange information in an interactive manner with dispersed groups of recipients,[21] or as applications that allow for UGC.[22]

Common to these definitions is the recognition that social media platforms diminish the distinction between the amateur and the professional content creator. They comprise 'social' technologies that allow users to create, modify and disseminate content. This is an allowance previously afforded to a small group of content producers who decided which content would be distributed. Social media platforms are thus unique in that they enable users to be both producers and consumers of content.[23] Furthermore, they extend the 'dis-intermediating' power of the internet to the masses[24] in relation to the creation, modification and dissemination of content. Firstly, in respect of creation, all users, not only professionals,[25] are encouraged to create content because it is easy to do so with the technological features made available to them on the platforms. Secondly, in respect of modification, such platforms create interactivity between their content and their users, thereby allowing a range of different forms of modification by readers of content, who go beyond their previously passive roles on the internet to various levels of activity on social media. Thirdly, in respect of dissemination, the extended reach that the platforms have is unprecedented. For instance, when an Australian political commentator decided to share a witty observation on Twitter, her single message reached 149,000 'followers'.[26] Moreover, content can be distributed much faster than before, as users experience a new degree of autonomy in cyberspace.[27] On this note, Elkin-Koren has observed that the emerging structures of digital production are no longer bilaterally confined to the producer-consumer or author-user relationships. Rather, they constitute a tripartite relationship consisting of the relevant individual user, a wider community of networked users and the facilitating commercial platform.[28] This tripartite relationship is especially pronounced on social media, where the content shared by users is easily accessible by a broad community.

Furthermore, social media platforms have facilitated changes in content which is part of a continually evolving discussion, rather than a fixed product.[29] Social media platforms effect these changes by lowering the threshold required for user participation through their technologies – even regular unskilled users can now make minor contributions to an overall collaborative work.[30] In allowing for these minor contributions,[31] users are given the opportunity to experience participation with simple activities[32] before moving on to activities requiring greater personal effort and engagement.[33] Additionally, most users have social, rather than financial, motivations for creating, modifying and disseminating content. For example, users who contribute entries to the Wikipedia platform do so because of the shared sense of community among users and the desire for reciprocity, among other things.[34]

Social media platforms have also changed the economics of content creation and distribution. The costs of running these platforms are irrecoverable via the traditional route carved by copyright laws, given that such platforms do not own the content on them under their terms of service and are not the copyright holders.[35] Notwithstanding this, revenue is earned usually through the building of value-added services around the content available, such as an advertising or a micropayments licensing system.[36] Advertising remains the most common revenue model for social media platforms, where the advertiser pays only when a user clicks on an advertisement.[37] Indeed, most social media platforms offer free services to their users and are known to adopt advertiser-supported business models[38] that, among other things, sort, aggregate, monetise or otherwise create social and economic value around content.[39] Social media platforms can thus increase the revenue they earn by attracting more users to their platforms, so that there will be a correspondingly higher volume of advertising clicks and actions.[40]

Social media platforms therefore have a strong incentive to grow their audiences. Moreover, network effects, or the effects that the number of users of a service has on the value of that service to others,[41] also play a part. Other users will be incentivised to join a social media platform when it expands its user base. This is due to the fact that social media platforms appear to be designed around users' interactions with the content available on such platforms. Thus the probability of a user finding content on a social media platform useful is likely to increase when there are more users contributing to the shared pool of content. Social media platforms want their users to share content with other users in their networks. When there are more users on a network and access to content is effortless, advertisers will be willing to engage the platforms, making them more economically viable.[42] In light of the business models adopted by social media platforms and their financial incentive to increase the volume of content shared, the question of governance *by* social media becomes all the more important to address.[43] I direct myself, in this book, to answering the consequential question that necessarily arises: how can this influence of social media platforms, as exemplified by their terms of service and technological features, affect users' compliance with copyright laws when they engage in content-generative activities?

II. Regulation of content-generative behaviours from a copyright perspective

Many users on social media are, with startling regularity, engaging in behaviours that could potentially fall within the scope of copyright infringement.[44] The ubiquitous employment of social media platforms by users to create, modify and disseminate content has expanded the possibilities of copyright laws applying to the content-generative activities in which users engage. As noted by Wu, a giant 'grey zone' exists in copyright legislation, which includes millions of uses that 'do not fall in a clear category but are often infringing'.[45] This grey zone arguably grows larger with the proliferation of social media platforms, and their increasing technological enablement. Moreover, because the sharing of content on social media transcends national borders, the application of laws in these virtual spaces is uncertain.[46] The restricted abilities of countries to enforce their legislation, including copyright laws, owing to the sheer volume of content and the de-centralisation of media producers,[47] make this uncertainty more acute.

Against this backdrop, recent movements highlight that copyright laws are perceived to be restrictive and in urgent need of reform.[48] Scholars have called for reforms to copyright laws, so that they reflect the way users actually behave in their digital interactions.[49] This, however, raises the question of whether the law should be adjusted simply because this is the way users behave: in some cases the behaviours may be ones that, as a matter of policy, the law should not acknowledge. At the same time, the rhetoric of the intellectual property industries calling for stronger intellectual property rights comprises terms such as 'innovation', 'wealth creation', 'incentive' and 'creative'[50] – precisely the terms that also appear to support the resistance against expanding copyright on social media.

The regularity of technical infringement, the uncertain application of copyright laws and the merging of arguments *for* and *against* copyright make a strong case for copyright reform to look beyond striking a balance between interests that are less distinct. Social media users who are both producers and consumers not only require the incentives[51] to create under copyright laws; they also need the freedom to use content to express themselves through copyright exceptions. My inquiry into how the terms of service and the technological features of social media platforms can influence users' content-generative behaviours provides cause to reflect on the extent to which copyright laws actually regulate the ways in which users behave.

On a broader level, understanding the ability of copyright laws to regulate the content-generative behaviours of social media users may prove to be a good springboard upon which the abilities of other laws[52] to regulate behaviours on social media can be examined. In this book I choose to take the copyright perspective, and to use copyright laws as a pivot for my analysis. Through surveying the influences that cause dilemmas in one area of law such as copyright, broader lessons may be drawn from the book in relation to other applicable laws on social media. This goes beyond a consideration of how the challenges posed to copyright's effective regulation of content-generative behaviours can be resolved.

If society moves towards the ambient networked computing environment described by Hildebrandt[53] – a world in which the impact of technological features on user behaviours is less explicit and visible – decisions may be made instead by an active set of cooperating devices, not by the users themselves. When this happens, users exercise less autonomy in decision-making and are hence more vulnerable to influence. While the copyright regime is *expected* to regulate content-generative behaviours on social media, I question the extent to which copyright laws continue to govern the content-generative activities of users in reality. Subjecting users to the risks of copyright infringement on social media may then be tantamount to adopting the copyright view of the universe Litman describes, which does not take the vantage point of these users into account.[54] In spite of copyright's purported regulation of content-generative behaviours, I argue that users act in response to 'nudges'.[55] These 'nudges', or the influences users face on social media when they generate content, arise from the governance of users' behaviours by social media. In particular, the terms of service and the technological features on social media platforms can affect the awareness and perceptions of copyright laws in users, and so influence such behaviours. This gives rise to the question as to whether it is unfair, in this environment of mixed signals and conflicting expectations, that users continue to be widely exposed to the risks of copyright infringement for the activities they regularly undertake on these platforms.

Studies on social media can be the subject of research from a variety of fields including communications,[56] human factors,[57] computer science,[58] sociology[59] and political science.[60] The governance of and by social media is a subset of the wider study of internet governance, situated within an even broader realm of internet studies.[61] In this book, my aim is to develop a line of inquiry and to extract the arguments resulting from such inquiry, rather than to advance existing theoretical foundations.[62] My focus is on the practical implications for users, whose compliance with copyright laws can be affected by social media platforms. Throughout my inquiry I ask and answer questions in a way that acknowledges the multiple influences users face on social media platforms. This ultimately makes a case for future areas of research – whether for copyright reform or relating to the form of contribution such platforms can make towards aligning their terms of service and technological features with copyright laws.

While I am not furnishing neatly packaged solutions in the book, my analysis of the factors regulating content-generative behaviours makes it more comprehensible for users to understand the influences to which they are subject on social media. The book belongs to the field of critical information studies that describes the multidisciplinary confluence of work that focuses on the ways in which information and culture are regulated by their relationships with creativity, commerce and other human affairs.[63] The orientation of this field allows researchers to put laws in dialogue with other forces, whether economic, technological, cultural or otherwise. With my inquiry in the book, I offer interested users and regulators a way of considering whether the behaviours encouraged or constrained on social media are in line with laws, whether those of copyright or other laws.

III. Approach

The scholarship around the regulation of cyberspace serves as a good starting point for my inquiry in this book, notwithstanding that social media platforms warrant separate analyses from those conducted on cyberspace. More than a decade ago the regulation of cyberspace, or cyberlaw, emerged as a new legal domain to be studied.[64] Opponents to cyberlaw's emergence argued against its usefulness as a distinct field by claiming that cyberspace, by its very nature, could not be regulated, not even by the government.[65] In response, other scholars have contended that cyberlaw is a unique field of study because of the regulation of cyberspace through technological standards, premised on the argument that 'code is the law'.[66] Another view might well be that cyberspace is not too different from any other area of human activity to be in need of special study in its own right.

In this book I consider the application of copyright laws to various uses on social media, and explore how this application is aligned with the terms of service and the technological features of the selected social media platforms.[67] Where there are inconsistencies between the application of either of the regulatory factors with copyright laws, I argue that they can compromise the effectiveness of copyright laws in regulating content-generative behaviours. I have chosen to examine these two factors as they constitute the points of contact between the social media platforms and their users when the latter generate content on these platforms. While users have to accept the terms of service of such platforms before they use their services,[68] the technological features are the interfaces users interact with when they generate content on the platforms.[69] Both factors can be readily observed for the purpose of the book and are hence included in my inquiry.

To illustrate more specifically the ways in which the surveyed factors (ie, copyright laws, the terms of service and the technological features) regulate the content-generative behaviours of users, I employ a case study that details the content-generative activities undertaken by a hypothetical user, Jane Doe, and other users on the selected social media platforms. This case study is modelled after the activities of users that can occur on these platforms; it provides an anchor around which the discussions can be conducted. This takes place one activity at a time.

Notwithstanding my attempt in this book to depict the usual content-generative activities that can occur on the five social media platforms, including Facebook, Pinterest, YouTube, Twitter and Wikipedia using the case study, it has its limitations. I can never fully replicate the varied phenomena on social media nor capture the complete range of diverse activities that occur on social media platforms in the book. In addition, the terms of service and the technological features are not static features and will be frequently updated by the platforms. The terms and the features referred to here are those of the platforms as at 7 June 2017. Nevertheless, in trying to compare copyright laws with these other regulatory factors, I have developed a structured way to assess how the effectiveness (or ineffectiveness) of copyright laws in regulating content-generative behaviours is affected by such factors on social media.

In my consideration of the application of copyright laws, I will refer to the copyright laws of three jurisdictions – the United States (US), the United Kingdom (UK) and Australia. I will also draw from earlier empirical studies that illuminate users' perspectives and awareness of copyright laws. The US is the country in which the entities operating the social media platforms are registered.[70] The copyright laws of the other two common law jurisdictions are referred to in order to illustrate how variations between the copyright laws of these three jurisdictions, in spite of some commonalities, may yield different outcomes when a user considers: firstly, if content is copyright protected; and secondly, if his or her content-generative activity is copyright infringing. Having different laws apply to the questions of subsistence and infringement of copyright,[71] given that the generation of content on social media occurs online and cannot be confined geographically, is now a reality – social media users come from all over the world.

IV. Structure

With this approach in mind, Chapter One sets the foundation upon which I make my arguments in this book. In Chapter One, I discuss the adopted definitions of 'social media', together with those of 'UGC'. I also set out the types of UGC that are included within the scope of the book. In this chapter I explain my reasons for confining the discussion in the book to the content-generative activities of users resulting in content across four categories of social media platforms – namely, collaborative projects, blogs, content communities and social networking sites. At the end of the chapter I narrate a case study detailing the content-generative activities of a hypothetical user, Jane Doe, and other users on the selected social media platforms.

In Chapter Two I discuss the copyright subsistence and infringement issues that arise from the application of copyright laws to content-generative activities on social media platforms, and highlight the challenges posed in addressing these issues. I then apply the specific copyright laws of the US, the UK and Australia to the content-generative activities of Jane Doe and other users in the case study, in order to illustrate how these issues may be resolved in relation to each activity. This application of copyright laws constitutes the first of four hypothetical scenarios, which allows for the subsequent evaluation of the consistency of the copyright regimes with each of the private regimes (ie, the terms of service and the technological features). Through scenario one, I demonstrate why it is not possible for any regular user of social media to have the requisite understanding of copyright laws to know how they apply to the content-generative activities he or she undertakes. I also show that the application of the copyright laws of the three jurisdictions to the same activities can result in different outcomes being reached on the copyright liabilities of users based in each jurisdiction.

In Chapter Three I examine the standard form contracts entered into by users across the five selected social media platforms, in order to identify the key terms that govern or have implications for the content-generative activities of these users. I also apply the terms of service to the content-generative activities of Jane and other users in the case study under scenario two. This scenario shows that the application of the terms of service to content-generative activities cannot be conducted on a comprehensive basis as there is a dearth of case law in this area – particularly in the UK and Australia. I then consider the extent of alignment and incompatibility that the terms of service have with the copyright regimes, and note that there are potential incompatibilities on a number of issues among the regimes.

In Chapter Four I identify the technological features that encourage and constrain users from creating, modifying and disseminating content. I also consider how the technological features encourage or constrain the content-generative activities Jane Doe and other users undertake in the case study under scenario three. I then go on to examine the extent of alignment and incompatibility the technological features have with the copyright regimes, and discuss the implications of the spread of the technological features on social media platforms which encourages and constrains users when they engage in content-generative activities. In rounding up, I set out what the observations from the discussion in Chapter Four, and from scenario three, mean for users.

In Chapter Five I review earlier empirical studies conducted on the perceptions and awareness users have of either intellectual property in general or of copyright laws more specifically. I analyse these findings with the discussions conducted in the earlier chapters of the book. I then draw on scenarios one, two and three – considered in Chapters Two, Three and Four respectively – to understand how copyright laws, the terms of service and the technological features regulate, *in toto*, the content-generative behaviours of users across the five selected social media platforms. Under scenario four of Chapter Five I bring together the conclusions arrived at in the earlier hypothetical scenarios to evaluate the consistency of regulatory signals that users receive from each of these factors regarding the content-generative activities that are legitimate on the platforms.

To do so, I assess the extent to which the positions reached are the same in relation to the application of the following pairs of factors: the copyright regimes and the terms of service; the copyright regimes and the technological features; and the terms of service and the technological features. Through this evaluation I arrive at some observations.

Finally, in my concluding chapter, I summarise the arguments that I have made in the earlier chapters and my recommendations for law reform. I also outline future areas of research.

Notes

1. Facebook, YouTube and Twitter are among the most utilised social media platforms in the world. As of December 2012, there were approximately 693 million active users on Facebook, 300 million active users on YouTube and 288 million active users on Twitter. See, for example, International Business Times, *Google Plus Becomes World's No 2 Social Network after Facebook, Knocking off Twitter* (28 January 2013) <http://www.ibtimes.com/google-plus-becomes-worlds-no-2-social-network-after-facebook-knocking-twitter-1042956>; ZDNet, *Facebook remains top social network, Google+, YouTube battle for second* (14 May 2013) <http://www.zdnet.com/facebook-remains-top-social-network-google-youtube-battle-for-second-7000015303/>. In fact, as of 31 March 2015, Facebook declared that it had 1.44 billion monthly active users, see Facebook, *Facebook Reports First Quarter 2015 Results* (22 April 2015) <http://investor.fb.com/releasedetail.cfm?ReleaseID=908022>. As of 17 September 2015, Pinterest announced that 100 million people use the service each month, see Quartz, *Pinterest, which just hit 100 million users, is growing much faster than expected* (17 September 2015) <http://qz.com/504823/pinterest-which-just-hit-100-million-users-is-growing-much-faster-than-expected/>.
2. Andreas M. Kaplan and Michael Haenlein, 'Users of the World, Unite! The Challenges and Opportunities of Social Media' (2010) 53(1) *Business Horizons* 59, 62.
3. See Nielsen, *Social Media Report 2012* (8 January 2013) <http://blog.nielsen.com/nielsenwire/social/2012/>, which found that internet users spend more time on social media than on other internet sites. See also Global Web Index, *Daily time spent on social networks rises to 1.72 hours* (26 January 2015) <https://www.globalwebindex.net/blog/daily-time-spent-on-social-networks-rises-to-1-72-hours>, which found that social networking accounts for about 30 per cent of the time spent online, while micro-blogging accounts for about 15 per cent of the time spent.

4. The term 'internet governance' is often used to described the design and administration of the technical infrastructure necessary to keep the internet operational and the enactment of substantive policies around these technologies. See Laura DeNardis, *The Global War for Internet Governance* (Yale University Press, 2014). See also Milton L. Mueller, *Networks and States: The Global Politics of Internet Governance* (The MIT Press, 2010) 9, where he explains that 'internet governance' is a direct and inclusive label for the ongoing set of disputes and deliberations over how the internet is coordinated and managed to reflect policies.
5. L. DeNardis and W.M. Hackl, 'Internet Governance *by* Social Media Platforms' (2015) *Telecommunications Policy* 1, 2. One dominant theme examines the policymaking role of new global institutions, such as the Internet Corporation for Assigned Names and Numbers (ICANN), the Internet Engineering Task Force (IETF) and the World Wide Web Consortium (W3C). See, eg, A. Michael Froomkin, 'ICANN 2.0: Meet the New Boss' (2003) 36 *Loyola of Los Angeles Law Review* 1087; Hans Klein, 'ICANN and Internet Governance: Leveraging Technical Coordination to Realize Global Public Policy' (2002) 18(3) *Information Society* 193. Another theme is the role of nation states or intergovernmental organisations in regulating or coordinating the internet in areas such as antitrust, net neutrality, computer fraud, privacy or hate speech. See Laura De Nardis, *Protocol Politics: The Globalization of Internet Governance* (The MIT Press, 2009); Jack Goldsmith and Tim Wu, *Who Controls the Internet? Illusions of a Borderless World* (Oxford University Press, 2006); Mueller, M.L. 2010.
6. DeNardis, L. and Hackl, W.M. 2015, 1.
7. DeNardis, L. and Hackl, W.M. 2015, 1. See also Philip N. Howard et al, 'Opening Closed Regimes: What was the Role of Social Media during the Arab Spring?' (2011) 1 *Project on Information Technology and Political Islam* 1; Renee Marlin-Bennett and E. Nicole Thornton, 'Governance Within Social Media Websites: Ruling New Frontiers' (2012) 36 *Telecommunications Policy* 493; Council of Europe – Commissioner for Human Rights, *Social Media and Human Rights* (February 2012) <www.commissioner.coe.int>; Danah M. Boyd and Nicole B. Ellison, 'Social Network Sites: Definition, History and Scholarship' (2007) 13 *Journal of Computer-Mediated Communication* 210; Teresa Correa, Amber Willard Hinsley and Homero Gil de Zuniga, 'Who Interacts on the Web?: The Intersection of Users' Personality and Social Media Use' (2010) 26(2) *Computers in Human Behaviour* 247.
8. DeNardis, L. and Hackl, W.M. 2015, 2.
9. DeNardis, L. and Hackl, W.M. 2015, 2–3.
10. For example, Facebook's manipulation of the news feeds of users to influence their moods highlights the importance of being aware of how social media platforms could be designed to reach the objectives of the platforms. See, for example, Robert Shrimsley, *Facebook: why we're all lab rats now* (4 July 2014) <http://www.ft.com/cms/s/2/81196950-023c-11e4-ab5b-00144feab7de.html#axzz37quSJedp>; Thomas Jones, *Short Cuts* (17 July 2014) <http://www.lrb.co.uk/v36/n14/thomas-jones/short-cuts>; Forbes, *Facebook NewsFeed Manipulation Prompts FTC Complaint, Investigation Possible* (4 July 2014) <http://www.forbes.com/sites/gregorymcneal/2014/07/04/facebook-faces-possible-ftc-investigation-for-manipulation-study/>.
11. *Kristen Pierson v Twitter Inc*, Case 15-5669 (United States District Court for the Central District of California at Los Angeles, 27 July 2015); *Christopher Boffoli v Twitter Inc*, Case 12-01534 (United States District Court for the Washington District at Seattle, 10 September 2012). See also Matt Kamen, *Twitter sued over photo copyright* (29 July 2015) <http://www.wired.co.uk/news/archive/2015-07/29/twitter-sued-over-photo-copyright>.
12. See, for example, The Guardian, *Twitter removes lifted jokes over copyright infringement claims* (27 July 2015) <http://www.theguardian.com/technology/2015/jul/27/twitter-removes-lifted-jokes-copyright-infringment-claims>; Dante D'Orazio, *Twitter is deleting stolen jokes on copyright grounds* (25 July 2015) <http://www.theverge.com/2015/7/25/9039127/twitter-deletes-stolen-joke-dmca-takedown>.
13. See, for example, Colton Valentine, *Richard Prince Sold Strangers' Instagram Photos for $90k – And It's Probably Legal* <http://www.huffingtonpost.com/2015/06/30/richard-prince-appropriation-art_n_7674786.html>; Lizzie Plaugic, *The story of Richard Prince and his $100,000 Instagram art: When does appropriation go too far?* <http://www.theverge.com/2015/5/30/8691257/richard-prince-instagram-photos-copyright-law-fair-use>.
14. DeNardis, L. 2014, 154.
15. DeNardis, L. 2014, 154.

16. See, for example, Council of Europe – Commissioner for Human Rights 2012; Eva Lievens, Peggy Valcke and Pieter Jan Valgaeren, *State of the art on regulatory trends in media* (December 2011) <https://lirias.kuleuven.be/bitstream/123456789/350852/1/EMSOC_ICRI_D+1+2+1_2011.pdf>. The latter work is an example of research on the regulation of social media written with a broader focus. In this work a number of regulatory trends that are of interest for the regulation of social media were identified, and the shift from provider-oriented to user-oriented media regulation was also highlighted.
17. In respect of being 'nudged', see generally Richard Thaler and Cass Sunstein, *Nudge: Improving Decisions about Health, Wealth and Happiness* (Penguin Books, 2008).
18. Antony Mayfield, *What is social media* (1 August 2008) <http://www.repromax.com/docs/113/854427515.pdf>. See also Sylvia M. Chan-Olmsted, Moonhee Cho and Sangwon Lee, 'User Perceptions of Social Media: A Comparative Study of Perceived Characteristics and User Profiles by Social Media' (October 2013) 3(4) *Online Journal of Communication and Media Technologies* 149.
19. See, for example, Trisha Dowerah Baruah, 'Effectiveness of Social Media as a Tool of Communication and its Potential for Technology Enabled Connections: A micro-level Study' (May 2012) 2(5) *International Journal of Scientific and Research Publications* 1.
20. DeNardis, L. and Hackl, W.M. 2015, 2.
21. Bernie Hogan and Anabel Quan-Haase, 'Persistence and Change in Social Media' (2010) 30(5) *Bulletin of Science, Technology & Society* 309.
22. Kaplan, A.M. and Haenlein, M. 2010. 61. This definition is accompanied by classifications that will be discussed further in Chapter One.
23. These users are called 'prosumers' or 'produsers'. The term 'prosumers' was developed by Alvin Toffler (1980) while the term 'produsers' was developed by Alex Bruns (2009), as has been referred to in Bhuva Narayan, 'From Everyday Information Behaviours to Clickable Solidarity in a Place called Social Media' (2013) 5(3) *Cosmopolitan Civil Societies Journal* 32, 34. See also Ola Erstad, 'The Agency of Content Creators: Implications for Personal Engagement and Media Industries' (2013) 20(2) *Javnost – The Public* 67, 73.
24. See McKinsey Global Institute, *The social economy: Unlocking value and productivity through social technologies* (July 2012) <http://www.mckinsey.com/insights/high_tech_telecoms_internet/the_social_economy>. See also Bhuva Narayan, 'From Everyday Information Behaviours to Clickable Solidarity in a Place called Social Media' (2013) 5(3) *Cosmopolitan Civil Societies Journal* 32, 35; Nicola Lucchi, 'Internet Content Governance and Human Rights' (2014) 16(4) *Vanderbilt Journal of Entertainment and Technology Law* 809, 854.
25. See generally Dan Hunter et al (eds), *Amateur Media: Social, Cultural and Legal Perspectives* (Routledge, 2013). This edited collection provides an interdisciplinary contextualisation of amateur media before and after web 2.0, where amateur producers are seen as the key drivers of the creative economy.
26. See, for example, Chris Kenny, *Insidious Twitter not always as it seems* <http://www.theaustralian.com.au/opinion/columnists/insidious-twitter-not-always-as-it-seems/story-fn8qlm5e-1227018479199?nk=39a974840f8300ebf91be8676821d82e>. A user's 'followers' on Twitter are the other users who receive his or her 'tweets'.
27. It has been suggested that when users engage in content-generative activities such as the creation, modification and dissemination of content on social media platforms, they are in effect exercising these values of autonomy, freedom and democracy. See Greg Lastowka, 'Minecraft as Web 2.0' in Dan Hunter et al (eds), *Amateur Media: Social, Cultural and Legal Perspectives* (Routledge, 2013) 153, 162.
28. See Niva Elkin-Koren, 'Tailoring Copyright to Social Production' (2011) 12 *Theoretical Inquiries of Law* 309, 311.
29. See McKinsey Global Institute 2012. See also Yochai Benkler, *The Wealth of Networks: How Social Production Transforms Markets and Freedom* (Yale University Press, 2007), in which he argues that digital media has inspired the peer production of knowledge, with individuals working collaboratively on creative projects.
30. See Axel Bruns and Mark Bahnisch, *Social Media: Tools for User-Generated Content – Social Drivers behind Growing Consumer Participation in User-Led Content Generation* (March 2009) Volume 1 <http://www.smartservicescrc.com.au/files/files/Social_Media_State_of_the%20Art_March2009.pdf>.
31. Bruns, A. and Bahnisch, M. 2009.

32. For example, this could be: the posting of a brief 'status update' on Facebook; 'pinning' an image on Pinterest; commenting on a video clip on YouTube; 're-tweeting' a 'tweet' on Twitter; and accessing shared content on Wikipedia.
33. For example, this could be: the posting of a longer 'status update' with other content such as a photograph on Facebook; creating a themed 'pin-board' and 'pinning' more than one image on it; creating a video clip and sharing it on YouTube; creating and 'tweeting' a comment on Twitter; and contributing a page on Wikipedia.
34. See Elkin-Koren, N. 2011, 321–2.
35. In fact, the abilities of copyright holders to control the use, as well as receive remuneration from the use of copyright protected material, have been eroded by technological and social shifts experienced on social media. See, for example, Olufunmilayo B. Arewa, 'YouTube, UGC, and Digital Music: Competing Business and Cultural Models in the Internet Age' (2010) 104(2) *Northwestern University Law Review* 431, 442.
36. See, for example, Pew Research Internet Project, *The Future of the Internet III - Scenario 3: The Evolution of IP Law and Copyright Protection* <http://www.pewinternet.org/2008/12/14/scenario-3-the-evolution-of-ip-law-and-copyright-protection/>.
37. See, for example, McKinsey Global Institute 2012; Kenneth Olmstead and Kristine Lu, *Digital News: Revenue – Fact Sheet* (29 April 2015) <http://www.journalism.org/2015/04/29/digital-news-revenue-fact-sheet/>.
38. These business models have developed to fill the gaps resulting from the erosion of copyright holders' control over their content. They threaten the businesses of traditional content intermediaries, since anyone with a mobile device or a personal computer can distribute his or her work at little or no cost to others online, including on social media platforms. See, for example, Benkler, Y. 2007, 99–106; Don Tapscott and Anthony D. Williams, *Wikinomics: How Mass Collaboration Changes Everything* (Penguin Group, 2006) 10–1.
39. See, for example, Greg McFarlane, *How Facebook, Twitter, Social Media Make Money From You* (2 September 2014) <http://www.investopedia.com/stock-analysis/032114/how-facebook-twitter-social-media-make-money-you-twtr-lnkd-fb-goog.aspx>; L.J. Rich, *How can social networks make money* (15 April 2011) <http://news.bbc.co.uk/2/hi/programmes/click_online/9457946.stm>; The Market Oracle, *How do social media companies like Facebook and Twitter make money* (11 October 2013) <http://www.marketoracle.co.uk/Article42647.html>.
40. See, for example, McKinsey Global Institute 2012. It is noted further that some platforms adopt targeted advertising, in which advertisements are inserted more skilfully into a user's experience so that they do not impact on the user negatively in any way. See The Market Oracle, *How do social media companies like Facebook and Twitter make money* (11 October 2013) <http://www.marketoracle.co.uk/Article42647.html>. See also DeNardis, L. 2014, 29.
41. Carl Shapiro and Hal R. Varian, *Information Rules: A Strategic Guide to the Network Economy* (Harvard Business Press, 1999).
42. More viable than they would be otherwise, if they were to adopt subscription-based business models. See McFarlane, G. 2014.
43. According to DeNardis, such governance responsibility exists in relation to the exchange of products and social capital. See DeNardis, L. 2014, 29.
44. See, for example, Arewa, O.B. 2010, 439; John Tehranian, *Infringement Nation: Copyright 2.0 and You* (Oxford University Press, 2011) 2.
45. See Tim Wu, 'Tolerated Use' (2007–8) 31 *Columbia Journal of Law & Arts* 617.
46. This is due to the ambiguity introduced by conflict of laws issues. See, for example, Uta Kohl, *Jurisdiction and the Internet: Regulatory Competence over Online Activity* (Cambridge University Press, 2007); Pew Research Internet Project, *Summary: 15 Theses about the Digital Future* (11 March 2014) <http://www.pewinternet.org/2014/03/11/digital-life-in-2025/>.
47. See, for example, Australian Law Reform Commission (ALRC), *Classification – Content Regulation and Convergent Media* (February 2012) <http://www.alrc.gov.au/sites/default/files/pdfs/publications/final_report_118_for_web.pdf>; Kate Crawford and Catharine Lumby, *The Adaptive Moment: A Fresh Approach to Convergent Media in Australia* (2011) <http://www.crr.unsw.edu.au/media/File/The_Adaptive_Moment_Convergent_media1.pdf>.
48. These movements include the 'Creative Commons' and 'Open Source' movements promoting various licences which authors can adopt to allow others to exercise some or all of their rights. See, for example, Craig Collins and Heather Forrest, *Intellectual Property Law* (LexisNexis Butterworths, 2nd ed., 2014) 15–16.

49. See, for example, Jessica Litman, *Digital Copyright* (Prometheus Books, 2006); Tehranian, J. 2011. See also Hector Postigo, *The Digital Rights Movement: The Role of Technology in Subverting Digital Copyright* (The MIT Press, 2012) 50.
50. See Amy Kapczynski, 'The Access to Knowledge Mobilization and the New Politics of Intellectual Property' (2008) 117 *The Yale Law Journal* 804, 855, in which she highlights the use of narrower frames by both sides (for and against the expansion of intellectual property rights) to create common arguments to support their respective agendas.
51. These incentives are both economic and non-economic (ie, status, prestige and moral rights). They encourage authors to create content they perceive to be socially valuable. See, for example, John Quiggin and Dan Hunter, 'Money Ruins Everything' (2008) 30 *Hastings Commerce and Entertainment Law Journal* 203, 244; William M. Landes and Richard A. Posner, 'An Economic Analysis of Copyright Law' (1989) 18 *Journal of Legal Studies* 325; Joseph P. Liu, 'Copyright Law's Theory of the Consumer' (2003) 44 *Boston College Law Review* 397.
52. Regulation of social media by other laws including privacy laws, censorship laws, personal data protection laws, antitrust laws and defamation laws warrant separate consideration.
53. See generally Mireille Hildebrandt, 'A Vision of Ambient Law' in Roger Brownsword and Karen Yeung (eds), *Regulating Technologies* (Hart Publishing, 2008) 175.
54. See Litman, J. 2006, 28 and 179.
55. See generally Thaler, R. and Sunstein, C. 2008.
56. See, for example, Lee Humphreys, 'Cellphones in Public: Social Interactions in a Wireless Era' (2005) 7(6) *New Media & Society* 810.
57. See, for example, Damian Ballam and Chris Fullwood, 'Fluidity of Personal Boundaries in Online Social Media: Implications for Netiquette' in Martin Anderson (ed.), *Contemporary Ergonomics and Human Factors: Annual Conference of the Institute of Ergonomics and Human Factors* (Taylor & Francis, 2010) 391.
58. See, for example, Kittichote Rojanakul and Hu Liang, 'Initiatives and Challenges in Countering Inappropriate Internet Use' (2009) *Proceedings of International Conference on Computer Technology and Development* 516.
59. See, for example, Piotr Konieczny, 'Governance, Organisation and Democracy on the Internet: The Iron Law and the Evolution of Wikipedia' (2009) 24(1) *Sociological Forum* 162.
60. See, for example, Barbel R. Dorbeck-Jung et al, 'Contested Hybridization of Regulation: Failure of the Dutch Regulatory System to Protect Minors from Harmful Media' (2010) 4(2) *Regulation and Governance* 154; Wilson Wong and Eric Welch, 'Does E-government Promote Accountability? A Comparative Analysis of Website Openness and Government Accountability' (2004) 17(2) *Governance – An International Journal of Policy and Administration* 275. See also Renee Marlin-Bennett and E. Nicole Thornton, 'Governance within Social Media Websites: Ruling New Frontiers' (2012) 36 *Telecommunications Policy* 493, 493.
61. Dutton explains that internet research draws on multiple disciplines to focus theory and research on questions concerning the social implications of the widespread diffusion and diverse uses of the internet, web, related media, information and communication technologies. See William Dutton (ed.), *Oxford Handbook of Internet Studies* (Oxford University Press, 2013) 1.
62. See, for example, L. Edwards et al, 'Framing the Consumer, Copyright Regulation and the Public' (2013) 19(1) *Convergence: The International Journal of Research into New Media Technologies* 9, in which the authors seek to advance existing theoretical foundations, through considering various policy approaches to understanding users and introducing an analytical framework that re-evaluates user resistance to copyright laws. The authors argue for a democratic copyright policymaking process that allows copyright laws to reconnect with public interest goals.
63. Said Vaidhyanathan, 'Afterword: Critical Information Studies' (2006) 29 (2–3) *Cultural Studies* 292. See also Aram Sinnreich, *The Piracy Crusade: How the Music Industry's War on Sharing Destroys Markets and Erodes Civil Liberties* (University of Massachusetts Press, 2013) 8.
64. See, for example, David R. Johnson and David Post, 'Law and Borders – The Rise of Law in Cyberspace' (1996) 48(5) *Stanford Law Review* 1367; Needham J. Boddie II et al, 'A Review of Copyright and the Internet' (1998) 20(2) *Campbell Law Review* 193; Steven R. Salbu, 'Who Should Govern the Internet?: Monitoring and Supporting a New Frontier' (1998) 11 *Harvard Journal of Law & Technology* 429; Jack Goldsmith, 'Against Cyberanarchy' (1998) 65 *University of Chicago Law Review* 1199.
65. See, for example, Frank H. Easterbrook, 'Cyberspace and the Law of the Horse' (1996) *University of Chicago Legal Forum* 207, 213; Joseph H. Sommer, 'Against Cyberlaw' (2000) 15

Berkeley Technology Law Journal 1145, 1147; John Perry Barlow, *A Declaration of the Independence of Cyberspace* (8 February 1996) <https://projects.eff.org/~barlow/Declaration-Final.html>.

66. See, for example, Joel Reidenberg, 'Lex Informatica: The Formulation of Information Policy Rules through Technology' (1998) 76 *Texas Law Review* 553; Mitchell, William, *City of Bits: Space, Place and the Infobahn* (The MIT Press, 1996) 111; James Boyle, 'Foucault in Cyberspace: Surveillance, Sovereignty and Hardwired Censors' (1997) 66 *University of Cincinnati Law Review* 177; Lawrence Lessig, 'The Law of the Horse: What Cyberlaw Might Teach' (1999a) 113 *Harvard Law Review* 501. Among these scholars, Lessig's seminal work is recognised to have developed this argument the most persuasively. See Lawrence Lessig, *Code and Other Laws of Cyberspace* (Basic Books, 1999b); Lawrence Lessig, *Code Version 2.0* (Basic Books, 2nd ed., 2006). See also Viktor Mayer-Schonberger, 'The Shape of Governance: Analyzing the World of Internet Regulation' (2003) 43 *Vanderbilt Journal of International Law* 605, 609; Murray, Andrew and Colin Scott, 'Controlling the New Media: Hybrid Responses to New Forms of Power' (2002) 65(4) *The Modern Law Review* 491, 500. In particular, Murray and Scott highlighted that Lessig's theory is widely regarded as one of the most complete analytical attempts to capture the variety of forms that the regulation of new media takes.
67. This approach draws, to some extent, on Lessig. See Lessig, L. 1999b; Lessig, L. 2006. The 'modalities' of regulation under Lessig's regulatory theory of cyberspace include not just law, but also architecture, markets and social norms. Not only is Lessig's theory a useful regulatory for cyberspace of which social media platforms are a subset, but the 'modalities' are also expressed as broad terms open to interpretation. I note further that Wiseman and Sherman have highlighted that the role of technology in copyright law is contradictory. Technology can be 'both hero and villain, creator of opportunities and problems, generator of solutions as well as the means to counteract or circumvent those solutions'. See Leanne Wiseman and Brad Sherman, 'Facilitating Access to Information: Understanding the Role of Technology in Copyright Law' in Susy Frankel and Daniel Gervais (eds), *The Evolution and Equilibrium of Copyright in the Digital Age* (Cambridge University Press, 2014) 221, 221.
68. The terms of service arguably constitute the way in which the market, of which the platforms are a part, attempts to regulate user behaviours. Furthermore, the positions of dominance held by the companies operating these popular social media platforms, vis-à-vis their users, empower them to dictate their terms of service. The 'markets' are also argued to stimulate the use of contracts. See, for example, Lee A. Bygrave, *Internet Governance by Contract* (Oxford University Press, 2015) 1.
69. These technological features embody the technologies that can influence individual (and societal) action. This is in line with a technologically deterministic view, in which individuals conform to the technical infrastructures that are imposed on them. The theory of technological determinism is countered by the theory of social constructivism (ie, the 'social construction of technology'), which expounds that a society has a hand in technological regulation and a choice in the technologies that it adopts. See, for example, Langdon Winner, 'Do Artifacts have Politics?' (Winter 1980) 109(1) *Daedalus* 121, 121–35; Postigo, H. 2012, 11–12.
70. Facebook is operated by Facebook, Inc.; Pinterest by Pinterest, Inc.; YouTube by Google, Inc.; Twitter by Twitter, Inc.; and Wikipedia by the Wikimedia Foundation. These entities are incorporated or registered in the United States (US).
71. See Peter K. Yu, 'Conflict of Laws Issues in International Copyright Cases' on GigaLaw.com (2001) <http://www.peteryu.com/gigalaw0401.pdf>; Part III of Chapter Three, sub-section (B)(3)(d). See also Kohl, U. 2007.

Chapter One
Scope of study and a day in the life of Jane Doe

In this chapter I first set out the adopted definitions of social media and UGC (ie, user-generated content), along with the inclusions of certain types of UGC within the scope of this book. I then explain why I have chosen to confine the discussion in the book to content-generative activities occurring on certain categories of social media platforms.

At the end of this chapter I describe a day in the life of Jane Doe, a hypothetical user of social media. Together with other users, she engages in content-generative activities across a few social media platforms, including those surveyed in this book. These activities constitute a case study, which assist in anchoring the discussions in the later chapters of the book.

I. Defining social media and user-generated content

Among the characterisations of social media discussed earlier,[1] social media has been defined specifically to mean 'a group of internet-based applications that build on the ideological and technological foundations of web 2.0, and that allow the creation and exchange of UGC'.[2] The term 'social media' is distinct from the related concepts of web 2.0 and UGC. While web 2.0 refers collectively to the 'architecture of participation'[3] or the technological platforms for the evolution of social media, UGC describes instead the various forms of content that are created and shared with the public by users of social media services.[4] Due to the characteristics embodied by web 2.0 involving the development of internet-based applications designed to be user-centric and to facilitate collaboration among users in the creation and modification of content, there is an increased generation of both original and derivative UGC online.[5]

UGC is referred to under a few labels. The Organisation for Economic Cooperation and Development (OECD) has defined 'user-created content' in a 2007 study as: (i) content 'made publicly available over the internet'; (ii) content which reflects a 'certain amount of creative effort'; and (iii) content which is 'created outside of professional routines and practices'.[6] This OECD definition of 'user-created content' has been frequently cited in other research.[7]

Another term, 'amateur creative digital content' (ACDC),[8] similarly refers to UGC. The word 'creative' in ACDC conveys the sense that the content on social media platforms is derived from the creative labour of amateurs.[9] This arguably mirrors the substance of the second limb of the OECD definition. On the other hand, the word 'amateur' in ACDC implies both the positive sense of a commitment to a pastime and the negative sense of a lack of skill or knowledge.[10] The quality of 'non-professionalism' conveyed by the latter brings to mind the substance of the third limb of the OECD definition.

Ultimately, the existence of these alternative labels for UGC is of little significance – they are discussed mainly to clarify the type of content with which this book is concerned. For my purpose in the book, the term UGC will be employed over other substitute terms including 'user-created content' or ACDC. To substantiate the meaning given to UGC further, I note that there is also a definition of UGC as content possessing 'an element of either originality, transformativity or a combination of the two'.[11] This definition seems to complement the OECD definition – this is because content possessing either originality or resulting from transformative uses, or indeed encompassing both qualities, will also reflect an adequate amount of creative effort to satisfy the second limb of the OECD definition. To develop further on its meaning, not all UGC comprises content originally authored by the relevant users. Instead, UGC can be produced from transformative uses. For instance, when one draws on myriad pieces of original content in remixing video clips (on a platform such as YouTube), or juxtaposes two or more different images to create mash-ups of photographs (on a platform such as Pinterest), UGC results from these transformative uses.

Given these broad definitions of UGC, it is appropriate to set out the types of UGC that are excluded from, and included within, this book's scope. With reference to the first limb of the OECD definition, UGC refers to content that is publicly accessible and that is published in some context. This *publication* requirement excludes *bilateral* messages such as emails.[12]

With reference to the second limb of the OECD definition, UGC refers to new or adapted content embodying *creative* effort. As UGC that is a by-product of transformation raises concerns of copyright infringement by users,[13] therefore, I am concerned with the activities resulting in adapted content, in relation to my consideration of users' compliance with copyright laws when undertaking these activities. UGC that is original content involving no adaptation, derivation or copying on the part of a user[14] is also within the book's purview, mainly in relation to addressing first if such UGC is copyright protected, before the question of infringement follows.

At the same time, it has been suggested that UGC should not refer to content that has been appropriated wholesale from another source. For instance, an episode of a television show copied by a user and shared on a content platform such as YouTube is not classified as UGC.[15] Nonetheless, such content taken wholesale will be included within this book's scope, as infringement issues clearly arise for consideration where content is uploaded without the permission of copyright holders.

With reference to the third limb of the OECD definition, UGC refers to content created *outside of professional practices*, and that does not have a commercial market.[16] At the initial stages of the participative web, UGC was produced with social incentives in mind, such as the desire for self-expression and status, rather than with the expectation of remuneration.[17] This last characteristic of non-commercialism is increasingly unreliable as an identifying element of UGC,[18] as amateur users often evolve into professionals after an initial phase of non-commercial activity. Indeed, commercial interests can co-exist with altruistic motivations behind the production of content on social media.[19]

Moreover, the point of time when commercial motivations arise in an amateur creator requires a subjective enquiry into his or her intention, which may not be ascertainable. In applying this qualifier in the third limb, more allowance for deviation should be tolerated. If the requirement for absence of commercial motivation is applied restrictively, it can effectively exclude a substantially large amount of UGC from this book's scope. The creation of content beyond a professional routine nevertheless remains a useful concept in general to distinguish UGC from content conventionally produced by commercial entities.[20] Notwithstanding this, given the limitations of the third limb of the OECD definition, it should not be rigidly applied in determining if any content in question is UGC.

In the following section, I will explain – with reference to existing classifications of UGC and social media – why I have chosen to look at the content-generative activities occurring across certain categories of social media platforms.

II. Choice of social media platforms

It is important to identify both the type of UGC with which the book is concerned and the context in which the UGC is created, modified and disseminated, in order to decide which social media platforms to survey for the book. This is because the production of different types of UGC is linked to the specific UGC distribution platforms.[21]

In this respect I have decided to confine the book to evaluating the activities which generate what Troscrow et al identify as 'creative content'[22] or 'individual textual, audio, image, video and multimedia productions that are distributed online through software platforms including blogs and podcast repositories'. These platforms include, among others, Facebook, Pinterest, Twitter, YouTube (four out of five social media platforms surveyed for this book), Tumblr and Flickr, as well as citizen journalism sites.[23]

At the same time I have drawn on Kaplan and Haenlein's classification of social media[24] to focus on four specific categories of social media.[25] These categories are: collaborative projects; blogs; content communities; and social networking sites.[26] Because virtual game and social worlds raise special issues, I have excluded the last two categories of Kaplan and Heinlein's classification from consideration.[27] Given the chosen focus of the book, I will investigate in particular the application of copyright laws to the content-generative activities, and explore how these align with the terms of service and the technological features, across selected social media platforms from the four categories. I have selected at least one platform[28] from each of these four categories for survey in the book.

III. A day in the life of Jane

It is timely to give examples of how content can be created, modified and shared on multiple social media platforms by a hypothetical user named Jane Doe, along with other users, all in a single day. In this case study my focus on content-generative activities resulting in 'creative content' on four categories of social media informs my choice of the social media platforms Jane and other users generate content on. The platforms surveyed for the purpose of the book and henceforth included as platforms used under the case study will include: the social networking site Facebook;[29] the content communities Pinterest[30] and YouTube;[31] the blog Twitter;[32] and the collaborative project Wikipedia.[33] With the case study modelled after the usual content-generative activities occurring on social media, I can then consider how the similar activities of Jane and the other users are practically regulated by copyright laws, the terms of service and the technological features in the subsequent chapters of the book. I have also made references in the case study to social media platforms not surveyed in the book, such as the blog WordPress. Such references are useful in illustrating the methodical way in which the regulatory factors on another social media platform outside the book's scope can be considered.

Jane wakes up one morning to a 'bespoke' alarm call from an application on her mobile device.[34] Her friend Elly has recommended to her a music video clip of her favourite singer uploaded by the singer's managers on YouTube, and Jane has chosen to have the video clip played, through the application, as her alarm this morning. She is pleasantly surprised with her friend's good choice, opens her Pinterest account while still in bed and 'pins' the video on her pin-board named 'My Favourite Things', with the comment 'Use as your wake-up call!' This addition on her pin-board is viewed by over two hundred of her 'followers' in their 'home feeds', comprising both close friends and strangers, all of whom have decided to 'follow'[35] Jane's interests on Pinterest.

Jane jumps out of bed and promptly dresses for work. Her workplace is an hour's ride from her home, but this does not concern her. There are just so many ways she can entertain herself on the train, as she has done every single weekday morning. She whips out her mobile phone and logs into her Facebook account to check what her friends are up to. Through her 'news feed' she gets to view the posts of others within her network. One of her friends, Evangeline, wrote a commentary about income inequality – Jane reads it, and could not help agreeing more, so much so that she is inspired to share the post with others. To re-post this commentary of Evangeline's on her own 'Timeline', there are a few options available to Jane. She can choose either to do a manual selection of the text, followed by a 'copy and paste', or she can choose more conveniently to click the 'Share' option tab positioned right under her friend's commentary. In the first scenario, it may not be clear to a third party reading the post from Jane's 'Timeline' that Evangeline is the original author, unless Jane makes the effort to attribute Evangeline as the author, perhaps by incorporating a short note to that effect. In the latter scenario, if Jane chooses to use the 'Share' option, the source of the content, being Evangeline, will be clearly reflected in the post on Jane's 'Timeline'.

What if Jane decided to include her views and to incorporate them as part of the post, just above or below the original commentary written by Evangeline? In this case, Jane's comment is not distinguishable from Evangeline's original commentary, at least to readers of such post. What if these views of Jane's are substantive in quantum and quality, and not mere one-liner comments to Evangeline's original post? Alternatively Jane may simply decide to insert her views as a 'comment' on Facebook, placed under the original post from Evangeline. Running through these options in her head, Jane decides instead to weave her views into Evangeline's commentary, such that the commentary as a whole puts forward a coherent argument. Unfortunately, the content contributed by Evangeline can no longer be separately identified in Jane's commentary. Nevertheless, Jane posts this commentary, which incorporates her comments to Evangeline's original commentary, on her Facebook 'Timeline'.

If Jane does not expressly attribute Evangeline as the original author of the content that Jane drew from in her commentary, Evangeline's identity will be obscured. Is Jane's commentary copyright protected? What are Evangeline's rights in relation to preventing Jane's use in this instance? Does Facebook, through its terms of service and technological features, encourage Jane and other users to engage in content-generative activities that respect the copyrights of other users such as Evangeline, or is one witnessing the contrary instead?

Still logged into her Facebook account, Jane glances at her watch and realises that she has half an hour to go before she arrives at her destination. Her Twitter account runs in the background and she decides to take this time to check her 'Twitter feed'. She notes, to her delight, that her favourite celebrity blogger Small-Steps[36] just 'tweeted' 'New Post – Welcoming a New Member into our Family'. A link to this latest post on Small-Steps' WordPress site has been included within the 'tweet'. Jane immediately clicks on this link, and at the top of Small-Steps' blog post, she spots a photograph of Small-Steps' newborn baby, just delivered yesterday evening at a local hospital.

A brilliant idea comes to Jane's mind, and she immediately searches for other photographs of newborn babies on the pin-boards of other Pinterest users using the key search term 'newborn'. To her delight, lots of results show up on this search. Jane carefully selects the photographs that appeal to her, crops some of them and forms a collage with the selected images. In creating this collage, Jane uses the aid of some photo-editing applications on her mobile phone. She is proud of this collage and decides to title it 'Remedy for an Aging Population' before sharing the collage on her pin-board on Pinterest. She is given the option, on Pinterest's interface, as to whether she wants to simultaneously share the 'pin' on Facebook. Feeling it a waste not to share it, she decides to do so, and her collage appears accordingly on her Facebook 'Timeline'. She also shares the collage on Twitter, by incorporating the link to her pin-board in a 'tweet'. At the same time Jane decides to log into her WordPress account, so that she can share her collage with the readers of her blog and express at greater length the thoughts she had while creating the collage.

When Jane finally reaches work, a group of her colleagues approaches her and tell her that they agree very much with her latest commentary on income inequality on Facebook – in fact, they think that her commentary makes a very original and credible argument. One of her colleagues Zee has strong convictions in sharing information for public benefit and decides unilaterally to add this information on 'income inequality' posted by Jane on her 'Timeline' to the content page on 'income inequality' on Wikipedia. Zee holds the opinion that listing the source of the new information he contributed (ie, being a user's Facebook 'Timeline') may defeat the credibility of the information, and he decides against attributing Jane as the source of the comment. Jane is not aware of this, nor that subsequent to Zee's sharing of her commentary, other content contributors to Wikipedia will eventually develop on Jane's original expression of her idea. Due to Zee's contribution of Jane's commentary, the content page on 'income inequality' on Wikipedia is modified into something quite different from what it once was.

On returning home after a hard day at work, Jane winds down by watching video clips on YouTube. Feeling her creative juices churning again, she decides to share a new video clip on YouTube, as well as on the 'Timeline' of her Facebook page, created by way of 'vidding',[37] so that her final clip comprises extracted footages from different video clips available on YouTube. This video clip she creates incorporates scenes shared by the producers of her favourite television series, 'Making Good', with scenes from other random video clips shared of the same television series, albeit not uploaded by the producers nor with their consent. This video clip is intended to reflect Jane's interpretation and thoughts of how a character, by whom she is particularly intrigued, develops in the series. Later that evening Cheryl – someone Jane does not know – chances on Jane's video clip on YouTube. She decides to take screen captures of a few images from the clip and to display these screenshots as thumbnail images on her website, for aesthetic purposes and to tell a different story.

With reference to the events above, what are Jane's rights against Zee and Cheryl, in relation to her commentary and her video clip respectively, under copyright laws? What are the rights of the producers of the television series 'Making Good' against Jane? How can social media platforms such as Facebook, Wikipedia and YouTube influence Jane, Zee and Cheryl's compliance with copyright laws, when they generate content on these platforms?

Before going to sleep that night, Jane thinks of her use of multiple social media platforms and the comments that she has received – from friends, colleagues, and readers whom she does not personally know – for the content she has shared on Facebook, Pinterest, Twitter, WordPress and YouTube. She is grateful that through technology she can widen her reach to so many different audiences. She does not anticipate that, in the next couple of weeks, the collage she shared on Pinterest, Facebook and Twitter, while on her way to work that morning, will spread like wildfire on social media, and that the original photographs included in the collage will be recognised by all the mothers of the newborns featured. Some of the photographs have been cropped, while others, remaining un-cropped, have been photo-edited such that the edited photographs can be differentiated from the originals.

Quite a few avid social media users adopt Jane's style of creating this collage. Several selectively crop a portion of her collage to create their own versions for dissemination on Pinterest, Facebook and Twitter. Meanwhile Jane's collage also catches the attention of a magazine editor, Jasper. He considers using it on the cover page for his magazine's next issue, since its feature article will be on the falling birth rates in developed countries.

Further questions arise from these events. What are the rights of the users who own the copyrights to the original photographs against Jane? Will other users who have adapted and disseminated Jane's collage fall foul of copyright laws? What are the rights of Jane, as well as of the users who own the copyrights to the original photographs, against Jasper, if he uses Jane's collage as described? Is an application of the terms of service and the technological features on platforms such as Pinterest, Facebook and Twitter consistent with an application of copyright laws to the content-generative activities of Jane and other users?

There could be more questions raised than there are answers for them. Indeed, there are endless possibilities for the content-generative activities that can occur on social media and their consequential implications under copyright laws. Within this book's limitations, my focus on the activities described in the case study will make more tangible the ways in which copyright laws, the terms of service and the technological features regulate the content-generative behaviours of social media users.

Table 1.1 Overview of the formats of content generated and the content-generative activities occurring across four categories of social media

Type of social media platform	Examples	Description of main activities on social media platform	Formats and descriptions of content	Content-generative activities that may attract copyright liabilities
Collaborative Projects	*Wikis* **Wikipedia** Wikia	To add, delete and/or modify content	Text: Original works written or adapted from other works	Using, in part, the original work of another person to contribute to the content on wikis
			Photographs or images: Photographs or images taken, modified and/or posted	Using, in part, the derivative or transformative work of another person (not being the original author) to contribute to the content on wikis
			Music and audio: Music and audio files recorded, edited and/or posted	
			Videos: Video files recorded, edited and/or posted, such video files being remixes of existing content, original home-made content or a combination of the two	

(continued)

Table 1.1 *(Cont.)*

Type of social media platform	Examples	Description of main activities on social media platform	Formats and descriptions of content	Content-generative activities that may attract copyright liabilities
Blogs	*Single-Author or Multi-Author Blogs*: Blogger WordPress LiveJournal	To create entries at desired intervals on any topic, for the purpose of providing commentaries on various subjects, to serve as online diaries and/or to advertise brands online To allow for interactivity with readers, who are in most instances allowed to leave comments and respond to other readers via widgets	All of the above pertaining to Collaborative Projects apply here	All of the above pertaining to Collaborative Projects apply here, but in respect of contributing to the content on blogs Commenting on, criticising or targeting the original work of another person for ridicule Using, in part, the original work of another person to comment on something else, although the secondary work retains its underlying relevance to the original work Re-contextualising the original work without modification, but changing the meaning of the original work, so that the secondary work is perceived differently by others Changing the purpose of the original work within an expressive context[i]
	Micro-blogs: Tumblr **Twitter**	Same as above, but entries of digital content are smaller To allow for more interactivity with readers, who are allowed to re-post the entries to demonstrate consensus	All of the above pertaining to Collaborative Projects apply here	All of the above pertaining to Single-Author or Multi-Author Blogs apply here, in respect of the smaller entries

Content Communities	**YouTube** Vimeo Instagram IMDB Rotten Tomatoes **Pinterest** HubPages Etsy	To upload and/or view content To allow for interactivity, since viewers are allowed to leave comments	All of the above pertaining to Collaborative Projects apply here	All of the above pertaining to Single-Author or Multi-Author Blogs apply here, particularly in respect of mash-ups and remixes
Social Networking Sites	**Facebook** LinkedIn Google Plus	All of the above pertaining to blogs and Content Communities apply here What is written on Collaborative Projects applies only to a limited extent (particularly in respect of deleting or modifying content, other than by way of giving comments to an original post), mainly due to the absence of the common goal to produce content with combined effort	All of the above pertaining to Collaborative Projects apply here	All of the above pertaining to Single-Author or Multi-Author Blogs apply here

i These categories of uses are the types of transformative uses for which the fair use doctrine in the US arises for consideration. See David Tan, 'The Transformative Use Doctrine and Fair Dealing in Singapore' (2012) 24 *Singapore Academy of Law Journal* 832, 846–8. A fifth category was recognised in David Tan, 'The Lost Language of the First Amendment in Copyright Fair Use: Leval's "Transformative Use" Doctrine Twenty-Five Years On' (2016) 26 *Fordham Intellectual Property, Media & Entertainment Law Journal* 311, 324–5. This fifth category relates to changing the purpose of the original work within a technological context (for example, time-shifting for later viewing) and is therefore not relevant for consideration in respect of the content-generative activities occurring on social media.

IV. Conclusion

Table 1.1 above lists the content-generative activities that occur on social media platforms such as collaborative projects, blogs, content communities and social networking sites. It also articulates an overview of the formats of content that is generated and the activities that potentially attract copyright liabilities. The platforms surveyed in this book are highlighted in bold.

With the defined focus of this chapter in mind, I will discuss, in the next chapter, copyright's regulation of the content-generative behaviours of social media users, especially the challenges posed by the copyright laws of the US, the UK and Australia. I will also consider the implications of the strict application of copyright laws to the content-generative activities of Jane and the other users in the case study.

Notes

1. See, for example, Mayfield, A. 2008; DeNardis, L. and Hackl, W.M. 2015; Hogan, B. and Quan-Haase, A. 2010.
2. Kaplan, A.M. and Haenlein, M. 2010, 61. See also Bruns, A. and Bahnisch, M. 2009.
3. See generally Tim O' Reilly, 'What is Web 2.0: Design Patterns and Business Models for the Next Generation of Software' (2007) 65 *Commerce and Strategies* 17.
4. Kaplan, A.M. and Haenlein, M. 2010, 61.
5. See Warren Chik, 'Paying it Forward: The Case for a Specific Statutory Limitation on Exclusive Rights for User-Generated Content under Copyright Law' (2011) 11 *The John Marshall Review of Intellectual Property Law* 240, 244.
6. Sacha Wunsch-Vincent and Graham Vickery, *Participative Web: User-Created Content* (12 April 2007) <http://www.oecd.org/sti/38393115.pdf>.
7. See, for example, Daniel Gervais, 'The Tangled Web of UGC: Making Copyright Sense of User-Generated Content' (2009) 11(4) *Vanderbilt Journal of Entertainment and Technology Law* 841, 857; Chik, W. 2011, 248; Kaplan, A.M. and Haenlein, M. 2010, 61; Pamela J. McKenzie et al, 'User-generated online content 1: Overview, current state and context' (4 June 2012) 17(6) *First Monday* 1, 3 <http://firstmonday.org/htbin/cgiwrap/bin/ojs/index.php/fm/article/view/3912/3266>; Michael B. McNally et al, 'User-generated online content 2: Policy implications' (4 June 2012) 17(6) *First Monday* 1, 3 <http://firstmonday.org/htbin/cgiwrap/bin/ojs/index.php/fm/article/viewArticle/3913/3267>; Patricia Aufderheide and Peter Jaszi, *Recut, Reframe, Recycle: Quoting Copyrighted Material in User-Generated Video* (January 2008) <http://www.centerforsocialmedia.org/sites/default/files/CSM_Recut_Reframe_Recycle_report.pdf>.
8. See Steven Hetcher, 'Amateur Creative Digital Content and Proportional Commerce' in Dan Hunter et al (eds), *Amateur Media: Social, Cultural and Legal Perspectives* (Routledge, 2013) 35, 35.
9. See Preface in Hunter, D. et al. 2013.
10. Hunter, D. et al. 2013. Alternatively this could mean that the pastime or activity is not done for remuneration alone.
11. McNally, M.B. et al. 2012, 4.
12. Wunsch-Vincent, S. and Vickery, G. 2007.
13. Wunsch-Vincent, S. and Vickery, G. 2007.
14. See, for example, Gervais, D. 2009, 858.
15. McNally, M.B. et al. 2012, 4.
16. Wunsch-Vincent, S. and Vickery, G. 2007.

17. See, for example, Wunsch-Vincent, S. and Vickery, G. 2007.
18. Wunsch-Vincent, S. and Vickery, G. 2007.
19. Kimberlee Weatherall, 'The Relationship between User-generated Content and Commerce' in Dan Hunter et al. 2013, 59, 61.
20. Wunsch-Vincent, S. and Vickery, G. 2007.
21. Wunsch-Vincent, S. and Vickery, G. 2007.
22. I have referred to one classification of user-generated content (UGC), proposing that there are three principal intersecting and overarching models of content creation and distribution; see Samuel E. Troscow et al, *Mobilizing User-Generated Content for Canada's Advantage* (1 December 2010) Faculty of Information and Media Studies at the University of Western Ontario <ir.lib.uwo.ca/fimspub/21/>. The classification was borne out of an earlier study conducted by a group of researchers, most of whom co-authored the subsequent article proposing this classification; see McKenzie, P.J. et al. 2012. The reference made to *creative content* (ie, content under the first model) under this classification is general; it may not always include content that meets the requisite modicum of creativity and is hence copyright-protectable. Under the second model, there are *small-scale tools* that are software applications or modifications written to provide access to pre-existing data sets, or to augment software and hardware platforms. These tools can include, among others, user-created applications for mobile devices or for social media platforms such as Facebook, modifications and virtual objects created by users of virtual social worlds (for instance, Second Life) or virtual game worlds (for instance, World of Warcraft). Under the third model there is *collaborative content*, which refers to content collaboratively produced and distributed by individuals or companies. This content includes, among others, content on wikis such as Wikipedia and open-source software such as the Mozilla Firefox web browser. These categories are not mutually exclusive – for example, collaborative content, comprising individual and collective contributions, is typically also creative content (as is the case with content on Wikipedia).
23. Hunter, D. et al. 2013, 2.
24. Kaplan, A.M. and Haenlein, M. 2010, 59–61. The classification relies on a set of theories in the dual fields of media research and social processes. While the former field is defined by properties such as social presence and media richness, the latter field is defined by properties such as self-presentation and self-disclosure. In relation to the first field – the media dimension in the term 'social media' – the element of social presence is dependent on the intimacy and immediacy of the medium of communication, while the concept of media richness is premised on the assumption that the goal of communicating to another is the reduction of ambiguity. See Richard L. Daft and Robert H. Lengel, 'Organisational Information Requirements, Media Richness and Structural Design' (1986) 32(5) *Management Science* 554. In relation to the second field – the social-related component of the term 'social media' – presentation of the self by an individual comes with the desire to control others' impressions of him or her. See Erving Goffman, *The Presentation of Self in Everyday Life* (Doubleday Anchor Books, 1959); see also John Short et al, *Social Psychology of Telecommunications* (John Wiley & Sons, 1976). Just as is the case with UGC, the categories are not mutually exclusive – for example, a social networking platform such as Facebook has characteristics associated with content communities. A Facebook user can not only establish connections with other users, but he or she can also share content in various formats with such other users.
25. This classification is proposed together with their oft-cited definition of social media. See, for example, The Social Media Guys, *The Complete Guide to Social Media* (8 November 2010) <http://www.thesocialmediaguys.co.uk/wp-content/uploads/downloads/2011/03/CompleteGuidetoSocialMedia.pdf>; Julia Ying-Chao Lin et al, 'Social Media Usage and Work Values: The Example of Facebook in Taiwan' (2012) 40(2) *Social Media and Personality* 195, 196; Wikipedia, *Social media* <http://en.wikipedia.org/wiki/Social_media>; Jan H. Kietzmann et al, 'Social Media? Get Serious! Understanding the Functional Building Blocks of Social Media' (2011) 54 *Business Horizons* 241, 242; James Benjamin, 'Tweets, Blogs and the Ethics of 21st-Century Communication Technology' in Hana S. Noor Al-Deen and Hohn Allen Hendricks (eds), *Social Media: Usage and Impact* (Lexington, 2011) 271, 277.
26. Collaborative projects enable the concurrent creation of content by multiple users, and include wikis as well as social bookmarking applications. Blogs are platforms that display posts typically in reverse chronological order; they can include personal journals as well as collations of information in specific content areas of interest. Content communities allow primarily for the sharing of media content between users. Social networking sites allow users primarily to

establish social networks online. Virtual game and social worlds are online communities that simulate real life by enabling users to appear in the form of personalised avatars to interact with one another; see Kaplan, A.M. and Haenlein, M. 2010. Virtual game and social worlds are excluded from consideration as the content generated in these environments constitutes small-scale tools. On the other hand, the content on platforms hosting collaborating projects is both collaborative and creative.

27. See, for example, Melissa de Zwart, 'For Fun rather than Profit: Playing around with Online Games' (2013) 18 *Media and Arts Law Review* 106; Melissa de Zwart and Sal Humphreys, 'Playing in Contested Zones: Norms, Laws and Rules in MMOGs' (2012) 17(1) *Media and Arts Law Review* 1.
28. Pinterest and YouTube are both content communities selected for the survey. This choice has been made so that a wider range of activities can be included in the case study and considered in this book. However, most formats of content can be shared on both platforms – Pinterest remains primarily an image-sharing platform and YouTube a platform to share video clips.
29. Facebook, *Facebook* <https//www.facebook.com>. Users of Facebook typically start using the service by creating profiles with their personal information and develop this further by establishing connections with others within the network. Users can communicate with 'friends' or other users – ie, those with whom the aforementioned users have not established virtual friendships – by sending private messages, utilising a chat feature or posting messages on the 'timelines' of these other 'friends' or users. The visibility of posts on the 'timelines' of Facebook users, whether to the public, 'friends' of such users or only to the users themselves, is dependent on the privacy settings of these Facebook users. As with most other social networking sites, Facebook allows users to 'post' photographs, audio files, video files and comments to the 'posts' or 'status updates' of other users.
30. See Wikipedia, *Pinterest* <en.wikipedia.org/wiki/Pinterest>. See also Pinterest, *pinterest.com* <www.pinterest.com>. Pinterest allows for the sharing of photographs, audio and video files on pin-boards. Users can also comment on other users' 'pins', as well as choose to re-share these 'pins' on Facebook and Twitter.
31. YouTube, *YouTube* <https://www.youtube.com>. On YouTube video files can be uploaded, viewed and shared (including on other social media platforms a user is registered on, such as Facebook, Google Plus, Tumblr, Twitter, and so on). A user can also comment on the video files shared by others.
32. See Wikipedia, *Twitter* <en.wikipedia.org/wiki/Twitter>. See also Twitter, *twitter.com* <www.twitter.com>. On a micro-blog such as Twitter, the main constraint is on the number of characters that a 'tweet' can have. Although primarily text-based, the text in a message can include the link to content in alternative media formats on other social media platforms such as YouTube, Pinterest, and so on.
33. Wikipedia, *Wikipedia* <https://www.wikipedia.org/>. Content can be added, deleted or modified on most Wikipedia pages, except where such pages are protected and can only be edited by established registered users.
34. For instance, the application Easy Alarm YouTube that allows users to play YouTube video clips as their clock alarms. This can be purchased from Google Play, *Easy Alarm YouTube* <https://play.google.com/store/apps/details?id=com.cimleah.easyalarm&hl=en>.
35. People typically 'follow' other users either due to associations in real life or due to similar interests.
36. A pseudonym used by the blogger.
37. 'Vidding' is the practice of creating video clips from the footage of one or more media sources. See, for example, Wikipedia, *Vidding* <http://en.wikipedia.org/wiki/Vidding>.

Chapter Two
Regulation by copyright laws

In this chapter I consider the application of copyright laws of the US, the UK and Australia to the content-generative activities of social media users. I begin by discussing the following copyright subsistence and infringement issues: the types of subject matter that are protected by copyright laws; originality and authorship requirements; fixation, recording or reduction to material form; the scope of rights protected, including moral rights; available remedies; exceptions to copyright infringement, in particular, the fair use doctrine in the US and the fair dealing exceptions in the UK and in Australia; and finally, conflict of laws issues. I also outline the challenges posed in addressing these issues.

I then apply the copyright laws of each of the three jurisdictions to the content-generative activities undertaken by Jane and other users in the case study, under the first of four hypothetical scenarios in this book. I do not seek here to determine with finality how the copyright issues will be resolved in relation to each activity. Specific analysis is possible only in the context of particular disputes. My purpose is rather to provide a general overview of the interaction between copyright laws and the generation of content in the social media context.

The application of copyright laws in this chapter to the case study constitutes scenario one of this book. It allows for the evaluation of the consistency of the copyright regimes, with each of the terms of service and the technological features, under subsequent scenarios in the later chapters.

I. Relevant copyright standards

The clause on intellectual property rights in the US Constitution provides for the promotion of 'the progress of science and useful arts, by securing for limited times to authors and inventors the exclusive right to their respective writings and discoveries'.[1] The US Supreme Court has reiterated in its decisions that copyright exists to promote creative expression and its dissemination, so as to encourage others to build freely upon the ideas contained within copyright works.[2] In the UK the goal for copyright is similarly articulated in the first statute providing for the regulation of copyright, the *Statute of Anne 1709*;[3] its preamble described the act as one for 'the encouragement of learning'.[4] Australian copyright law has this same goal as its British counterpart.[5]

The respective copyright statutes in the US, the UK and Australia have been shaped, to some extent, by the obligations assumed by each country under international instruments such as the *Berne Convention for the Protection of Literary and Artistic Works* (*Berne Convention*)[6] and the *Trade-Related Aspects of Intellectual Property Rights Agreement* (*TRIPS Agreement*).[7] In the following sub-sections I will refer to the copyright principles contained in the *Copyright Act of 1976* in the US (*US Copyright Act*),[8] the *Copyright, Patents and Designs Act 1988* in the UK (*UK Copyright Act*)[9] and Australia's *Copyright Act 1968* (Cth) (*Australian Copyright Act*).[10] In particular, given that copyright laws protect digital content, including content on social media, I will discuss the potential application of the copyright laws of these three jurisdictions to the content-generative activities on social media. I will also set out the challenges faced in addressing copyright issues pertaining to these activities. This will enable me to examine how social media platforms can alter the effectiveness of copyright laws in regulating users' content-generative behaviours.

A. Subsistence: works and other subject matter protected by copyright

Given the dual role of users as producers and consumers of content on social media, it is important for users to know whether the content they create and share on social media is copyright protected, and if this entitles them to rights against other users. In addition, users may like to know whether the primary content they use from social media to create secondary content is entitled to copyright protection in its own right. For example, are 'status updates' on Facebook and 'tweets' on Twitter protected under the copyright laws of the US, the UK and Australia? Addressing questions on copyright subsistence requires a preliminary assessment as to whether the particular content falls under the categories of works and other subject matter protected.

The categories of copyright-protected works are set out in a non-exhaustive list protected under the *US Copyright Act*. The content available across the five social media platforms surveyed is in textual, image, audio and video formats, and the categories of works that are principally relevant to this book include: literary works; musical works; dramatic works; 'pictorial, graphic and sculptural works';[11] audiovisual works; sound recordings; and architectural works.[12] Additionally, compilations of pre-existing materials or data, as well as derivative works – albeit not of materials used unlawfully or not contributed by the author in question[13] – are copyright protected.

In contrast, copyright protection under the *UK Copyright Act*[14] and the *Australian Copyright Act*[15] extends to a finite group of works and other subject matter.[16] This group includes literary, dramatic, musical and artistic works, as well as sound recordings and films. As a 'broadcast' is broadly defined in the UK[17] to include any internet transmission that takes place simultaneously on the internet, broadcasts are relevant for consideration in the book. On the other hand, a 'broadcast' in Australia[18] is more narrowly defined and will not be relevant. Additionally, because of the limited definitions of 'published editions' in the UK[19] and the references made to 'published editions' in Australia,[20] published editions are not relevant to this book.

At the same time, as minor contributions of content are incorporated through incremental activities on social media and are regular occurrences on social media, users are likely to be confused on whether content created or used by them with minimal effort is protected under copyright laws. Mature copyright systems protect expressions, but not ideas, facts and other building blocks of literary and artistic expression.[21] In the US such material, whether or not embodied in copyright-protected works and subject matter, is expressly excluded from copyright protection.[22] For instance, the *US Copyright Office Regulations* provide, as examples of materials not protected by copyright and of which applications for registrations will not be entertained, 'words and short phrases such as names, titles and slogans' and, among other things, ideas, plans and so on.[23] The axiom that copyright protection only covers the expression of ideas has been described as an amorphous characterisation rather than a principled guidepost.[24] As such, courts in the US have developed two doctrines to fill the gaps.[25]

With reference to Goldstein and Hugenholtz's description of the doctrines, the first is the *doctrine of merger* and the second, '*scènes à faire*'. Under these two doctrines expressions will not be copyright protected if the underlying ideas can be expressed in only one or a limited number of ways.[26] While the first doctrine usually applies to functional works, such as rules, forms and computer programs, the second applies mainly to fictional works, including novels and dramas.[27] Because the second doctrine withholds copyright protection from elements such as narrated incidents that are preordained by un-protectable ideas, including basic plot,[28] this could mean that a fair amount of content on social media platforms – being expressions which flow from the commonplace ideas shared on the platforms – is not copyright protected. An example of such content is a status update on Facebook, say a photograph of the blue skies on a sunny day, accompanied by a comment that reads: 'Perfect weather for a stroll today!' This comment on its own will not be copyright protected. Also, as users can undertake content-generative activities simultaneously in relation to the same content on social media, they may frequently arrive at similar expressions that necessarily follow the same idea.

The two doctrines in the US described above are employed to effectuate the distinction between ideas and expressions.[29] This idea–expression dichotomy similarly applies in the UK and in Australia, and results in the non-protection of ideas under copyright laws.[30]

B. Subsistence: originality

Whether content generated on social media is protected under copyright laws will be determined by the originality of such content. This concept of originality under copyright laws[31] is closely linked to the concept of authorship, which will be discussed next.

The measure for originality entitling a work to copyright protection is the independent creation by its author (as opposed to copying from other works) and the exercise of some minimal degree of creativity.[32] In the US, originality is the touchstone of copyright protection.[33] Differentiating between a mechanical arrangement of content that is not copyright protected and a compilation that is – provided that there is some creative effort found in the arrangement or selection of material – can be challenging.[34] For example, is a collage incorporating a few images shared previously on Pinterest deserving of copyright protection on this measure? If the material variation test[35] is used to counter the ambiguity of the definition of 'creativity',[36] the question that arises will be whether the secondary work contained more than a trivial variation vis-à-vis the original work and is hence copyright protected. Nevertheless, the analysis to be undertaken in respect of such variations in terms of number, size, abstract significance and so on necessarily entails multiple subjective judgements which can result in different outcomes.

In the UK[37] and in Australia,[38] the statutory requirement of originality for copyright protection only applies in relation to literary, dramatic, musical and dramatic works; it does not apply in relation to other subject matter such as sound recordings, films and broadcasts.[39] In both jurisdictions, copyright protection has to be the result of a person's 'skill, labour or experience', in addition to being more than a copy of earlier content.[40] It is worth noting that the threshold to be met for the originality requirement in all three jurisdictions is fairly low.[41]

Further, in the UK, the requirement of sufficient skill and/or labour is suggested to operate as a *proviso de minimis* (ie, a court will refuse to consider trifling matters) and henceforth excludes works in which the degree of literary composition is slight from copyright protection.[42] Similarly, in Australia, Ricketson has suggested that the application of the *de minimis* principle results in the denial of copyright protection in works on the basis that they are not original, or alternatively are 'insubstantial' in purely quantitative terms.[43] There is also the consideration that conferring copyright protection on single words or phrases may intrude too much on the rights of the public,[44] in the case of which the real reason for denying copyright protection is suggested to be one of public policy.[45] In this respect English and Australian courts have not recognised as copyright-protected works the following: an advertisement consisting of four common sentences;[46] the title of a song;[47] the word 'Exxon', which is a well-known trademark;[48] a short series of words communicating the need for assistance;[49] and headlines.[50]

The question then is whether simple activities such as the posting of a brief 'status update' on Facebook, commenting on content shared on Pinterest or YouTube and 'tweeting' on Twitter, as well as making minor edits on Wikipedia, result in content that is copyright protected. Given that much of the content on social media platforms will be short or insubstantial works, add-ons and revisions, ascertaining whether content is copyright protected in an instance will require consideration of the following:

(i) The application of the idea–expression dichotomy discussed in sub-section (A);
(ii) The satisfaction of the originality requirement; and/or
(iii) The application of the *de minimis* principle (ie, copyright-protected works need to comprise a certain minimal amount of content).

For example, a 'tweet' – limited to a maximum of 140 characters on Twitter – may not be copyright protected because of either *or* all of the following reasons: the 'tweet' consists of facts or ideas; the 'tweet' is insufficiently original; or the 'tweet' fails to meet the basic quantitative requirement.[51] The joke of the freelance writer Olga Lexell, which reads: 'Saw someone spill their high end juice cleanse all over the sidewalk and now I know God is on my side'[52] is therefore more likely to be copyright protected than a 'tweet' that reads: 'Loving the sunny Melbourne', given that all three of the reasons apply in the case of the latter 'tweet'.

The rate at which content is simultaneously created, modified and disseminated by social media users gives rise to additional considerations. The degree of originality between successive versions of content[53] (for instance, where derivative material is based upon pre-existing material)[54] required for copyright protection, as well as the point at which content contributed as an add-on or revision becomes a copyright-protected work in terms of quantum, raise issues that are difficult to resolve.[55] Richard Prince's recent sale of the enlarged images shared by other users on Instagram as artworks comes to mind here.[56] In between an original image first shared by the relevant Instagram user and the subsequent artwork incorporating this image sold by Prince, a few successive versions of the modified image were possibly generated on Instagram – this happens when users, including Prince, comment on the image. The 'modified composites' of the images circulating on Instagram which incorporate other users' (including Prince's) comments are arguably not derivative works; there is little originality and authorial activity[57] to qualify them as warranting separate consideration. It is far from certain, however, whether Prince's artworks will qualify as copyright-protected derivative works by virtue of his enlargement and re-contextualisation of the relevant images.

Indeed, there is no clear approach under existing authorities that can definitively address the issues raised above, to give certainty as to whether specific content on social media (whether new or a successive version of content) is copyright protected. Moreover, given the three criteria highlighted above, it is foreseeable that a large volume of content on social media may not be copyright protected under the copyright laws of all three jurisdictions.

C. Subsistence: authorship

Next the authors of content on social media, in whom copyright resides, have to be identified. While the *US Copyright Act* expressly provides that copyright vests in the author or authors of the work, and that the authors of a joint work are co-owners of the copyright of such work,[58] the term 'author' remains undefined. A 'joint work' has been defined as a work prepared by two or more authors with the intention that their contributions be merged into inseparable parts of a unitary whole.[59] This requirement for contemporaneous intention has been suggested to be satisfied even where participants do not know one another and have not worked within the same time frame, so long as each participant contributed with the intention of integrating his or her contribution into a unitary product.[60] Examples of such joint works, each created by multiple authors holding the intention to merge their contributions into a single product, are the content pages on Wikipedia.

At the same time, under the *UK Copyright Act*, an 'author' is defined as the person who creates a work,[61] and 'a work of joint authorship' is defined as a work produced by the collaboration of two or more authors and in which the contribution of each author is not distinct from the other(s).[62] In Australia the term 'author' is defined only in relation to a photograph under the *Australian Copyright Act*;[63] similarly, 'a work of joint authorship' refers to a work that is produced by the collaboration of two or more authors and in which the contributions of each author are inseparable from one another.[64] In view of these definitions in the UK and in Australia, it is less clear if content pages on Wikipedia are 'works of joint authorship'. Although the history of a content page sets out the individual contribution made to that page by each user, each user's contribution to, or editing of, a single sentence in the page can be so minor that it may be practically unfeasible to distinguish the individual contribution of one user from another. If this is the case, such content pages on Wikipedia are 'works of joint authorship'.

Further, in spite of the provision for joint authorship under the copyright laws of all three jurisdictions, it may be arduous to identify the users who have authored content on social media together. This is because such content frequently comprises parts from several users that are inseparable from one another, as per the definitions given for works jointly authored. Previous criticisms of copyright laws for failing to accommodate the realities of contemporary writing practices still hold true today,[65] as collaborative writing practices are shoehorned into the conventional human-centric concept of authorship.[66] While it remains crucial to identify the human authors of works jointly authored, it may be tedious to do so in relation to all such content on social media. For example, a user can write a segment for an article that incorporates existing contributions from other contributors on Wikipedia. Although all of the authors of this article are joint authors, their identification through their usernames[67] is subject to their retention of their Wikipedia user accounts. Also, more often than not, the Wikipedia platform will be attributed as the source of the relevant content – in this sense, the identification of the joint authors of content on Wikipedia takes a back seat.

In this respect Ginsburg, in critiquing the techno-postmodernist view of the 'death of the author' and the rising importance of the reader,[68] highlights that under this view, the reader no longer draws from the authored works of others. Instead, the reader casts the contents of his or her bucket into the 'constantly changing stream of reader-modified creations'.[69] In this sense, the reader is characterised as a creator, as reading is an act of creative interpretation in which readers give meaning to the texts they peruse.[70] Social media users are active participants: they interact with, and continuously contribute to, existing works, often to the same extent as the original producers of these works.[71] At the same time, Bently's observation that the author is a notion to be sustained only for an instant[72] is also relevant to the generation of content on social media. This is particularly the case as social media platforms are designed to allow for a great extent of collaborative participation from their users, in creating, modifying and disseminating content. Because active interaction with content is so often encouraged on social media, with no single user able to impose his or her unilateral significance as creator[73] over a piece of content, the palpable challenge faced is in deciding on whom copyright protection is vested.[74] For the reasons given above, these dilemmas around the designation of authorship (whether single, joint or multiple) and the identification of authors are amplified when it comes to content generated on collaborative projects such as Wikipedia.[75]

D. Subsistence: fixation, recording or reduction to material form

Where originality and authorship requirements standards are met, the issue of fixation, recording or reduction to material form comes into play. It has been argued that the content created on some categories of social media – for instance, social networking platforms such as Facebook and blogs (especially micro-blogs such as Twitter) – and which is not stored separately elsewhere does not meet the fixation standard, or its equivalent, for copyright protection.[76] This is because content on such platforms is incredibly fluid, and hence can be deleted just as quickly as it is posted.[77] For example, Twitter only displays the 3,200 most recent 'tweets'.[78] Although old 'tweets' are not displayed on Twitter, these 'tweets' are stored and hence copyright protected; moreover, they can still be located.[79] Further, some social media platforms may invite the continual participation of users with regard to the collaborative content on such platforms. Wikipedia, a long-term collaborative project that is open-ended, and that allows users to create, modify and share content over an indefinite period of time, is one example of such a platform. On the Wikipedia platform, given that content is constantly evolving, it is difficult to identify *at which point* content, and further *what content*, is fixed, recorded or reduced to material form, and thus copyright protected.[80]

In the US copyright protection is conferred on an original work when it is 'fixed in any tangible medium of expression' by or under the authority of the author.[81] So long as the embodiment of the work in a copy 'is sufficiently *permanent* or *stable* to permit it to be perceived, reproduced, or otherwise communicated for a period of *more than transitory duration*',[82] the nature of the medium is immaterial. In this respect the term 'copies' is broadly defined and refers to material objects, other than phonorecords, in which a work is fixed by any known method (whether existing now *or* later developed) and from which a work can be communicated, either *directly* or with the aid of a machine or *device*. Therefore copyright protection is granted to a work that is fixed, wherever that fixation takes place, whether on a web page of a social media platform or otherwise.

In the UK copyright only subsists in literary, dramatic and musical works that are '*recorded*, in writing or *otherwise*'.[83] Furthermore, an 'artistic work' is defined to mean, among others, a painting, drawing or photograph (ie, defined also as a recording of light or other radiation on any medium).[84] In addition, 'sound recordings' and 'films' are broadly defined to include recordings on *any* medium.[85] Similarly, in Australia, in respect of literary, dramatic, musical and artistic works, reference is made instead to works that are *reduced* to writing or some other *material form*,[86] the latter of which is defined to include *any* form of storage of the work.[87] 'Sound recordings' and 'cinematograph films' in Australia are also broadly defined.[88] Thus, in both the UK and in Australia, I argue that the wide definitions in relation to recording or reduction to material form, as the case may be, include the recording or storing of content on social media – such content can thus be copyright protected.

Finally, following the satisfaction of the fixation requirement, or its equivalent, copyright subsists in works and other subject matter only when conditions tied to the publication or authored status of such works or other subject matter are met. For instance, in the US published works (being literary, musical, dramatic, pictorial, graphic, sculptural, audiovisual or architectural works, as well as sound recordings, compilations and derivative works)[89] are copyright protected if, among other things,[90] they are first published in the US or in a foreign nation that is a treaty party.[91] Sound recordings are copyright protected only if they are first fixed in a treaty party.[92] Unpublished works, on the other hand, are granted copyright protection regardless of the nationality or domicile of the author.[93]

It is noted that the term 'publication' is defined as the distribution of copies of a work to the public by sale or other transfer of ownership.[94] On the face of this definition, content on social media may be considered *unpublished* in the US, as such content is not distributed to the public by sale or other transfer of ownership. Thus copyright's protection of content on social media could exist irrespective of the nationality or domicile of the relevant author.[95] There is hence no need to determine the precise venue of first publication or fixation of content on social media platforms: the treatment of content on social media as unpublished obviates this difficulty.[96] This would mean that content created by social media users without any connection to the US, but which meets the other copyright subsistence requirements discussed above, is copyright protected in the US.

In the UK a literary, dramatic, musical or artistic work, sound recording or film qualifies for copyright protection if such work, sound recording or film is first published in the UK, or the author is a qualifying person (such as a British citizen or a person resident in the UK).[97] The term 'publication' is, however, defined more broadly than in the US to include not only the issue of copies, but also the making available of literary, dramatic, musical or artistic works to the public by means of an electronic retrieval system.[98] While there is no definition of the term 'copies', the definition of 'copying' is instructive. In this respect 'copying' can include, among other things, the storing of a literary, dramatic, musical or artistic work in *any* medium by *electronic* means, as well as the making of copies that are *transient* or *incidental* to the use of such work.[99] By the application of these definitions, content shared on social media constitute *published* works in the UK.

In Australia the requirements for copyright protection are similar and refer, among other things, to the place of first publication, or the nationality or domicile of the author if the relevant work is published.[100] The term 'publication' is widely defined as occurring when reproductions of literary, dramatic, musical or artistic works are supplied, whether by sale or *otherwise*, to the public.[101] Therefore content on social media can constitute *published* works in Australia, just as in the UK. For such works to be copyright protected in either jurisdiction, the first publication, nationality or residency requirements mentioned earlier will need to be met.[102] While nationality and domicile are relatively easy to ascertain if the users who authored the content can be identified, the same cannot be said of identifying the country of first publication, given the global reach of content shared on social media.

This problem is somewhat mitigated by the principle of national treatment stipulated under article 5(1) of the *Berne Convention* which requires the country in which protection is claimed to treat foreign and domestic authors alike.[103] Although it may be challenging to identify the venue of first publication, it is more likely than not that the nationality and domicile of a user is that of a contracting party to the *Berne Convention*, given that very few countries are not contracting parties.[104] In general, so long as a user is a national or resident in a *Berne Convention* country, and other copyright subsistence requirements are met, the content he or she creates on social media will be copyright protected, even if the venue of first publication (if published) cannot be ascertained.

This means that, because all three countries are members of the *Berne Convention*,[105] just as content created by a social media user resident in the UK can receive copyright protection as unpublished content in the US, content created on social media by a person resident in the US will similarly receive copyright protection as published content in the UK, pursuant to *The Copyright (Application to Other Countries) Order 1993* in the UK.[106] The same content, if available online in Australia, being published in a *Berne Convention* country, is hence copyright protected by virtue of the *Copyright (International Protection) Regulations 1969* in Australia.[107]

E. Infringement: scope of protection

Once the copyright subsistence requirements are satisfied and the relevant content (whether on social media or otherwise) is found to be copyright protected, the next step is to inquire into the specific rights infringed by the activities undertaken with regard to such content. A copyright holder is entitled to a bundle of exclusive rights under the *US Copyright Act*.[108] Unless otherwise stated, these rights are held by authors of the full range of works that content on social media platforms can constitute, namely: literary works; musical works; dramatic works; pictorial, graphic and sculptural works; motion pictures and other audiovisual works; sound recordings; and architectural works.[109] The most basic right in the bundle to which a copyright holder is entitled is the right of *reproduction*.[110] As mentioned earlier, the term 'copies' is liberally defined. It refers to the material objects in which a work is fixed and from which a work can be *communicated*, either directly or with the aid of a machine or *device*.[111] This broad definition of 'copies' includes the reproductions of pre-existing content when users interact with such content on social media. Such reproductions can occur, for example, when users share another user's 'status update' on Facebook, 're-pin' a 'pin' on Pinterest or 're-tweet' another user's 'tweet' on Twitter.

Under the *UK Copyright Act*, the right of reproduction is one among others in a similar bundle of rights.[112] 'Copying'[113] can mean, among others: the storing of a literary, dramatic, musical or artistic work in *any* medium by *electronic means* (ie, in a material form);[114] the making of a copy in two dimensions of a three-dimensional work;[115] in relation to a film or broadcast, the making of a photograph of the whole or substantial part of any image forming part of the film or broadcast;[116] and the making of copies that are *transient* or *incidental* to some other use of a work.[117] This right of reproduction of a literary, dramatic, musical or artistic work in a material form is similarly set out under the *Australian Copyright Act*.[118] In respect of sound recordings and cinematograph films, copyright holders have the equivalent right to make copies of the relevant subject matter.[119]

The term 'material form' is widely defined to include *any* form of *storage* of a work or adaptation, or a substantial part of the work or adaptation; at the same time the term 'copy' refers to *any* article or thing in which the visual images or sounds comprising a cinematograph film are embodied.[120] Further, a work, sound recording or film is reproduced if it is converted into or from a digital or machine-readable format.[121] In addition, the right of reproduction under Australian copyright legislation can be infringed when a two-dimensional work is produced from a three-dimensional artistic work.[122] There are some exceptions from infringement, including one that applies to the taking of a photograph of a sculpture situated permanently in a public place.[123] There will, however, be an infringement if a photograph of a privately owned sculpture is shared on a platform such as Pinterest. Therefore some content-generative activities on social media, such as those described above, can involve the infringement of the right to reproduce existing content, whether reference is made to this right in the US, the UK or Australia.

The challenge faced is in differentiating these activities from other activities which involve *de minimis* uses (ie, the forms of copying that are too trivial for copyright laws to apply) and hence do not amount to infringement. In the US, whether the right of reproduction has been infringed is determined by the standard of substantial similarity. The allegedly infringing work is compared with the original work – both to ascertain the amount of the original work that has been copied, as well as the observability of the original work in the allegedly infringing work (particularly in the case of visual works).[124] In the UK and in Australia, the standard is couched in different terms. The reproduction of the whole or a substantial part of the original work in the allegedly infringing work can amount to infringement.[125] In any case, the application of the standard of substantial similarity in the US may not give rise to a different outcome from that reached in the UK and in Australia (ie, when the test of whether a substantial part of the original work has been reproduced is applied). This is given that the latter also involves looking at the similarities between the original and the allegedly infringing works.[126]

Secondly, the right of a copyright holder to *prepare derivative works* under the *US Copyright Act*[127] may be infringed, for example, when other users' 'pins' are modified to form collages on Pinterest or when 'vidding' results in new video clips on YouTube. The definition of a 'derivative work' under the *US Copyright Act* refers to 'a work based upon one or more preexisting works, such as a translation, musical arrangement, dramatization, fictionalization, motion picture version, sound recording, art reproduction, abridgement, condensation or any other form in which a work may be recast, transformed or *adapted*' and further states that 'a work consisting of editorial revisions … or other modifications which, as a *whole*, represent an *original* work of authorship' is a 'derivative work'.[128] The allegedly infringing derivative work also has to be 'substantially similar' to the original before it is seen as infringing.[129]

Further, the scope of application of this right to prepare derivative works is unclear. There are uncertainties as to whether material derived from an original work which does not qualify for copyright protection separately as a secondary work can infringe the derivative works right[130] (although, in any case, the right of reproduction could still be infringed if there is substantial similarity). If the view that a derivative work must be original and qualify for copyright protection for the derivative work's right to be infringed is adopted, the derivative work's right will only be relevant in a fairly narrow range of situations[131] with respect to content on social media.

Notwithstanding this, Prince's sale of art works comprising images shared on Instagram could be an example falling within this range of situations.[132] These resulting art works can be argued to be sufficiently modified (ie, in presentation and scale) by virtue of Prince changing the purpose[133] of the Instagram images to create original works of authorship, and are hence derivative works. They may also appear to be substantially similar to the original images as these images are readily observable in the art works[134] (although the wholesale embodiment of the images within the art works alone is not determinative), such that they are infringing of the rights to prepare derivative works.[135]

In the UK there is instead the right to *make adaptations* of works, or to do anything in relation to such adaptations.[136] This right of adaptation is only restricted by copyright in a literary, dramatic or musical work (but not an artistic work).[137] 'Adaptation' is further defined under the *UK Copyright Act.* The forms of adaptations include, among others: in relation to a literary work, a translation of the work or a version of the work in which the story is conveyed mainly by pictures in a form suitable for reproduction; or, in relation to a musical work, an arrangement or transcription of the work.[138] Under the *Australian Copyright Act*, this right is also referred to as the right of adaptation, and only attaches to a literary, dramatic or musical work (but not an artistic work).[139] What an 'adaptation' means is also similarly defined.[140] Additionally, in both jurisdictions, a copyright holder enjoys further rights to do anything in relation to the adaptation of a literary, dramatic or musical work.[141] In the UK and in Australia, given that the definitions of 'adaptation' are different from the definition of a 'derivative work' in the US, the right to make adaptations or to do anything in relation to these adaptations is potentially relevant for consideration in relation to different types of content-generative activities. The modification of content, undertaken by users on social media discussed earlier (ie, those that result in derivative works in the US), can, however, be considered in relation as to whether the right of reproduction has been infringed.

Thirdly, the right to *distribute*[142] is another right in the bundle. It is described, under the *US Copyright Act*, as the right 'to distribute copies or phonorecords of the copyright work to the public by *sale* or *any other transfer of ownership*, or by rental, lease or lending'.[143] As mentioned earlier, the term 'copies' refers to material objects in which a work is fixed and from which a work is communicated.[144] In spite of the lack of express stipulation, the digital transmission of content has been held to fall within the exercise of the exclusive right to distribute.[145] Further, although the transmission of content on social media platforms to the users of such platforms – for example, the sharing of a 'status update' on Facebook, a 'tweet' on Twitter or information on Wikipedia – is not occurring by sale or any other transfer of ownership, a US court is expected to take a broader view of a copyright holder's right to distribute his or her content, so as to uphold the exclusive rights held by copyright holders in the digital age.[146] In this respect, the right to distribute can be infringed through the usual dissemination or making available[147] of content on social media.

In the UK the equivalent to the right to distribute is the right *to issue copies of a work to the public.*[148] In light of the express exclusion of the subsequent distribution of copies previously put into circulation (from the exercise of this right) under the *UK Copyright Act*,[149] this right will not be infringed by the regular dissemination of content on social media, insofar as such dissemination involves content already circulated. Under the *Australian Copyright Act*, the right to *publish* is provided for in relation to literary, dramatic, musical and artistic works.[150] This right to (*first*) publish under section 31(1)[151] is distinguished from the notion of publication for the subsistence of copyright under section 32.[152] As in the UK, the right to publish is arguably not infringed by the typical dissemination of content on social media, so long as the content has already been made available to the public. Nonetheless, there are limited situations – such as the sharing of content known privately on social media for the first time (for example, when a private copy of a copyright-protected collage is converted into a digital copy and shared on social media, or when an image of a private sculpture is disseminated for the first time) – which can infringe this right of first publication.

Fourthly, a copyright holder has the right to *perform publicly*,[153] among others, works such as literary, dramatic or musical works, motion pictures or audiovisual works, as well as sound recordings (by means of digital audio transmissions). The term 'performance' is defined broadly. Also, the *US Copyright Act* makes clear that there is actionable infringement when there is a transmission of a performance of a copyright work, and explains what performing a work publicly means (includes performing at a place open to the public *or* transmitting or otherwise communicating a performance to the public, by means of any *device* or *process*, notwithstanding that the performance is *received in separate places at different times*).[154] Furthermore, the right to *display publicly*[155] applies (in addition to literary, musical or dramatic works) to pictorial, graphic and sculptural works, as well as individual images of motion pictures and other audiovisual works, and is defined broadly enough to include the showing of a copy of a work, either directly or by means of a 'film, slide, television image, or any other *device* or *process*'.[156]

Displaying a work publicly is as widely defined as performing a work publicly, and includes displaying the work at a place open to the public *or* transmitting or otherwise communicating the display of the work, by means of any *device* or *process*, notwithstanding that the display is *received in separate places at different times.*[157] A place open to the public can include a limited space which can accommodate only a few people at any one time, and the performance and display of a work are considered as 'public' irrespective of the composition of the audience.[158] Additionally, a copyright holder has the right to perform a sound recording publicly by means of a digital audio transmission.[159]

These broad definitions of public performance and display are intended to accommodate technological changes. This means that some content-generative activities on social media – in particular, the dissemination of content – can infringe the exclusive right of a copyright holder to perform and display publicly his or her content. An example of the former (ie, right to perform publicly) is the uploading of a television episode on YouTube, while an example of the latter (ie, right to display publicly) is the 'pinning' of a photograph of a private sculpture on Pinterest – both without the relevant copyright holders' consent.

In the UK the equivalent rights are the rights to *perform, show or play a work in public* and to *communicate a work to the public*.[160] The performance of a literary, dramatic or musical work includes any mode of visual or acoustic presentation, including a presentation by means of a sound recording, film or broadcast of the work.[161] The *UK Copyright Act* further provides that where copyright is infringed by virtue of the performance, playing or showing of a work, 'by *means* of *apparatus for receiving visual images* or *sounds conveyed by electronic means*', the person by whom the images or sounds are sent is not responsible for the infringement.[162] Moreover, the communication to the public of a literary, dramatic, musical or artistic work, sound recording, film or broadcast has been broadly defined to include the *broadcasting* of the work or the *making available* of the work to the public by *electronic transmission*, in a way that members of the public access such copyright work from a *place* and at a *time individually chosen* by them.[163]

Given these technologically neutral definitions, the dissemination of content on social media can infringe the rights to perform, play, show or communicate to the public in the UK. This 'public', whether in relation to the rights to issue copies (as discussed earlier), to perform, show or play, *or* to communicate,[164] has been construed as referring to an indeterminate number of recipients, or a fairly large number of persons.[165] More specifically, in respect of a performance made to a limited group of persons, the 'public' has been interpreted to refer to a 'copyright owner's public'.[166] Such public is considered in relation to the copyright owner – where a copyright owner would be exercising his or her statutory right in performing before an audience described as the owner's 'public' or part of his or her 'public', any performance without the owner's consent to this audience or 'public' will infringe his or her copyright.[167]

In relation to the right to communicate, the concept of 'public' has been recently qualified in a decision made by the European Court of Justice to refer to a 'new public' that was not taken into account by the copyright holder when he or she authorised the initial exercise of his or her copyright.[168] The consent of the copyright holder is needed for a communication made to the 'new public'.[169] Given that the applicability of the concept of 'new public' in the UK is uncertain,[170] some content-generative activities, such as those discussed above (ie, the activities on YouTube and Pinterest) will likely involve the (unauthorised) exercise of the right to communicate.

In the same vein, a copyright holder of a literary, dramatic or musical work has the exclusive right to *perform* the work *in public* under the *Australian Copyright Act*,[171] as well as the right to *communicate* a literary, dramatic, musical or artistic work *to the public*.[172] 'Performance' has been defined broadly to refer to 'any mode of visual or aural presentation ... by the use of a record or by any other means'.[173] The term 'communicate' is also defined widely to refer to the *making available online* or *electronic transmission* of a work or subject matter.[174] There are equivalent rights in respect of sound recordings and cinematograph films, namely, the right to *cause* the sound recording or film *to be seen or heard in public* and the right to *communicate* the sound recording or film *to the public*.[175] While the term 'public' includes a small portion of the public, the phrase 'to the public' emphasises the nature of the recipient as a member of the public, even if in a private situation.[176] Audiences in a private situation can constitute the 'copyright owner's public' if a work is performed in a commercial setting.[177] It is further noted that 'to the public' is defined as the public within or outside Australia.[178] Thus these rights to perform, communicate *or* cause to be seen or heard in public can be infringed on social media. Like in the UK, the right to communicate to the public, in particular, is frequently infringed through similar activities to those given in the earlier examples.

Among the exclusive rights discussed above, I note that the rights to reproduce,[179] to make available (in the US)[180] and to communicate to the public (in the UK[181] and in Australia[182]) will be the most relevant rights for consideration in relation to content-generative activities on social media.

F. Infringement: other rights

Further to the copyrights above, other rights – such as moral rights – held by the authors of content can be infringed on social media. Moral rights essentially allow the creators of works to control the treatment and presentation of such works by others.[183] The infringement of these rights is relevant for consideration in the UK or in Australia, but not in the US, for the reasons given below.

The *Visual Artists Rights Act* (*VARA*)[184] that provides for the 'rights of attribution and integrity'[185] in the US applies to a very narrow subset of works of visual art. This includes paintings, drawings, prints, sculptures and still photographic images produced for exhibition purposes, existing in single copies or as limited editions.[186] As such, moral rights of attribution and integrity vest only in a very narrow group of persons, being the authors of works of visual art.[187]

Pursuant to the *VARA*, an author is entitled to: the right of attribution (ie, the right to claim authorship);[188] the right against false attribution (ie, to prevent use of his or her name as the author of any work he or she did not create);[189] the right to prevent use of his or her name where there is a distortion, mutilation or modification of the work that would be prejudicial to his or her honour or reputation;[190] the right to prevent modification of his or her work that would be prejudicial to his or her honour or reputation;[191] and the right to prevent any intentional or grossly negligent destruction of a work of recognised stature.[192] The right of attribution is suggested to be broad enough to object to misattribution – this happens, for example, when one's work is plagiarised by another and the plagiarist is credited for the work instead of the author.[193] The right of integrity is, however, limited by the condition that a cause of action for its violation only arises where there is a distortion, mutilation or modification that is prejudicial to the author's honour or reputation.[194]

On the other hand, in the UK, moral rights are held in a broader range of works and films. For instance, an author of a literary, dramatic, musical or artistic work[195] or the director of a film has the right of attribution (ie, right to be identified) under the *UK Copyright Act*.[196] Although the right against misattribution of a work or film to another is not expressly provided for, such right to object to incorrect attribution is one that is assumed to fall under the general right to attribution.[197] In general, this right of attribution arises when literary, dramatic, musical and artistic works, as well as films, are published commercially or made available to the public, whether by way of issue of sound recordings, films or other communication to the public, as applicable.[198] There can, however, only be infringement of the right of attribution if the author or director has previously asserted his or her moral rights – this assertion may be general or specific.[199]

Separately, there is a right against the false attribution of authorship in the UK.[200] In the same way, the right of integrity is held in a similarly broad range of works and films, and is violated when a modified or adapted work is distorted, mutilated[201] or otherwise prejudicial to the honour or reputation[202] of the author or director.[203] Because of the wider application of moral rights in the UK, these rights can be infringed on social media. For example, the author's moral right of attribution[204] may be infringed when a commentary shared as a 'status update' by a Facebook user is plagiarised by another user and shared on Facebook or another platform, without identification of the first user as the author. A separate example in which the author's moral right of integrity[205] is potentially infringed occurs when a user takes a photograph of an art work and vandalises it digitally.

Likewise moral rights under the *Australian Copyright Act* are held broadly in, among others, literary, dramatic, musical and artistic works, as well as cinematograph films,[206] but without the requirement of assertion. In Australia these basic authorial entitlements are divided into three main rights: the right of attribution of authorship; the right of integrity; and the right not to have the authorship falsely attributed.[207] The right against false attribution of authorship differs from its namesake in the UK and refers instead to an author's right not to have another identified as the author of his or her work,[208] as well as his or her right not to have such work altered by another and dealt with so as to indicate that the alterations were made by the latter.[209] Separately, the author's right of integrity to a work is defined as the right not to have the work subject to derogatory treatment,[210] or that which results in a material distortion, mutilation or alteration to the work, or otherwise, that is prejudicial to the author's honour and reputation.[211] Moral rights in Australia can be similarly infringed through the undertaking of the content-generative activities discussed in the paragraph above.

Even where content resulting from generative activities on social media meets the subsistence requirements under copyright laws for authorship, originality and fixation – and is henceforth copyright protected – users who are authors of content on social media will not be entitled to the moral rights specified under the *VARA*. This is because digitised content on social media falls outside the narrow definition of works of visual art under the *VARA*.[212] Although moral rights have a broader scope of application in the UK than in the US, there is a requirement of assertion to be fulfilled[213] in relation to the right of attribution. Typically, this requirement will not be met on social media.[214]

The right of attribution has, however, a broader scope of application in Australia, given the lack of a requirement of assertion there. Therefore, with reference to copyright laws in the UK or in Australia, a user will hold moral rights (other than the right of attribution in the UK) to content resulting from his or her generative activities on social media, provided that other subsistence requirements under the respective copyright laws are met. Such moral rights can be infringed when other social media users interact with this content, through modifying and disseminating such content.

There are alternative avenues to protect the rights of attribution of authors in each of the US, the UK and Australia. They are, however, imperfect[215] and subject to the satisfaction of substantive requirements under the relevant rights management provisions. Under the *Digital Millennium Copyright Act* (*DMCA*),[216] the *intentional removal* or *alteration* of 'copyright management information' – by a person knowing, or having reasonable grounds to know, that the removal or alteration will, among others, facilitate or conceal an infringement of any right – is prohibited. The term 'copyright management information' is defined to include the information conveyed in connection with digital copies or displays of a work, such as the name of and other identifying information about the author or the copyright holder of the work, as well as about the writer, performer or director of an audiovisual work (with the exception of public performances of works by radio and television broadcast stations).[217]

'Copyright management information' is interpreted to extend to any information embedded in a copyright work, independent of the use of an automated copyright protection or management system to do so – this includes, for instance, information crediting the author of a photograph.[218] The copyright management provisions allow for the enforcement of moral rights – in particular, the right of attribution[219] – except that such rights to prevent the removal or alteration of 'copyright management information' extend more broadly to other categories of works[220] beyond works of visual art under the *VARA*.

It has been suggested that the provisions are ineffective in ensuring, among other things, the maintenance of authorship attribution, as many claims against the alteration or removal of 'copyright management information' are likely to flounder on the statutory double intent standard.[221] There is, first, a requirement of knowledge (or reasonable grounds for such knowledge) for the removal or alteration to, inter alia, facilitate or conceal copyright infringement, and secondly, another requirement of knowledge that the information is removed or altered without the copyright holder's authorisation.[222] Thus, so long as the double intent standard is met, these provisions are breached in similar circumstances to those in which the moral right of attribution is infringed (for instance, when the commentary of a Facebook user is plagiarised by another or when the information identifying the author of an image digitally created and shared on Pinterest is removed).

The equivalent provision to this under the *UK Copyright Act* refers to the rights of a copyright holder against a person's *knowing removal* or *alteration* of 'electronic rights management information' that is associated with a copy of a copyright work, or appears in connection with the communication of the copyright work to the public, by a person who knows, or has reason to believe, that by doing so, he or she is, inter alia, facilitating or concealing a copyright infringement.[223] Further, it is required that the person knows that he or she has no authority from the copyright holder to do so.[224]

Also, the rights management provisions extend to prohibit the removal or alteration of such information when a person, among other things, distributes or communicates to the public copies of a copyright work.[225] The term 'rights management information' is similarly defined to include information which identifies the author or the copyright holder of the work.[226] These provisions are breached where the moral right of attribution[227] is infringed, in the same situations as those highlighted above. Just as in the US, the double intent standard needs to be satisfied for the prohibition to apply.[228]

At the same time, under the *Australian Copyright Act*, a copyright holder can bring an action against a person who *removes* or *alters* electronic rights management information relating to a work or subject matter – if the person knew, or ought reasonably to know, that such removal or alteration would, inter alia, facilitate or conceal a copyright infringement of the work or subject matter.[229] In addition, the person has removed or altered the information without the permission of the copyright holder.[230] This right to bring an action extends to when such person, among other things, distributes or communicates a copy of the work or subject matter to the public in which the electronic rights management information has been removed or altered.[231] The term 'electronic management rights information' is defined to refer to *electronic* information that is attached to, or embodied in, a copy of the work or subject matter, or appears in connection with a communication of such work or subject matter, and which, among other things, identifies the author or copyright holder of the work or subject matter.[232] Again, the right to bring an action potentially arises where the moral right of attribution is infringed.[233] This can happen in relation to the examples given earlier, so long as the double intent standard is satisfied (as in the US and the UK).[234]

G. Infringement: remedies

Where there is infringement of copyright-protected content on social media, the next step will be to ascertain the remedies available to the relevant copyright holder. This consequentially highlights the risks that users face in undertaking content-generative activities that potentially infringe the copyrights held by others. Generally, if a copyright work originated in the US, or in a country with which the US does not have copyright treaty relations, registration is a pre-requisite to the commencement of copyright infringement actions.[235] In addition, the requirement of timely registration (ie, before commencing an action for infringement of copyright in an unpublished work, *or* within three months after the first publication of the published work) has to be satisfied if the copyright holder intends to elect to recover statutory damages,[236] in addition to the usual remedies of inter alia, injunctions, damages and account of profits.[237]

The implications of registration (and non-registration) are significant, particularly if one considers that the statutory damages recoverable with respect to infringement for any one work is in a wide range – between US$ 750 and US$ 30,000, 'as the court considers just'.[238] Additionally, if the copyright holder proves wilful infringement, the court may in its discretion award up to US$ 150,000 of statutory damages.[239] A case where the maximum statutory damages were awarded is *Agence France Presse v Morel* (*Morel*).[240] In this case the jury found that there was wilful infringement by the news agencies of the photojournalist Daniel Morel's copyrights in his eight photographs of the Haitian earthquake shared on Twitter. Morel was awarded in excess of US$ 300,000 in actual damages and profits, as well as the maximum US$ 1.2 million in statutory damages (based on the award of US$ 150,000 for each of the eight photographs).[241] Notwithstanding that infringing users are potentially subject to hefty copyright damages – in view of the availability of a large volume of content, including the images shared on social media, and the ease with which images can be extracted for publication offline (as illustrated by the *Morel* case) – registering copyrights in the content on social media may not be an easy burden for copyright holders to discharge, particularly within the short time frame of three months provided.[242]

On the other hand, it is not necessary to register for copyright protection in the UK and in Australia, nor are there any registration systems in these countries. In the UK the remedies available to copyright holders include injunctions, damages and accounts of profits.[243] Where the defendant in an action for infringement did not know, and had no reason to believe, that copyright subsisted in the work, the copyright holder is not entitled to damages, but can still be awarded an injunction and/or account of profits.[244] Additional damages may be awarded in special circumstances, as 'the justice of the case' requires.[245] Such circumstances considered by the court include the flagrancy of the infringement and the defendant's benefit from the infringement.[246]

Similarly, in Australia either damages or an account of profits can be awarded, together with an injunction, to compensate copyright holders whose copyrights are infringed.[247] Damages are not available to a copyright holder, if the defendant in question was not aware, and had no reasonable grounds to suspect, that his or her act constituted an infringement. In such a situation, an account of profits may be awarded instead.[248] Additional damages, if appropriate in the specific circumstances, can also be awarded.[249] The circumstances considered in Australia in the court's assessment of damages are wider than those in the UK. They include, in addition to the flagrancy of the infringement and the defendant's benefit from the infringement, the conduct of the defendant after the infringing act and whether the infringement involved the conversion of a work or other subject matter from hard copy into digital form.[250]

Therefore, under the *US Copyright Act*, copyright holders of content[251] on social media can choose to register their content, prior to commencing copyright infringement actions against their respective defendants. The millions of users interacting with such content on social media on an everyday basis are therefore vulnerably positioned, as they are exposed to potentially massive awards of statutory damages. In contrast, under the *UK Copyright Act* and *Australian Copyright Act*, the quantum of damages awarded (whether ordinary or additional) does not fall within as wide a range as the statutory damages in the US.[252] Moreover, defendant-users may be able to establish, within the social media context, that they had no reasonable grounds to suspect that copyright subsisted in the (allegedly) infringed works[253] *or* that their acts constituted infringement.[254] If that is the case, social media users who infringe the copyrights of others through their content-generative activities will likely be subject to the imposition of injunctions and/or accounts of profits, instead of damages.

H. Infringement: fair use and fair dealing exceptions

Users who infringe the copyrights held by others when they engage in content-generative activities on social media can consider whether their uses are exempt from copyright infringement under copyright exceptions, such as the fair use and fair dealing exceptions.[255] Through permitting some exercise of the copyright holders' exclusive rights by others, even without their consent, these copyright exceptions balance the rights of copyright holders to remuneration against the public's interest in accessing copyright-protected works. These exceptions have been argued to create space for cultural engagement on social media by allowing for the re-interpretation and remixing of copyright-protected content.[256]

Content-generative activities undertaken by users on social media platforms can give rise to concerns of the infringement of more than one right. For example, when a user creates a collage with photographs taken by others of sculptures, including private sculptures, he or she potentially infringes multiple rights under the *US Copyright Act*.[257] The scope of copyright exceptions becomes a more pressing concern than before, because the creation, modification and dissemination of content on social media often – as illustrated earlier – involve the rights to reproduce,[258] to make available (in the US)[259] and to communicate to the public (in the UK[260] and in Australia).[261] The possibilities for infringement increase in proportion to the frequency of these activities. As noted above, the prospect of statutory damages is a particularly grave concern for potential infringers.

In this respect, the fair use doctrine in the US serves as a safety valve against the rigid application of copyright laws and remedies.[262] It exempts uses for purposes such as criticism, comment, news reporting, teaching, scholarship and research from copyright infringement, as well as acts of parody, satire and even artistic appropriation.[263] Further, in ascertaining whether the use made of a work is a fair use, the four factors to be considered include: the purpose and character of the use; the nature of the copyright work; the substantiality of the portion used in relation to the copyright work; and the effect of the use on the potential market for or value of the copyright work.[264]

At the same time the 'transformative-ness' (of a use) – or the alteration of the original work with new expression, meaning or message[265] – has been recognised as a key element of the fair use analysis in the US.[266] Broad categories of transformative uses demonstrating a change in purpose or character under the fair use doctrine[267] have been identified.[268] These include, among other things: commenting on or criticising the original work, or targeting the original work for parody;[269] using the original work to comment on something else;[270] re-contextualising the original work through changing the meaning of the work;[271] and changing the purpose of the original work within an expressive context.[272] Although a large number of content-generative activities on social media are arguably for purposes such as criticism and comment, it will be impossible to predict which specific activity is exempt as fair use and which is not, as each of the four factors can be decided differently on the facts of each case. Unsurprisingly then, the application of the doctrine confounds not only judges,[273] but also users of content.

The fair dealing exceptions in the UK and in Australia exempt specified categories of purposes from copyright infringement. Although a balance is also sought between the private interests of copyright holders and the wider public interests in the dissemination of ideas, British and Australian legislators have taken a more prescriptive approach. In the UK there are fair dealing exceptions for the purpose of research and private study,[274] as well as for the purpose of criticism, review and news reporting.[275] These exceptions are conditional on a sufficient acknowledgement being made, except in respect of fair dealing for the purpose of private study.[276] Further, fair dealing exceptions for the purposes of quotation, as well as for caricature, parody or pastiche, were introduced recently, pursuant to *The Copyright and Rights in Performances (Quotation and Parody) Regulations 2014*.[277] Unlike the newly extended fair dealing exception for the purpose of criticism, review, *quotation* and news reporting, there is no requirement of acknowledgement under the new fair dealing exception for the purpose of caricature, parody or pastiche.[278]

In Australia the fair dealing exceptions are similar and are for the purposes of criticism or review,[279] reporting news[280] and research or study.[281] An additional category of fair dealing for the purpose of parody or satire[282] was introduced under the *Copyright Amendment Act 2006*.[283] As in the UK, the application of the fair dealing exceptions for the purposes of criticism or review, or for reporting news, are conditional upon giving the requisite acknowledgement of the relevant copyright work – there is no similar condition in relation to the fair dealing exception for the purpose of parody or satire.[284] It is worth noting that the Australian Law Reform Commission has recommended in its report on copyright reform that the fair use exception be introduced as an extension of Australia's existing fair dealing exceptions.[285] This recommendation has recently been provisionally endorsed by the Productivity Commission in its Draft Report on Intellectual Property Arrangements.[286]

Among these available categories of fair dealing in the UK and in Australia, I argue that the fair dealing exception for the purpose of research or study will be of lesser use to users keen to defend their content-generative activities undertaken on social media platforms against copyright infringement than the exceptions for other purposes. In particular, the fair dealing exceptions for the purposes of caricature, parody or pastiche in the UK,[287] as well as for parody or satire in Australia[288] respectively, are arguably the most relevant to social media users. This is in view of the nature of the content-generative activities in which they engage on social media. Taking the example of Australia, before the new exception was introduced into the *Australian Copyright Act* in 2006, the other fair dealing exceptions, including the exception for the purpose of criticism or review,[289] were hard to rely on to excuse parodic or satirical uses due to their restrictive interpretations.[290]

Notwithstanding this, both fair dealing exceptions – whether for the purpose of caricature, parody or pastiche in the UK *or* for the purpose of parody or satire in Australia – are still untested by litigation.[291] In addition, the terms 'caricature, parody or pastiche', as well as 'parody or satire', remain undefined in their respective statutes, giving courts a considerable scope to interpret these terms. In this respect, as a pastiche refers to a work made from a selection of materials and styles from one or more sources,[292] its broader meaning may make the 'caricature, parody or pastiche' defence in the UK more suited for exempting uses – particularly when users modify content on social media – than the 'parody or satire' defence in Australia.

On the other hand, however, the newly extended fair dealing exception for the purpose of quotation (whether for criticism, review or otherwise) in the UK may be of limited use in exempting social media uses. This is given that it is conditional upon: the availability of the original work to the public; the use of the quotation being a fair dealing of the work; the extent of quotation being no more than is required for its specific purpose; and its accompaniment by a sufficient acknowledgement (unless this is impossible for reasons of practicality or otherwise).[293] On the face of it, while the first condition may be easily satisfied on social media, the same cannot be said for the other three conditions.[294]

On the whole, because the fair dealing exceptions in the UK and in Australia are more prescriptive than the fair use doctrine in the US, ascertaining whether a use is exempt as a fair dealing exception is more straightforward. Nonetheless, this too involves addressing questions of degree and impression, and can reasonably lead to different determinations.[295]

I. Conflict of laws issues

Before social media users can ascertain whether they have infringed the copyrights held by others, they have to decide which laws govern the subsistence of copyright in the relevant content, as well as their potentially infringing activities. In general, the expansion of digital communications compromises the reach and practicality (of enforcement) of territoriality-based domestic copyright laws.[296] The rapid generation of huge volumes of content on social media exacerbates the problems introduced by the fact that cyberspace is inherently borderless. Due to the global reach of social media platforms, the creation, modification and dissemination of content consequentially occur among users situated in different jurisdictions. However, the principle of territoriality to which copyright laws are subject makes it difficult to localise any dispute around content on a social media platform to a single jurisdiction.

These transnational disputes occur, for example, when the copyright in a work held by a copyright holder in the US is infringed by users resident in other jurisdictions, such as the UK and Australia. If the infringement action is commenced in either the UK or Australia, reference may be made to the rights of the copyright holder of such work in the US. On the other hand, if the action is instead commenced in the US, it will be related to infringing activities occurring outside the US, including but not limited to the UK and Australia (given the nature of the internet).[297] A user is exposed to the challenge of identifying which copyright laws apply and hence faces greater uncertainty over the legitimacy of the content-generative activities he or she undertakes.[298]

Currently, there is no clear direction provided under existing international conventions, or otherwise, on the private international law of intellectual property. It has been suggested that this lack of direction may explain why provisions in international intellectual property instruments resembling conflicts principles are sometimes adopted without any attempt to relate them to any coherent principle of private international law.[299] For instance, while the principle of national treatment stipulated in article 5(1) of the *Berne Convention* requires the country in which protection is claimed to treat foreign and domestic authors alike, it is not read as a conflicts rule.[300] Also, notwithstanding the reaffirmation of the principle of national treatment in article 3(1) of the *TRIPS Agreement*, the article is seen to operate as a constraint on the choice of law rules that a country adopts rather than as a mandate of a particular rule.[301]

In addition, the view that article 5(2) of the *Berne Convention* endorses the *lex loci protectionis* (ie, the law of the jurisdiction for which protection is sought) is the majority view, but one not without its detractors.[302] The international flow of copyright-protected content and the ubiquity of content disseminated online – both effects amplified on social media – have evoked doubts around the applicability of the *lex loci protectionis* choice of law rule, given that *lex loci protectionis* may not capture the complete set of 'affinities', or connecting factors, that govern the conduct of users online.[303] As such, the breadth of private international intellectual property law today gives little guidance to potential litigants involved in copyright disputes relating to content on social media.

There are, however, initiatives that have proposed possible solutions regarding the jurisdiction, choice of law and the enforcement of judgements in transnational intellectual property disputes, such as the principles adopted by the American Law Institute (*ALI Principles*) in 2007[304] and the Principles on Conflict of Laws in Intellectual Property prepared by the European Max Planck Group (*CLIP Principles*) in 2011.[305] Under both the *ALI Principles*[306] and the *CLIP Principles*,[307] a person may be sued in any state in which he or she is resident. The same person can also be sued in any state in which he or she has acted to initiate or further the alleged infringement, *or* if such person has directed his or her activities to that state.[308] Thus there is more than one jurisdiction in which the action can be commenced. Finally, there are rules dealing with ubiquitous infringement under both sets of principles that recognise the problem of having a multitude of applicable laws and attempt to solve that by referring to the law or laws of the state or states with the closest connection to the dispute.[309] The difference between the two is that the *ALI Principles* refer to both parties,[310] but the *CLIP Principles* refer mainly to the infringer's location.[311] Even with the guidance of these principles, the factors taken into account to ascertain the state (and hence the applicable law) having the closest connection with the infringement – including the residency of the parties[312] (*or* the infringer),[313] as well as the principal markets toward which the parties directed their activities[314] (*or* the place where the harm caused by the infringement is substantial in relation to the infringement in its entirety)[315] – will prove challenging to identify in the case of social media.

While there are no clear answers, the following preliminary questions could guide a copyright holder in ascertaining where he or she can enforce his or her rights in relation to content-generative activities on social media:

(i) Which court has the jurisdiction to govern the dispute?
(ii) Which governing law will this court apply? Will the same governing law apply across the various copyright subsistence and infringement issues?
(iii) Will judgements given by the court be recognised and enforced in other jurisdictions?

In the next chapter, I will discuss how the terms of service of social media platforms attempt to address some of the above questions and the resulting implications for social media users.

J. Summary

Table 2.1 below serves as a summary of the above discussion relating to the application of copyright laws in the US, the UK and Australia to the content-generative activities of social media users, and the unique challenges arising from such application.

Table 2.1 Summary of the application of copyright laws in the US, the UK and Australia to the content-generative activities of social media users

No.	Copyright issues	Jurisdictions			Other comments
		US	UK	Australia	
1	Subject matter protected	Literary works Musical works Dramatic works Pictorial works Graphic works Sculptural works Audiovisual works Sound recordings Architectural works	Literary works Dramatic works Musical works Artistic works Broadcasts Sound recordings Films	Literary works Dramatic works Musical works Artistic works Sound recordings Cinematograph films	Idea–expression dichotomy across the three jurisdictions (ie, only expressions, not ideas, are entitled to copyright protection)
		Compilations and derivative works (excluding material used unlawfully or pre-existing material not contributed by the author in question)			Doctrine of merger and '*scènes à faire*' are concepts that fill the gaps in this distinction in the US
2	Originality	Requirement of creativity	Result of 'skill, labour or experience'	Result of 'skill, labour or experience'	Even then, original words on their own, or short phrases, may not qualify for copyright protection in the UK and in Australia
		'Sweat of the brow' insufficient			Whether content crosses the threshold for originality is always a question of degree and depends on the factual circumstances
					Consider also the application of the *de minimis* principle (ie, copyright-protected works need to comprise a minimal amount of content)

(continued)

Table 2.1 *(Cont.)*

No.	Copyright issues	Jurisdictions			Other comments
		US	UK	Australia	
3	Authorship	Term 'author' is not defined, although the term 'joint work' is	Term 'author' is defined simply (ie, person who creates a work)	Term 'author' is defined (only in relation to a photograph)	May be tedious to identify all the human authors of content on social media
		Requirement of contemporaneous intentions of joint authors for the creation of a joint work	'Work of joint authorship' is also defined	'Work of joint authorship' is also defined	Dilemmas around the designation of authorship (whether single, joint or multiple) and the identification of the authors are amplified with regard to content generated on collaborative projects such as Wikipedia
4	Fixation, recording or reduction to material form	Requirement of fixation in a tangible medium of expression – work has to be sufficiently stable to permit its communication, or otherwise communicated for more than a transitory period	Requirement of being recorded, in writing or otherwise (for literary, dramatic and musical works) See also the definitions for an artistic work (means, inter alia, any painting, photograph [also defined as a recording of light or other radiation on any medium], and so on) and broadcast Sound recordings and films – requirement of being recordings on any medium	Requirement of being reduced to writing or some other material form (for literary, dramatic, musical or artistic works) See also the broad definitions for sound recordings and cinematograph films	Content on social networking sites and blogs (especially micro-blogs) may not meet the fixation requirement – or its equivalent – for copyright protection, since it may be deleted after a short while and is not stored separately There are also long-term collaborative projects such as the Wikipedia platform, where the continual participation of users is invited, and as such it is challenging to identify at which point content (and what content, if so) is fixed, recorded, or reduced to material form

	Limited definitions of 'publication' (ie, distribution of copies … by sale or other transfer of ownership) and 'copies' (ie, material objects) apply, such that content on social media is taken to be unpublished – copyright subsists irrespective of the nationality or domicile of the author	Definitions of 'publication' and 'copying' much broader, such that content on social media will constitute published works – copyright will only subsist if the author is a British citizen or resident, or if the country of first publication is the UK	Definition of 'publication' is broadly defined, such that content on social media will constitute published works – copyright will only subsist if the author is an Australian citizen or resident, or if the country of first publication is Australia	Furthermore, the venue of first publication may be hard to ascertain on social media
	Therefore, there is no need to determine the precise venue of first publication or fixation	Need to determine the precise venue of first publication, if the requirement of nationality or domicile is not met	Need to determine the precise venue of first publication, if the requirement of nationality or domicile is not met	In the US, this issue is obviated from consideration. In the UK and in Australia identifying the venue of first publication may be needed – although this problem is mitigated in view of the principle of national treatment in the *Berne Convention* and the convention's wide membership So long as the user is a national or resident of a *Berne Convention* country, the content is likely to be copyright protected if other subsistence requirements are met, regardless of where the content is first published (if published)

(continued)

Table 2.1 *(Cont.)*

No.	Copyright issues	Jurisdictions			Other comments
		US	UK	Australia	
5	Scope of protection	Right of reproduction (applies to, inter alia: literary, musical and dramatic works; pictorial, graphic and sculptural works; motion pictures and other audiovisual works; sound recordings; and architectural works)	Right of reproduction (applies to, inter alia, literary, dramatic, musical and artistic works, as well as films)	Right of reproduction (applies to, inter alia, literary, dramatic, musical or artistic works, as well as to sound recordings and cinematograph films)	The right of reproduction in the US, the UK and Australia can be infringed when users engage in some content-generative activities on social media
		Note that the term 'copies' is liberally defined to refer to material objects in which a work is fixed, and from which a work can be communicated, either directly or with the aid of a machine or device	Note that the references to 'copying' are broad and can include the storing of a work in any medium by electronic means, as well as the making of copies that are transient or incidental to some other use of the work	Note that in relation to this right, references are made to conversion into or from a digital format	

	Right to prepare derivative works (applies to, inter alia, all the categories of works listed above) – note the preparation of a derivative work, even prior to fixation, can be an infringement	Right to make adaptations of works, or to do anything in relation to these adaptations (applies to, inter alia, literary, dramatic and musical works, but not artistic works)	Right to make adaptations of works, or to do anything in relation to these adaptations (applies to, inter alia, literary, dramatic and musical works, but not artistic works)	Given the differences in the definitions of a 'derivative work' in the US and 'adaptation' in the UK and in Australia, the right to make adaptations or to do anything in relation to such adaptations is potentially relevant for consideration in relation to different types of content-generative activities on social media
	Uncertainties as to whether material derived from original work which does not qualify for copyright protection separately as a secondary work can infringe the derivative work's right	May be exercised when undertaking content-generative activities (for instance, the translation of a literary work, conveying a story in a different version with pictures, arranging or transcribing a musical work, and so on)	May be exercised when undertaking content-generative activities (for instance, the translation of a literary work, conveying a story in a different version with pictures, arranging or transcribing a musical work, and so on)	

(continued)

Table 2.1 *(Cont.)*

No.	Copyright issues	Jurisdictions			Other comments
		US	UK	Australia	
		Right to distribute (applies to, inter alia, all the categories of works listed above). Note that this right is broadly interpreted such that digital transmission (including the transmission of content on social media) is included within the exercise of this right	Right to issue copies to the public (applies to, inter alia, literary, dramatic, musical and artistic works, as well as sound recordings and films). Note that the description of this right excludes subsequent distribution of copies already put into circulation; as such, this right will not be infringed by the regular dissemination of content on social media (insofar as such dissemination involves content already circulated)	Right to (first) publish (applies to, inter alia, literary, dramatic, musical and artistic works) – distinguished from the notion of publication for the subsistence of copyright	The rights to distribute in the US can be infringed by the usual dissemination of content on social media
				This right will only be infringed in limited circumstances (ie, in relation to content that has not been made available to the public)	The rights to issue copies to the public in the UK, as well as to (first) publish in Australia, are not infringed by the usual dissemination of content on social media

	Right to perform (applies to, inter alia, literary, musical and dramatic works, motion pictures, other audiovisual works and sound recordings [ie, by digital audio transmission]) and the right to display (applies to, inter alia, literary, musical and dramatic works, pictorial, graphic and sculptural works, as well as individual images of motion pictures and other audiovisual works). Note that 'audiovisual works', as well as what it means to perform or display a work publicly, are very broadly defined – these rights are frequently exercised on social media	Right to perform, show or play a work in public (applies to, inter alia, literary, dramatic and musical works, sound recordings, films and broadcasts) and the right to communicate a work to the public (applies to, inter alia, literary, dramatic, musical and artistic works, sound recordings, films and broadcasts) – note that the right to perform, show or play, as well as the right to communicate, is defined very broadly to include electronic means and transmissions. In particular, the right to communicate is frequently exercised on social media	Right to perform a work in public (applies to, inter alia, literary, dramatic and musical works) and the right to communicate a work to the public (applies to, inter alia, literary, dramatic, musical and artistic works) – note that the terms 'performance' and 'communicate' are defined broadly to include electronic transmissions Equivalent rights are available in respect of sound recordings and cinematograph films (ie, right to cause to be seen or heard in public [as applicable], as well as the right to communicate to the public) In particular, the right to communicate is frequently exercised on social media	Among the bundle of rights, the rights to reproduce, to make available in the US (ie, to distribute, perform and display) and to communicate in the UK and in Australia are the most relevant rights for consideration in relation to content-generative activities on social media

(continued)

Table 2.1 *(Cont.)*

No.	Copyright issues	Jurisdictions			Other comments
		US	UK	Australia	
6	Other rights	Moral rights of attribution and integrity apply only to works of visual art	Moral rights of attribution and integrity apply to, inter alia, literary, dramatic, musical and artistic works, as well as films	Moral rights of attribution and integrity apply to, inter alia, literary, dramatic, musical and artistic works, as well as cinematograph films	Users who are authors of content on social media will not hold moral rights to such digitised content, which falls outside the definition of works of visual art under the *VARA*
		Right of attribution – possibly broad enough to object to misattribution	Right of attribution – note that right against misattribution assumed to exist, even if not clearly provided for	Right of attribution of authorship	On the other hand, users who are authors of content on social media can hold moral rights in their content resulting from content-generative activities under both the *UK Copyright Act* (other than the right of attribution, as the requirement of assertion will not likely be fulfilled) and the *Australian Copyright Act*, provided that other copyright subsistence requirements are met – these moral rights of attribution and integrity can conceivably be infringed when users interact with such content, through modifying and disseminating the content
		Right against false attribution	Right against false attribution	Right against false attribution (note that this refers instead to what is called misattribution in the US and in the UK [ie, the right of an author or director not to have another identified as the author or director of his or her work or film])	
			Not withstanding the above, there is a requirement of assertion (ie, that the author or director has asserted his or her moral right of attribution)	No requirement for assertion	

Under the right of integrity, the right of an author to prevent use of his or her name when there is distortion of a work that would be prejudicial to his or her honour or reputation	Right of integrity to work (which can be violated when a modified work is, inter alia, distorted or otherwise prejudicial to the honour or reputation of the author of a work, or director of a film)	Under the right of integrity, the right not to have the work subject to derogatory treatment (further defined to mean anything that results in, inter alia, a distortion to the work or is prejudicial to the author's honour or reputation)
Under the right of integrity, the right to prevent modification of his or her work that would be prejudicial to his or her honour or reputation	In general, moral rights are of a broader application as they are held by copyright holders in a broader range of works (including literary, dramatic, musical and artistic works, as well as films)	Clearly stipulated that the right of integrity is violated by a person who engages in various acts in respect of the derogatorily treated
Under the right of integrity, the right to prevent any intentional or grossly negligent destruction of a work of recognised stature		In general, moral rights are of a broader application as they are held by copyright holders in a broader range of works (including literary, dramatic, musical and artistic works, as well as films)

(continued)

Table 2.1 *(Cont.)*

No.	Copyright issues	Jurisdictions			Other comments
		US	UK	Australia	
		Right to prohibit the removal or alteration of 'copyright management information' – the relevant provision allows for the enforcement of moral rights, except that it extends more broadly to other categories of works (ie, literary, musical, dramatic, pictorial, graphic, sculptural and audiovisual works, as well as sound-recordings, architectural works, compilations and derivative works)	Right against a person's knowing removal or alteration of 'electronic rights management information', which is associated with a copy of a copyright work or appears in connection with the communication to the public of a copyright work (includes a literary, dramatic, musical or artistic work, broadcast, sound recording or film)	Right against a person's removal or alteration of 'electronic rights management information relating to a work or subject matter (includes a literary, dramatic, musical or artistic work, sound recording or cinematograph film)	These rights arise for enforcement where the moral right of attribution is infringed, except that there is a requirement for knowledge (or reasonable grounds for knowledge or belief) that the removal or alteration will, inter alia, facilitate or conceal a copyright infringement, in addition to the requisite knowledge that the removal or alteration is done without the authorisation of the copyright holder – the relevant provisions provide an alternative avenue for the enforcement of the rights of attribution, albeit imperfect and subject to the satisfaction of the double intent standard
7	Remedies for infringement	Registration is a pre-requisite to the institution of copyright infringement actions	No registration requirement	No registration requirement	Registration requirement in the US is not an easy burden to discharge, but when discharged, a very large sum of damages can be awarded if infringement is found to be wilful
		Additional requirement of timely registration for statutory damages (ie, three months after the first publication of a work, or before the commencement of a copyright action for an unpublished work)	Grant of injunctions, damages and/or accounts of profits are possible remedies	Grant of injunctions, damages and/or accounts of profits are possible remedies	Users are therefore exposed to a wider range of statutory damages in the US than in the UK and Australia (although the awards of additional damages can still be high in Australia)

		Statutory damages recoverable in a wide range of between US$ 750 and US$ 30,000, with respect to an infringement for any one work In the case of wilful infringement, court can award up to US$ 150,000 of statutory damages	Note that damages are not likely to be awarded when the defendant did not know, and had no reason to believe, that copyright subsisted in the relevant work	Note that damages are not likely to be awarded when the defendant was not aware, and had no reasonable grounds to suspect, that his or her act constituted an infringement	Also, in the UK and in Australia, defendant-users may be able to defend themselves against awards of damages for infringement, through establishing that they had no reason to believe copyright subsisted in the relevant content on social media, or that they had no reasonable grounds to suspect that their acts were infringing
8	Defences such as fair use and fair dealing	Fair use doctrine	Fair dealing exceptions (ie, for the purposes of criticism, review, quotation and news reporting, as well as caricature, parody or pastiche)	Fair dealing exceptions (ie, for the purposes of criticism or review, reporting news and parody or satire)	Unpredictability around the application of the fair use doctrine in the US to the content-generative activities of social media users The fair dealing exceptions for the purpose of caricature, parody or pastiche in the UK, and for the purpose of parody or satire in Australia, are the more relevant defences to social media users – although both are untested, the UK defence is possibly wider than its Australian counterpart

(continued)

Table 2.1 *(Cont.)*

No.	Copyright issues	Jurisdictions			Other comments
		US	UK	Australia	
9	Conflict of laws	Little guidance on the private international law of intellectual property Principle of national treatment articulated in the *Berne Convention* and the *TRIPS Agreement* is not a conflicts rule *Lex loci protectionis* (ie, law of the jurisdiction for which protection is sought) is the default view – but has its detractors, since it does not capture the complete set of affinities that govern the conduct of users online More than one jurisdiction, as well as applicable law, can be identified under both the *ALI Principles* and the *CLIP Principles*, in transnational disputes			Challenge of identifying the jurisdiction, as well as applicable law, for disputes relating to copyright-protected content on social media. It is thus uncertain for social media users to ascertain the legitimacy of their content-generative activities under copyright laws

II. Scenario one: the application of copyright laws

The case study of Jane in Chapter One serves as the basis on which the copyright laws discussed in this chapter can be applied to the content-generative activities undertaken by Jane and other users. Jane's day will be dissected to allow for a consideration of the copyright issues arising from each activity she and other users undertake, in chronological order. I then consider the possible grounds of liability and whether exceptions apply under the respective copyright laws for each activity. For this purpose, I assume that the relevant connecting factors for protection under each law (nationality, residence, place of first publication and so on) are met.[316]

A. Jane's use of the music video clip on YouTube as her morning alarm

Under the *US Copyright Act* the video clip in its entirety is a copyright-protected 'audiovisual work'; the lyrics in it constitute a literary work, while the music in it constitutes a musical work. This same video clip is a copyright-protected film comprising a literary work (ie, in the lyrics) and a musical work (ie, in the musical score) under the *UK Copyright Act* and the *Australian Copyright Act*. I argue that Jane's use of the video clip infringes the right of *reproduction* in the US, the UK and Australia.[317]

Although the right of reproduction is arguably infringed, Jane's use is likely to qualify as a fair use in the US. Given that her use is private and non-commercial, at least two of the four fair use factors – the purpose and character of use, as well as the effect of the use on the potential market for the copyright work – are likely to tip the balance in her favour.[318] This is in spite of the possibility that another factor, being the substantiality of the portion used,[319] does otherwise. In the UK Jane's use does not fall within the fair dealing exceptions, including the exceptions for the purposes of criticism, review, quotation and news reporting,[320] *or* caricature, parody or pastiche.[321] Furthermore, the private copying exception under *The Copyright and Rights in Performances (Personal Copies for Private Use) Regulations 2014*[322] is fairly narrow and may not excuse Jane's use. Although Jane makes a personal copy for private use each time she uses the video clip as her morning alarm, I argue that she does not satisfy the condition of having lawfully acquired the video clip on a *permanent* basis, by her use of the relevant application on her mobile phone. Finally, Jane's use is not exempt in Australia, as her use does not fall within the fair dealing exceptions for the purposes of criticism or review,[323] parody or satire,[324] *or* reporting news.[325] In addition, the exceptions for private and domestic uses will not apply to Jane's use for two reasons. Firstly, the video clip is not included within the categories of copyright-protected material under these private and domestic use exceptions;[326] secondly, there is a condition of ownership under most of these provisions.[327]

The above suggests that Jane has infringed the copyright laws in the UK and Australia, but not in the US.[328]

B. Jane's 'pinning' of the YouTube music video clip on her pin-board titled 'My Favourite Things' on Pinterest

Jane's 'pinning' of the video clip on Pinterest may infringe the right to *distribute*[329] held by the copyright holder of the video clip under the *US Copyright Act*. The position is different under the *UK Copyright Act*, as the description of the right to *issue copies to the public*[330] specifically excludes subsequent distribution of copies already put into circulation – in this case, the video clip is already shared on YouTube. Under the *Australian Copyright Act* the right to *(first) publish*[331] is also not infringed by Jane's 'pinning', given that the video clip has already been made available to the public on YouTube.

In addition, a case can likely be made out for Jane's infringement of the copyright holder's rights to *perform* and to *display* a work *publicly* in the US;[332] to *perform, show or play* a work *in public*, as well as to *communicate the work to the public* in the UK;[333] and to *perform, cause to be seen or heard in public*, as well as to *communicate the work and copyright protected subject matter to the public* in Australia.[334] As the audience of the video clip shared on Jane's pin-board comprises an expanding group of users who choose to 'follow' Jane or this pin-board in particular, and who can access the video clip in separate places at different times on the Pinterest platform, the requirement for performing or displaying a work 'publicly' is met in the US.[335] At the same time this falls within the broad definition of a communication to the public in the UK.[336] Further, the indeterminate number of Pinterest users to whom the video clip is performed, showed, played *and* communicated constitutes this 'public' in the UK,[337] and also in Australia (in relation to the performance *and* causing to be seen or heard).[338] Finally, Jane's use falls under the broad concept of a communication to the public in Australia.[339]

Jane's use is *less* likely to qualify as a fair use in the US than is the case under sub-section (A) above, as her 'pinning' of the video clip is more likely to have an adverse impact on the potential market for the video clip, even if the purpose of sharing the video clip remains non-commercial in nature. Jane's 'pinning' is similarly not exempt as a fair dealing or private use in the UK and in Australia.

The above indicates that Jane has infringed the copyright laws in all three jurisdictions.

C. Jane's use of Evangeline's earlier commentary on Facebook to create her own commentary

Evangeline's commentary constitutes a literary work, whether in the US, the UK or Australia, if other subsistence requirements such as originality, authorship and fixation (or their equivalents) are met. In general, it will be *more* likely for the commentary to qualify for copyright protection in the UK and Australia *than* in the US, given the higher originality requirement in the last. As the author can be identified (ie, Evangeline), the requirement of authorship is not likely to pose a barrier to the recognition of the commentary as a copyright-protected literary work. In addition, fixation (and its equivalent) requirements are broadly defined, and are therefore likely to be satisfied. When the other copyright subsistence requirements are met, Evangeline's commentary will be copyright protected, whether she is a national or resident of the US, the UK or Australia.[340]

On the basis that the original commentary is copyright protected, I argue that Jane will not infringe Evangeline's right to *prepare derivative works*.[341] This is because Jane's commentary has to be 'substantially similar' to Evangeline's before it can be considered to be an infringing work. Given that Jane has woven her views into Evangeline's commentary to create a new one and that Evangeline's contribution is no longer identifiable in Jane's commentary, there is arguably no infringement of the derivative works right as there is no substantial similarity[342] between the original commentary and Jane's new commentary.[343]

In the UK and in Australia, an equivalent to this right is the right to *make adaptations* of works and such an adaptation includes, among other things, the translation of a literary work.[344] While the term 'translation' is not defined, Jane's creation of her own commentary using Evangeline's commentary is not a translation, by the term's ordinary meaning. In spite of the non-infringement of this right, Jane may infringe Evangeline's right to *reproduce* in both the UK and Australia,[345] particularly if Jane is seen to have taken a substantial part of Evangeline's commentary.[346] In this case, it will not matter if Jane's commentary is otherwise different from Evangeline's.

Additionally, I argue that Jane infringes Evangeline's right of attribution as an author of the commentary under the *Australian Copyright Act*.[347] This is not the case under the *US Copyright Act*, which applies very narrowly to works of visual art,[348] or the *UK Copyright Act*. In the case of the latter, the assertion requirement in the UK[349] has not been met as Evangeline has not asserted her right to be identified. This is in spite of the fact that the identity of Evangeline as the author of the commentary is known to Jane, who extracted Evangeline's commentary from her Facebook 'Timeline'.

As no rights are infringed in the US, discussing whether the fair use doctrine will apply to excuse Jane's use of Evangeline's commentary is not necessary. The UK fair dealing exception for the purpose of criticism, review, quotation and news reporting,[350] as well as the Australian fair dealing exception for the purpose of criticism or review,[351] could have applied to exempt Jane's use, *but for* the lack of acknowledgement of Evangeline's earlier commentary. Further, Jane's infringement of Evangeline's right of attribution (ie, non-identification of Evangeline) under the *Australian Copyright Act* is not likely to be reasonable in the circumstances.[352]

This suggests that Jane has infringed the copyright laws in the UK and Australia, but not in the US.

D. Jane's use of multiple photographs of newborn babies available on the pin-boards of other Pinterest users to create a collage to share on Pinterest

Under the *US Copyright Act* each of the photographs, as well as the overall collage that Jane creates, will fall under the definition of 'pictorial, graphic and sculptural' works. Under the *UK Copyright Act* and the *Australian Copyright Act,* each of the photographs and the overall collage is an artistic work.

The originality, authorship and fixation (or their equivalents) requirements are easily met for copyright to subsist in the individual photographs and in the collage. The collage is not however a 'joint work' in the US, as the mutual intention of the individual authors (ie, of each photograph) to merge their works into a joint piece is absent. Similarly, in the UK and in Australia, the collage will not qualify as a 'work of joint authorship' as there is no collaboration among the authors of each of the photographs forming the collage. As such, Jane is the sole author of the collage.

Furthermore, it is noted that Jane crops only some of the original photographs, but not all, to create the collage. At first appearance, she could have exercised more than one exclusive right in the bundle of rights held by the copyright holder to each photograph, namely, the right to *reproduce*, the right to *prepare derivative works*, the right to *distribute* and the right to *display* in the US, as well as the equivalent rights in the UK and in Australia. Firstly, the discussion under sub-section (A) can be referred to in respect of the right of *reproduction* – Jane's use infringes this right under the *US Copyright Act*, the *UK Copyright Act* and the *Australian Copyright Act*.

Secondly, in respect of the right to *prepare derivative works*, because the individual components in Jane's collage can be recognised in the overall collage, there is arguably substantial similarity between each of these components (ie, photographs) and Jane's collage. Hence the right to prepare derivative works held by the relevant copyright holder(s) in the US is probably infringed. The equivalent right to *make adaptations of works* in the UK and in Australia does not apply in respect of artistic works such as photographs, therefore addressing the issue of such infringement is not necessary.

Thirdly, the discussion under sub-section (B) can be referred to in respect of the rights to *distribute* and to *display*. While Jane's sharing of the collage infringes the right to distribute in the US, the right to *issue copies to the public* in the UK and the right to (*first*) *publish* in Australia will not be infringed. On the other hand, Jane's use infringes each copyright holder's rights to display (in the US) and to *communicate the work to the public* (in the UK and in Australia).

In summary, Jane's use has infringed: the rights to reproduce, to prepare derivative works, to distribute and to display under the *US Copyright Act*; the rights to reproduce and to communicate the work to the public under the *UK Copyright Act*; as well as the rights to reproduce and to communicate the work to the public under the *Australian Copyright Act*. More than one right under the copyright laws of each jurisdiction is infringed by Jane's use. Her use may be transformative enough to qualify as a fair use under the fair use doctrine in the US, particularly as the use is non-commercial and *if* there is no market for the photographs (ie, the photographs are not taken by professional photographers who licence their use in return for fees). Regardless of the commerciality of the use or existence of a market for the photographs, Jane's use is still likely to qualify as a fair use, given that she has used the original photographs to comment on something else (ie, the ageing population),[353] and that she has changed the composition, presentation and scale of the original photographs so as to have sufficiently transformed them[354] in creating her collage. At the same time, the fair dealing exception for the purpose of caricature, parody or pastiche in the UK[355] could exempt Jane's use, as she has created her collage – a pastiche – using selected photographs shared by other Pinterest users. However, no exceptions, including the fair dealing exception for criticism or review,[356] will likely apply to exempt Jane's use in Australia. In any event, the condition of acknowledgement of the source of each photograph is not satisfied.

Based on the above, Jane has infringed the copyright laws in Australia, but not in the US and the UK.[357]

E. Jane's simultaneous sharing of the collage on Facebook and Twitter

The discussion under sub-section (D) can be referred to in respect of the rights to *reproduce*, to *prepare derivative works*, to *distribute* and to *display* under the *US Copyright Act*, as well as the equivalent rights under the *UK Copyright Act* and the *Australian Copyright Act*. The application of copyright exceptions such as fair use and fair dealing, as the case may be, is also similar.

For the same reasons as under sub-section (D), the above indicates that Jane has infringed the copyright laws in Australia, but not in the US and the UK.

F. Jane's sharing of the same collage in her blog post on WordPress

The discussion under sub-section (D) can be referred to in respect of the rights to *reproduce*, to *prepare derivative works*, to *distribute* and to *display*, as well as the equivalent rights under the *UK Copyright Act* and the *Australian Copyright Act*. The application of copyright exceptions such as fair use and fair dealing, as the case may be, is also similar.

For the same reasons as under sub-section (D), the above suggests that Jane has infringed the copyright laws in Australia, but not in the US and the UK.

G. Zee's contribution to Wikipedia on 'income inequality' using what Jane has written

With reference to the discussion on copyright subsistence in Evangeline's commentary under sub-section (C), the discussion in this sub-section is conducted on the assumption that Jane's commentary enjoys copyright protection as a literary work in all three jurisdictions. I argue that Zee, in contributing Jane's commentary to Wikipedia, infringes Jane's rights to *reproduce* and to *display* the commentary under the *US Copyright Act*; to *reproduce* and to *communicate her work to the public* under the *UK*

Copyright Act; and to *reproduce* and to *communicate her work to the public* under the *Australian Copyright Act.*

Zee also infringes a moral right – the right of *attribution* – under the *Australian Copyright Act*. This is not the case under the *US Copyright Act*, as it applies very narrowly to works of visual art.[358] Further, although Zee extracted Jane's commentary from her Facebook 'Timeline' and is aware of her authorship, the assertion requirement under the *UK Copyright Act* is not satisfied, as Jane has not asserted her right to be identified. Therefore there is no infringement of this moral right in the UK.

In any case, more than one right under the copyright laws of each jurisdiction is infringed by Zee's use. The fair use doctrine in the US will arguably exempt Zee's use from infringement, as the purpose of Zee's use is non-commercial and there is no existing market for Jane's commentary.[359] Neither of the fair dealing exceptions for the purpose of review or criticism, whether in the UK or in Australia,[360] will apply to exempt Zee's use, given the lack of acknowledgement of Jane as the original author of the commentary. Finally, on the facts given, Zee's infringement of Jane's right of attribution under the *Australian Copyright Act* will not likely be seen as reasonable in the circumstances.[361]

Based on the above, Zee has infringed the copyright laws in the UK and Australia, but not in the US.[362]

H. Jane's creation and sharing of a new video clip by way of 'vidding' on YouTube, and subsequently on Facebook

Under the *US Copyright Act*, each of the random video clips from which scenes are extracted, as well as the new video clip Jane created, is an 'audiovisual work'. These video clips are 'films' under the *UK Copyright Act* and 'cinematograph films' under the *Australian Copyright Act.*

Copyright subsists in each video clip and in the new video clip created by Jane, so long as the originality, authorship and fixation (or their equivalent) requirements are met. However, the new video clip is not a 'joint work' in the US, as the mutual intention of the individual authors (ie, of each video clip) to merge their works into a joint piece is absent. Similarly the new video clip will not qualify as a 'work of joint authorship' in the UK and Australia, as there is no collaboration involved among the authors of the original video clips. As such, Jane is the sole author of the new video clip.

The discussion under sub-section (D) can be referred to in respect of the rights to *reproduce*, *prepare derivative works*, *distribute*, *perform* and *display* in the US, as well as the equivalent rights, as applicable, in the UK and in Australia. I argue that Jane's use infringes the rights of the copyright holder (ie, the producer of the television series) to reproduce, prepare derivative works, distribute, perform and display in the US; *reproduce, show or play* and *communicate to the public in the UK*; as well as *reproduce, cause to be seen or heard and communicate to the public* in Australia.

More than one right under the copyright laws of each jurisdiction is infringed by Jane's use. Jane's use will arguably not qualify as a fair use in the US. While her use is non-commercial, it may be argued to interfere with the existing market for the television series. On the other hand, the fair dealing exception for the purpose of caricature, parody or pastiche in the UK[363] could exempt Jane's use as she has created the new video clip – a pastiche – through drawing on other video clips shared on YouTube. No exceptions, however, including the fair dealing exception for criticism or review,[364] will apply to exempt Jane's use in Australia. In any event, the requirement for sufficient acknowledgement is not met.

The above indicates that Jane has infringed the copyright laws in the US and Australia, but not in the UK.[365]

I. Cheryl's use of 'stills' from Jane's video clip as thumbnail images on her website

I discuss the extent to which each of the extracted 'stills', or individual images, is protected under the *US Copyright Act*, the *UK Copyright Act* and the *Australian Copyright Act* below.

As mentioned in sub-section (H), the individual images are extracted from 'audiovisual works' (being the random video clips, as well as Jane's new video clip) as defined under the *US Copyright Act*. These images are extracted from 'films' under the *UK Copyright Act* and 'cinematograph films' under the *Australian Copyright Act*.

At first appearance Cheryl may have exercised more than one exclusive right in the bundle of rights held by the producer of the television series in the audiovisual works from which these images are extracted – namely the rights to *reproduce, prepare derivative works* and *display* in the US. On further analysis, I argue that Cheryl does not infringe the right of reproduction. As she has only extracted a few images for her website, the amount she has copied from the original works is minimal and the standard of substantial similarity is not met. In addition, Cheryl does not infringe the right to prepare derivative works as there is no substantial similarity between her web page incorporating the images as thumbnails and the original audiovisual works. However, Cheryl's use does infringe the right to display the individual images from the original works. The term 'display' means, in the case of an audiovisual work, 'to show individual images nonsequentially'.[366]

I argue that in the UK Cheryl's use of the individual images infringes the right to *reproduce*. This is because the definition of 'copying' in relation to a film 'includes making a photograph of the whole or any substantial part of *any* image forming part of the film'.[367] On the other hand, in Australia the position is less clear. Given the definition of 'cinematograph films' to be the 'aggregate of the visual images',[368] as well as the nature of copyright in these films,[369] no copyright appears to be infringed in relation to Cheryl's use. Notwithstanding this, the individual images are arguably protected as 'artistic works',[370] and Cheryl's use infringes the rights to *reproduce* and to *communicate the works to the public*.

Based on the above, at least one right under the copyright laws of each jurisdiction is prima facie infringed by Cheryl's use. Her use is likely to qualify as a fair use in the US. Not only is her use non-commercial, such use is not one that can foreseeably interfere with the market for the television series.[371] Additionally, her use of only a few images as thumbnails on her website is likely to tip the balance in her favour.[372] Cheryl's use may also be transformative enough to qualify as a fair use under the fair use doctrine in the US. By using the 'stills' as thumbnail images on her website, she has arguably re-contextualised the original video clips through changing their meaning (ie, using the 'stills' from them to decorate the website). Furthermore, in using the thumbnail images for aesthetic reasons she has changed the purpose of these clips from the television series. In the UK and in Australia this is not the case, as Cheryl's use is not for a specified purpose exempt under any fair dealing exception.

Therefore this suggests that Cheryl has infringed the copyright laws in the UK and Australia, but not in the US.[373]

J. Other users' partial use of Jane's collage to create their own, and sharing the same on Pinterest, Facebook and Twitter

The discussion under sub-section (D) can be referred to in respect of the rights to *reproduce*, to *prepare derivative works*, to *distribute* and to *display* under the *US Copyright Act*, as well as the equivalent rights under the *UK Copyright Act* and the *Australian Copyright Act*. In particular, the rights (held by Jane in the collage and the author of each photograph used in such collage) to reproduce, to prepare derivative works, to distribute and to display in the US; as well as to *reproduce* and to *communicate the work to the public* in the UK and in Australia, are arguably infringed by other users' partial use of Jane's collage. The application of copyright exceptions such as fair use and fair dealing, as the case may be, is largely similar. In relation to the application of the fair use doctrine in the US, the users' transformation of Jane's collage may additionally be their way of commenting on, criticising or parodying Jane's collage, depending on the collages resulting from their uses. At the same time, the fair dealing exception for the purpose of caricature, parody or pastiche in the UK[374] could exempt these uses, as the collages (or pastiches) are created using Jane's collage, as well as other selected materials.

Based on the above, these users have infringed the copyright laws in Australia, but not in the US and the UK.[375]

K. Editor Jasper's use of Jane's collage on the cover page of his magazine

As mentioned earlier, Jane's collage is a 'pictorial, graphic and sculptural work' under the *US Copyright Act*, and an artistic work under the *UK Copyright Act* and the *Australian Copyright Act*. By his use, I argue that Jasper infringes Jane's rights to *reproduce* and to *distribute* the collage in the US; to *reproduce* and to *issue copies of the collage to the public* in the UK; as well as to *reproduce*[376] and to (*first*) *publish* the collage in Australia. Similar rights held by the author of each photograph used in such collage are also infringed by Jasper's use.

Given that Jasper's use of Jane's collage is commercial in nature (ie, the magazine copies will be purchased by interested readers), his use is *less* likely to be exempt as a fair use in the US. Moreover, such use will have an adverse effect upon the potential market for Jane's collage (and the photographs in the collage) *if* Jane (or the relevant author) decides to license the use of the collage (or each photograph in the collage) in return for a fee. In addition, Jasper's use is not exempt as a specified purpose under any fair dealing exception in the UK and in Australia.

This suggests that Jasper has infringed the copyright laws in all three jurisdictions.

III. Conclusion

In this chapter I have considered the application of copyright laws in the US, the UK and Australia to the content-generative activities of social media users. This allows me to compare copyright laws with other regulatory factors on social media – namely the terms of service and the technological features – in regulating the content-generative behaviours of users. In particular, I am concerned with the consistency of the copyright regimes with each of the private regimes explored in the subsequent chapters of this book.

I have demonstrated, through my discussion of the application of copyright subsistence and infringement issues and the challenges posed to the content-generative activities on social media, as well as through scenario one, the following:

(i) Whether content used on social media is copyright protected requires one to address the multiple copyright subsistence issues set out;
(ii) Any single content-generative activity can raise concerns of copyright infringement of more than one right;
(iii) There is uncertainty as to whether any exceptions to copyright laws apply, although the fair use doctrine in the US is found to be more permissive than the fair dealing exceptions in the UK and Australia; and
(iv) Conflict of laws issues will make it hard for users to ascertain the applicable law and the relevant jurisdiction in which a court can adjudicate a copyright-related dispute with respect to content on social media.

In this sense, it is not possible for any regular social media user to have the level of understanding of copyright laws required to assess the legitimacy of the content-generative activities he or she undertakes, through the application of copyright laws to these activities.

With scenario one, I have shown how the application of the copyright laws of the three jurisdictions to the same content-generative activities under the case study can result in varied positions being reached on the copyright liabilities of users based in each jurisdiction. In particular, the application of the copyright laws of the US, the UK and Australia in scenario one yields different outcomes under the *US Copyright Act*, as against the *UK Copyright Act* and the *Australian Copyright Act*. Out of a total of *eleven* content-generative activities extracted from the case study for scenario one, the application of copyright laws to as many as *nine* of these activities results in contrasting positions on the copyright liabilities of the respective users.

In the next chapter I will survey the terms of service of the five selected social media platforms that purport to regulate the content-generative behaviours of users. I will also assess the interaction of these terms of service with the copyright regimes in each of the US, the UK and Australia for alignment and incompatibility. I then present the second of four scenarios in the book to demonstrate how the terms of service can apply to the content-generative activities of Jane and other users in the case study.

Notes

1. *United States Constitution* art I § 8, cl 8 (1787). The terms 'science' and 'useful arts' are used in their eighteenth-century sense: the term 'science' relates to knowledge, while the term 'useful arts' relates to inventions. See, for example, Tyler T. Ochoa, 'Copyright Duration: Theories and Practice' in Peter K. Yu (ed.), *Intellectual Property and Information Wealth: Copyright and Related Rights* (Green Publishing Group, 2007) 133; Malla Pollack, 'What is Congress Supposed to Promote?: Defining "Progress" in Article I, Section 8, Clause 8 of the United States Constitution or Introducing the Progress Clause' (2001) 80 *Nebraska Law Review* 754.
2. See, for example, *Harper & Row Publishers Inc v Nation Enterprises,* 471 US 539 (1985) (*Harper*); *Golan v Holder*, 132 S Ct 873 (2012).
3. *Statute of Anne 1709* (UK) c 19, as repealed by the *Copyright Act 1842.*
4. *Statute of Anne 1709* (UK) c 19.
5. The copyright laws of Australia and the UK did not evolve in lockstep. For instance, Australian copyright law was still based upon the *Copyright Act 1911* (UK), even after the United Kingdom (UK) modernised its copyright laws under the *Copyright Act 1956* (UK). Despite a strong resemblance between copyright laws in Australia and the UK between the years 1968 and 1988, subsequent reforms under the *Copyright, Designs and Patents Act 1988* (UK) c 48 were not followed by Australia. The British Copyright Act of 1911 applied in Australia until the *Copyright Act 1968* (Cth) came into force in 1969. See, for example, *Copyright Owners Reproduction Society v EMI (Australia) Pty Ltd* [1958] HCA 54; James Lahore, *Intellectual Property in Australia: Copyright* (Butterworths, 1977) [102].
6. *Berne Convention for the Protection of Literary and Artistic Works*, signed 9 September 1886 (entered into force 5 December 1886) (*Berne Convention*). The US was the last of these three countries to join the *Berne Convention*. See *Berne Convention Implementation Act,* 17 USC § 101 (1988).
7. *Agreement on Trade-Related Aspects of Intellectual Property Rights,* signed 15 April 1994 (entered into force 1 January 1996) (*TRIPS Agreement*).
8. *Copyright Act of 1976*, 17 USC §§ 101–810 (*US Copyright Act*).
9. *Copyright, Patents and Designs Act 1988* (UK) c 48 (*UK Copyright Act*).
10. *Copyright Act 1968* (Cth) (*Australian Copyright Act*).
11. Sculptural works are grouped together with pictorial and graphic works under the *US Copyright Act* and hence mentioned as part of this broad category. However, sculptural works *per se* are not the types of content currently available on social media, as we now know it to be.
12. See *US Copyright Act*, §§ 101 and 102 (a).
13. *US Copyright Act*, § 103.
14. *UK Copyright Act*, s 1(1).
15. *Australian Copyright Act*, ss 32, 89–92. Copyright protection is conferred on 'works' (comprising literary, dramatic, musical and artistic works) and other forms of subject matter not being 'works' (such as sound recordings, cinematograph films, television broadcasts, sound broadcasts and published editions of works).
16. This closed list of works may have less significance in the UK, particularly if creativity becomes the only relevant determinant of entitlement to copyright protection. See Jonathan Griffiths, 'Dematerialization, Pragmatism and the European Copyright Revolution' (2013) 33(4) *Oxford Journal of Legal Studies* 767, 782. See also *Infopaq International A/S v Danske Dagblades*

Forening (Court of Justice of the European Union, C-5/08, 16 July 2009) (*Infopaq*), where it was decided that the 'author's own intellectual creation' threshold for copyright protection is relevant not only to those categories of work to which it has been explicitly applied in legislation, but also to all forms of copyright-protected work under the *Directive 2001/29/EC of the European Parliament and of the Council of 22 May 2001 on the harmonisation of certain aspects of copyright and related rights in the information society* [2001] OJ L 167 (*Information Society Directive*). But see *The Newspaper Licensing Agency and others v Meltwater Holding BV and others* [2011] EWCA Civ 890 (*Meltwater*), where the court found that the *Infopaq* (Court of Justice of the European Union, C-5/08, 16 July 2009) decision did not qualify the long-standing English test of originality, and that the test of being an author's intellectual creation relates to the question of origin, rather than of novelty.

17. *UK Copyright Act*, s 6.
18. *Australian Copyright Act*, s 10. A 'broadcast' is defined to refer to a communication to the public delivered by a broadcasting service within the meaning of the *Broadcasting Services Act 1992* (Cth).
19. *UK Copyright Act*, s 8.
20. *Australian Copyright Act*, s 88.
21. See art 9(2) of the *TRIPS Agreement* and art 2 of the *WIPO Copyright Treaty*, signed 20 December 1996 (entered into force 6 March 2002) (*WIPO Copyright Treaty*). See also Paul Goldstein and Bernt Hugenholtz, *International Copyright: Principles, Law and Practice* (Oxford University Press, 3rd ed., 2013) 220.
22. *US Copyright Act*, § 102 (b).
23. *Code of Federal Regulations*, 37 CFR § 202.1 (1991).
24. Sheldon W. Halpern, Craig Allen Nard and Kenneth L. Port, *Fundamentals of United States Intellectual Property Law: Copyright, Patent and Trademark* (Kluwer Law International, 4th ed., 2012) 9.
25. *Chuck Blore & Don Richman Inc v 20/20 Advertising Inc*, 674 F Supp 671, 676 (D Minn, 1987). See also Halpern, S.W., Nard, C.A. and Port, K.L. 2012, 9; Goldstein, P. and Hugenholtz, B. 2013, 220–1.
26. Goldstein, P. and Hugenholtz, B. 2013, 220. See also *Baker v Selden*, 101 US 99 (1879); *Morissey v Proctor & Gamble Co*, 379 F 2d 675 (1st Cir, 1967) (*Morissey*) (in relation to the first doctrine); *Murray Hill Publications Inc v Twentieth Century Fox*, 361 F 3d 312 (6th Cir), *cert denied*, 543 US 959 (2004); *Reyher v Children's Television Workshop*, 533 F 2d 87 (2nd Cir), *cert denied*, 429 US 980, 97 S Ct 492 (1976) (in relation to the second doctrine).
27. Goldstein, P. and Hugenholtz, B. 2013, 220–1.
28. Goldstein, P. and Hugenholtz, B. 2013, 221. See also *Walker v Time-Life Films Inc*, 784 F 2d 44, 50 (2nd Cir) ('Elements such as drunks, prostitutes, vermin and derelict cars would appear in any realistic work of policemen in the South Bronx. These similarities are therefore unprotectable as 'scènes à faire', that is, scenes that necessarily result from the choice of a setting or situation'), *cert denied*, 476 US 1159 (1986).
29. Goldstein, P. and Hugenholtz, B. 2013, 220. The US Supreme Court has stated that the idea–expression dichotomy strikes a balance between the First Amendment and the *US Copyright Act* by permitting the free communication of facts while still protecting an author's expression. See *Harper*, 471 US 539 at 556 (1985).
30. See, for example, *Kenrick v Lawrence* (1890) 25 QBD 99; *Donoghue v Allied Newspapers Limited* (1938) Ch 106; *Jones v London Borough of Tower Hamlets* [2001] RPC (14) 379; *Autodesk Inc v Dyason (No 1)* (1992) 173 CLR 330 at 334; *Victoria Park Racing and Recreation Grounds Co. Ltd v Taylor* (1937) 58 CLR 479 (*VPR*). See also Lionel Bently and Brad Sherman, *Intellectual Property Law* (Oxford University Press, 3rd ed., 2009) 181; Sam Ricketson and Chris Cresswell, *The Law of Intellectual Property: Copyright, Designs and Confidential Information* (Thomson Reuters, 2015) [4.65].
31. See *US Copyright Act*, § 102(a); *UK Copyright Act*, s 1(1); *Australian Copyright Act*, ss 32(1) and 32(2).
32. See, for example, *Feist Publications Inc v Rural Telephone Service Company*, 499 US 340 (1991) (*Feist*); *L Batlin & Son Inc v Synder*, 536 F 2d 486, 490 (2nd Cir, 1976) (*Batlin*); *Baltimore Orioles v Major League Baseball Players*, 805 F 2d 663 (7th Cir, 1986).
33. The 'sweat of the brow' doctrine was rejected in *Feist*, 499 US 340 (1991), where the court held that the selection, coordination and arrangement of the pages in telephone directories did not satisfy the minimum standard of originality for copyright protection in the US.

34. See, for example, *Feist*, 499 US 340 (1991); *Warren Publishing Inc v Microdos Data Corp*, 115 F 3d 1509 (11th Cir, 1997); *BUC International Corp v International Yacht Council Ltd*, 489 F 3d 1129 (11th Cir, 2007); *CCC Information Services Inc v Maclean Hunter Market Reports Inc*, 44 F 3d 61 (2nd Cir, 1994), *cert denied*, 116 S Ct 72 (1995).
35. See, for example, *Alfred Bell & Co v Catalda Fine Arts Inc*, 191 F 2d 99, 103 (2nd Cir, 1951), which articulated that an author had to contribute something more than a 'merely trivial' variation which is recognisably his or her own for the author's work to be copyright protected. See also cases after *Feist*, 499 US 340 (1991), which relied in part or employed similar language to this test: *Atari Games Corp v Oman,* 979 F 2d 242, 246 (DC Cir, 1992) (*Atari*); *Silverstein v Penguin Putnam*, 368 F 3d 77 (2nd Cir, 2004); *Assessment Technologies v Wiredata*, 350 F 3d 640 (7th Cir, 2003).
36. Russ VerSteeg, 'Originality and Creativity in Copyright Law' in Peter K. Yu (ed.), *Intellectual Property and Information Wealth: Issues and Practices in the Digital Age* (Praeger Publishers, 2007) 1, 17.
37. *UK Copyright Act*, ss 1(a) and 1(b). See also Kevin Garnett, Gillian Davies and Gwilym Harbottle, *Copinger and Skone James on Copyright* (Thomson Reuters, 16th ed., 2011) [3–150]–[3–151].
38. *Australian Copyright Act*, s 32(1). See also Ricketson, S. and Cresswell, C. 2015 [4.35].
39. Ricketson and Cresswell suggest that there are two aspects of the requirement of 'originality'. The first is that the particular work must have originated from the author and must not have been copied. The second is that the author has used some skill and/or labour in the making of the work. Although there is no statutory requirement of originality in Australia, there is still a minimum requirement for protection in relation to other subject matter, in the sense that such subject matter should not be taken or copied from another source. See Ricketson, S. and Cresswell, C. 2015 [4.35]. See also *UK Copyright Act*, ss 5A(2) and 5B(4), which provides for this minimum requirement.
40. See, for example, *University of London Press Ltd v University Tutorial Press Ltd* [1916] 2 Ch 601 at 608–9; *Ladbroke (Football) Ltd v William Hill (Football) Ltd* [1964] 1 All ER 465 (*Ladbroke*); *CBD Records Australia Ltd v Gross* (1989) 15 IPR 385 (Federal Court of Australia); *VPR* (1937) 58 CLR 479 at 511; *IceTV Pty Ltd v Nine Network Australia Pty Ltd* [2009] HCA 14 (*IceTV*). In *IceTV* the High Court held that although the plaintiff invested the required 'skill and labour' in the programming decisions and selection of programme information, the action for infringement failed as this 'skill and labour' was not directed to the expression of time and title information in the programme guide that the defendant appropriated.
41. See, for example, *Feist*, 499 US 340 (1991); *Atari*, 979 F 2d 242 (DC Cir, 1992); *American Dental Association v Delta Dental Plans Association*, 126 F 3d 977, 979 (7th Cir, 1997); *Ladbroke* [1964] 1 All ER 465; *Data Access v Powerflex* [1999] HCA 49. See also Goldstein, P. and Hugenholtz, B. 2013, 194; Halpern, S.W., Nard, C.A. and Port, K.L. 2012, 914; VerSteeg, R. 2007, 21.
42. William Cornish, David Llewelyn and Tanya Aplin, *Intellectual Property: Patents, Copyrights, Trademarks and Allied Rights* (Sweet & Maxwell, 7th ed., 2010) [11–05].
43. Ricketson, S. and Cresswell, C. 2015 [7.215]. Ricketson also suggests that an alternative explanation is that such works have no intelligible meaning on their own.
44. Ricketson, S. and Cresswell, C. 2015 [7.215].
45. See, for example, *State of Victoria v Pacific Technologies (Australia) Pty Ltd* (No 2) [2009] FCA 737 (*Pacific Technologies*); *Fairfax Media Publications Pty Ltd v Reed International Books Australia Pty Ltd* [2010] 88 IPR 11 (Federal Court of Australia) (*Fairfax*). Ricketson, S. and Cresswell, C. 2015 [7.220].
46. *Kirk v Fleming* [1928–35] Mac CC 44.
47. *Francis, Day & Hunter v Twentieth Century Fox Film Corporation* [1940] AC 112 at 123 (*Francis, Day & Hunter*) (see Lord Wright).
48. *Exxon Corp. v. Exxon Insurance Consultants International Ltd* [1982] Ch 119. See also Megan Richardson, 'Copyright in Trademarks? On Understanding Trade Mark Dilution' [2000] *Intellectual Property Quarterly* 66, 72–4, where Richardson notes that the lack of originality is not the primary consideration for denying copyright protection to the word 'Exxon', and the reference Stephenson LJ made to the *de minimis* principle in the case (at 139).
49. *Pacific Technologies* [2009] FCA 737.
50. See, for example, *Fairfax* [2010] 88 IPR 11 (Federal Court of Australia). But see also *Meltwater* [2011] EWCA Civ 890, which suggests that news headlines can be copyright protected if they are worthy of being original literary works on their own.

51. Ricketson, S. and Cresswell, C. 2015 [7.215]. See also *Pacific Technologies* [2009] FCA 737; *Fairfax* [2010] 88 IPR 11 (Federal Court of Australia).
52. See, for example, *The Guardian* 2015; D'Orazio, D. 2015.
53. See Sam Ricketson, 'Reflections on Authorship and the Meaning of a "Work" in Australian and Singapore Copyright Law' (2012) 24 *Singapore Academy of Law Journal* 792, 831.
54. In the US some courts have set a higher standard of originality for derivative works than that for non-derivative works. See, for example, *Batlin*, F 2d 486 (2nd Cir, 1976); *Gracen v Bradford Exchange*, 698 F 2d 300 (7th Cir, 1983). But see *Schrock v Learning Curve International Inc*, 586 F 3d 513, 519–20 (7th Cir, 2009) (where the court observed the historically lower standard in finding originality in the photographs, which were derivative works).
55. Ricketson, S. 2012.
56. See Valentine, C. 2015; Plaugic, L. 2015.
57. See Ricketson, S. 2012.
58. *US Copyright Act*, § 201(a). In addition, under the *US Copyright Act*, in the case of a work made for hire the employer is deemed to be the author of the work; see *US Copyright Act*, § 201(b).
59. *US Copyright Act*, § 101.
60. Halpern, S.W., Nard, C.A. and Port, K.L. 2012, 46.
61. *UK Copyright Act*, s 9(1).
62. *UK Copyright Act*, s 10(1).
63. *Australian Copyright Act*, s 10.
64. *Australian Copyright Act*, s 10.
65. See Peter Jaszi, 'On the Author Effect: Contemporary Copyright and Collective Creativity' in Martha Woodmansee and Peter Jaszi (eds), *The Construction of Authorship: Textual Appropriation in Law and Literature* (Duke University Press, 1994) 35, 50.
66. Jaszi, P. 1994, 50. See also Megan Richardson and Jake Goldenfein, 'Competing Myths of Informal Economies' in Dan Hunter et al (eds), *Amateur Media: Social, Cultural and Legal Perspectives* (Routledge, 2013) 18, 23. But see Ricketson, S. 2012. Where there is no human author identifiable for content, the question to ask could be whether the time, effort and investment of resources to create such content, if unprotected by copyright's author-centric framework, should be protected under a neighbouring rights regime instead. It appears that there is no current protection for such content under present laws, except, perhaps, under the *UK Copyright Act*, s 9(3).
67. As indicated on the history of the relevant page. See also *Fairfax* [2010] 88 IPR 11 (Federal Court of Australia), which highlights the growing problem of identifying authorship in a work. In *Fairfax*, the plaintiff chose to rely on s 129(2) of the *Australian Copyright Act* that presumes the originality of published works where it is not established that 'the identity of the author is generally known or can be ascertained by reasonable inquiry', instead of adducing evidence regarding the authorship of the works in question. Bennett J noted that the plaintiff did not attempt to ascertain the identity of the authors from its own employment and attendance; as such, she found that the presumption under s 129(2) was not available to the plaintiff in proving the originality of the headlines. This presumption of originality under s 129(2) (including that the publication is alleged to be pseudonymous) may, however, be useful in relation to articles shared on Wikipedia.
68. See, for example, Jessica Litman, 'Lawful Personal Use' (2007) 85 *Texas Law Review* 1871; Roland Barthes, 'The Death of the Author' in Stephen Heath (trans.), *Image, Music, Text* (Hill and Wang, 1977) 142; Michel Foucault, 'What is an Author?' in James D. Faubion (ed., translated by Josue V. Harari) in *Aesthetics, Method and Epistemology* (The New Press, 1994) 205.
69. Jane C. Ginsburg, 'The Author's Place in the Future of Copyright' (2009) 153(2) *Proceedings of the American Philosophical Society* 147, 152–3. Ginsburg argues that the concept of professional authorship will persist, notwithstanding that professional authors will be joined by a host of newcomers.
70. Ginsburg, J.C. 2009, 151.
71. See Erez Reuveni, 'Authorship in the Age of the Conducer' (2007) 54 *Journal of the Copyright Society of the U.S.A.* 1801, 1802.
72. Lionel Bently, 'Copyright and the Death of the Author in Literature and Law' (1994) 5 *The Modern Law Review* 973, 981.
73. Ginsburg, J.C. 2009, 151.
74. See *Telstra Corporation Ltd v Phone Directories Company Pty Ltd* (2010) 194 FCR 142, where individual human contributions to telephone directories produced by Telstra could not be

discerned clearly, in part because the ultimate work was produced by technology. As such, it was held that copyright did not subsist in Telstra's phone directories. It was also decided that the collaboration between staff members did not warrant the deployment of the concept of joint authorship, and that the intellectual effort to organise the listings did not represent sufficient literary effort warranting protection.

75. But see Melissa Dolin, 'Note: Joint Authorship and Collaborative Artwork Created through Social Media' (2011) 39(4) *American Intellectual Property Law Association Quarterly Journal* 535, 561, where she suggests that in order to encourage artists to continue creating works and to further the goals of copyright, collaborative content created on social media platforms should generally be found to satisfy the requirements for copyright protection. Users who have jointly collaborated to create such works should be considered joint authors, unless there are contractual stipulations to the contrary or a person is contributing anonymously.
76. Elizabeth White, 'The Berne Convention's Flexible Fixation Requirement: A Problematic Provision for User-Generated Content' (2012–2013) 13(2) *Chicago Journal of International Law* 685, 689–99.
77. White, E. 2012–2013, 689–99.
78. Twitter, *Help Center: I'm missing Tweets* <https://support.twitter.com/articles/277671#>.
79. See, for example, Elisa Gabbert, *Find Your Old Tweets: How to See Your First (Worst?) Tweet* (10 October 2013) <http://www.wordstream.com/blog/ws/2013/10/10/how-to-find-your-old-tweets>. This guide provides users with steps to take to locate their old 'tweets'.
80. This challenge persists although US courts are observed to be generous in their interpretation of the fixation requirement, so long as the expressions of ideas in content on social media are tangible. See Dolin, M. 2011, 553.
81. *US Copyright Act*, § 102.
82. *US Copyright Act*, § 101. In particular, see the definition of a work that is 'fixed'.
83. *UK Copyright Act*, s 3(2).
84. *UK Copyright Act*, s 4.
85. *UK Copyright Act*, ss 5A and 5B.
86. *Australian Copyright Act*, s 22(1).
87. *Australian Copyright Act*, s 10.
88. *Australian Copyright Act*, s 10. See particularly the definitions for 'sound recording', 'record' (which includes an electronic file), 'cinematograph film' and 'sound-track'.
89. *US Copyright Act*, §§ 102 and 103.
90. This includes that one or more of the authors of the works (wherever published) is a national or domiciliary of the US on the date of first publication; see *US Copyright Act*, § 104(b)(1).
91. *US Copyright Act*, § 104(b)(2). A treaty party is a country or intergovernmental organisation that is a party to an international agreement; see *US Copyright Act*, § 101.
92. *US Copyright Act*, § 104(b)(3).
93. *US Copyright Act*, § 104(a).
94. *US Copyright Act*, § 101. In spite of this definition of the term 'publication', which mirrors the reference to the exclusive right of distribution under § 106(3), publication has been found to be 'an important subsidiary right' subsumed within the right of distribution; see *Harper,* 471 US 539, 549 (1985). It is a narrower right than the right of distribution.
95. In spite of the *US Copyright Act*, § 104(b)(1).
96. This difficulty arises from the fact that the fixation of content on social media occurs online. Regardless of where the user creating the content is situated, the content is ultimately accessible from all over the world.
97. *UK Copyright Act*, ss 153–5.
98. *UK Copyright Act*, s 175(1).
99. *UK Copyright Act*, s 17.
100. *Australian Copyright Act*, s 32(2).
101. *Australian Copyright Act*, s 29. The term 'copy' is defined to relate narrowly to a cinematograph film; see *Australian Copyright Act*, s 10.
102. See *UK Copyright Act*, ss 153–5; *Australian Copyright Act*, s 32(2).
103. This principle of national treatment is established in other international instruments including but not limited to the *TRIPS Agreement* (art 3(1)), as well as the *WIPO Copyright Treaty* (through incorporating arts 2 to 6 of the *Berne Convention* under art 3) and the *WIPO Performances and Phonograms Treaty* (art 4), signed 20 December 1996 (entered into force 20 May 2002) (together, the *WIPO Internet Treaties*).

104. To date the *Berne Convention* has 172 contracting parties. See World Intellectual Property Organisation (WIPO), *WIPO-Administered Treaties: Contracting Parties – Berne Convention* <http://www.wipo.int/treaties/en/ShowResults.jsp?treaty_id=15>.
105. The US acceded the instrument on 16 November 1988, which came into force on 1 March 1989; and the UK ratified the instrument on 5 September 1887, which came into force on 5 December 1887. The instrument came into force in Australia on 14 April 1928. See WIPO.
106. See *UK Copyright Act*, s 159 and *The Copyright (Application to Other Countries) Order 1993* (UK) SI 1993/942, Schedule One.
107. *Copyright (International Protection) Regulations 1969* (Cth) reg 4.
108. *US Copyright Act*, § 106.
109. *US Copyright Act*, § 102.
110. *US Copyright Act*, § 106(1).
111. *US Copyright Act*, § 101.
112. *UK Copyright Act*, s 16(1).
113. *UK Copyright Act*, s 17.
114. *UK Copyright Act*, s 17(2).
115. *UK Copyright Act*, s 17(3).
116. *UK Copyright Act*, s 17(4).
117. *UK Copyright Act*, s 17(6).
118. *Australian Copyright Act*, ss 31(1)(a)(i) and 31(1)(b)(i).
119. *Australian Copyright Act*, ss 85(1)(a) and 86(a).
120. *Australian Copyright Act*, s 10.
121. *Australian Copyright Act*, ss 21(1A) and 21(6).
122. *Australian Copyright Act*, s 21(3)(b).
123. *Australian Copyright Act*, s 65(2). See also *Australian Copyright Act*, ss 66 and 67.
124. See, for example, *Sandoval v New Line Cinema Corp*, 147 F 3d 215 (2nd Cir, 1998) (*Sandoval*); *Ringgold v Black Entertainment Television Inc*, 1996 WL 535547 (USDC SDNY, 19 September 1996) (*Ringgold*). See also Paul C. Weiler and Gary Myers, *Entertainment, Media, and the Law: Text, Cases and Problems* (Thomson Reuters, 4th ed., 2011) 347.
125. In relation to the application of this principle in the UK see *UK Copyright Act*, s 16(3). See, for example, *Designers Guild Ltd v Russell Williams (Textiles) Ltd* [2000] UKHL 58 (*Designers Guild*); *Ladbroke* [1964] 1 All ER 465; *Francis, Day & Hunter* [1940] AC 112. See also William Cornish, David Llewelyn and Tanya Aplin, *Intellectual Property: Patents, Copyrights, Trademarks and Allied Rights* (Sweet & Maxwell, 7th ed., 2010) [12–06]. In the case of Australia, see *Australian Copyright Act*, s 14(1). See, for example, *EMI Songs Australia Pty Ltd v Larrikin Music Publishing Pty Ltd* [2011] FCAFC 47 (*EMI Songs*); *IceTV* [2009] HCA 14; *Elwood Clothing Pty Ltd v Cotton On Clothing Pty Ltd* [2008] FCAFC 197 (*Elwood Clothing*). See also Ricketson, S. and Cresswell, C. 2015 [9.80]; Sam Ricketson, Megan Richardson and Mark Davison, *Intellectual Property: Cases, Materials and Commentary* (Lexis Nexis Butterworths, 5th ed., 2013) 247–71. Whether an author has copied a substantial part may depend more on quality (ie, whether an important part of the subject matter is taken) than on the quantity of what he has taken. This could make the assessment a difficult one to make.
126. See, for example, *Designers Guild* [2000] UKHL 58; *EMI Songs* [2011] FCAFC 47; *Elwood Clothing* [2008] FCAFC 197.
127. *US Copyright Act*, § 106(2).
128. *US Copyright Act*, § 101. The definition of 'derivative work' also means that, to be copyright protected, such work must pass the threshold for originality and be fixed as tangible expression. The implications of the concept of originality on content on social media have been highlighted earlier.
129. Even where there is incorporation of the original work in the secondary work, the secondary work is not infringing if the final product is not substantially similar to the original work. See *Castle Rock Entertainment Inc v Carol Publishing Group Inc*, 150 F 3d 132 (2nd Cir, 1998) (*Castle Rock*), for the proposition that if the secondary work sufficiently transforms the expression of the original work such that the two works are not substantially similar, then the secondary work is not a derivative work and, as such, does not infringe the copyright of the original work. It is noted that no distinction was made between the two forms of infringement (ie, of the rights of reproduction and to produce derivative works) in *Castle Rock*. See also *Well-Made Toy Manufacturing Corp v Goffa International Corp*, 354 F 3d 112 (2nd Cir, 2003).

130. See, for example, *Batlin*, F 2d 486 (2nd Cir, 1976) for the view that a derivative work must qualify for copyright protection on its own in order to infringe the derivative works right. But see *Lone Ranger Television Inc v Program Radio Corp*, 740 F 2d 718, 722 (9th Cir, 1984) for the alternative view that a derivative work (of which derivative rights can be infringed) may not qualify for copyright protection. See also *Lee v A.R.T. Co*, 125 F 3d 580 (7th Cir, 1997). In this case the district court initially concluded that as the tile art created by the defendants with the plaintiff's copyrighted note cards was not original enough to be copyright protected, it was not an infringing derivative work. Subsequently the Seventh Circuit affirmed the judgement on slightly different grounds. Although the tile art was seen by itself to be a derivative work, it was not considered an infringement as 'an alteration that includes (or consumes) the original lacks economic significance'. In addition, a split in case law and in scholarly commentary was noted by Judge Easterbook, who then concluded that in the case it was not necessary to choose either view (at 582). The first view results in the paradoxical result that a defendant could gain more protection against liability for *not* being creative than if he or she had been; see Amy B. Cohen, 'When does a Work Infringe the Derivative Works Right of a Copyright Owner?' (1999) 17 *Cardozo Arts and Entertainment Law Journal* 623, 639.
131. See, for example, *Eden Toys v Florelee Undergarment Co*, 697 F 2d 27 (2nd Cir, 1982). In this case Judge Mansfield noted that a work may make non-trivial contributions to an existing one, and hence be copyright protected as a derivative work. The author of the work may be liable for copyright infringement if permission from the owner holding the copyright to the original work is not sought, *and* if the secondary work retains the same aesthetic appeal as the original work. He gave the example of a second edition of a textbook that is copyright protected as a derivative work. This second edition can infringe the original copyright work if it is created without permission.
132. If this case goes to trial its outcome would, however, likely depend on whether Prince's use qualified for the fair use defence in the US; see *US Copyright Act*, § 107.
133. See *Cariou v Prince*, 714 F 3d 694 (2nd Cir, 2013) (*Cariou*). In this case Prince was noted to have created the collages on canvases which incorporate colour, feature distorted forms and settings, and measure between 10 and nearly 100 times the size of the original photographs. Prince's composition, presentation, scale, colour palette and media, as is the expressive nature of his works, were observed to be fundamentally different from the original photographs.
134. See *Sandoval*, 147 F 3d 215 (2nd Cir, 1998) citing *Ringgold*, 1996 WL 535547 (USDC SDNY, 19 September 1996).
135. Although this relates to content on social media, it should be noted that Prince's use occurred, in part, off site. See Valentine, C. 2015; Plaugic, L. 2015. See also sub-section (B).
136. *UK Copyright Act*, s 16(1).
137. *UK Copyright Act*, s 21.
138. *UK Copyright Act*, s 21(3).
139. *Australian Copyright Act*, s 31(1)(a)(vi).
140. *Australian Copyright Act*, s 10.
141. See *UK Copyright Act*, s 21(2); *Australian Copyright Act*, s 31(1)(a)(vii).
142. *US Copyright Act*, § 106 (3).
143. *US Copyright Act*, § 106 (3). This description overlaps with the given definition of the term 'publication' in § 101.
144. *US Copyright Act*, § 101.
145. See *A&M Records v Napster*, 239 F 3d 1004 (9th Cir, 2001), where the court held that the internet transmission of a sound recording is an infringing 'distribution' of the sound recording and of the copyright-protected music contained therein.
146. This is consistent with the obligations of the US under the *WIPO Internet Treaties*. See also United States Copyright Office, *The Making Available Right in the United States* (February 2016) <http://copyright.gov/docs/making_available/making-available-right.pdf>; Jane C. Ginsburg, *Comments in response to the US Copyright Office's Notice soliciting further comments on the 'Right of Making Available' dated 15 July 2014* (3 September 2014) <http://copyright.gov/docs/making_available/comments/docket2014_2/reply/Ginsburg_Jane.pdf>. See, for example, *BMG Rights Management (US) LLC v Cox Communications Inc et al*, 2015 WL 7756130 (ED Va, 1 December 2015) [transferring electronic files (also 'material objects') using the BitTorrent protocol satisfies the transactional element of distribution].

147. The making available right, although not expressly provided for, is said to be implemented through the *US Copyright Act*'s rights of distribution, public performance and display. The making available right is noted to be narrower than the rights to communicate a work to the public under the *UK Copyright Act* (ss 16(1) and 20(2)) and the *Australian Copyright Act* (ss 31(1)(a)(iv), 31(1)(b)(iii) and 10). See United States Copyright Office 2016.
148. *UK Copyright Act*, s 16(1).
149. *UK Copyright Act*, s 18(3).
150. *Australian Copyright Act*, ss 31(1)(a)(ii) and 31(1)(b)(ii).
151. The right to publish under Section 31(1) is confined to 'first publication' (ie, as a right which can be violated under an infringement action), unlike publication for the subsistence of copyright under Section 32. See *Avel Pty Ltd v Multicoin Amusements Pty Ltd* (1990) 171 CLR 88. In this case it was established that the right to publish a work extends only to the right of first publication (ie, supplying copies of a work not previously made public in the relevant territory to the public). See also Ricketson, S. and Cresswell, C. 2015 [16.280]; Ricketson, S., Richardson, M. and Davison, M. 2013, 353–4.
152. *Australian Copyright Act*, s 29. When a work 'deemed to have been published' is further defined, and references are made, among others: to reproductions of a work being supplied to the public, by sale or otherwise; copies of films being sold or let on hire to the public; and records of sound recordings being supplied by sale or otherwise to the public.
153. *US Copyright Act*, § 106(4).
154. *US Copyright Act*, § 101. The same applies to displaying a work publicly.
155. *US Copyright Act*, § 106(5).
156. In the case of a motion picture or other audiovisual work, to show individual images non-sequentially; see *US Copyright Act*, § 101.
157. *US Copyright Act*, § 101.
158. *Columbia Pictures Industries Inc v Redd Horne Inc*, 749 F 2d 154 (3rd Cir, 1984).
159. *US Copyright Act*, § 106(6).
160. *UK Copyright Act*, s 16(1).
161. *UK Copyright Act*, s 19(2).
162. *UK Copyright Act*, s 19(4).
163. *UK Copyright Act*, s 20(2).
164. *UK Copyright Act*, s 16(1).
165. Reference can be made to the decisions made at the European Union (EU) level. See *Information Society Directive*, art 3(1). See also *ITV Broadcasting Ltd And Others* (Court of Justice of the European Union, C-607/11, 7 March 2013) (*ITV Broadcasting Ltd*) [32].
166. See, for example, *Jennings v Stephens* [1936] Ch 469 (*Jennings*); *Ernest Turner Electrical Instruments Ltd v Performing Right Society Ltd* [1943] Ch 167; *Performing Right Society Ltd v Harlequin Record Shops Ltd* [1979] 2 All ER 828 at 833 (where Browne-Wilkinson J, as he then was, adopted the view of Greene LJ in the earlier cases, and said that it is important to see whether the composer would expect to receive a fee for the performance given to the audience).
167. *Jennings* [1936] Ch 469.
168. See, for example, *Nils Svensson et al v Retriever Sverige AB* (Court of Justice of the European Union, C-466/12, 13 February 2014) (*Svensson*) [24]–[30], which introduced the concept of the 'new public'. It was held that as making available the relevant works through hyperlinks did not lead the works in question to be communicated to a new public, the authorisation of the copyright holders is not required.
169. *Svensson* (Court of Justice of the European Union, C-466/12, 13 February 2014).
170. *Svensson* (Court of Justice of the European Union, C-466/12, 13 February 2014). It should be noted that this is a contentious decision which may not be relevant to the UK in future, in any case, owing to the country's forthcoming exit from the EU (or 'Brexit').
171. *Australian Copyright Act*, s 31(1)(a)(vi).
172. *Australian Copyright Act*, ss 31(1)(a)(iv) and 31(1)(b)(iii).
173. *Australian Copyright Act*, s 27(1)(a).
174. *Australian Copyright Act*, s 10.
175. *Australian Copyright Act*, ss 85(1)(c) and 86(c).
176. See, for example, *Rank Film Production Ltd v Colin S Dodds* (1983) 2 IPE 113 (*Rank Film Production*); *Telstra Corporation v Australasian Performing Right Association* (1997) 38 IPR 294.

177. *Telstra Corporation v Australasian Performing Right Association* (1997) 38 IPR 294 at 295.
178. *Australia Copyright Act*, s 10.
179. See *US Copyright Act*, § 106(1); *UK Copyright Act*, ss 16(1) and 17; *Australian Copyright Act*, ss 31(1)(a)(i), 31(1)(b)(i), 85(1)(a) and 86(a).
180. *US Copyright Act*, §§ 106(3)–(6).
181. *UK Copyright Act*, ss 16(1) and 20.
182. *Australian Copyright Act*, ss 31(1)(a)(iv), 31(1)(b)(iii), 85(1)(c) and 86(c).
183. Elizabeth Adeney, *The Moral Rights of Authors and Performers: An International and Comparative Analysis* (Oxford University Press, 2006) 1. See also art 6bis of the *Berne Convention*, which provides that an author is entitled to moral rights (ie, the rights of attribution and integrity) that exist independently of economic rights.
184. *Visual Artists Rights Act (VARA)*, 17 USC § 106A (1990).
185. Prior to the enactment of *VARA*, some state legislatures have enacted moral rights laws. These states include California, New York and Maine. Not all state moral rights protection has been pre-empted by *VARA*, although the Artists Authorship Rights Act in New York has been held to be so (pre-empted); see *Board of Managers of Soho International Arts Condominimum v City of New York*, US Dist LEXIS 10221 (SDNY, 2003).
186. In the case of limited editions of 200 copies or fewer, these are signed and consecutively numbered by the author; see *US Copyright Act*, § 101.
187. In general there is the question as to whether digital works of visual art can be protected under the *VARA*. It has been suggested that artists who seek *VARA*'s protection will need to fix their art works in a physical medium and arrange for subsequent dealings in a manner that is consistent with the *VARA* paradigm. An example is given of a photographer who never prints his digital photograph; instead, he sells the photograph in a digital format (for instance, by placing it in a thumb drive or by permitting the collector to download the digital work). See Joseph Gibbons Llewellyn, 'Visual Artists Rights Act and the Protection of Digital Works of Photographic Art' (2010) 11(3) *North Carolina Journal of Law and Technology* 531, 552.
188. *VARA*, § 106A(a)(1)(A).
189. *VARA*, § 106A(a)(1)(B).
190. *VARA*, § 106A(a)(2).
191. *VARA*, § 106A(a)(3)(A). The formulation for determining whether harm to honour or reputation exists is flexible – the reputation need not be derived independently of the art work that is the subject of the dispute (ie, author need not prove a pre-existing standing in the artistic community). See *Carter v Helmsley-Spear* 71 F 3d 77 (2nd Cir, 1995).
192. *VARA*, § 106A(a)(3)(B). The rights under § 106A(a)(2) and § 106A(a)(3) are noted to be rights of integrity.
193. See, for example, Adeney, E. 2006, 487.
194. *VARA*, §§ 106A(a)(2) and 106A(a)(3)(A). It is noted that the requirements for prejudice are conjunctive as the provision reads 'which would be prejudicial to his or her honour or reputation', therefore suggesting the non-inevitability of the harm. This can be contrasted with the equivalent provisions in the UK and in Australia. See also Adeney, E. 2006, 494.
195. Dramatic works are again omitted from the discussion, as they are not relevant to this book.
196. *UK Copyright Act*, s 77.
197. See, for example, Adeney, E. 2006, 395.
198. *UK Copyright Act*, ss 77(2)–(6).
199. Specific assertion can be made by a statement included in an assignment of copyright in the work, where the author or director asserts his or her right to be identified, *or* by an instrument in writing signed by the author or director; see *UK Copyright Act*, ss 77(1) and 78(2).
200. The right of a person not to have a work or film falsely attributed to him or her if the person is not the author or director; see *UK Copyright Act*, s 84(1).
201. See, for example, *Pasterfield v Denham* [1999] FSR 168 (*Pasterfield*), 182, where it was held that the colour variations and minor variations of detail between the two works are not considered to be 'derogatory treatment' and that 'gross differences' would be required.
202. See *Pasterfield* [1999] FSR 168, 181–2, where it was considered that the honour or reputation test applied to mutilations and distortions. See also *Confetti Records* [a firm] *v Warner Music UK Ltd (trading as East West Records)* [2003] EWJC 1274, [149]–[150]; Adeney, E. 2006, 407–9. Like in the US, the honour or reputation test applies conjunctively.
203. *UK Copyright Act*, ss 80(1) and 80(2).

204. See *UK Copyright Act*, s 77(2)(a), in respect of the right to attribution where a literary work is communicated to the public.
205. See *UK Copyright Act*, s 80(4), in respect of the respect of the right to integrity where a visual image of a derogatorily treated artistic work is communicated to the public.
206. *Australian Copyright Act*, Part IX.
207. *Australian Copyright Act*, Part IX, Divisions 2–4.
208. *Australian Copyright Act*, ss 195AC–AF.
209. *Australian Copyright Act*, ss 195AG and 195AH.
210. *Australian Copyright Act*, s 195AI.
211. *Australian Copyright Act*, ss 195AJ–AL. It has been suggested that proving the propensity to produce harm to honour or reputation through present action is sufficient to establish prejudice. See Adeney, E. 2006, 583.
212. Such content will not fall under the definition of a work of visual art, being a painting, drawing, print, sculpture or a still photographic image produced for exhibition purposes only; see *US Copyright Act*, § 101.
213. Doubt has been expressed as to whether this requirement is compliant with the *Berne Convention*. See, for example, Garnett, K., Davies, G. and Harbottle, G. 2011 [111.18].
214. This is because the right is not likely to have been asserted generally or specifically (ie, in an assignment through a statement of the author or director, or by an instrument in writing); see *UK Copyright Act*, ss 78(1) and 78(2).
215. For instance, the right of attribution of an *author* is only protected under rights management provisions if his or her name is included as part of the information accompanying the copyright work. There is no obligation imposed on the *owner* of the work to do so.
216. *Digital Millennium Copyright Act*, 17 USC § 1202(b)(1) (1998) (*DMCA*).
217. *Digital Millennium Copyright Act*, § 1202(c).
218. *Murphy v Millennium Radio Group LLC*, 650 F 3d 295 (3rd Cir, 2011).
219. *VARA*, § 106A(a)(1)(A).
220. This will include literary, musical, dramatic, pictorial, graphic, sculptural and audiovisual works, as well as sound recordings, architectural works, compilations and derivative works. See *US Copyright Act*, §§ 102 and 103.
221. See Jane Ginsburg, 'Moral Rights in the U.S.: Still in Need of a Guardian *Ad Litem*' (2012) 30 *Cardozo Arts & Entertainment Law Journal* 73, 78.
222. *DMCA*, § 1202(b)(1).
223. *UK Copyright Act*, s 296ZG(1).
224. *UK Copyright Act*, s 296ZG(1).
225. *UK Copyright Act*, s 296ZG(2).
226. *UK Copyright Act*, s 296ZG(7)(b).
227. *UK Copyright Act*, s 77.
228. *UK Copyright Act*, ss 296ZG(1)–(2).
229. *Australian Copyright Act*, s 116B.
230. *Australian Copyright Act*, s 116B.
231. *Australian Copyright Act*, s 116C.
232. *Australian Copyright Act*, s 10.
233. *Australian Copyright Act*, ss 195AC–AF.
234. *Australian Copyright Act*, s 116B(1)(c).
235. See *US Copyright Act*, §§ 411 and 101. See Goldstein, P. and Hugenholtz, B. 2013, 227.
236. *US Copyright Act*, § 412.
237. *US Copyright Act*, §§ 502–504.
238. *US Copyright Act*, § 504(c)(1).
239. *US Copyright Act*, § 504(c)(2).
240. *Agence France Presse v Morel*, 10 Civ 02730 (USDC SDNY, 14 January 2013) (*Morel*); *Morel*, 10 Civ 02730 (USDC SDNY, 21 May 2013); *Morel*, 10 Civ 02730 (USDC SDNY, 22 November 2013); *Morel*, 10 Civ 02730 (USDC SDNY, 13 August 2014).
241. *Morel* (USDC SDNY, 14 January 2013); *Morel* (USDC SDNY, 21 May 2013); *Morel* (USDC SDNY, 22 November 2013); *Morel* (USDC SDNY, 13 August 2014).
242. See, for example, Eugene Reznik, *How the photo community would reimagine copyright* (16 July 2015) <http://www.americanphotomag.com/how-photo-community-reimagines-copyright>. A photojournalist named Yunghi Kim commented that there is a burden both

in terms of time and money for photographers to protect their works through registration. In addition, he recommended giving photographers up to a year to register their works. See also United States Copyright Office, *eCO Registration System* <http://copyright.gov/eco/>, where the current processing time for the electronic filing of a copyright (registration) application is stated to take up to 8 months and that for the filing of such an application through paper forms is 13 months.

243. *UK Copyright Act*, s 96.
244. *UK Copyright Act*, s 97(1).
245. *UK Copyright Act*, s 97(2).
246. *UK Copyright Act*, s 97(2).
247. *Australian Copyright Act*, s 115(2).
248. *Australian Copyright Act*, s 115(3).
249. *Australian Copyright Act*, s 115(4).
250. *Australian Copyright Act*, s 115(4).
251. This content is likely to be considered as *unpublished*. Reference is made to the limited definitions of the terms 'publication' and 'copies' discussed earlier; see sub-section (D).
252. The awards of additional damages can, however, be high in Australia. See, for example, *Aristocrat Technologies Australia Pty Ltd v DAP Services (Kempsey) Pty Ltd (in liq)* (2007) 71 IPR 437.
253. *UK Copyright Act*, s 97(1).
254. *Australian Copyright Act*, s 115(3).
255. The fair use doctrine exempts a fair use from copyright infringement in the US, while the fair dealing exceptions exempt specified categories of purposes from copyright infringement in the UK and in Australia.
256. See Matthew Sag, 'Predicting Fair Use' (2012) 73(1) *Ohio State Law Journal* 47, 85, where Sag makes this comment of fair use.
257. The right of reproduction (of the photographs), the right to prepare derivative works (also of the photographs), as well as the right to display publicly (in respect of the sculptures that are private); see *US Copyright Act*, §§ 106(1), 106(2) and 106(5).
258. *US Copyright Act*, § 106(1); *UK Copyright Act*, ss 16(1) and 17; *Australian Copyright Act*, ss 31(1)(a)(i), 31(1)(b)(i), 85(1)(a) and 86(a).
259. *US Copyright Act*, §§ 106(3)–(6).
260. *UK Copyright Act*, ss 16(1) and 20.
261. *Australian Copyright Act*, ss 31(1)(a)(iv), 31(1)(b)(iii), 85(1)(c) and 86(c). See also sub-section (E).
262. See, for example, *Harper*, 471 US 539 (1985); *Eldred v Ashcroft*, 537 US 186 (2003).
263. *US Copyright Act*, § 107.
264. *US Copyright Act*, § 107.
265. *Campbell v Acuff-Rose Music Inc*, 510 US 569 (1994) (*Campbell*).
266. See, for example, *Campbell*, 510 US 569 (1994); *Suntrust Bank v Houghton Mifflin Co*, 268 F 3d 1257 (11th Cir, 2001) (*Suntrust Bank*); *Blanch v Koons*, 467 F 3d 244 (2nd Cir, 2006) (*Koons II*); *Mattel Inc v Walking Mountain Productions*, 353 F 3d 792 (9th Cir, 2003) (*Mattel Inc*); *Bill Graham Archives v Dorling Kindersley Ltd*, 448 F 3d 605 (2nd Cir, 2006) (*Bill Graham*); *Kelly v Arriba Soft Corporation*, 336 F 3d 811 (9th Cir, 2003) (*Kelly*); *Perfect 10 Inc v Amazon.com Inc*, 508 F 3d 1146 (9th Cir, 2007) (*Perfect 10*). See also Tan, D. 2016, 321; Barton Beebe, 'An Empirical Study of U.S. Copyright Fair Use Opinions, 1978–2005' (2008) 156 *University of Pennsylvania Law Review* 549; Sag, M. 2012, 369. Tan highlighted that both Beebe's empirical study of fair use decisions in the US and Sag's statistical analysis – which focused on the ex-ante predictability of fair use based on fair use cases in the US – affirmed the salient role that transformative use (as part of the fair use inquiry for the first statutory factor, being the purpose and the character of the use) plays in the evaluation of fair use.
267. *US Copyright Act*, § 107(1).
268. Tan, D. 2016.
269. See, for example, *Campbell*, 510 US 569 (1994); *Suntrust Bank*, 268 F 3d 1257 (11th Cir, 2001).
270. See, for example, *Koons II*, 467 F 3d 244 (2nd Cir, 2006); *Mattel Inc*, 353 F 3d 792 (9th Cir, 2003).
271. See, for example, *Bill Graham*, 448 F 3d 605 (2nd Cir, 2006).

272. See, for example, *Kelly*, 336 F 3d 811 (9th Cir, 2003); *Perfect 10*, 508 F 3d 1146 (9th Cir, 2007).
273. See, for example, Pierre Leval, 'Toward a Fair Use Standard' (1990) 103 *Harvard Law Review* 1111, 1105–7.
274. *UK Copyright Act*, s 29.
275. *UK Copyright Act*, s 30.
276. *UK Copyright Act*, s 29(1C).
277. *The Copyright and Rights in Performances (Quotation and Parody) Regulations 2014* (UK) SI 2014/2356 (*UK Copyright Regulations 2014*), reg 5. The regulation introduced, among other things, the new sections 30(1ZA), 30A and a new paragraph 2A (to Schedule 2) to the *UK Copyright Act*.
278. This is practical given that the subtle humour of a parody can be diminished by such a requirement.
279. *Australian Copyright Act*, ss 41 and 103A.
280. *Australian Copyright Act*, ss 42 and 103B.
281. *Australian Copyright Act*, ss 40 and 103C.
282. *Australian Copyright Act*, ss 41A and 103AA.
283. *The Copyright Amendment Act 2006* (Cth). Part 3 introduced the new sections 41A and 103AA.
284. *Australian Copyright Act*, ss 41, 41A, 42, 103A, 103AA and 103B.
285. ALRC, *Copyright and the Digital Economy* (November 2013) <http://www.alrc.gov.au/sites/default/files/pdfs/publications/final_report_alrc_122_2nd_december_2013_.pdf>. The ALRC recommended that a fair use exception should be applied when determining whether quotation infringes copyright, and that 'quotation' should be one of the illustrative purposes in the fair use analysis. Alternatively, if fair use is not enacted, the ALRC recommended consolidating the existing fair dealing exceptions and to provide for certain new purposes in a closed list (including for the purpose of quotation) which do not infringe copyright. In this instance, fairness factors will have to be considered in determining if a dealing is fair.
286. Productivity Commission, Australian Government, *Productivity Commission Draft Report on Intellectual Property Arrangements* (April 2016).
287. *UK Copyright Act*, s 30A.
288. *Australian Copyright Act*, 41A and 103AA.
289. *Australian Copyright Act*, ss 41 and 103A.
290. See, for example, *Network Ten Pty Ltd v TCN Channel Nine Pty Ltd* [2004] HCA 14. In this case, Network Ten's show 'The Panel' played short clips from the recorded broadcasts made by Channel Nine (and other networks) – its hosts discussed these short clips. Channel Nine brought suit for Network Ten's copyright infringement of its broadcasts. The finding that some of The Panel's uses infringed copyright provides little certainty for users of copyright-protected material that their parodic or satirical commentaries are exempt. See also Nicolas Suzor, 'Where the Bloody Hell Does Parody Fit in Australian Copyright Law?' (2008) 13 *Media and Arts Law Review* 218, 224. Suzor noted that the definitions of 'criticism', 'review' and 'news' are drawn restrictively in *De Garis v Neville Jefress Pidler* (1990) 37 FCR 99 at 107, and that there is little room for unlicensed use of copyright-protected material to make a general comment on society or unrelated works.
291. Although a recent European Court of Justice's decision suggests a sophisticated interpretation of the expression 'parody', which takes into account the striking of a 'fair balance' between the interests and rights of copyright holders and the freedom of expression of users. Furthermore, whether a defendant has used the original copyright work to convey a discriminatory message is potentially relevant to the assessment of this 'fair balance'; see *Johan Deckmyn and Vrijheidsfonds VZW v Helena Vandersteen and Others* (Court of Justice of the European Union, C-201/13, 3 September 2014) [26]. The relevance of this decision to the UK (owing to Brexit) is uncertain. See also Jonathan Griffiths, 'Fair Dealing after Deckmyn: The United Kingdom's Defence for Caricature, Parody or Pastiche' in Megan Richardson and Sam Ricketson (eds), *Research Handbook on Intellectual Property in Media and Entertainment* (Edward Elgar, 2017) 64.
292. For example, pastiche is listed in Lesley Brown (ed.), *The New Shorter Oxford English Dictionary* (Clarendon Press, 1993); Macquarie Dictionary, *Pastiche* <https://www.macquariedictionary.com.au/features/word/search/?word=pastiche&search_word_type=Dictionary>.
293. *UK Copyright Act*, s 30(1ZA).

294. In respect of the second condition, the UK Intellectual Office's guidelines suggest that it would be a matter of fact, degree and impression in each case, and of asking how a fair-minded and honest person would have dealt with the work. Relevant factors considered include the amount of the work quoted and if the use would affect the market for the original work. For the third condition, the use has to be fair and reasonable (ie, a shorter quotation is likely to be more permissible than a longer extract). In respect of the last condition, I see few instances on social media where sufficient acknowledgement could be impossible for reasons of practicality or otherwise. See Intellectual Property Office, *Exceptions to Copyright: Guidance for Creators and Copyright Owners* (October 2014) <https://www.gov.uk/government/uploads/system/uploads/attachment_data/file/448274/Exceptions_to_copyright_-_Guidance_for_creators_and_copyright_owners.pdf>.
295. See, for example, *TCN Channel Nine Pty Ltd v Network Ten Pty Ltd* (2002) 55 IPR 112 (Full Federal Court, see particularly Sundberg J's judgement at [2]); *Hubbard v Vosper* [1972] 2 QB 84 at 94.
296. See, for example, Kevin Taylor, 'Copyright in Practice: The Publisher Perspective' in Trevor Fenwick and Ian Locks (eds), *Copyright in the Digital Age: Industry Issues and Impacts* (Wildy, Simmons & Hill Publishing on behalf of The Stationers Company and individual contributors, 2010) 159, 162.
297. See, for example, American Law Institute, *Intellectual Property: Principles Governing Jurisdiction, Choice of Law, and Judgments in Transnational Disputes* (2007) (*ALI Principles*) § 101(6). A 'transnational civil dispute' is defined to mean a civil action in a court of the forum state in which there is a claim or defence under the intellectual property rights of another state (ie, non-forum state), *or* a claim arising out of activities that implicate intellectual property rights where the activities occur, at least in part, outside the forum state.
298. This uncertainty can be caused as much by conflicting demands imposed under varied copyright provisions from different jurisdictions, as well as by overlapping rights under the same. See Graeme B. Dinwoodie, Rochelle Dreyfuss and Annette Kur, 'The Law Applicable to Secondary Liability in Intellectual Property Cases' (2010) 42 *New York University Journal of International Law and Politics* 201, 206.
299. See, for example, Graeme Dinwoodie, 'Developing a Private International Intellectual Property Law: The Demise of Territoriality' (2009) 51 *William & Mary Law Review* 711, 716.
300. See Dinwoodie, G. 2009, 716. See also *Tod's SpA v. Heyraud SA*, Case C-28/04, 2005 ECR I-05781; Sam Ricketson and Jane C. Ginsburg, *International Copyright and Neighbouring Rights: The Berne Convention and Beyond* (Oxford University Press, 2nd ed., 2005) [20.08].
301. See, for example, Dinwoodie, G. 2009, 718.
302. See Dinwoodie, G. 2009, 718. Dinwoodie has also argued that the unexamined invocation of the principle of territoriality has undermined the maturing of a properly developed private international law of intellectual property, as the principle has led erroneously to the vesting of exclusive jurisdiction over intellectual property litigation in the courts of the country for which protection is sought (788–9). He noted further that article 5(2) has been alternatively read to institute a rule of *lex fori*, as the forum is 'the country where protection is claimed', although the accepted reading is that the article refers to the country where the infringement is alleged to have occurred (ie, the country in which protection is claimed). See also Graeme W. Austin, 'Domestic Laws and Foreign Rights: Choice of Law in Transnational Copyright Infringement Litigation' (1999) 23 *Columbia-VLA Journal of Law & Arts* 1, 24–5.
303. See Dinwoodie, G. 2009, 730. In this respect Dinwoodie noted that the US courts have articulated choice of law rules that admit greater flexibility on the question of infringement, without jettisoning respect for the claims of the *lex loci protectionis*. Instead the *lex loci delicti* (ie, the law of the place where the wrong was committed) is identified as the applicable choice of law rule in the infringement context.
304. *ALI Principles*.
305. European Max Planck Group, *Principles on Conflict of Laws in Intellectual Property* (1 December 2011) <http://www.ip.mpg.de/fileadmin/ipmpg/content/clip/Final_Text_1_December_2011.pdf> (*CLIP Principles*).
306. *ALI Principles*, § 201(1).
307. *CLIP Principles*, art 2.101.
308. *ALI Principles*, § 204(1) – (2) (the person must have *substantially* acted, or taken *substantial* preparatory acts, to initiate or further the infringement); *CLIP Principles*, art 2.202.
309. *ALI Principles*, § 321(1); *CLIP Principles*, art 3.603(1).

310. *ALI Principles*, § 321(1).
311. *CLIP Principles*, art 3.603(2).
312. *ALI Principles*, § 321(1)(a).
313. *CLIP Principles*, art 3.603(2)(a).
314. *ALI Principles*, § 321 (1)(d).
315. *CLIP Principles*, art 3.603(2)(d). See also Rita Matulionyte, 'IP and Applicable Law in Recent International Proposals: Report for the International Law Association' (2012) 3(2) *Journal of Intellectual Property, Information Technology and Electronic Commerce Law* 263, 289, where it is noted that the ubiquitous infringement rules provide little legal certainty and foreseeability; Andrew F. Christie, *Private International Law Issues in Online Intellectual Property Infringement Disputes with Cross-Border Elements: An Analysis of National Approaches* (2015) <http://www.wipo.int/edocs/pubdocs/en/wipo_rep_rfip_2015_1.pdf>.
316. See *UK Copyright Act*, ss 153–5; *Australian Copyright Act*, s 32(2). These factors are less relevant when we consider if the same content is copyright protected in the US, as such content (likely considered to be unpublished instead) is copyright protected irrespective of the nationality or domicile of the relevant author. See *US Copyright Act*, § 104(a). See also the discussion in Part I, sub-section (D).
317. See *US Copyright Act*, § 106(1); *UK Copyright Act*, ss 16(1) and 17; *Australian Copyright Act*, ss 31(1)(a)(i), 31(1)(b)(i), 85(1)(a) and 86(a).
318. *US Copyright Act*, §§ 107(1) and (4). The second fair use factor (ie, the nature of the copyright-protected work) is likely to be neutral to both the copyright holder and Jane; see § 107(2).
319. See *US Copyright Act*, § 107(3).
320. *UK Copyright Act*, s 30.
321. *UK Copyright Act*, s 30A.
322. *The Copyright and Rights in Performances (Personal Copies for Private Use) Regulations 2014* (UK) SI 2014/2361 (*UK Copyright Regulations 2014*), reg 3.
323. *Australian Copyright Act*, ss 41 and 103A.
324. *Australian Copyright Act*, ss 41A and 103AA.
325. *Australian Copyright Act*, ss 42 and 103B.
326. See *Australian Copyright Act*, ss 43C, 47J, 109A, 110AA and 111.
327. *Australian Copyright Act*, ss 43C, 47J, 109A and 110AA.
328. Jane's use is likely exempt as a fair use in the US.
329. *US Copyright Act*, § 106(3).
330. *UK Copyright Act*, s 16(1).
331. *Australian Copyright Act*, s 31(1).
332. *US Copyright Act*, §§ 106(4) and 106(5).
333. *UK Copyright Act*, s 16(1).
334. *Australian Copyright Act*, ss 31(1)(a)(vi), 31(1)(a)(iv), 31(1)(b)(iii), 85(1)(c) and 86(c).
335. *US Copyright Act*, § 101.
336. *UK Copyright Act*, s 20(2).
337. See *Information Society Directive*, art 3(1); *ITV Broadcasting Ltd* (Court of Justice of the European Union, C-607/11, 7 March 2013) [32].
338. The expression 'in public' is considered in relation to the owner of the copyright (ie, the copyright holder's public). The question is whether the audience is one which the copyright holder would fairly consider to be a part of his or her public (ie, whom the copyright holder would expect to receive remuneration from). This can refer to a small portion of the public and neither the size of the audience nor the privacy of the surroundings is decisive. See, for example, *Rank Film Production Ltd* (1983) 2 IPE 113 (*Rank Film*); *Telstra Corporation v Australasian Performing Right Association* (1997) 191 CLR 140.
339. 'To the public' (in relation to the right to communicate) conveys a broader concept than 'in public' (in relation to the right to perform, show or play). A communication to the public includes a communication to individual members of the public in a private setting. See, for example, *Rank Film* (1983) 2 IPE 113; *Telstra Corporation v Australasian Performing Right Association* (1997) 191 CLR 140. Apart from defining 'to the public' to refer to the public within or outside Australia, see *Australian Copyright Act*, s 10, 'in public' and 'to the public' is left largely to judicial determination. See also Ricketson, S., Richardson, M. and Davison, M. 2013, 358–61.

340. These countries are contracting parties to the *Berne Convention*. Copyright protection will be conferred even if the venue of first publication (if published) cannot be ascertained. See the discussion in Part I, sub-section (D).
341. *US Copyright Act*, § 106(2).
342. I note that substantial similarity appears to be an elusive concept, not subject to precise definition. See, for example, *Concrete Machinery Co Inc v Classic Lawn Ornaments Inc*, 843 F 2d 600 (1st Cir, 1988); *Atari Inc v North American Philips Consumer Electronics Corp*, 672 F 2d 607 (7th Cir, 1982). Under the 'ordinary observer' test, as the original commentary is not identifiable in Jane's new commentary, an ordinary, reasonable person is not likely to conclude that the two commentaries are substantially similar, and that Jane has appropriated Evangeline's expression.
343. This is regardless of whether the allegedly infringing work is original enough to constitute a separate, copyright-protected, derivative work.
344. See *UK Copyright Act*, ss 16(1) and 21(3); *Australian Copyright Act*, ss 31(1)(a)(vi) and 10.
345. See *UK Copyright Act*, ss 16(1) and 17; *Australian Copyright Act*, ss 31(1)(a)(i), 31(1)(b)(i), 85(1)(a) and 86(a).
346. Although Evangeline's commentary is not reproduced substantially so as to be recognisable by any person, the quality of what is copied (linked to the factor of originality of the part copied) is critical to the assessment as to whether a substantial part is copied. See *UK Copyright Act*, s 16(3); *Australian Copyright Act*, s 14. See also *Hawkes & Son (London) Ltd v Paramount Films Service Ltd* [1934] 1 Ch 593; *Ice TV* [2009] HCA 14.
347. In particular, the right against false attribution; see *Australian Copyright Act*, ss 195AC–AH.
348. See *US Copyright Act*, § 101. There is also no breach of the right to prohibit the removal or alteration of copyright management information under the *DMCA*, § 1202(b), given that there are no facts in the case study which establish that Jane knows, or has reasonable grounds to know, that she is assisting or hiding an infringement of Evangeline's copyright.
349. *UK Copyright Act*, ss 77(1) and 78(2).
350. *UK Copyright Act*, s 30. I add that Jane will not likely be able to satisfy all the conditions to avail herself of the newly extended fair dealing exception for the purpose of quotation under s 30(1ZA) [in particular, that sufficient acknowledgement is impossible for reasons of practicality or otherwise under s30(1ZA)(d)]. On the facts, it cannot be ascertained if Jane's use is a fair dealing and if the amount of material quoted from Evangeline's commentary is required for the specific purpose. These will be matters of fact, degree and impression.
351. *Australian Copyright Act*, ss 41 and 103A.
352. Circumstances such as the purpose for which the work is used, the context, any practice and so on will be taken into account; see *Australian Copyright Act*, s 195AR.
353. See, for example, *Koons II*, 467 F 3d 244 (2nd Cir, 2006).
354. See *Cariou v Prince*, 714 F 3d 694 (2nd Cir, 2013), 714 F 3d 694 (2nd Cir, 2013).
355. *UK Copyright Act*, s 30A.
356. *Australian Copyright Act*, ss 41 and 103A. This exception has been restrictively interpreted. This is also the case under the *UK Copyright Act*, s 30.
357. Jane's use is likely exempt as a fair use in the US and a fair dealing in the UK.
358. There are no facts in the case study which establish that Zee knows, or has reasonable grounds to know, that he is assisting or hiding an infringement of Jane's copyright. As such, there is no breach of the right to prohibit the removal or alteration of copyright management information under the *DMCA*, § 1202(b).
359. This is although Zee has copied Jane's commentary substantially onto the relevant Wikipedia page.
360. *UK Copyright Act*, s 30; *Australian Copyright Act*, ss 41 and 103A. I also add that Zee will not likely be able to satisfy all the conditions to avail himself of the newly extended fair dealing exception for the purpose of quotation under s 30(1ZA) [in particular, that sufficient acknowledgement is impossible for reasons of practicality or otherwise under s30(1ZA)(d)].
361. Again circumstances such as the purpose for which the work is used, the context, any practice and so on will be taken into account; see *Australian Copyright Act*, s 195AR.
362. Zee's use is likely exempt as a fair use in the US.
363. *UK Copyright Act*, s 30A.
364. *Australian Copyright Act*, ss 41 and 103A. This exception has been restrictively interpreted. This is also the case under the *UK Copyright Act*, s 30.

365. Jane's use is likely exempt as a fair dealing in the UK.
366. *US Copyright Act*, § 101.
367. *UK Copyright Act*, s 17(4).
368. *Australian Copyright Act*, s 10.
369. *Australian Copyright Act*, s 86. This includes the exclusive right to make a copy of the film, cause the film to be seen or heard in public and to communicate the film to the public.
370. *Australian Copyright Act*, s 10. See also *Australian Olympic Committee Inc v The Big Fights Inc* (1999) 46 IPR 53; Ricketson, S. and Cresswell, C. 2015 [7.290].
371. *US Copyright Act*, §§ 107(1) and (4).
372. *US Copyright Act*, § 107(3). The third factor refers to the 'amount and substantiality of the portion used in relation to the copyrighted work as a whole'.
373. Cheryl's use is likely exempt as a fair use in the US.
374. *UK Copyright Act*, s 30A.
375. These uses are likely exempt as fair uses in the US and fair dealings in the UK.
376. The reproduction occurs through the conversion of the collage from a digital form. Each magazine embodying the collage is taken to be a single reproduction. See *Australian Copyright Act*, s 21(1A).

Chapter Three
Application of the terms of service

In this chapter I examine the standard terms of service (TOS) that users agree to when they use the services offered on the five selected social media platforms, namely Facebook, Pinterest, YouTube, Twitter and Wikipedia. I begin by identifying the key TOS that govern or have implications on the content-generative activities undertaken by users on these platforms. These TOS address the following: the ownership and licensing of the content generated; the copyright policies adopted by the platforms; the indemnification and limitation of liability of such platforms; and the choice of a governing law and jurisdiction. I then apply the relevant terms to the content-generative activities undertaken by Jane and other users in the case study, under the second of four scenarios in this book. My application of the TOS to each content-generative activity will not be conducted on a comprehensive basis as there is a dearth of case law in this area, particularly in the UK and in Australia.

I then examine the extent of alignment and incompatibility the TOS have with the copyright regimes in the US, the UK and Australia. The clauses that deal with the ownership and licensing of the content, as well as the copyright policies that expressly incorporate the *Digital Millennium Copyright Act* (*DMCA*)'s notice and takedown mechanism, are the most relevant with regard to the content-generative behaviours of users. While the incorporation of the *DMCA* reflects the way in which social media platforms align themselves with copyright laws (particularly those of the US, where these platforms are registered), there are three areas that give rise to potential incompatibilities between the TOS and the copyright regimes.

The other clauses identified, such as those providing for the indemnification and limitation of liability of the platforms, have implications for the content-generative activities of users. In particular, these clauses underscore the vulnerability of users who are exposed to the risks of copyright infringement through the generation of content on such platforms.

This chapter provides further support for the book's argument that current inconsistencies existing between the TOS and the copyright regimes compromise the effectiveness of those laws in regulating the content-generative behaviours of social media users. The TOS are also found to reflect the unilateral interests of the social media platforms surveyed, at the expense of their users. Finally, the application of the TOS in the chapter to the case study constitutes scenario two in the book. This allows – through a juxtaposition of the outcomes reached under scenarios one (from Chapter Two) and two (from this chapter) – for a specific evaluation of the consistency between the copyright regimes and the TOS.

I. Terms of service

Users have to tread through a labyrinth of terms and policies set out in separate documents across multiple web pages to ascertain their rights and obligations on social media platforms, including those pertaining to their content-generative activities on such platforms. For instance, the main TOS for Facebook that outline its users' rights and responsibilities are comprised within Facebook's 'Statement of Rights and Responsibilities' (Facebook Statement).[1] In addition, many links to separate documents[2] are provided under the Facebook Statement, and these have a bearing on the overall position of a user when it comes to issues relating to his or her content-generative activities. The TOS for Pinterest (Pinterest Terms),[3] YouTube (YouTube Terms),[4] Twitter (Twitter Terms)[5] and Wikipedia (Wikipedia Terms)[6] are similarly presented across multiple documents. In the following sub-sections I will look at the primary types of provisions under the TOS that seek to regulate the content-generative behaviours of users on the five social media platforms surveyed. The types of provisions which otherwise have implications on these activities are also studied.

A. Ownership and licensing

The ownership and licensing clauses under the TOS of social media platforms govern the content-generative activities undertaken by social media users. They identify users who hold the copyrights to the content created, modified and disseminated on these platforms, as well as provide for the rights of users to use copyright-protected content generated by others on such platforms.

1. Facebook

Pursuant to the Facebook Statement, a user grants to Facebook, in respect of content 'covered by intellectual property rights', a '*non-exclusive, transferable, sub-licensable, royalty-free, worldwide* license' to *use* any content covered by intellectual property rights that he or she posts on the Facebook platform.[7] This licence is effectively unencumbered (ie, unrestricted by copyright), although a user owns all the content that he or she posts.[8] The licence ends when the user deletes the relevant content, or closes his or her account, *unless* such 'content has been shared with others, and they have not deleted it'.[9] The Facebook Statement further clarifies that where a user publishes content and chooses the 'Public setting', the user is in effect allowing *everyone*, including non-Facebook users, 'to access and use that information'.[10] At the same time the term 'use' is broadly defined and includes the acts of running, copying, public performance or display, distribution, modification, translation and the creation of derivative works.[11]

2. Pinterest

Under the Pinterest Terms, a user retains all rights in the content he or she has posted on the Pinterest platform.[12] Further, each of Pinterest and *other users* acquire a 'non-exclusive, royalty-free, transferable, sub-licensable, worldwide' licence to, among other things, use, display, reproduce, 're-pin', modify, create derivative works from, perform and distribute a user's content *solely* for 'the purposes of operating, developing, providing and using' the Pinterest products.[13] This qualifier limits the scope of the licences granted – the broad range of acts is permissible only to the extent that these are carried out on the Pinterest platform and for the purposes of developing and using the services and products on Pinterest. After a user has deactivated his or her account, Pinterest and other users can continue, in relation to the user's content, to engage in acts consistent with the rights granted under the licence when the Pinterest account was active, if such content has already been stored or shared by other users.[14]

3. YouTube

The YouTube Terms provide that a user retains all ownership rights, although the user, through submitting his or her content to YouTube, grants to the latter a similarly unencumbered 'worldwide, non-exclusive, royalty-free, sub-licensable and transferable' licence to, inter alia, use, reproduce, distribute, *prepare derivative works of*, display, *adapt*, electronically transmit and perform his or her content[15] in connection with the service, as well as YouTube's, and its successors' and affiliates' business.[16] While content on the YouTube platform is 'owned by or licensed to YouTube', it is subject to 'copyright and other intellectual property rights under the law'.[17] In relation to the sharing of content by a user, *other users* of YouTube are also expressly granted a licence with similar rights as can be exercised through the functionality of the YouTube service, except that the rights of adaptation, and to prepare derivative works, are specifically omitted.[18] Further, notwithstanding the termination of licences granted to YouTube within a 'commercially reasonable time' after a user removes the relevant video clips from his or her YouTube account, YouTube may retain the deleted video clips that are not displayed.[19] In addition, the licences in respect of comments a user submits (ie, to video clips shared on YouTube) are irrevocable and perpetual.[20]

4. Twitter

Under the Twitter Terms, while a user retains the rights to his or her content,[21] a 'worldwide, non-exclusive, royalty-free license (with the right to sublicense)' is granted to Twitter to, inter alia, use, copy, reproduce, adapt, modify, publish, display and distribute such content in 'any and all media or distribution methods'.[22] The provision further clarifies that the licence authorises Twitter to make a user's 'tweets' available to the public and to let *others* do the same.[23]

5. Wikipedia

The Wikipedia Terms are the TOS that apply to all of the collaborative projects started by the Wikimedia Foundation. Its summary states that while a user can share and re-use articles and other media on the Wikipedia platform under *free* and *open* licences, such users also license his or her individual contributions to Wikipedia under *free* and *open* licences, except where these contributions fall within the public domain.[24] It is emphasised under the Wikipedia Terms that the Wikimedia Foundation merely *hosts* the content, which is created and managed by users.[25] In general, *all* content submitted to Wikipedia has to be *licensed* so that it is freely re-usable by anyone who is interested in accessing it.[26] In particular, users contributing content to Wikipedia are required to 'grant broad permissions to the general public to *re-distribute* and *re-use*' their content freely, so long as there is proper *attribution* of the use and the *same freedom to re-use and re-distribute* is granted to resulting *derivative works*.[27] The licensing requirements for text in respect of which a user holds the copyright are set out under the 'Creative Commons Attribution-Share Alike 3.0 Unported License'[28] and the 'GNU Free Documentation

License'.[29] These licences allow for *commercial* uses of the content, so long as users are compliant with the licensing terms.[30] Furthermore, under the Wikipedia Terms, the licences granted by a user in relation to his or her contributed content are irrevocable, even after a user terminates his or her use of the services.[31] Overall, the clauses relating to the ownership and licensing of the content are presented differently from the equivalent clauses under the TOS of the other four social media platforms. For instance, the Wikipedia Terms make a point of specifying that the re-use of content on the Wikipedia platform is acceptable.[32]

6. Observations

Under the TOS surveyed, a user not only grants the relevant social media platform an unencumbered licence to use his or her content under the respective TOS; he or she also grants other users the licence to use his or her content. The rights of other users in relation to a user's content are more equivocal and vague under the Facebook Statement and the Twitter Terms as compared to the Pinterest Terms, the YouTube Terms and the Wikipedia Terms.

In respect of the Pinterest platform, the scope of the licence granted by a user to other users is fairly limited – such licence covers mainly the activities occurring on the Pinterest platform. With regard to the Wikipedia platform, on the other hand, the expansive grant of rights from a user to other users, in relation to his or her content, could be explained by the purpose of a collaborative project such as Wikipedia. Its main purpose is to expand the commons of free culture and knowledge,[33] so hosting freely accessible and re-usable content is consistent with the project's overall ethos. Finally, it is noted that YouTube users are granted limited rights (in comparison to those granted to YouTube) to re-use a user's content, which do not include the rights of adaptation and to prepare derivative works.[34]

B. Copyright policy

Under the *DMCA*,[35] there is a safe harbour provision that can, subject to the meeting of other conditions,[36] exempt social media platforms (being service providers)[37] from liability for monetary relief, in relation to secondary liability for copyright infringement[38] by their users. The conditions that have to be met by a social media platform are as follows:

(i) the platform does not have either actual or constructive knowledge of the infringing activity;[39]

(ii) the platform does not receive any direct financial benefit from the infringing activity, where such platform has the right and ability to control such activity;[40] and

(iii) where notified of infringement, the platform responds expeditiously to remove infringing material.[41]

Another condition to be met is that the relevant social media platform has a termination policy in respect of the accounts of users who are repeat copyright infringers.[42] Moreover, the platform is also protected from liability to users if the removals of content were done in good faith, even if the content is later found to be non-copyright infringing and erroneously removed.[43]

At the same time there are safeguards built into the *DMCA* to prevent abuse by copyright holders of the notice and takedown process available to them. These include the user's option to issue a counter-notice where his or her content has been erroneously removed[44] and the award of damages where a copyright holder knowingly and materially misrepresents that content is infringing.[45] Separately, the *DMCA* also lists the requisite elements for a notice alleging copyright infringement[46] and a counter-notice disputing the same.[47]

In this sub-section, the copyright policies of the social media platforms are examined. These policies set out the recourses (legal or otherwise) available to copyright holders, in relation to the infringing content and the relevant users, as well as the positions taken by such platforms against users who repeatedly infringe the copyrights of others. In either respect, it is noted that the *DMCA* mechanism is incorporated into the TOS of the five platforms.

1. Facebook

The Facebook Statement prohibits a user from sharing content that infringes another user's rights.[48] Facebook can remove content that violates the rights of a copyright holder, and also disable a user's account for repeated infringements.[49] In this respect Facebook has created a page, accessible via a link,[50] which specifically advises users on copyright and trademark infringements. A user is warned against misrepresenting that an activity is infringing,[51] as he or she may be liable for damages under the *DMCA*,[52] including costs and fees incurred by Facebook or other users. Other alternatives are proposed to a copyright holder (often also a user) – namely, resolving the issue directly with another user whom he or she believes is infringing his or her copyright or seeking legal advice before reporting the infringement under the *DMCA*.[53] A copyright holder who nonetheless wishes to notify Facebook of copyright infringement has to fill in a *DMCA* compliant form made available online.[54] He or she can alternatively submit a report to Facebook's designated agent, which includes all elements of a copyright notice under the *DMCA*.[55] If there is a wrongful removal of content by Facebook, a user can appeal against such removal.[56]

2. Pinterest

Under Pinterest's acceptable use policy, a user agrees that he or she will not post content that is infringing of, among other things, another user's intellectual property rights.[57] On the other hand, pursuant to its copyright policy, Pinterest has the discretion to terminate the account of a user who repeatedly infringes, or is repeatedly charged, with infringing the intellectual property rights, including copyrights, of others.[58] A copyright holder, or a person acting on his or her behalf, is asked to report copyright infringements, *either* by completing a *DMCA* compliant form of notice and delivering it to Pinterest's designated agent *or* by taking the more convenient option and submitting a *DMCA* compliant form made available online.[59] A user who believes that his or her content was mistakenly removed is entitled to file a counter-notice by sending an email to Pinterest, in the format suggested under Pinterest's copyright policy.[60]

3. YouTube

Under the YouTube Terms, YouTube can terminate the account of a repeat infringer who has been notified of infringing activity for the third time.[61] In addition, under its community guidelines, YouTube users are reminded not to upload video clips they did not make, or to use content within their video clips that someone else owns the copyright to.[62] The mechanism under the *DMCA* is similarly available to a copyright holder – the copyright holder can notify YouTube of copyright infringement using a *DMCA* compliant online form,[63] while a counter-notice using another online form can be submitted to YouTube if the latter has removed content erroneously.[64]

4. Twitter

The Twitter Terms provide that Twitter respects the intellectual property rights of others and expects its users to do the same.[65] As with the other social media platforms discussed, Twitter can terminate the account of a repeat infringer.[66] A copyright holder can avail him- or herself of the *DMCA* notice and takedown procedure and submit an online form for this purpose;[67] a user can submit a counter-notice to Twitter, in response to a wrongful removal of content.[68]

5. Wikipedia

Users are prohibited under the Wikipedia Terms from infringing intellectual property rights;[69] further, the Wikimedia Foundation can terminate the account of a repeat infringer.[70] In addition to the notice and takedown mechanism under the *DMCA*,[71] the Wikimedia Foundation offers two alternative mechanisms to a copyright holder.[72] The first alternative is to submit a request to the Wikimedia community, which, in the Wikimedia Foundation's own words, 'handles copyright issues faster and more effectively than prescribed under the *DMCA*'.[73] The copyright holder can post a notice stating his or her copyright concerns on a relevant page created for this purpose.[74] The second alternative is for the copyright holder to send an email to the community, at the email address provided.[75]

6. Observations

The *DMCA* mechanism is available to copyright holders (often also users) under all of the TOS examined. Beyond the *DMCA*, Facebook, YouTube and the Wikimedia Foundation have flagged out other self-help alternatives to copyright holders. Indeed, Facebook appears to encourage copyright holders to seek self-help firsthand when they have copyright concerns. YouTube offers, under its 'Copyright Center', a vast source of self-help options[76] for copyright holders of content, as well as users.[77] Finally, the Wikimedia Foundation, in respect of its projects including Wikipedia, also directs copyright holders to take up community self-help options, instead of the legal route under the *DMCA*.

C. Indemnification and limitation of liability

The indemnification and limitation of liability clauses under the TOS of social media platforms provide for the position taken by these platforms if the content-generative activities undertaken by social media users are found to be copyright infringing, as well as such platforms' right to indemnity in these circumstances. The clauses further limit the liability of the platforms.

1. Facebook

Facebook disclaims all responsibility for the acts of a user on Facebook, including his or her sharing of content.[78] If there is any claim brought against Facebook in relation to a user's actions or content, such user is required to indemnify Facebook against all damages, losses and expenses related to the claim.[79] Facebook further excludes or limits, to the fullest extent permissible under applicable law, its liability to a user.[80]

2. Pinterest

Pinterest similarly disclaims any responsibility for content shared on the Pinterest platform.[81] The Pinterest Terms contain an indemnity clause, albeit a narrower one, since it applies only if there are damages, losses, expenses, and so on, arising from a use of Pinterest for *commercial* purposes.[82] Pinterest also excludes or limits – to the maximum extent permitted by law – its liability to a user for, among other things, damages or losses arising from his or her use of the Pinterest platform or the content shared on Pinterest.[83]

3. YouTube

YouTube too disclaims all responsibility relating to content shared on its platform.[84] The YouTube Terms further provide that a user agrees to indemnify YouTube and its affiliates, and so on, to the fullest extent permitted by law, for matters relating to his or her use of YouTube,[85] including a violation of the copyright of a third party[86] (often also a user). Additionally, YouTube's liability to a user for, among other things, losses, expenses or damages resulting from his or her use of its service or the content on the YouTube platform is excluded or limited, to the fullest extent permitted by law. [87]

4. Twitter

Twitter also disclaims responsibility for any content posted on Twitter.[88] Furthermore, pursuant to the Twitter Terms, Twitter's liability to a user is excluded or limited – to the maximum extent permissible under applicable law – for matters resulting from the use of Twitter or the content on Twitter.[89]

5. Wikipedia

Under the Wikipedia Terms, the Wikimedia Foundation disclaims, among other things, responsibility for the content or acts of third parties.[90] The

Wikipedia Foundation also limits or excludes its liability to a user, to the fullest extent permitted by law.[91]

6. Observations

As can be seen, all the social media platforms examined disclaim liability for the content available and for the use of such content. In any case, if these platforms are found liable and the disclaimers are ineffective, the liability clauses under the TOS will apply, to the maximum extent legally permissible, to limit or exclude their liabilities. In addition, a user has the contractual obligation to indemnify Facebook, Pinterest and YouTube under their respective TOS, if the platforms incur losses as a result of his or her use. Notably, the indemnity and liability clauses have been drafted to be inclusive – in respect of the scope of circumstances they can apply to as well as the parties involved (ie, users of such platforms or other third parties).

D. Governing law and jurisdiction

When there is a copyright-related dispute relating to content, the governing law and jurisdiction clauses under the TOS of social media platforms will naturally be the first point of reference as to the law that governs such dispute, and the jurisdiction in which a court can adjudicate the dispute.

1. Facebook

The laws of the state of California govern the Facebook Statement and any dispute arising between Facebook and a user, 'without regard to conflict of law provisions'.[92] The user further agrees to have any dispute resolved exclusively in the US District Court for the Northern District of California or a state court located in San Mateo County, and to submit to the personal jurisdiction of these courts for the purpose of all litigation claims.[93]

2. Pinterest

Under the Pinterest Terms a user agrees to contact Pinterest first to resolve a dispute informally. If the dispute remains unresolved, it will be subject to binding arbitration by the American Arbitration Association, with reference to the applicable arbitration rules.[94]

The laws of the state of California similarly govern the Pinterest Terms, 'without respect to its conflict of laws principles'.[95] The user also consents to submit to the personal jurisdiction of a state court located in San Francisco County, California, or the US District Court for the Northern District of California, for actions not subject to arbitration.[96]

3. YouTube

The YouTube Terms are governed by the laws of California, 'excluding California's choice of law rules', and a user consents to submit to the personal jurisdiction of the courts in Santa Clara County, California.[97] The user further agrees that the YouTube service is deemed 'solely based in California' and that YouTube is 'a passive website that does not give rise to personal jurisdiction over YouTube', in jurisdictions other than California.[98]

4. Twitter

Under the Twitter Terms, the governing law is that of the state of California, 'excluding its choice of law provisions'.[99] Further, the user agrees that the federal or state courts located in San Francisco County, California will have jurisdiction over the litigation claims arising from his or her use of the Twitter service.[100]

5. Wikipedia

Where there is a dispute, a user is encouraged to seek resolution through the alternative dispute resolution mechanisms provided by the project.[101] Similar to the Pinterest Terms and the Twitter Terms, the Wikipedia Terms provide that the laws of the state of California, without reference to conflict of laws principles, constitute the governing law. The user also submits to the personal jurisdiction of the federal or state courts in San Francisco County, California.[102]

6. Observations

The social media platforms studied have chosen as the governing law of their TOS the laws of the state in which their headquarters are based.[103] A user also agrees to submit to the jurisdiction of various federal, state or district courts in the US, as the case may be, in the event of a dispute.

E. Summary

Table 3.1 below serves as a summary of the above discussion on the key terms that govern or have implications on the content-generative activities of users on Facebook, Pinterest, YouTube, Twitter and Wikipedia.

Table 3.1 Summary of the key terms applicable to the content-generative activities of users across the five selected social media platforms

Social media platform & terms of service	Ownership and licensing	Copyright policy	Indemnification and limitation of liability	Governing law and jurisdiction
Facebook 1. Facebook Statement 2. Facebook Principles 3. Data Policy 4. Facebook Copyright Policy 5. Community Standards	In general, a user owns the content he or she shares Unencumbered licence granted to Facebook It is implied that other users can use the content made available to them by a user, although this is equivocal Note: Broad definition of the term 'use'	Notice and takedown, as well as counter-notice procedures under the *DMCA* Facebook will disable a user's account for repeated infringements Online form to notify Facebook of copyright infringement available Encourages self-help by a copyright holder before reporting copyright infringement under the *DMCA*	User indemnification of Facebook against all damages, losses and expenses incurred, in relation to a user's actions or content Broad exclusion and limitation of liability	Laws of the state of California US District Court for the Northern District of California or a state court located in San Mateo County

(continued)

Table 3.1 *(Cont.)*

Social media platform & terms of service	Ownership and licensing	Copyright policy	Indemnification and limitation of liability	Governing law and jurisdiction
Pinterest 1. Pinterest Terms 2. Pinterest Acceptable Use Policy 3. Privacy Policy 4. Pinterest Copyright Policy	In general, a user owns the content he or she shares Licence granted to Pinterest Licence granted to *other users* However, the broad range of acts licensed must be *solely* for the purposes of developing and using the services and products on Pinterest	Notice and takedown, as well as counter-notice procedures under the *DMCA* Pinterest will disable a user's account for repeated infringements Online form to notify Pinterest of copyright infringement available	User indemnification of Pinterest where there are damages, losses, expenses and so on arising from his or her use of Pinterest for *commercial* purposes Broad exclusion and limitation of liability	Laws of the state of California US District Court for the Northern District of California or a state court located in San Francisco County Note: In general, an attempt must be made to resolve the dispute informally, before submitting it for binding arbitration
YouTube 1. YouTube Terms 2. Privacy Guidelines 3. YouTube Copyright Policy 4. Community Guidelines	In general, a user owns the content he or she shares Unencumbered licence granted to YouTube More limited licence granted to *other users* – this does not include the rights to *adapt* and *prepare derivative works*	Notice and takedown, as well as counter-notice procedures under the *DMCA* YouTube will disable a user's account for repeated infringements Online forms to notify YouTube of copyright infringement, as well as to lodge a counter-notice for content mistakenly removed, are available	User indemnification of YouTube in matters relating to his or her use of YouTube Broad exclusion and limitation of liability	Laws of the state of California Courts of Santa Clara County, California

Twitter 1. Twitter Terms 2. Privacy Policy 3. Twitter Copyright Policy 4. Twitter Rules	In general, a user owns the content he or she shares Unencumbered licence granted to Twitter	Notice and takedown, as well as counter-notice procedures under the *DMCA* Twitter will disable a user's account for repeated infringements Online form to notify Twitter of copyright infringement available	Broad limitation and exclusion of liability	Laws of the state of California Federal or state courts of San Francisco County
Wikipedia 1. Wikipedia Terms 2. Privacy Policy 3. Creative Commons Attribution-ShareAlike3.0 4. GNU Licence 5. Wikipedia Copyright Policy	No express reference to the ownership of content on Wikipedia Content on Wikipedia can be shared and re-used under free and open licences Free and open licences *also* granted by a user over his or her contributions to the project Note: *Commercial* uses of content are permitted, so long as the user is compliant with the licensing terms	Notice and takedown, as well as counter-notice procedures under the *DMCA* Wikimedia Foundation will disable a user's account for repeated infringements Encourages community self-help as alternatives (ie, submit a request by posting a notice on a relevant page or by sending an email to the Wikimedia community)	Broad limitation and exclusion of liability	Laws of the state of California Federal or state courts of San Francisco County

II. Scenario two: the application of the terms of service

The case study on Jane in Chapter One serves as the basis on which the TOS discussed in this chapter can be applied to the content-generative activities undertaken by Jane and other users. I consider these activities in the same order as in Chapter Two, where the copyright laws discussed were applied to such activities.

A. Jane's use of the music video clip on YouTube as her morning alarm

As the singer's managers have uploaded the video clip to YouTube they are bound by the YouTube Terms, which provides that they grant a licence to other users, including Jane, to use the video clip in the way Jane has. In this instance, Jane is acting within the scope of the limited licence granted from one YouTube user to another, as there is no preparation of derivative works from, or adaptation of, the said video clip.[104]

This suggests that Jane has not acted in breach of the YouTube Terms.

B. Jane's 'pinning' of the YouTube music video clip on her pin-board titled 'My Favourite Things' on Pinterest

Jane can directly 'pin' the video clip on her Pinterest pin-board by utilising the 'share' function available on the YouTube platform. Through its provision of the social plug-in[105] for Pinterest, among other social media platforms, YouTube arguably anticipates and permits[106] this use (ie, the sharing of a video clip on YouTube with users of such other platforms).

This indicates that Jane has not acted in breach of the YouTube Terms.

C. Jane's use of Evangeline's earlier commentary on Facebook to create her own commentary

Whether Jane's use complies with the Facebook Statement is less straightforward to evaluate than in the earlier two instances. Pursuant to the Facebook Statement, while an unencumbered licence is expressly granted to Facebook by a user in respect of his or her content, it is less clear what other users are permitted to do in relation to such user's content.[107] Notwithstanding this lack of clarity, Jane's use is arguably permitted under the Facebook Statement. An example is made, under the Facebook Statement, of a user who publishes content using the 'Public' setting – this user is said to have allowed everyone, including others not on Facebook, to use the information shared.[108] I argue that Jane's use falls within the wide definition of 'use' which includes the modification and translation of, as well as the creation of derivative works from, original content.[109] The Facebook Statement further emphasises that a user controls how content is shared with his or her privacy settings.[110] In this instance, Evangeline's Facebook settings are permissive enough to enable Jane to view and receive notifications of Evangeline's posts on Facebook. Thus, in consideration of the Facebook Statement in its entirety, Jane's use is likely to be licensed.

Based on the above, Jane has not acted in breach of the Facebook Statement.

D. Jane's use of multiple photographs of newborn babies available on the pin-boards of other Pinterest users to create a collage to share on Pinterest

Jane has modified the images of other Pinterest users to create the collage, a derivative work. Her use is permitted under the licences granted by these users to Jane.[111] Further, since the collage is shared on Pinterest, the condition that certain acts are permitted so long as they are carried out for the purpose of using the Pinterest service is satisfied.[112]

This suggests that Jane has not acted in breach of the Pinterest Terms.

E. Jane's simultaneous sharing of the collage on Facebook and Twitter

The licences granted by the other Pinterest users to Jane, in respect of their images, permit acts for the limited purposes of developing or using Pinterest.[113] At first glance, Jane's sharing of the collage off the Pinterest platform does not fall within the scope of the licences granted. However, it is noted that users who access the 'pin' on Facebook are linked back to the Pinterest platform. This is the same for users who access the 'tweet' incorporating the link on Twitter.

Based on the above, Jane has not acted in breach of the Pinterest Terms. Also, as her use is licensed, she has not breached the Facebook Statement[114] and the Twitter Terms[115] (ie, for infringing the rights of others in general) when she shares the collage hosted on Pinterest on these two platforms.

F. Jane's use of the same collage in her blog post on WordPress

To ascertain if Jane is in breach of WordPress's TOS, its terms will have to be examined separately. While WordPress is not one of five social media platforms selected for the purpose of this book, its mention in the case study serves to depict the common situation where content derived from one social media platform (ie, Pinterest) is reproduced on another platform. In such an instance, the terms of the latter platform (ie, WordPress) will be relevant for consideration.

For the purpose of conducting a discussion distinct from that under sub-section (E), assuming that Jane directly attaches the collage to her blog post on WordPress – instead of sharing the link to the collage on Pinterest – her use is not licensed under the Pinterest Terms.[116] Because Jane, as a user of WordPress, represents and warrants under its TOS that she does not infringe the intellectual property rights of any third party through her use,[117] she is at first appearance in breach of WordPress's TOS.

The above indicates that Jane has breached both the Pinterest Terms and WordPress's TOS.

G. Zee's contribution to Wikipedia on 'income inequality' using what Jane has written

Zee's use is arguably permitted under the Facebook Statement, in view of its reference to a user who publishes content under the 'Public' setting – such user is said to allow everyone, including non-Facebook users, to access and use the information.[118] Zee's use also falls within the broad definition of 'use' given under the Facebook Statement.[119] In this instance, Jane's Facebook settings are permissive enough to enable her colleagues, including Zee, to access her posts.

As is the case under sub-section (C), the above suggests that Zee has not acted in breach of the Facebook Statement considered in its entirety. On this basis Zee has also not breached the Wikipedia Terms.[120]

H. Jane's creation and sharing of a new video clip by way of 'vidding' on YouTube and subsequently on Facebook

Jane's 'vidding' to create a new video clip (being a derivative work) is not a permitted use under the limited licence granted by the relevant YouTube users to Jane, pursuant to the YouTube Terms.[121] Moreover, Jane has not sought the consent of the copyright holder (ie, the producer of the television series), although she is seen to have represented that the new video clip she shares on the YouTube platform does not contain the copyright-protected material of third parties.[122] At the same time Jane is prohibited from posting content that infringes another person's rights on Facebook.[123]

The above indicates that Jane has breached both the YouTube Terms and the Facebook Statement by her sharing of the new video clip on YouTube and Facebook.

I. Cheryl's use of 'stills' from Jane's video clip as thumbnail images on her website

Similar to Jane's 'vidding' discussed under sub-section (H), Cheryl's use (being an adaptation) is not a permitted use under the limited licence granted by Jane to other users on YouTube, pursuant to the YouTube Terms.[124] In this instance, the content is shared on another website. With reference to the discussion under sub-section (F), if this website happens to be a standard one hosting a blog such as WordPress, Cheryl is taken to represent and warrant – through her use – that she does not infringe the intellectual property rights of any third party.[125]

Regardless of which website Cheryl is displaying the images on, the above suggests that she has breached at least one set of TOS (ie, the YouTube Terms).

J. Other users' partial use of Jane's collage to create their own, and sharing the same on Pinterest, Facebook and Twitter

The discussion under sub-section (D) can be referred to. In this instance, other users instead of Jane are creating the collages for sharing across the three social media platforms. Although multiple scenarios, dependent on the social media platform on which the collage is first accessed, present themselves for consideration here, it is assumed – for the purpose of discussion in this sub-section – that the collage is first accessed on the Pinterest platform and thereafter edited for sharing on Pinterest, Facebook and Twitter by these users. Unlike the case under sub-section (E), the users are sharing their collages by uploading them directly on the Pinterest, Facebook and Twitter platforms. Facebook and Twitter users accessing these collages are not linked back to the Pinterest platform.

Each user's modification of Jane's collage and other users' images to create his or her own collage, a derivative work, for sharing on Pinterest is a permitted use under the licences granted to him or her (ie, by Jane and such other users) under the Pinterest Terms.[126] Therefore the creation of a new collage for sharing on the Pinterest platform by such users does not (per se) breach the Pinterest Terms.

On the other hand, if the user accesses Jane's collage on the Pinterest platform and creates a new collage to share on Facebook and Twitter, the licences granted to him or her will not extend to cover this sharing off the Pinterest platform.[127] Under the Facebook Statement, a user is prohibited from posting content that infringes another user's rights.[128] The Twitter Terms also contain a similar obligation to respect the intellectual property rights of others.[129] In this respect the above indicates that the user has breached not only the Pinterest Terms, but also the Facebook Statement and the Twitter Terms.

K. Editor Jasper's use of Jane's collage on the cover page of his magazine

It is not clear from which social media platform (ie, Pinterest, Facebook or Twitter) Jasper extracted Jane's collage. Therefore the possibility of each platform being the platform on which Jasper accessed the collage will be considered in turn. Consistent with the earlier discussion, any use that is not carried out for the purpose of developing or using the Pinterest service is unlicensed under the Pinterest Terms.[130] The Facebook Statement, on the other hand, is equivocal as to the rights of other users to a user's content:[131] Jasper's specific use of the collage for his magazine cover arguably falls outside the scope of the licence granted by Jane. Finally, the Twitter Terms are also fairly equivocal in this respect. Any use by a third party user of a user's content, other than for the purpose of 're-tweeting', is likely to be unlicensed.[132]

Based on the above, Jasper has breached each of the Pinterest Terms, the Facebook Statement and the Twitter Terms by extracting the collage for commercial use.

III. Relationship with the copyright regimes

In this section, I will analyse the relationship that the TOS have with the copyright regimes, with reference to the discussions in this chapter and in Chapter Two. I argue that while the TOS are aligned with the copyright regimes to some extent, there are potential incompatibilities between the regimes in three areas. I have elaborated on the alignment and incompatibilities in the following sub-sections.

A. Alignment with the copyright regimes

As evidenced by the discussion in Part I, a copyright holder who observes infringing use of his or her content on any of the five social media platforms surveyed can initiate the notice and takedown process under the *DMCA* integrated into the copyright policy of each platform.[133] The requisite conditions for service providers, such as social media platforms hosting content online to qualify for protection under the safe harbour provision,[134] give these platforms great incentive to incorporate the *DMCA* mechanism[135] into their copyright policies – in order to be free from liability for monetary relief, in relation to any secondary liability for copyright infringement.[136]

One way to assess the effectiveness of the contractual regime in deterring users against undertaking potentially copyright infringing activities when these users generate content is to look at the frequency of use of the *DMCA* mechanism on the social media platforms examined. In this respect, there is some information made available by these platforms.

In a transparency report published online by Twitter detailing information including, among other things, the number of notices issued under the *DMCA*, it is recorded that between 1 July 2015 and 31 December 2015 there were a total of 19,039 takedown notices received by Twitter – 71 per cent of these notices resulted in the removal of content.[137] That is more than a twofold increase in the number of takedown notices received compared to two years earlier.[138] In contrast, with reference to a similar report published by the Wikimedia Foundation for the same period, 20 notices were received by the Wikimedia Foundation for its various projects, including Wikipedia. Only 45 per cent of these notices (ie, less than one in two) resulted in the removal of content.[139]

On a related note, Facebook also has a transparency report – albeit a less useful one for the purpose of this book, since it records only the number of government requests,[140] rather than the number of takedown notices under the *DMCA* issued by copyright holders. Pinterest's report has similar limitations.[141] Although Google's transparency report details information including, among other things, the requests to remove uniform resource locators (URLs) from various governments and copyright holders, the records furnished in the report exclude requests sent to Google's search engine directed to other Google products, such as YouTube.[142] The report also excludes requests relating to content appearing on other Google products, such as content accessible through YouTube URLs,[143] and is therefore of little relevance to this book.

Overall, social media platforms are solicitous about being perceived to caution users, through their reminders, from undertaking content-generative activities that do not respect the copyrights held by copyright holders. In addition to the removal of content under the *DMCA*, these platforms are entitled to disable the accounts of users for repeated infringements. This right is usually exercised when more than one *DMCA* takedown notice has been received in relation to content from the same user.[144] The possibility of expulsion from a social media platform for repeated infringements – noted to be a condition for the platform to be eligible for the safe harbour provision[145] – could have an additional deterrent effect on users, in respect of their engaging in potentially copyright-infringing activities. I argue that, where the TOS are aligned with the relevant copyright regime,[146] the two regimes reinforce one another.

Where the regimes are not aligned, I argue that the effectiveness of copyright laws in securing compliance from social media users when they generate content is compromised. This non-alignment is represented by the inconsistencies between the two regimes, which will be outlined in the following sub-section.

B. Potential incompatibilities with the copyright regimes

There are three main areas of potential incompatibilities to be considered here.

1. Vesting of 'ownership' under the terms of service

The vesting of 'ownership' on a user of a post on Facebook, a 'pin' on Pinterest, a video clip on YouTube, a 'tweet' on Twitter and a contribution on the Wikipedia platform under the TOS does not per se entitle him or her to copyright protection of his or her content. A foreseeable barrier to the grant of copyright protection to content on social media is where it comprises banal words, phrases and language of widespread usage.[147] As such, not all content on social media will qualify as independent works containing the requisite modicums of creativity entitling such content to copyright protection.

As mentioned earlier, the minimal originality threshold to be met for copyright protection in the US, the UK and Australia is not high.[148] While there can be no generalisations – all other things being equal – *if* the relevant content originates directly from the user, each of a post on Facebook, a 'pin' on Pinterest, a video clip on YouTube and a contribution on Wikipedia is more likely to meet the originality requirement than a 'tweet' on Twitter, given the latter platform's imposition on its users of a limit of 140 characters or less, per 'tweet'.[149] Because there is a need for a higher level of creativity to qualify a short textual work for copyright protection, a brief work such as a 'tweet' is less likely to be copyrightable as it affords fewer opportunities for originality.[150] It is nonetheless possible for some 'tweets' to cross the originality threshold and hence to be copyright protected.[151]

In addition, works such as status updates on Facebook, comments to 'pins' on Pinterest and to video clips on YouTube, as well as 'tweets' on Twitter, are less likely to be copyrightable for another reason – that of not meeting the fixation requirement or its equivalent.[152] Unlike photographs and video clips on Facebook, such updates, comments and 'tweets' do not concurrently exist as stored formats in separate media. Indeed, it has been suggested that the Facebook Statement recognises the distinction between a) photographs and video clips and b) status updates, when it expressly states that photographs and video clips are content covered by intellectual property rights, but silently leaves open to debate the same question in respect of status updates.[153] Status updates on Facebook and 'tweets' on Twitter will arguably meet the general fixation requirement in the US[154] or the equivalent requirements in the UK[155] and in Australia,[156] particularly if they can still be found. For example, subject to a Facebook user's privacy settings, status updates from years back may remain accessible on the Facebook platform. At the same time, although recent 'tweets' by a Twitter user who 'tweets' frequently may be inaccessible for the reason that Twitter only allows retrieval of up to 3,200 'tweets',[157] such 'tweets' can still be located through taking specific steps. In the case of transient (or inaccessible) content, the evidentiary purpose of fixation is argued to be defeated, as the author's contribution to public discourse cannot be preserved nor can reliable proof of the bounds of his or her copyright-protected expression be provided.[158]

On the other hand, this non-fulfilment of the evidentiary purpose of fixation conceivably applies to the comments made to 'pins' on Pinterest and to video clips on YouTube. In the case of the Wikipedia platform, the fixation requirement, or its equivalent, will likely pose less of a challenge to the copyright-ability of content shared on Wikipedia. This is because of its purpose as a platform. Wikipedia serves as a repository of the cumulative knowledge upon which its users build and consult for a longer period of time than the other social media platforms.

That a substantial volume of the content 'owned' is not copyright protectable in the first place leads to the inference that social media platforms are employing precautionary measures in their acquisitions of licences from their users.[159] Furthermore, even if the relevant content is copyright protected, the grant of an unencumbered licence to the social media platform means that the copyright holder (also a user of the platform) has limited rights to his or her content.[160] On this basis, I argue that the 'ownership' conferred on a user over his or her content under the TOS is not meaningful, as it does not mirror the exclusive rights to which a copyright holder is ordinarily entitled.

2. Imposition of the terms of service on third parties

Generally the doctrine of privity provides that contracts, such as the TOS entered into by social media users, cannot confer rights or impose obligations on any third party, other than the direct parties to such contracts. To varying degrees, the TOS of the respective social media platforms make reference to the rights of others[161] to use the content made available by a user on the relevant platform. Accordingly, a strict application of the doctrine of privity means that third party users may not be able to invoke these provisions under the TOS to justify their uses of content.

There are exceptions to the doctrine of privity. This doctrine is relaxed, for example, by way of development of the common law in the US[162] and the introduction of the *Contracts (Rights of Third Parties) Act 1999* in the UK.[163] Therefore, in either of these two jurisdictions, a third party to a contract can enforce a contractual term if it is clearly intended to benefit him or her. With reference to the TOS examined, it can be argued that this intention to benefit third party users (ie, to confer licences on third party users which permit uses of a user's content) is less clearly expressed under the Facebook Statement and the Twitter Terms than under the Pinterest Terms, the YouTube Terms and the Wikipedia Terms – the latter platforms are more unequivocal in this respect.[164] On the other hand, in Australia, the exception to the doctrine of privity applies narrowly to insurance contracts.[165]

In this respect the *Morel* case[166] lends support to the argument that the intention to benefit third parties is unclear under the Twitter Terms. It also confirms the copyright-ability of Twitter-related content (ie, a photograph).[167] In *Morel* the trial court rejected Agence France Presse's (AFP) argument that there was an implied licence for AFP to use Morel's works under the Twitter Terms, finding instead that the unencumbered copyright licence granted to Twitter under the Twitter Terms did not extend to benefit third parties.[168] As such, AFP, which has its own user account on Twitter,[169] was held liable for copyright infringement when – together with its distribution partner Getty Images in the US – it distributed and licensed the photographs shared on Morel's Twitter page, without his permission, for commercial use by other third party news agencies.

Although the licence granted by a user to Twitter under the Twitter Terms allows Twitter to make a user's 'tweets' available to the public and to let others do the same,[170] the licence did not extend to include AFP's use in this instance. Moreover, Twitter has issued guidelines for the use of content shared by its users on Twitter – these guidelines remind other users, in disseminating images found on Twitter, to display the full text of 'tweets' with their accompanying images and to include the respective names of the user accounts.[171] Through suggesting that content such as images should not be disassociated from the 'tweets' with which they are shared, the guidelines are found to support the interpretation that the Twitter Terms do not manifest the intention of a user to confer a benefit on the world at large commercially to use his or her content,[172] other than for the limited purpose of 're-tweeting'.

Therefore, while US courts appear prepared to recognise a user's rights to his or her copyrightable content on social media, they are inclined to interpret narrowly any incursions on a user's rights. This will include the scope of licence to a user's content granted under the TOS he or she accepts, particularly if the TOS are not adequately clear in this respect. The position is likely to be similar in the UK.[173] On this note, Australian courts will be *more* likely than in the US or the UK to hold that a third party user of content on social media is not licensed to do so under the TOS, given that there is no general exception to the doctrine of privity.[174]

The provision for voluntary licensing by users under the TOS of social media platforms – to obviate the risk of copyright infringement for other users who undertake content-generative activities in relation to the content shared – is premised on the assumption that such content is copyright protectable. As seen earlier, this is not always the case. Even if the content is copyright protected, the licensing terms under the TOS have to be clear enough for the use of (one user's) content by third party users to be permitted. In this sense, the principles relating to contractual interpretation may render ineffective the attempt made by social media platforms to make legitimate their users' interactions with copyright-protected content.

3. Choice of governing law and jurisdiction

The choice of governing law and jurisdiction clauses under the TOS may be unenforceable, as against a user resident in a state outside California or in another country. In sub-sections (a) and (b) below, I will consider the application of conventions, treaties and mandatory domestic laws to which a user resident in a jurisdiction outside California is subject. Through this discussion, the contradictions between the TOS and other laws are highlighted.

I will also consider, in sub-section (c) below, the governing law for copyright-related disputes arising from content-generative activities on social media. The discussion will underscore the inconsistencies between the TOS and the copyright regimes. It is convenient to conduct the analyses in these sub-sections together, although sub-sections (a) and (b) do not point to an inconsistency between the TOS and the copyright regimes, unlike sub-section (c). These analyses are relevant to ascertaining the governing law that will apply to a copyright-related dispute, and the jurisdiction in which a court can adjudicate the dispute.

In these respects, I confine my discussion to what is necessary to illustrate that the enforceability of the choice of governing law and jurisdiction provisions under the TOS is limited. The logical corollary of the non-enforceability of the choice of governing law and jurisdictions clauses is that the legal positions in other jurisdictions beyond that specified under the TOS – whether in the US (and outside of California), the UK, Australia or otherwise – and further, in relation to contract, copyright or other laws, are relevant to users of social media platforms. This supports this book's approach of considering the copyright laws in jurisdictions such as the UK and Australia, in addition to those of the US. There is no intention for the discussion below to accommodate the intricate details of broader conflict of laws issues, beyond what is needed for the narrower purpose of the book.

(a) Choice of law

Although the Restatement (Second) of Conflict of Laws in the US (*Second Restatement*) supports the application of the contractual choice of governing law under the TOS,[175] an alternative governing law can apply, particularly where the contractually chosen governing law would be contrary to a fundamental policy of another state that has a materially greater interest.[176] Therefore, if a user is resident in another state other than California in the US, the content of such state's laws will be relevant to an inquiry made on the applicable governing law. The *Second Restatement* further provides that a fundamental policy is a substantial one, which may be embodied in laws that make one or more kinds of contracts illegal or which protect a person against the oppressive use of superior bargaining power.[177] An example of such a law is one that involves the rights of an insured individual against an insurance company.[178]

On the other hand, with respect to a user in the UK, *Regulation (EC) No 593/2008 of the European Parliament and of the Council of 17 June 2008 on the law applicable to contractual obligations* (*Rome I Regulation*)[179] applicable to member states of the European Union (EU) has to be taken into account. While the freedom of the parties to choose a governing law for the contract entered into is to some extent respected, the rules under the *Rome I Regulation* recognise that the contractual choice of law clause will not override provisions that cannot be derogated from by way of private agreement.[180] These provisions are overriding mandatory provisions regarded as crucial by a country for safeguarding its public interests and (similar to the position in the US) include the provisions which, on application, can render the performance of some contracts unlawful.[181] Furthermore, the US-registered entities operating the relevant social media platforms are taken to direct their activities to users in Europe.[182] Because there are mandatory provisions under the law of the country where the consumer has his or her habitual residence that cannot be derogated from,[183] this means that the relevant court adjudicating the dispute – in assessing the validity of the governing law contractually chosen – has to take into account the fact that there may be no similar protection of the British user under the mandatory laws of the UK.[184]

There is no equivalent regime applicable to a user in Australia. However, since English and Australian choice of law rules are non-mandatory and there is no obligation on the part of plaintiffs in these two jurisdictions to plead foreign law, the *implied* permissible choice of governing law is effectively that of the forum or jurisdiction where the dispute is heard.[185] As a result of the closely connected relationship between the test for *forum non conveniens* and the pleading of foreign law, when the adjudicating court is an English or Australian court and there is a failure to plead foreign law effects, the governing law will likely be that of the UK or Australia, as the case may be.

Thus an alternative law may govern a dispute between a user resident in a state outside California, *or* in a country such as the UK and Australia, and the respective US-registered entity operating the social media platform, despite the express election of a governing law under the TOS.

(b) Choice of jurisdiction

Notwithstanding that the governing law chosen under the TOS will likely be honoured, in relation to a dispute between a user in the US and the US-registered entity operating the relevant social media platform, state laws may limit the enforceability of a choice of jurisdiction clause with respect to users who are not resident in California.[186]

With respect to a user in the UK, *Regulation (EU) No 1215/2012 of 12 December 2012 on jurisdiction and the recognition and enforcement of judgments in civil and commercial matters* (*Brussels I Regulation*)[187] applicable to member states of the EU has to be considered. While the autonomy of parties to determine the court having jurisdiction over their dispute is respected – albeit within some limits – there are specific rules under the *Brussels I Regulation*[188] which will apply to the TOS, in view that these TOS are consumer contracts and that the US-registered entities running the social media platforms have directed their activities to the UK where the user resides.[189] For example, under the home court rule, proceedings against the user can only be brought in a court of the UK, although the user has the option of bringing proceedings either in the US or the UK.[190] Even where the user does not exercise his or her right to sue the US-registered entity in an English court, it has been suggested that such a court will likely refuse to enforce a judgement if the user was summoned to a court in a distant forum such as the US for litigation.[191]

On a related note, an English court adopts the doctrine of *forum non conveniens*, or the *Spiliada Maritime Corporation v Consulex Ltd* (*Spiliada*)[192] test, and will *only* stay proceedings if there is *clearly* a *more appropriate* court for trial. Therefore a user resident in the UK is unlikely to be turned away by an English court at which he or she decides to commence proceedings, in spite of the chosen jurisdiction under the TOS. The effect of this doctrine is consistent with the home court rule.

There is no equivalent regime applicable to a user in Australia.[193] In general the jurisdiction agreement incorporated under the TOS will likely be respected by an Australian court,[194] although such a court may refuse to enforce a choice of jurisdiction clause where doing so would be tantamount to allowing the parties to contract out of applicable legislation.[195] Nonetheless, in light of *Voth v Manildra Flour Mills Pty Ltd*,[196] an Australian court is unlikely to order a stay of its proceedings against an Australian user who commences litigation proceedings in a court of Australia unless it considers itself a *clearly inappropriate* forum. As such, it appears to be rarer for an Australian plaintiff to be turned away by an Australian court on grounds of jurisdiction,[197] in comparison to a British plaintiff who brings proceedings in an English court under the *Spiliada* test.[198]

Thus, particularly in respect of a dispute concerning a user resident in a country such as the UK and Australia, the applicability of the choice of jurisdiction clause under the TOS is limited.

(c) Applicable copyright legislation

Outside the contractual elements of the TOS, conflict of laws issues in respect of the non-contractual elements, such as those relating to copyright, will be considered further. If the governing law is still determined to be the law of the state of California as contractually provided under the TOS, after taking into account the other factors above, the principle of presumption against extraterritoriality developed under US case law[199] generally applies to limit the application of US copyright legislation to content-generative activities occurring within the territorial limits of the US.[200] This defeats the attempt made by social media platforms under their TOS to include such activities occurring outside of the US[201] under the purview of US copyright legislation.

There is a dearth of detailed guidance on this issue in the UK and in Australia.[202] The *Berne Convention*, to which the US, the UK and Australia are contracting parties, may shed some light on this. Although article 5(1) of the *Berne Convention* is not a conflicts rule, the principle of national treatment in the article requires a member state to treat foreign and domestic copyright holders alike.[203] This means that, independent of the existence of protection in the country of origin of a copyright work,[204] protection is conferred on the work by the law of the country for which protection is sought (or *lex loci protectionis*).[205] Such law will apply to issues pertaining to the extent of protection and redress available to the copyright holder, and could be different from the law governing the rights and obligations of the parties under the TOS.

At the same time, the difficulty of characterising issues arising under and relating to the TOS into contractual and non-contractual issues further complicates the determination of the governing law that applies to a copyright-related dispute, and the jurisdiction in which a court can adjudicate such dispute. For instance, the choice of governing law and jurisdiction clauses may be valid in relation to the grant of non-exclusive licences under the TOS.[206] These licences are not seen to affect the proprietary rights of copyright holders – as such, the conventional choice of law principles continues to apply in this respect.[207]

(d) Implications

In line with this book's approach, I consider the implications of the earlier discussion on a user resident in the UK or in Australia. Notwithstanding the expected enforcement of the choice of governing law and jurisdiction clauses by courts in the US, the mandatory consumer protection provisions comprised in the EU regimes discussed above[208] could mean that the governing law and jurisdiction clauses under the TOS are largely unenforceable against users resident in most of Europe, including the UK – this is due to the potential violation of the *Rome I Regulation* and the *Brussels I Regulation*.[209] A similar outcome will be reached with respect to a user resident in Australia because of the improbability of an Australian court turning a plaintiff away on grounds that it is clearly an 'inappropriate forum'.[210]

Where an English or Australian court adjudicates a copyright-related dispute involving a user in the UK or Australia (as the case may be) arising from or related to the TOS, such a court – even with the requisite jurisdiction for adjudication in respect of foreign copyrights,[211] and in spite of having elected the governing law under the TOS – may apply an alternative law to the dispute at hand. Even where the applicable governing law is that elected under the TOS, different laws can apply to questions of subsistence and infringement of copyright.[212] For instance, in respect of the originality requirement for a copyright-related dispute, a court in the US is not likely to apply the more lenient originality standard of another jurisdiction.[213] With reference to the ownership[214] requirement, the law of the country of origin, being the jurisdiction with the most significant relationship to the copyright-protected content, could be the law applied by a US court.[215] On the other hand, the law of the state where infringement has occurred may apply to the infringement issue.[216] These examples are in no way intended to be exhaustive. Instead, they demonstrate that there will be such foreseeable issues presenting themselves for consideration, in view of the reach of social media platforms in a 'flatter'[217] globalised world.

I argue that the choice of governing law and jurisdiction clauses represents the unsuccessful attempts made by social media platforms to ameliorate the uncertainties posed by conflict of laws issues[218] when it comes to determining the governing law applicable to a copyright-related dispute arising under and relating to the TOS, as well as the jurisdiction in which a court can apply such governing law. These clauses can be unenforceable if they are incompatible with the relevant copyright regime and other laws. Moreover, even if such clauses are valid, they apply to disputes arising between the parties to the TOS (ie, the social media platforms and their users). This leaves open the question of the applicable governing law and the jurisdiction in which a court can adjudicate a copyright-related dispute which arises between a social media user and a copyright holder (whether another user or a third party who has not accepted the TOS).

IV. Conclusion

This chapter, together with Chapter Two, form the basis for my evaluation in this book of the consistency of the TOS with the copyright regimes in the US, the UK and Australia. I have identified the key terms of the five selected social media platforms that govern or have implications on users' content-generative behaviours. I have also applied, under scenario two, the TOS to the content-generative activities undertaken by Jane and other users in the case study. Out of the total of *eleven* content-generative activities considered, the application of the TOS to as many as *five* of these activities results in breaches of the respective TOS.

I have further discussed the relationship the TOS have with the copyright regimes, in particular, the extent of alignment and incompatibility between the regimes. The TOS are aligned with the copyright regimes to some extent – this is reflected by the incorporation of the notice and takedown mechanism under the *DMCA* into the copyright policies of the five social media platforms studied. In addition, each of these platforms has adopted a termination policy for repeat infringers, in order to be eligible for the *DMCA* safe harbour provision.[219] I have argued that the TOS and the relevant copyright regime reinforce one another when they are in alignment. Copyright infringing acts by users can lead to legal consequences under the *DMCA*, and users who repeatedly receive copyright takedown notices may be expelled from such platforms.

On the other hand, three areas give rise to potential incompatibilities between the TOS and the copyright regimes. These incompatibilities are arguably obscured by the oversimplification of complex contractual and copyright issues under the TOS.

The first is that the conferment of 'ownership' of content on a user who creates it under the TOS is not consistent with the concept of ownership under the copyright regime. This label of 'ownership' is misleading: it does not per se entitle the user to the exclusive copyrights to which a copyright holder is entitled under copyright laws, as not all content on social media will be copyright protectable in the first place. Even if the content in question is copyright protected, such content will typically be subject to an unencumbered licence granted in favour of the relevant social media platform. This renders the reference to the 'ownership' of content a limited one for the copyright holder of the content, as he or she has few rights to such content.

The second is that there must be adequate clarity in order for the licensing clauses effectively to allow third party users to use the content shared on social media, in spite of the doctrine of privity. Such an inquiry as to whether these clauses are clear enough will be premised on an assumption that the relevant content is copyright protected in the first place. A strict application of the doctrine of privity can thus undermine the attempt made by social media platforms to confer permissions on third party users to use copyright-protected content.

The third is that the choice of governing law and jurisdiction clauses may be unenforceable, as against a user resident in a state in the US outside California or in another country. This is due not only to a potential incompatibility between the TOS and the relevant copyright regime, but also the contradictions between the TOS and other laws to which a user is subject. On the one hand, in spite of the governing law elected under the TOS, different laws may apply to questions of subsistence and infringement of copyright; on the other, a user from a jurisdiction outside California is subject to the application of conventions, treaties and mandatory domestic laws, including consumer laws. The discussion on conflict of laws issues illustrates the difficulties of determining the governing law that applies to a dispute arising from or related to the TOS, as well as the jurisdiction in which a court can apply such law. Therefore laws in other jurisdictions – whether of contract, copyright or otherwise – may be relevant to a user. I have argued further that these incompatibilities between the TOS and the copyright regimes compromise the effectiveness of copyright laws in regulating the content-generative behaviours of users (ie, in securing users' compliance when they generate content).

Finally, I note that while social media platforms can be exempt under the *DMCA* safe harbour provision from liability for monetary relief, in relation to secondary liability for copyright infringement by their users if conditions are met,[220] users of such platforms remain vulnerable to the risks of copyright infringement arising from their content-generative activities on the platforms. Not only have these platforms excluded or limited their liabilities (to the fullest extent permitted by law) in relation to the activities of their users, but users of Facebook, Pinterest and YouTube also have the obligation to indemnify the platforms[221] if losses are incurred by such platforms through their uses. Furthermore, the ceding of control over content generated by users to social media platforms and other users under broad licences[222] allows for users' engagement in content-generative activities on such platforms. This in turn leads to the consequent increase in the volume of content available, an outcome which helps these platforms to sustain the advertiser-supported business models that most adopt.[223] Overall the TOS appear to reflect the unilateral interests of the social media platforms studied – at the expense of their users.

In the next chapter, I will survey the technological features of the five selected social media platforms that influence the content-generative activities undertaken by their users. I will also assess the interaction of these technological features with the copyright regimes in the US, the UK and Australia respectively for alignment and incompatibility. I then present the third of four scenarios in the book to illustrate how the technological features can influence the content-generative activities of Jane and other users in the case study.

Notes

1. Facebook, *Statement of Rights and Responsibilities* (30 January 2015) <https://www.facebook.com/terms> (Facebook Statement 2015).
2. See Facebook, *Facebook Principles* <https://www.facebook.com/principles.php>; Facebook, *Data Policy* <https://www.facebook.com/privacy>; Facebook, *Help Center: About Copyright* <https://www.facebook.com/help/249141925204375> (Facebook Copyright Policy); Facebook, *Community Standards* <https://www.facebook.com/communitystandards>.
3. See Pinterest, *Terms of Service* (1 November 2016) <https://about.pinterest.com/en/terms-service> (Pinterest Terms 2016). See also Pinterest, *Acceptable Use Policy* <https://about.pinterest.com/en/acceptable-use-policy> (Pinterest Acceptable Use Policy); Pinterest, *Privacy Policy* <https://about.pinterest.com/en/privacy-policy>; Pinterest, *Copyright* <https://about.pinterest.com/en/copyright> (Pinterest Copyright Policy).
4. See YouTube, *Terms of Service* (9 June 2010) <www.youtube.com/static?template=terms> (YouTube Terms 2010). See also YouTube, *Privacy Guidelines* <http://www.youtube.com/static?template=privacy_guidelines>; YouTube, *Copyright on YouTube* <http://www.youtube.com/yt/copyright/> (YouTube Copyright Policy); YouTube, *Community Guidelines* <http://www.youtube.com/t/policyandsafety/community_guidelines.html> (YouTube Community Guidelines).
5. See Twitter, *Terms of Service* (30 September 2016) <https://twitter.com/tos> (Twitter Terms 2016). See also Twitter, *Privacy Policy* (30 September 2016) <https://twitter.com/privacy>; Twitter, *Help Center: Copyright policy* <https://support.twitter.com/articles/15795#> (Twitter Copyright Policy); Twitter, *The Twitter Rules* <https://support.twitter.com/articles/18311#>.
6. See Wikimedia Foundation, *Terms of Use* (16 June 2014) <https://wikimediafoundation.org/wiki/Terms_of_Use> (Wikipedia Terms 2014). See also Wikimedia Foundation, *Privacy Policy* (6 June 2014) <https://wikimediafoundation.org/wiki/Privacy_policy>; Creative Commons, *Attribution-ShareAlike 3.0 Unported* <http://creativecommons.org/licenses/by-sa/3.0/> (Creative Commons Attribution-ShareAlike 3.0); GNU Operating System, *GNU Free Documentation License* (3 November 2008) <http://www.gnu.org/copyleft/fdl.html> (GNU Licence); Wikimedia Foundation, *Resolution: Licensing Policy* (23 March 2007) <https://wikimediafoundation.org/wiki/Resolution:Licensing_policy>; Wikimedia Foundation, *Commons: Licensing* <https://commons.wikimedia.org/wiki/Commons:Licensing>; Wikipedia, *Copyright Violations* <https://en.wikipedia.org/wiki/Wikipedia:Copyright_violations> (Wikipedia Copyright Policy); Wikipedia, *Wikipedia: Dispute Resolution* <https://en.wikipedia.org/wiki/Wikipedia:Dispute_resolution>.

7. Facebook Statement 2015, cl 2(1).
8. Facebook Statement 2015, cl 2(1).
9. Facebook Statement 2015, cl 2(1).
10. Facebook Statement 2015, cl 2(4).
11. Facebook Statement 2015, cl 17(7).
12. Pinterest Terms 2016, cl 2(a).
13. Pinterest Terms 2016, cl 2(b).
14. Pinterest Terms 2016, cl 2(c).
15. YouTube Terms 2010, cl 6(C).
16. This includes, without limitation, the promotion and redistribution of part or all of the YouTube's service through any media channels. See YouTube Terms 2010, cl 6(C).
17. YouTube Terms 2010, cl 5(A).
18. YouTube Terms 2010, cl 6(C).
19. YouTube Terms 2010, cl 6(C).
20. YouTube Terms 2010, cl 6(C). It is noted that user comments are subsumed under the broad definition of 'content' which includes, inter alia, text, software, photographs, video clips and audiovisual combinations that a user views or contributes to the platform. See YouTube Terms 2010, cl 2(A).
21. Twitter Terms 2016, cl 3.
22. Twitter Terms 2016, cl 3.
23. Twitter Terms 2016, cl 3.
24. Wikipedia Terms 2014.
25. Wikipedia Terms 2014, Overview.
26. Wikipedia Terms 2014, cl 7.
27. Wikipedia Terms 2014, cl 7.
28. Creative Commons Attribution-ShareAlike 3.0.
29. GNU Licence 2008.
30. Wikipedia Terms 2014, cl 7(a).
31. Wikipedia Terms 2014, cl 7(e).
32. It is added that exemptions exist for content contributed under 'fair use' or similar exceptions under copyright laws. See Wikipedia Terms 2014, cl 7(g).
33. Wikipedia Terms 2014, cl 7.
34. YouTube Terms 2010, cl 6(C).
35. *DMCA*, § 512.
36. *DMCA*, §§ 512(c)(1) and (i)(1).
37. Social media platforms fall under the broad definition of a 'service provider' under the *DMCA*, being, among other things, 'a provider of online services'; see *DMCA*, § 512(k)(1B).
38. This refers to contributory or vicarious infringement. For contributory infringement see *Gershwin Publishing Corp v Columbia Artists Management Inc*, 443 2d 1159, 1162 (2nd Cir, 1971); *Metro-Goldwyn-Mayer-Studios Inc v Grokster Ltd*, 380 F 3d 1154, 1660 (9th Cir, 2004) (*MGM Studios*); *Perfect 10*, 508 F 3d 1146 (9th Cir, 2007). For vicarious infringement see *MGM Studios*, 380 F 3d 1154, 1660 (9th Cir, 2004); *Parker v Google Inc*, 2007 WL 1989660, 4 (3rd Cir, 10 July 2007).
39. *DMCA*, § 512(c)(1A).
40. *DMCA*, § 512(c)(1B).
41. *DMCA*, § 512(c)(1C).
42. *DMCA*, § 512(i)(1A). This provision sets the requirement for service providers to adopt a termination policy for repeat infringers.
43. *DMCA*, § 512(g)(1).
44. *DMCA*, §§ 512(g)(2) and (g)(3).
45. *DMCA*, § 512(f).
46. *DMCA*, § 512(c)(3). The notice has to include, inter alia, the identification of the copyright work and infringing material, a statement of good faith belief in its infringing use and a statement, under penalty of perjury, that the complaining party is authorised to act on behalf of the copyright holder.
47. *DMCA*, § 512(g)(3). The counter-notice has to include, inter alia, the identification of the erroneously removed material and a statement, under penalty of perjury, of good faith belief in its wrongful removal.
48. Facebook Statement 2015, cl 5(1).

49. Facebook Statement 2015, cls 5(2) and 5(5).
50. Facebook, *Help Center: About Intellectual Property* <https://www.facebook.com/help/399224883474207>. See also Facebook Copyright Policy.
51. This warning is issued under a reminder that such misrepresentations are punishable under the *DMCA*. See Facebook Copyright Policy.
52. *DMCA*, § 512(f).
53. Facebook Copyright Policy.
54. Facebook Copyright Policy.
55. Facebook Copyright Policy. See also *DMCA*, § 512(c)(3).
56. Facebook Copyright Policy.
57. Pinterest Acceptable Use Policy.
58. Pinterest Copyright Policy.
59. Pinterest Copyright Policy.
60. Pinterest Copyright Policy.
61. YouTube Terms 2010, cl 8(B).
62. This is elaborated on and includes 'music tracks, snippets of copyright protected programmes, or videos made by other users' without the necessary consents. See YouTube Community Guidelines.
63. YouTube Copyright Policy.
64. YouTube Community Guidelines.
65. Twitter Terms 2016, cl 3.
66. Twitter Terms 2016, cl 4.
67. Twitter Copyright Policy.
68. Twitter Copyright Policy.
69. Wikipedia Terms 2014, cl 4.
70. Wikipedia Terms 2014, cl 8.
71. A copyright notice can be sent to the email address provided or through the post to the Wikimedia Foundation's designated agent. See Wikipedia Terms 2014, cl 8.
72. Wikipedia Terms 2014, cl 8.
73. Wikipedia Terms 2014, cl 8. See also Wikipedia Copyright Policy.
74. Wikipedia Terms 2014, cl 8. See also Wikimedia Foundation, *Copyright problems* <https://meta.wikimedia.org/wiki/Copyright_problems>.
75. Wikipedia Terms 2014, cl 8.
76. For instance, there is a self-help tool that can be utilised by content owners to identify and manage their content easily on YouTube. Videos uploaded are scanned against a database of files submitted to YouTube by content owners. When there is a match, content owners can choose to apply from a few policies available on YouTube, including blocking the relevant video with the matched content. See YouTube Help, *How Content ID works* <https://support.google.com/youtube/answer/2797370>.
77. YouTube Copyright Policy.
78. Facebook Statement 2015, cl 15(2).
79. Facebook Statement 2015, cl 15(2).
80. Limited to the greater of USD 100 or the amount paid to Facebook in the past 12 months. See Facebook Statement 2015. cl 15(3).
81. Pinterest Terms 2016, cl 8.
82. Pinterest Terms 2016, cl 7.
83. Limited to USD 100. See Pinterest Terms 2016, cl 9.
84. YouTube Terms 2010, cl 6(F).
85. YouTube Terms 2010, cl 5(D).
86. YouTube Terms 2010, cl 11.
87. Limited to either supplying the services again to the user or the cost of supplying the user the services again. See YouTube Terms 2010, cl 10.
88. Twitter Terms 2016, cl 3.
89. Limited to USD 100 or the amount paid to Twitter in the past six months for the services giving rise to the claim. See Twitter Terms 2016, cl 5.
90. Wikipedia Terms 2014, cl 14.
91. Limited to USD 1000. See Wikipedia Terms 2014, cl 15.
92. Facebook Statement 2015, cl 15(1).
93. Facebook Statement 2015, cl 15(1).

94. The Commercial Arbitration Rules (effective on 1 June 2009) and the Supplementary Procedures for Consumer Related Disputes (effective on 15 September 2005). See Pinterest Terms 2016, cl 10.
95. Pinterest Terms 2016, cl 11.
96. Pinterest Terms 2016, cl 11. Such actions may include those for seeking injunctive or equitable relief from the courts for matters relating to data security, intellectual property or unauthorised access. See Pinterest Terms 2016, cl 10.
97. YouTube Terms 2010, cl 14.
98. YouTube Terms 2010, cl 14.
99. Twitter Terms 2016, cl 6.
100. Twitter Terms 2016, cl 6.
101. Wikipedia Terms 2014, cl 13.
102. Wikipedia Terms 2014, cl 13.
103. Their headquarters are based in California. See, for example, Facebook, *Facebook HQ* <https://www.facebook.com/Facebook-HQ-166793820034304/>; Pinterest, *Pinterest's Brand-New San Francisco Office* <https://www.pinterest.com/owenthomas/pinterest-s-brand-new-san-francisco-office/>; Wikipedia, *YouTube* <https://en.wikipedia.org/wiki/YouTube>; Twitter, *Company* <https://about.twitter.com/company>; Wikimedia Foundation, *Contact us* <https://wikimediafoundation.org/wiki/Contact_us>.
104. YouTube Terms 2010, cl 6(C).
105. This is a tool that allows a user to share his or her experience of the Pinterest platform with other users on Pinterest.
106. YouTube Terms 2010, cl 6(C).
107. Facebook Statement 2015, cls 2(1) and 2(4).
108. Facebook Statement 2015, cl 2(4).
109. Facebook Statement 2015, cl 17(7).
110. Facebook Statement 2015, cl 2.
111. Pinterest Terms 2016, cl 2(b).
112. Pinterest Terms 2016, cl 2(b).
113. Pinterest Terms 2016, cl 2(b).
114. Facebook Statement 2015, cl 5(1).
115. Twitter Terms 2016, cl 3.
116. Pinterest Terms 2016, cl 2(b).
117. WordPress, *Terms of Service* <https://en.wordpress.com/tos/> (WordPress Terms). See cl 14.
118. Facebook Statement 2015, cl 2(4).
119. Facebook Statement 2015, cl 17(7).
120. Wikipedia Terms 2014, cl 4.
121. YouTube Terms 2010, cl 6(C).
122. YouTube Terms 2010, cl 6(D).
123. Facebook Statement 2015, cl 5(1).
124. YouTube Terms 2010, cl 6(C).
125. WordPress Terms, cl 14.
126. Pinterest Terms 2016, cl 2(b).
127. Pinterest Terms 2016, cl 2(b).
128. Facebook Statement 2015, cl 5(1).
129. Twitter Terms 2016, cl 3.
130. Pinterest Terms 2016, cl 2(b).
131. Facebook Statement 2015, cls 2(1) and 2(4).
132. Twitter Terms 2016, cl 3.
133. Facebook Copyright Policy; Pinterest Copyright Policy; YouTube Copyright Policy; Twitter Copyright Policy; Wikipedia Copyright Policy.
134. *DMCA*, § 512(c).
135. *DMCA*, § 512(c).
136. This could refer to either contributory or vicarious infringement.
137. Twitter, *Transparency Report: Copyright Notices* <https://transparency.twitter.com/copyright-notices/2015/jul-dec>.
138. In a similar transparency report published for the period between 1 July 2013 and 31 December 2013 a total of only 6,680 takedown notices was received, of which 62 per cent

resulted in the removal of content. See Twitter, *Transparency Report: Copyright Notices* <https://transparency.twitter.com/copyright-notices/2013/jul-dec>.

139. See Wikimedia Foundation, *Transparency Report – Requests for Content Alteration & Takedown* <https://transparency.wikimedia.org/content.html>.
140. These requests are for data and to restrict access to content on Facebook. See Facebook, *Government Requests Report* <https://govtrequests.facebook.com/>.
141. Pinterest, *Transparency Report* <https://help.pinterest.com/en/articles/transparency-report>. The report does not record the number of *DMCA* takedown notices issued by copyright holders. Instead it includes requests from US law enforcement agencies, national security requests, government content removal requests, and so on.
142. Google, *Transparency Report* <www.google.com/transparencyreport/removals/copyright/> (Google Transparency Report).
143. Google Transparency Report.
144. See, for example, Facebook Statement 2015, cl 5(5); Pinterest Copyright Policy; YouTube Terms 2010, cl 8(B); Twitter Terms 2016, cl 4; Wikipedia Terms 2014, cl 8.
145. *DMCA*, § 512(i)(1)(A).
146. Although there are similar mechanisms to the *DMCA* mechanism under the *UK Copyright Act* (s 97A) and the *Australian Copyright Act* (ss 116AE, 116AF and 116AH), these are excluded from specific consideration as they limit the remedies available against social media platforms registered in the UK and Australia respectively. My concern in this book is with the perspective of a user – whether resident in the US, the UK or Australia – in relation to the five selected social media platforms registered in the US.
147. See, for example, *Acuff-Rose Music Inc v Jostens Inc*, 155 F 3d 140, 144 (2d Cir, 1998); *Jean v Bug Music Inc*, 2002 WL 287786, 6 (SDNY, 27 February 2002). In the first case a phrase that was copied from a song was held to lack the requisite originality to be copyright protected. In the second case the short verbal and musical elements from a song were held to be non-protectable material that existed in prior art.
148. See Part I of Chapter Two, sub-section (B).
149. There are reports that Twitter is intending to expand its character limit in the near future. See, for example, Kurt Wagner and Jason Del Ray, *Twitter plans to go beyond its 140-character limit* (29 September 2015), <http://recode.net/2015/09/29/twitter-plans-to-go-beyond-its-140-character-limit/>; Matt Hickey, *Twitter likely expanding 140-character tweet limit with new product* (29 September 2015), <http://www.forbes.com/sites/matthickey/2015/09/29/twitter-likely-expanding-140-character-tweet-limit-with-new-product/>.
150. See Rebecca Haas, 'Twitter: New Challenges to Copyright Law in the Internet Age' (2010) 10 *The John Marshall Review of Intellectual Property Law* 231, 248. Further, the 'tweet' is more likely to comprise facts or ideas (ie, the application of the idea–expression dichotomy) or to not meet the quantitative requirement (ie, the application of the *de minimis* principle). See also Part I of Chapter Two, sub-section (B).
151. See Haas, R. 2010, 244.
152. See White, E. 2012–2013, 689.
153. White, E. 2012–2013, 689. See also Facebook Statement 2015, cl 2(1).
154. See *US Copyright Act*, §101; White, E. 2012–2013, 697; Haas, R. 2010, 245.
155. *UK Copyright Act*, s 3.
156. *Australian Copyright Act*, s 22.
157. Twitter, *Help Center: New user FAQs* <https://support.twitter.com/articles/13920#>.
158. See White, E. 2012–2013, 703. See also Aaron Perzanowski, 'Fixing RAM Copies' (2010) 104 *Northwestern University Law Review* 1067, 1095.
159. See Orit Fischman Afori, 'Flexible Remedies as a Means to Counteract Failures in Copyright Law' (2011) 29 *Cardozo Arts & Entertainment Law Journal* 2, 2.
160. The main right retained by the user after sharing the content is to delete the content. Even then, the content is still available if it has been shared with other users, particularly with respect to content on Facebook and Pinterest. At the same time the comments made to video clips on YouTube are irrevocable and perpetual, as are the licences granted by a user in relation to his or her contributed content on the Wikipedia platform. Twitter is silent on this point. See particularly Facebook Statement 2015, cl 2(1); Pinterest Terms 2016, cl 2(c); YouTube Terms 2010, cl 6(C); Wikipedia Terms 2014, cl 7(e). See also Part I of this chapter, sub-section (A).

161. Facebook Statement 2015, cl 2(4); Pinterest Terms 2016, cl 2(b); YouTube Terms 2010, cl 6(C); Twitter Terms 2016, cl 3; Wikipedia Terms 2014, cl 7.
162. See, for example, *Lawrence v Fox*, 20 NY 268 (1859); *Burr v Beers*, 24 NY 178 (1861).
163. *Contracts (Rights of Third Parties) Act 1999* (UK) c 31; *UK Rights of Third Parties Act*, s 1.
164. This has been discussed in greater detail under Part I of this chapter, sub-section (A).
165. See *Trident General Insurance Co Ltd v McNiece Bros Pty Ltd [1988] 165 CLR 107 (Trident)*, where it was held that a third party beneficiary may uphold a promise made for his or her benefit in a contract of insurance to which he or she is not a party. See also *Insurance Contracts Act 1984* (Cth), s 48.
166. *Morel*, 10 Civ 02730 (USDC SDNY, 14 January 2013); *Morel*, 10 Civ 02730 (USDC SDNY, 14 January 2013).
167. See also White, E. 2012–2013, 697.
168. *Morel*, 10 Civ 02730 (USDC SDNY, 14 January 2013).
169. Twitter, *@AFP* <https://twitter.com/AFP>.
170. Twitter Terms 2016, cl 3.
171. *Morel*, 10 Civ 02730 (USDC SDNY, 14 January 2013). See also Twitter, *Tweets in broadcast* <https://about.twitter.com/company/broadcast#>.
172. *Morel*, 10 Civ 02730 (USDC SDNY, 14 January 2013).
173. See *UK Rights of Third Parties Act*, s 1, where a third party to a contract can enforce a contractual term if it purported to confer a benefit on him or her and the parties to the contract intended for the term to be enforceable by him or her.
174. The *Trident* decision creates a limited exception to benefit third parties in insurance contracts, and the extent of its scope of flexibility is uncertain. It has been suggested that this decision may provide the basis for enforcing contracts where it would be unfair for the court not to recognise the third party's interest. See Katy Barnett, *Trident v McNiece twenty-five years on* (18 October 2013) <https://blogs.unimelb.edu.au/opinionsonhigh/2013/10/18/trident-v-mcniece-twenty-five-years-on/>. In addition to the *Insurance Contracts Act 1984* (Cth), s 48, some other statutory modifications made to the privity rule are encapsulated in the *Property Law Act 1969* (WA) s 11, *Property Law Act 1974* (Qld) s 55 and *Property Law Act 2000* (NT) s 56. There is no equivalent to the *UK Rights of Third Parties Act* in Australia at the moment, although the doctrines of trust, agency and estoppel may provide some respite from the strict application of the privity rule.
175. American Law Institute, *Restatement (Second) of Conflict of Laws*, §§ 186 and 187 (1998) (*Second Restatement*).
176. *Second Restatement*, §§ 187 (2)(b) and 188.
177. *Second Restatement*, comment (g). Usury laws which are designed to protect consumers are another example. See, for example, *American Express Travel Related Servs Co Inc v Assih*, 893 NYS 2d 438 (Civ Ct, Richmond County, 2009), where New York usury laws were applied to an agreement choosing the laws of Utah because New York had the most significant contacts, a strong policy against usury and a materially greater interest than Utah in this respect. See also Tribar Opinion Committee, *Supplemental Report: Opinions on Chosen-Law Provisions under the Restatement of Conflict of Laws* <http://www.americanbar.org/content/dam/aba/publications/business_lawyer/2013/68_4/report-chosen-law-provisions-201308.authcheckdam.pdf>.
178. *American Express Travel Related Servs Co Inc v Assih*, 893 NYS 2d 438 (Civ Ct, Richmond County, 2009).
179. *Regulation (EC) No 593/2008 of the European Parliament and of the Council of 17 June 2008 on the law applicable to contractual obligations* [4 July 2008] OJ L 177/6 (*Rome I Regulation*). Following Brexit, the UK would need to decide whether to implement the *Rome I Regulation* by way of statutory instrument or to allow it to lapse.
180. *Rome I Regulation*, art 3.
181. *Rome I Regulation*, art 9.
182. *Rome I Regulation*, art 6(1).
183. Art 6 of the *Rome I Regulation* adopts the consumer's home court rule, which means that the governing law for a consumer is where he or she is habitually resident.
184. These laws can include those prohibiting unfair contract terms and limiting the validity of standard form contracts. See Michael L. Rustad and Maria Vittoria Onufrio, 'Reconceptualising Consumer Terms of Use for a Globalized Knowledge Economy' (2011–2012) 14(4) *University of Pennsylvania Journal of Business Law* 1085, 1128.

185. See James McComish, 'Pleading and Proving Foreign Law in Australia' (2007) 31(2) *Melbourne University Law Review* 401, 408. See also Richard Fentiman, *Foreign Law in English Courts* (Oxford University Press, 1998).
186. In general, choice of jurisdiction clauses are enforced. See, for example, *The Bremen v Zapata Offshore Co*, 407 US 1 (1972); *Carnival Cruise Lines Inc v Shute* 499 US 585 (1991). But this may not be the case if a choice of jurisdiction clause points to a specific forum with express exclusion to others. See, for example, *Future Industries of America v Advanced UV Light GmBH*, 10-3928. The laws of individual states must also be considered.
187. *Regulation (EU) No 1215/2012 of 12 December 2012 on jurisdiction and the recognition and enforcement of judgments in civil and commercial matters* [20 December 2012] OJ L 351/1 (*Brussels I Regulation*). Following Brexit, the UK would need to decide whether to implement the *Brussels I Regulation* by way of statutory instrument or to allow it to lapse.
188. *Brussels I Regulation*, preamble [11] (that jurisdiction is generally based on the domicile of a defendant save in a few well-defined situations in which the subject matter of the litigation or the autonomy of the parties warrants a different linking factor) and [14] (noting that there is limited autonomy to determine the courts having jurisdiction when it comes to a consumer contract).
189. *Brussels I Regulation*, art 17(1c).
190. *Brussels I Regulation*, arts 18(1) and 18(2). See also Rustad, M.L. and Onufrio, M.V. 2012, 1124.
191. See Rustad, M.L. and Onufrio, M.V. 2012, 1127, for the suggestion that European courts are unlikely to enforce judgements where consumers have been summoned to courts in distant jurisdictions, such as the US.
192. *Spiliada Maritime Corporation v Consulex Ltd* [1987] 1 AC 460 (*Spiliada*).
193. It is noted that the Australian government is considering acceding to the Hague Choice of Court Convention (signed on 30 June 2005) (*Hague Convention*), and further that copyright and related rights (unlike other intellectual property rights) are not excluded from the application of the *Hague Convention*. See, for example, Richard Garnett, 'The Hague Choice of Court Convention: Magnum Opus or Much Ado about Nothing?' (2009) 5(1) *Journal of Private International Law* 161; Jack Wright Nelson, *The Hague Convention on Choice of Court Agreements: Return of the Litigators?* (30 April 2015) <http://www.youngicca-blog.com/the-hague-convention-on-choice-of-court-agreements-return-of-the-litigators/>.
194. See, for example, Andrew Bell, 'The Future of Private International Law in Australia' (2012) *Australian International Law Journal* 11, 15; Garnett, R. 2009, 163.
195. See Bell, A. 2012, 15.
196. *Voth v Manildra Flour Mills Pty Ltd* [1990] HCA 55.
197. See, for example, *Puttick v Fletcher Challenge Forests Ltd* [2006] VSC 370 (*Puttick*); *Neilson v Overseas Projects Corporation of Victoria Ltd* [2005] HCA 54 (*Neilson*).
198. *Spiliada* [1987] 1 AC 460.
199. *Equal Employment Opportunity Commission v Arabian American Oil Co*, 499 US 244 (26 March 1991); *Morrison v National Australian Bank*, 130 S Ct 2869 (2010); *Kiobel v Royal Dutch Petroleum*, 133 S Ct 1695 (2013). In the absence of a clear congressional intent to that effect, federal statutes (such as the copyright statute) are presumed not to have effect to conduct outside of the territorial jurisdiction of the US.
200. There are approaches departing from the territoriality principle that have developed in the US. One example is the 'root copy' approach (ie, where foreign conduct is subject to US copyright laws if the initial illegal copy is made in the US and later reproduced in foreign countries). See, for example, *Update Art Inc v Modiin Pub Ltd*, 843 F 2d 67, 73 (2nd Cir, 1988); *Sheldon v Metro-Goldwyn Pictures Corp*, 106 F 2d 45, 52 (2nd Cir, 1939). This approach has developed in relation to infringements on traditional media and has been heavily criticised. If this approach is extended to cover infringement on the internet, a single digital reproduction in the US could allow for the application of US copyright laws in respect of worldwide infringements. See also Rita Matulionyte, *Law Applicable to Copyright: A Comparison of the ALI and CLIP Proposals* (Edward Elgar Publishing, 2011) 71–3; Graeme W. Austin, 'Importing Kazaa-Exporting Grokster' (2006) 22 *Santa Clara Computer and High Tech Law Journal* 577, 596 (discussing the approach and suggesting that 'the territoriality principle should preclude application of US liability theories where the primary acts of infringement occur abroad').
201. This is a reality given the cross-border usage patterns of social media users.

202. See *UK Copyright Act*; *Australian Copyright Act*. See also James J Fawcett and Paul Torremans, *Intellectual Property and Private International Law* (Oxford University Press, 2nd ed., 2011) [13.41].
203. See the discussion of art 5 of the *Berne Convention* in Part I of Chapter Two, sub-section (I) (ie, under the conflict of laws discussion).
204. This can be the place of first publication or, for unpublished works, the nationality of the copyright holder. See *Berne Convention*, art 5(4).
205. *Berne Convention*, art 5(2). See also Fawcett, J.J. and Torremans, P. 2011.
206. Facebook Statement 2015, cl 2(1); Pinterest Terms 2016, cl 2(b); YouTube Terms 2010, cl 6(C); Twitter Terms 2016, cl 3; Wikipedia Terms 2014.
207. Fawcett, J.J. and Torremans, P. 2011 [14.14].
208. See *Rome I Regulation* and *Brussels I Regulation*.
209. See Rustad, M.L. and Onufrio, M.V. 2012, 1127–30.
210. See, for example, *Puttick* [2006] VSC 370; *Neilson* [2005] HCA 54.
211. See *Lucasfilm v Ainsworth* [2011] UKSC 39 (*Lucasfilm*), where the rule in *British South Africa Co v Companhia de Mocambique* [1893] AC 602 (ie, courts in the UK were denied the jurisdiction to hear an action concerning the title of land situated in Mocambique) was found to have no application with respect to copyright. But see *Potter v Broken Hill Proprietary Co Ltd* [1906] HCA 88, where it is held that an action cannot be maintained in Victoria for a New South Wales patent. See also P.E. Nygh and M. Davies, *Conflict of Laws in Australia* (LexisNexis Butterworths, 7th ed., 2002) [7.48]; Ricketson, S., Richardson, M. and Davison, M. 2013, 572 (it is suggested that the *Lucasfilm* decision is likely to be treated with considerable respect by the Australian High Court if the same issue comes before it).
212. Yu, P.K. 2001.
213. See, for example, *Feist*, 499 US 340 (1991) (on the standard for originality).
214. Or authorship, if the author is also the owner of the copyright-protected content.
215. See, for example, *Itar-Tass Russian News Agency v Russian Kurier Inc*, 153 F 3d 82 (2nd Cir, 1998), which refers to the *lex originis*.
216. See *Itar-Tass Russian News Agency v Russian Kurier Inc*, 153 F 3d 82 (2nd Cir, 1998), which refers to the *lex loci delicti*.
217. See generally Thomas Friedman, *The World is Flat: A Brief History of the Twenty-First Century* (Farrar, Strous and Giroux, 2005). See also Rustad, M.L. and Onufrio, M.V. 2012, 1189.
218. In this respect Facebook's provision of links to the World Intellectual Property Office directory – so that users can learn of the scope of copyright protection in other countries – and further, YouTube's statement that users are responsible for compliance with laws in other jurisdictions indicate their awareness of the potential applicability of the laws of other jurisdictions. See Facebook Copyright Policy; YouTube Terms 2010.
219. *DMCA*, § 512(i)(1A).
220. *DMCA*, §§ 512(c)(1) and (i)(1).
221. See Facebook Statement 2015, cl 15(2); Pinterest Terms 2016, cl 7; YouTube Terms 2010, cl 5(D).
222. The licence granted by a user to a social media platform is generally noted to be broader than that granted to other users.
223. This is with the exception of the Wikipedia project run by the Wikimedia Foundation, which is a non-profit organisation.

Chapter Four
Influence of the technological features

As I have shown in Chapters Two and Three, each of the copyright regimes and the TOS (ie, terms of service) of social media platforms regulates the content-generative behaviours of social media users in its own way. In Chapter Four I continue this analysis by examining the technological features of the five selected social media platforms, namely Facebook, Pinterest, YouTube, Twitter and Wikipedia. I begin by identifying the technological features that *encourage*, as well as those that *constrain*,[1] the content-generative activities undertaken by users of these platforms. For ease of reference, the platform interfaces on which these technological features are made available to users are captured as screenshots and set out in *Appendix 1*.[2] In particular I highlight the features that encourage the creation, modification and dissemination of content on the platforms surveyed, as well as the features that constrain the same activities. The latter group comprises those features that limit the modification of content; limit the opportunities to engage in further content-generative activities; allow for requests to remove content; and filter content.

I then illustrate, in the following section, under the third out of four scenarios examined in this book, how the identified technological features encourage the content-generative activities undertaken by Jane and other users in the case study. Next, in considering the extent of alignment and incompatibility that the technological features have with the copyright regimes, I discuss the implications of having the existing spread of technological features, which serve to encourage and constrain users in their engagement with content-generative activities. In this regard I argue that the features that encourage content-generative activities on social media platforms can be incompatible with the copyright regimes, as they increase the opportunities for users to engage in content-generative activities, hence on occasion infringing the copyrights held by others. The other features that constrain content generation are in this respect aligned with the copyright regimes, as they reduce the opportunities for users to engage in content-generative activities. In respect of the latter, I elaborate further on how some of the technological features reflect copyright considerations. I make specific references to the copyright regimes in the US, the UK and Australia – consistent with the approach taken in the rest of the book.

This chapter advances the argument in this book that the inconsistencies between the technological features and copyright regimes compromise the effectiveness of copyright laws in regulating the content-generative behaviours of social media users. On the whole, the technological features on social media are observed to 'nudge'[3] users towards engaging in content-generative activities – which increases their likelihood of infringing the copyrights of others when they generate content. Finally, the influence of the technological features considered in the chapter, with reference to the case study, constitutes scenario three in the book. This allows for the juxtapositions of the outcomes reached under scenarios one (from Chapter Two) and three (from this chapter), as well as those reached under scenarios two (from Chapter Three) and three (from this chapter). The consistencies between the copyright regimes and the TOS, as well as between the two private regimes (ie, the TOS and the technological features), can then be respectively evaluated.

I. Technological features

In identifying the technological features on the five social media platforms that encourage and constrain content-generative activities, I relate both the enabling features to the activities they allow users to undertake and the technical constraints to the activities users are restrained from doing. I also set out the screenshots of the platform interfaces incorporating these features in Appendix 1. Given the range of features available on each platform and the varied ends for which they may be employed, I am unable to be exhaustive in identifying and describing these features. Rather, I wish to offer a more systematic way to think about the influence of the technological features on users' content-generative behaviours.

A. Technological features that encourage content-generative activities

1. Creation

The following are the ways in which users can create content, using the technological features available on the five platforms.

There are options on a user's *Facebook* page to post a 'status update' that can comprise content in text, images or video clips, or any combination of these formats of content. Alternatively, a Facebook user can directly upload content for sharing with other users, in the form of an image or video clip, without writing a status update.[4] A user can also comment on the status update of another user.[5]

A user can share an image he or she has uploaded by 'pinning' it onto his or her pin-board on the *Pinterest* platform.[6] Additionally, a user can comment on the images shared on the pin-boards of other users.[7] Although images constitute the majority of content shared on Pinterest, a user can also 'pin' audio and video clips on pin-boards and share them with other users.[8]

The *YouTube* platform is designed in such a way that a user who selects the 'upload' option is directed to tools that allow him or her to create a slideshow from photographs and edit a video clip.[9] More specifically, the video editing tool enables a user, among other things, to create new video clips conveniently by combining other uploaded video clips and images,[10] as well as to add or substitute audio clips with a 'swapping tool' provided by YouTube, from YouTube's library of approved tracks.[11] In addition, on the YouTube platform, a user can also choose to comment on a video clip shared by another user.[12]

On the *Twitter* platform, a user can easily compose and share a short message called a 'tweet' with his or her followers.[13] A user can also respond to another user's 'tweet'.[14] The 'tweet' or response to another's 'tweet' can comprise an image or video clip, if the user wishes to upload one.

On the *Wikipedia* platform a user can contribute text, insert links and embed images, audio and video clips within his or her contribution.[15]

2. Modification

The following are the ways in which users can modify content, using the technological features available on the five platforms.

A *Facebook* user can choose to modify the content from another user or website in several ways. One form of modification occurs when a user selects the 'share' option on his or her Facebook page to share the post of another user, upon which he or she can comment on the shared post.[16] If the user decides to do so, the comment, together with the original post, is arguably a modified composite by the two users. Another form of modification occurs when the 'download' option, which is available when a user expands an image, is used.[17] While Facebook does not provide any content editing tools that allow users to re-arrange text, images, video clips and so on, the user can modify an image after downloading it with external tools such as Gimp[18] and Photoshop.[19]

When a *Pinterest* user fancies an image shared on another user's pin-board, the user can choose to 'pin' the same image on his or her own pin-board. If this option is selected by the user, the description provided by the preceding user is automatically re-generated as a comment and can appear to be from the user (instead of from the preceding user). The source of the 'pin' is also displayed below it as a link.[20] If the user decides to edit the information accompanying the image, he or she engages in an act of modification. The same can be said even if the user does not change this information, given that the comment and the image are presented on the user's pin-board as originating from the user.

On the *YouTube* platform a user is prompted to comment on a video clip he or she decides to share on other social media platforms, such as Facebook, Pinterest and Twitter, by selecting the 'share' tab on YouTube.[21] Given that the user's comment will be presented with the link to the relevant video clip on the YouTube platform when the sharing occurs, the user arguably engages in an act of modification, in respect of the modified composite displayed on such other platform. The video editing tool discussed earlier also enables the modification of content, including content downloaded from YouTube.[22] This happens, for example, when many video clips are modified to custom-create one new video clip.

A user on the *Twitter* platform arguably engages in an act of modification when he or she uses the 'reply' function available on Twitter to respond to a 'tweet' of another user.[23] The user also modifies a 'tweet' when he or she adds a comment to the original 'tweet' in his or her 're-tweet'.[24] There is little room for the user to engage in alternative forms of modification, in light of the fact that no content editing tools are made available to users on the Twitter platform.

There are sophisticated technical coordination mechanisms on the *Wikipedia* platform that separate contributions, mark them chronologically and attribute them to specific usernames or internet protocol addresses,[25] therefore allowing a contributor to edit content comfortably. The contributing user engages in an act of modification when he or she edits content. Modification can also occur when the user takes the option to download an image, audio or video clip on the platform,[26] and then stores the image for subsequent modification with external tools.[27] In contrast to the other social media platforms, I note that Wikipedia does not allow its users to comment on content, so there is little room for this alternative form of modification.[28]

3. Dissemination

The following are the ways in which users can disseminate content to a wide audience, using the technological features available on the five platforms.

A user can disseminate content in multiple ways on *Facebook*. This happens when the user: posts a 'status update'; comments on another user's post; uses the 'share' option; uses the 'embed post' option;[29] chooses to embed an image; or uses the 'send' option for an image.[30] Firstly, in respect of a status update, the user gets to choose the audience to whom his or her post is disseminated. This audience can be the public, the user's group of 'friends'[31] on Facebook or people on a customised list created by the user. Secondly, when a user comments on the post of another user, the audience will instead be the selected audience of the latter user. Thirdly – if, for instance, a user decides to use the 'share' option available on Facebook – he or she can again select the audience to whom such content is disseminated. The constituent members of the audience will depend on whether the user shares the content on his or her own 'Timeline'; on a friend's 'Timeline'; in a social group to which he or she belongs; or in a private message to a few selected friends on Facebook. Fourthly, a user can also choose the 'embed post' option to place the code of a post on another website, such as his or her personal blog, if such post is publicly available on Facebook. The relevant content is then additionally disseminated to the audience of the other website incorporating the original post. Fifthly, a user can also choose to 'embed' an image put up by another Facebook user on another website. Sixthly, subject to the other user's privacy settings, a user can employ the 'send' option on Facebook to send an image put up by the first user to selected friends on Facebook.

On the *Pinterest* platform a user can disseminate content (be it an image, audio or video clip) to other users who access his or her pin-board simply by 'pinning' such content to the relevant pin-board. In respect of any specific image, audio or video clip, the platform also allows a user to send a 'pin' to another person's email account or to share the 'pin' on platforms including Facebook and Twitter.[32] Unless a user 'pins' content on secret boards, visible only to the user and other invited users,[33] his or her 'pins' are generally available to other users.

Similar to the Facebook platform, a user can disseminate content in multiple ways on *YouTube*. This happens when the user: uploads a video clip; comments on the video clip of another user; using social plug-ins, shares the video clip on other social media platforms such as Facebook, Pinterest and Twitter; uses the 'embed' option in respect of the video clip, so that the content is accessible to readers of another website; or uses the 'email' option available to distribute the content.[34] Firstly, when a video clip is uploaded, the user gets to decide on the audience who can view it – by selecting, using a drop-down menu, whether his or her video clip will be public, private or unlisted.[35] Secondly, the audience to whom a user's comment is disseminated will depend on whether the relevant video clip is made public, private or unlisted. Thirdly, when a video clip is shared on other social media platforms, the constituent members of the audience will depend on the user's privacy setting on each of these platforms.[36] Fourthly, a video clip embedded on another website, such as a personal blog, will be accessible to readers of that blog. Fifthly, a user disseminates content to a select audience, whose email addresses are specified, when he or she emails the link to a video clip on YouTube to such addresses.

On the *Twitter* platform, a user has the option of embedding a 'tweet'.[37] The user can place the 'tweet' on another website where he or she has administrative rights, such as a blog, by using the code given to him or her. The 'tweet' is therefore disseminated to readers of the website. On the other hand, when a user chooses to 're-tweet' a post, or to respond to another user's 'tweet', he or she disseminates this content to a group of Twitter users – the constituent members of this group depends on the respective user's privacy settings.[38]

Any content, once published on the *Wikipedia* platform, is available to the public – this is consistent with the purpose of the project as an online encyclopedia. A user can either share the link of the Wikipedia page on which content in the form of images, audio and video clips is hosted, or embed such content on a separate website.[39] In the latter instance, the content can be accessed by the audience of the website. The user disseminates content in both cases.

B. Technological features that constrain content-generative activities

In identifying the technological features on the five platforms that constrain content-generative activities, I note that while a user interacts with some of these features at the point *before* the dissemination of content, other features limit subsequent generative possibilities *after* the content is disseminated. Although many of the features are accessible to third parties (including the copyright holders of content) who are not users, I consider the features mainly from a user's perspective for the purpose of this discussion.

1. Limiting the modification of content

The technological features on the platforms that allow for the retention of the initial presentation of the content and for the identification of the original generator[40] of the content arguably constrain content-generative activities. This is so because no matter the amount of modification a user intends to effect to another user's content, these technological features allow for limited modification or remixing of the content.

For example, when a user selects the 'share' option on *Facebook* and disseminates the content of another user in this way, the user who originally uploaded the content can still be identified by his or her username.[41] Also the post of user X, who shares the content of another user Y (who in turn extracts the content from another person's 'Timeline' or website), will incorporate the link to the source website.

On the other hand, when a user 'pins' content from another user's pin-board on the *Pinterest* platform, the preceding user is no longer attributed for the 'pin'.[42] While the comment accompanying the 'pin' is automatically generated, the user who 're-pins' the content of the preceding user can choose to modify such comment. Notwithstanding this, even if 'pinning' continues through a chain of users, the link to the source website is retained just below the 'pin' and the identification of the original generator of the content remains possible.

Whether a *YouTube* user uses social plug-ins to 'share' a video clip on other social media platforms or simply to 'email' a video clip to a few email addresses, the link to the video clip on the YouTube platform is provided. As such, the user who originally uploaded the video clip can still be identified through his or her username.[43] Even where the user decides to 'embed' the code of the video clip on another website such as a blog, viewers of the video clip on the blog can identify the YouTube user who originally uploaded the video clip through his or her username.

When a user decides to 're-tweet' the content of another user on the *Twitter* platform, there is no change to the original 'tweet' in its entirety if he or she does not add a comment to the 're-tweet'.[44] Even if a comment is added, the original 'tweet' is presented in an identical manner, just below the comment. Regardless of whether such comment is added, other users on Twitter reading a user's 're-tweet' can identify the user who originally generated the 'tweet' through his or her username. Moreover, even if 're-tweeting' continues through a chain of users, the original generator of the 'tweet' can still be identified if the 're-tweet' feature is used.

When a file such as an image or audio clip is uploaded, an associated file page is automatically created on the *Wikipedia* platform. This file page reflects the modifications made to the page to date, the list of pages that embed the file and other technical information about the file. In general, the information on the file traces the activities undertaken in relation to it, although some information such as the file description and copyright information can be edited. This ensures that contributions can mostly be traced back to the original generators of the content with some due diligence.[45]

2. Limiting the opportunities to engage in further content-generative activities

On the *Twitter* platform, there are word constraints imposed by Twitter on a 'tweet', a 're-tweet' and a response to a 'tweet'.[46] This essentially confines a user to a brief message in either instance. The range of content-generative activities that can be taken in relation to a brief text message is therefore a narrow one.

Separately, if a user decides to write an article on a subject that does not already exist in the *Wikipedia* repository, there are requirements to be met before the article is published on Wikipedia – any article that is not acceptable is deleted promptly.[47] These requirements make it impossible to access the article and hence arguably constrain a user from engaging in further generative activities in relation to the content in such article. Additionally, all content uploaded to the Wikipedia platform – whether in the form of images or otherwise – requires a source and a copyright tag, without which the relevant content will be deleted after a week.[48] The deletions obliterate the possibility of the user, and others, from engaging in further generative activities with respect to the same content on the platform.

There are no such equivalent features on the *Facebook, Pinterest* and *YouTube* platforms.

3. Allowing for requests to remove content

There are technological features on the platforms that a user can utilise to request the removal of content that he or she perceives to be harmful to the user.[49] This prevents others from interacting further with such content.

A user can, by selecting an option on a drop-down menu, report a post or image to *Facebook* for reasons including, among other things, offence to personal sensibilities and unauthorised use of intellectual property.[50] Facebook can decide to remove the content based on its assessment of the user's report. If the user proceeds with requesting the content's removal on the basis of its violation of his or her copyrights, he or she will be presented with two options. The first is to contact the party the user believes has infringed his or her rights directly, to request the removal of the content. The second is to complete the *DMCA*[51] compliant form, made available on the platform, to report a copyright violation on Facebook.[52]

A user on the *Pinterest* platform has the option to report a 'pin' (ie, of content such as an image, audio or video clip), for reasons including, among other things, that the 'pin' goes against Pinterest's policies and that the 'pin' is his or her intellectual property.[53] In the latter case, the user is directed to a page where he or she can complete a *DMCA* compliant online form to report a copyright infringement on Pinterest.[54]

On the *YouTube* platform, a user who would like a video clip removed can report it to YouTube for various reasons – including, among other things, that the video clip contains violent content and that the video clip infringes his or her rights – by selecting a flag icon positioned under the video clip.[55] If the user wishes to request the removal of the video clip on grounds of copyright infringement, he or she can use the *DMCA* compliant form made available on the platform to submit a notice of copyright infringement.[56] A user can also report the comment of another user to a video clip on YouTube, by clicking on a tiny arrow positioned at the top right-hand corner of the comment, for 'spam or abuse'.[57]

On the *Twitter* platform, a user can report a 'tweet' of another user for various reasons – including, among other things, that it displays a sensitive message or that it is abusive and harmful.[58] While a user can utilise a *DMCA* compliant online form to request the removal of content, I note that the user is not offered a direct link to the web form when he or she decides to report a 'tweet', unlike the other platforms discussed earlier. This is regardless of the options he or she selects from the lists given. This online form can, however, be accessed when the user searches for it on the platform.[59]

A user of the *Wikipedia* platform can request the removal of content based on reasons such as inaccuracy or inappropriateness.[60] The editor of an article can, for instance, initiate a contributor copyright investigation against a contributing user who is noticed to infringe the copyrights of others on a large scale. The content of this user will be subject to scrutiny and subsequently removed if suspected to be infringing.[61] Further, if a user believes that his or her copyright work is infringed on the platform, he or she can send an email to the Wikimedia community to seek resolution, or post a notice stating his or her copyright concerns on a web page created for this purpose.[62] Unlike the other platforms discussed above, no *DMCA* compliant form is made available to users on the platform. This means that a *DMCA* compliant copyright notice has to be sent to the email address provided or dispatched by ordinary mail to the Wikimedia Foundation's designated agent.[63] In this sense the Wikipedia platform does not make the *DMCA* process readily available to its users through its technological features.

4. Filtering content

Filtering technologies such as YouTube's content identification (Content Id) system[64] that can apply at the point of dissemination of content, or after dissemination, limit subsequent generative possibilities.[65]

YouTube's Content Id software automatically scans all video clips uploaded on its platform to identify content that may be used without the permission of copyright holders. For this system to work, copyright holders have to provide information about their copyright-protected content to the system upfront, as well as selecting the policy for YouTube to follow when matches with their copyright-protected content are found. In this respect, YouTube allows copyright holders to choose from the following policies: to mute the audio which matches their music in the relevant video clip; to block the content from further access; to monetise the use of their content, by gaining revenue through advertisements; or to track the viewership statistics of such content.

C. Summary

Table 4.1 below serves as a summary of the above discussion on technological features which have been identified as factors that encourage or constrain content-generative activities on Facebook, Pinterest, YouTube, Twitter and Wikipedia.

Table 4.1 Summary of the technological features that influence the content-generative activities of users across the five selected social media platforms

Social media platform	Application of approach						
	Technological features that encourage content-generative activities			Technological features that constrain generative activities			
	Creation	Modification	Dissemination	Limiting modification	Limiting opportunities	Allowing for requests to remove content	Filtering content
Facebook	'Status update' or post (of text, images and/or video clips) Option to comment on the post of another user	Prompt to comment on a 'status update' or post that a user shares using the 'share' option Possible modification with external tools after an image is downloaded using the 'download' option	'Status update' or post Option to comment on another user's post 'Share' option 'Embed post' option 'Embed' option for an image 'Send' option for an image	'Share' option	Not applicable	Option to report a 'status update', post or image for various reasons, including for offence against personal sensibilities Option for copyright holders to contact a Facebook user directly to request removal Copyright holders also directed to *DMCA* compliant online form	Not applicable
Pinterest	'Pin' (of image, audio or video clip) Option to comment on the 'pin' of another	Possible modification if a user edits the information automatically generated with a 'pin'	'Pin' 'Send' option 'Share' option for sharing on Facebook and Twitter	'Pin.' option (ie, when 'pinning' content from another user's pin-board) – source website is still indicated	Not applicable	Option to report a 'pin' for various reasons, including for violation of Pinterest's policies Copyright holders directed to *DMCA* compliant online form	Not applicable

(continued)

Table 4.1 *(Cont.)*

Social media platform	Application of approach						
	Technological features that encourage content-generative activities			Technological features that constrain generative activities			
	Creation	**Modification**	**Dissemination**	**Limiting modification**	**Limiting opportunities**	**Allowing for requests to remove content**	**Filtering content**
YouTube	Tool to create a slide-show from images Video editing tool to create video clip with existing video clips Option to comment on the video clip of another user	Prompt to comment on a video clip that a user shares on other social media platforms using the 'share' option Video editing tool to modify existing video clips	Uploading a video clip Option to comment on the video clip uploaded by another user 'Share' option to share on other social media platforms 'Embed' option 'Email' option	'Share' option to share on other social media platforms 'Email' option 'Embed' option	Not applicable	Option to report a video clip for various reasons, including for containing violent content Copyright holders directed to *DMCA* compliant online form, in relation to a video clip shared	Content Id system identifies through detecting matches of content which could be used without the consent of copyright holders The policy elected by the relevant copyright holders can be applied thereafter (ie, among other things, the muting of audio in a video clip or the blocking of access to such content)

Twitter	'Tweet' (of text, image and/or video clip) Option to comment on another user's 'tweet'	Option to respond to another user's 'tweet' Option to add a comment when 're-tweeting' another user's 'tweet'	'Tweet' 'Embed' option 'Re-tweet' option Response to a 'tweet'	'Re-tweet' option	Word constraint of 140 charac-ters applies to a 'tweet', 're-tweet' and response to a 'tweet'	Option to report a 'tweet' for various reasons, including for abusive and harmful content *DMCA* compliant online form available – note that this form can be accessed only when searched for specifically, as a user is not directed to such form	Not applicable
Wikipedia	Contribution of text and links Option to embed images, audio and/or video clips	Can edit content with the assurance that the contributions are marked and separately attributed Possible modifica-tion with external tools after an image is downloaded using the 'download' option	Contribution of con-tent (whether text, links, images, audio and/or video clips) 'Share' option to share link to Wikipedia page 'Embed' option	File page created when content, such as an image or audio clip, is uploaded	Requirements to be met in an article contrib-uted by a user, without which the article will be deleted shortly after publication Media uploaded (ie, images or otherwise) each require a source and a copyright tag, without which they will be scheduled for deletion	Option to initiate a contributor copy-right investigation for infringement on a large scale Option to send email to the Wikimedia commu-nity to seek resolution for infringement of con-tent, or to post a notice on a web page created for this purpose No *DMCA* compliant online form available for copyright holders, but there is always the option to send a copyright takedown notice to the designated agent at the email address or mailing address provided	Not applicable

II. Scenario three: the influence of the technological features

The case study on Jane in Chapter One serves as the basis upon which the technological features identified in this chapter can be considered – in relation to their encouragement or constraint of the content-generative activities undertaken by Jane and other users. I consider these activities in the same order as in Chapters Two and Three, where the copyright laws were discussed and the TOS applied to such activities respectively.

It is worth noting that the technological features considered are self-executing to an extent[66] that copyright laws and the TOS are not. In this respect, the technological features that constrain content-generative activities are self-executing for a user who generates content. On the other hand, although the technological features that encourage content-generative activities facilitate the creation, modification and dissemination of content, the user retains his or her autonomy in deciding whether to do so.[67] As such, I can keep the discussion in this section brief, since the technological features *either* enable *or* constrain a user from engaging in content-generative activities.

A. Jane's use of the music video clip on YouTube as her morning alarm

The YouTube platform provides Jane with the option to download the video clip for later use (ie, as her morning alarm).[68] To play the video clip as her alarm, Jane needs to use an external application on her mobile device.

B. Jane's 'pinning' of the YouTube music video clip on her pin-board titled 'My Favourite Things' on Pinterest

The option to 'pin' is a main function on the Pinterest platform and has enabled Jane to share the video clip on one of her pin-boards. Moreover, YouTube provides the social plug-ins that enable Jane to share the video clip directly on other platforms, including Pinterest.

C. Jane's use of Evangeline's earlier commentary on Facebook to create her own commentary

It is noted that Jane did not choose to share or comment on Evangeline's post using the relevant functions on Facebook; instead, she incorporated her views into Evangeline's commentary to create her own. Jane is likely to have woven her views into the original commentary first by using external tools, such as the 'copy and paste' function on her operating system, before editing such commentary within the text box accessed (ie, using the function to post the 'status update'). The latter function is the main function on Facebook around which the sharing of content is premised.

D. Jane's use of multiple photographs of newborn babies available on the pin-boards of other Pinterest users to create a collage to share on Pinterest

The Pinterest platform does not provide Jane with the option to download the images shared on other users' pin-boards for later use; further, there is no image editing tool available on the platform. However, this constraint experienced by Jane can easily be bypassed using external tools. For example, Jane can choose to use the 'save image as' function on her web browser to save the images. She can then modify the images for her collage with image editing tools such as Gimp and Photoshop, before going on to share the collage on Pinterest.

E. Jane's simultaneous sharing of the collage on Facebook and Twitter

The social plug-ins available on the Pinterest platform give Jane the option to share a 'pin' on platforms including Facebook and Twitter. Here they have enabled her to share her collage on both platforms.

F. Jane's use of the same collage in her blog post on WordPress

Although WordPress is not one of the five social media platforms studied in this book, reproducing content derived from one social media platform on another platform is a common situation. In such an instance, the technological features on the WordPress platform will have to be examined. Similar to Facebook, the technological features on WordPress have enabled Jane, as a user, to write a textual post and to attach an image, such as the collage, with the post.[69]

G. Zee's contribution to Wikipedia on 'income inequality' using what Jane has written

If the specific content page on Wikipedia is unprotected and open for editing, Zee can select the 'edit' option available at the top of the page and type in his contribution. However, if the page is protected and locked, Zee can only request to edit the page by submitting an 'edit request' to the editor of the page.[70] In addition, there is a substantial amount of information on the Wikipedia platform for users who are keen to edit entries.[71] In this sense, the Wikipedia project has enabled Zee to make his contribution.

H. Jane's creation and sharing of a new video clip by way of 'vidding' on YouTube, and subsequently on Facebook

The YouTube platform provides Jane with the option to download the video clips from which the scenes are extracted. The video editing tool on YouTube can then be used to modify these video clips to create the new video clip. Jane can customise the lengths of incorporated video clips, as well as add special effects and songs from an approved library on YouTube, to such a video clip.[72] Further, while the 'upload' function can be used to share the new video clip on YouTube, the 'share' function allows Jane to share the video clip on other social media platforms such as Facebook. The technological features on both platforms have enabled Jane's use here.

I. Cheryl's use of 'stills' from Jane's video clip as thumbnail images on her website

Cheryl can download Jane's new video clip on YouTube. In order to extract 'stills' from Jane's video clip, however, she may choose to use YouTube's video editing tool first to pause the video clip at appropriate junctures, after which she can use the screen capture function of her device's operating system to capture the 'stills'. With reference to the discussion under sub-section (F), the technological features available on Cheryl's website are relevant for consideration. If Cheryl's website is a standard blog hosted on WordPress, her re-sizing and sharing of these 'stills' as thumbnail images on her blog are likely to be enabled by the technological features available. Notwithstanding this, because Cheryl needs to use an external tool to extract the 'stills' in the first place, her use is not enabled solely by the technological features on both platforms.

J. Other users' partial use of Jane's collage to create their own, and sharing the same on Pinterest, Facebook and Twitter

As multiple scenarios present themselves for consideration here, depending on which platform the collage is first accessed, it is assumed that the collage is first accessed on the Pinterest platform and thereafter shared by these users on Facebook and Twitter.[73] Although Pinterest does not provide such users with the option to download Jane's collage, this constraint can be easily bypassed with external tools such as the 'save image as' function available on their web browsers. Because there is no image editing tool available on all three platforms, the modifications of Jane's collage to create new collages will have to be carried out using other tools. The downloading and subsequent modifications of Jane's collage, as well as the sharing of the new collages across the three platforms, are not enabled solely by their technological features.

K. Editor Jasper's use of Jane's collage on the cover page of his magazine

It is not clear from which social media platform Jasper downloaded Jane's collage. While the 'download' option is available to a user accessing the collage on the Facebook platform, this is not the case for the Pinterest and Twitter platforms. To download the collage from either of these two platforms, Jasper can choose to use the 'save image as' function available on his web browser. The constraint experienced by users such as Jasper can therefore be easily bypassed with the external tools integrated into their web browsers, operating systems, and so on. In any case, even if the collage is extracted from Facebook, Jasper will still have to rely on external tools to edit Jane's collage for use on his magazine cover.

III. Relationship with the copyright regimes

In this section I will analyse the relationship the technological features have with the copyright regimes, with reference to the discussions in this chapter and Chapter Two.

As illustrated by the discussion in sub-section (A) of Part I, there are multiple ways in which a user can employ the technological features on the five social media platforms to create, modify and disseminate content. The technological features identified arguably contribute to the overall 'generativity'[74] on these platforms,[75] facilitating users in their generation of content. This enhanced 'generativity' distinguishes social media from cyberspace in general, and allows for social media's provision of the technological facilities, or 'affordances',[76] that further extend the internet's power in connecting people without the need for intermediaries. Such 'generativity' of social media platforms, owing in part to the technological features available on such platforms, encourages users to engage in content-generative activities.[77] The technological features that encourage content-generative activities – through increasing exponentially the volume of content on social media and users' opportunities to interact with such content – result in an increase of the possibilities for copyright infringement when users engage in content-generative activities on social media platforms.[78] I argue that these features can be incompatible with the copyright regimes.

On the other hand, there are technological features identified in sub-section (B) of Part I that constrain content-generative activities. These features limit the opportunities of users to interact with the relevant content, whether *at* or *after* the point of dissemination of such content. I argue further that such features can reduce the risks of copyright infringement by social media users, and are hence aligned with the copyright regimes. In any case, as illustrated under scenario three in Part II, any constraint on social media experienced by a user when he or she engages in content-generative activities can be readily bypassed with the external tools available on web browsers, operating systems, and so on. On balance, the social media platforms surveyed encourage content-generative activities more than they constrain them.

In addition, I also elaborate on how some of the technological features that constrain content-generative activities reflect copyright considerations.

A. Attribution of generator of content

The technological features that limit the modification of content arguably reflect copyright principles. In particular, these features operate to ensure, to some extent,[79] the identification of the original generator of content (ie, the first user who shares the material on a social media platform, who may or may not be the original author of such content), and also the source of the content. This is limited to the extent that a user can rely on external tools on his or her web browser, operating system and so on to edit the content. An example is Twitter's deletion of 'tweets' incorporating the jokes of freelance writer Olga Lexell after receipt of the copyright notices she submitted.[80] Although Twitter users can choose to share the jokes by using the 're-tweeting' function that will ensure the attribution of Olga as the original author of such jokes, users may often choose to do otherwise. Olga will not be attributed for her authorship of the 'tweets' in situations where users decide to re-type the entire jokes out as 'tweets' or to use the 'copy and paste' functions available to them on their operating systems to share the jokes.

With reference to the earlier discussion in Chapter Two[81] and the earlier discussion in this chapter,[82] I note that the technological features of four out of five platforms (ie, excluding Pinterest) – subject to the adoption of external tools by users – accommodate the right of an author to the attribution for his or her authorship of the relevant copyright work, through identification by username. These features apply consistently regardless of where the generator of content is based, the status of such content (whether copyright protected or not) and the different scopes of application of moral rights in different jurisdictions.

On the other hand, in respect of other moral rights such as the right of integrity, the same features that limit the modification of content[83] may nonetheless allow a user to modify a work by commenting on it, before sharing it with others – a situation that could compromise an author's right of integrity to his or her work.[84] This happens, for example, when a user modifies a work through commenting in such a manner that it could be prejudicial to the reputation of the author, whose username allows for his or her identification. It is paradoxical that the features that generally safeguard the right of an author to be attributed for the authorship of his or her work also create the opportunities for other moral rights to be violated, such as the author's right of integrity.

Social media platforms therefore appear to recognise that the clear attribution of contributions to individual users is important for users who identify with the content they create on platforms and wish to retain control over such material. This encourages continuing user-led creation, modification and dissemination of content, a key aspect of social media.[85] Notwithstanding this, the possibility of using the relevant features for purposes that conflict with copyright principles (in this instance, to violate the right of integrity to a work) dilutes their strength in upholding copyright considerations.

B. Notice and takedown mechanisms

As illustrated earlier,[86] the *DMCA* notice and takedown mechanism has been integrated into the interfaces with which a user interacts on four of the five platforms – namely Facebook, Pinterest, YouTube and Twitter. Each of these platforms make available to copyright holders *DMCA* compliant online forms that they can easily complete to notify the platforms of copyright infringement and to request the removal of content deemed to be copyright infringing. On the other hand, while the *DMCA* mechanism is part of the copyright policy of Wikipedia, the Wikipedia platform does not provide a similar online form to make the process of initiating the *DMCA* mechanism more convenient for copyright holders. Instead a copyright holder has to complete a notification of copyright infringement manually and arrange for this to be sent to the designated agent, through email or by post.

While social media platforms need to make the *DMCA* mechanism available to copyright holders in order to be exempt under the safe harbour provision from liability for monetary relief, in relation to secondary liability for copyright infringement by their users,[87] the accessibility to web forms on each of the Facebook, Pinterest, YouTube and Twitter platforms is a convenience granted to copyright holders on the initiatives of these platforms. On a related note, it is plausible that a substantial volume of non-copyright infringing content (for example, because the use resulting in such content falls under a copyright exception such as fair use in the US) is permanently removed pursuant to this mechanism. A user who receives a notification of copyright infringement may choose not to exercise his or her legal rights by responding with a counter-notice,[88] even if the relevant content has been mistakenly removed.[89]

The *DMCA* mechanism is only one of a few notice and takedown measures highlighted in sub-section (B3) of Part I. Among the five platforms studied, Facebook and Wikipedia additionally offer other self-help or community options through which copyright holders can request the removal of potentially infringing content *without* the initiation of the *DMCA* mechanism. Overall, the measures taken by the five platforms are found to extend beyond the prescriptions of copyright legislation. I argue that these measures reflect and reinforce copyright considerations.

There are similar mechanisms to the *DMCA* mechanism under the *UK Copyright Act*[90] and the *Australian Copyright Act*,[91] although these are not specifically considered in this book.

C. Filtering out content

Through the Content Id system mentioned above,[92] YouTube has integrated filtering technologies on its platform with the intention of filtering out potentially copyright-infringing content. As filtering is a form of technological control that applies automatically, there is often little room to raise disputes against its application, nor to exercise discretion in its implementation.[93] In the same vein, automatic enforcement through filtering results in an over-inclusive 'all or nothing' approach to governance that is non-proportionate; most filtering systems are not specific enough to restrict their application only to the targeted content.[94] Moreover, given that filtering technologies are better at implementing rules than imposing standards,[95] the relevant filtering software can be efficient in detecting matches with content claimed by copyright holders, but cannot assess – with reference to standards – whether a use is exempted under copyright laws, as a fair use or otherwise.[96]

Because of this limitation of filtering technologies in imposing standards on a case-by-case basis, many of the Content Id claims that result in the removal of content are erroneous. The policies elected by the copyright holders are immediately implemented, and no separate consideration is given to the possible application of copyright exceptions under these claims. It is only when the respondent user files a dispute to a claim, and the copyright holder does not respond within 30 days *or* chooses to release the claim, that the content and its previous settings are restored on YouTube.[97] Although this process shares some similarities with the *DMCA* mechanism that allows a respondent user to file a counter-notice in response to a copyright notice he or she receives, there are variations between the two.[98] Essentially, the Content Id system is a self-help system[99] that exists independently of the *DMCA* mechanism.

With respect to the use of the *DMCA* mechanism discussed earlier and the Content Id system, a case in point is *Lawrence Lessig v Liberation Music Pty Ltd*.[100] Lessig, with the backing of the Electronic Frontier Foundation (EFF), filed a complaint in a US federal court against Melbourne-based Liberation Music Pty Ltd (Liberation Music) for its aggressive enforcement of copyright – in insisting that YouTube remove the video clip of a lecture uploaded by Lessig featuring clips from the song 'Lisztomania' by the French band Phoenix (on Liberation Music's label).[101] The clips were included in Lessig's lecture delivered at a Creative Commons conference to demonstrate how young people are expressing themselves on the internet. Lessig's video clip was initially blocked by YouTube's Content Id system as having content licensed by US-based Viacom International Inc., and Lessig responded by filing a notice to dispute the block. Just as YouTube was about to restore access to the clip, Liberation Music submitted a copyright notice under the *DMCA*; in response Lessig filed a counter-notice, although he retracted this when Liberation Music threatened to sue him in the Massachusetts court. Subsequently Lessig and the EFF decided to file a complaint against Liberation Music, relying on the argument that Lessig's use of the clips for purposes such as criticism, comment, teaching and scholarship qualified as fair use.

The case was finally settled in favour of Lessig in February 2014 – with Liberation Music agreeing under a settlement agreement that Lessig's use qualified both as fair use under the copyright laws of US and as fair dealing under the copyright laws of Australia.[102] This case brings to light the possibility that a large volume of non-copyright infringing content can be removed under the *DMCA* mechanism and the Content Id system without due consideration being given to the application of copyright exceptions, including fair use. It is a unique situation, in that Lessig happens to be a renowned theorist on cyberspace who dared to challenge Liberation Music's claim.

Just as is the case with the requests to remove content – whether under the *DMCA* or otherwise – if the majority of Content Id claims go undisputed, the subsequent generative possibilities in relation to the content unjustifiably removed[103] will be obliterated. Thus the Content Id system results in a similar effect to the notice and takedown measures discussed in the earlier sub-section. Again I argue that it reflects and reinforces copyright considerations over and beyond legislative prescriptions.

IV. Conclusion

This chapter, together with Chapter Two, forms the basis for this book's evaluation of the consistency of the technological features of social media platforms with the application of copyright laws. I have identified the technological features that both encourage and constrain content-generative activities undertaken by users of these platforms. I have also illustrated, under scenario three, how the identified technological features on such platforms enable the content-generative activities of Jane and other users in the case study. Out of a total of *eleven* content-generative activities considered, as many as *four* of these activities can be carried out using solely the technological features on the relevant platforms. I have further noted that where Jane and the other users face constraints in their content-generative activities, these constraints can be readily bypassed with external tools.

I have discussed the relationship the technological features have with the copyright regimes of the US, the UK and Australia. I have argued that the 'generativity'[104] of social media platforms, in part due to their integration of technological features that encourage the creation, modification and dissemination of content, can increase the possibilities for copyright infringement on such platforms. These features can be incompatible with the copyright regimes. On the other hand, the technological features that constrain content-generative activities limit the opportunities for users to interact with content and hence correspondingly reduce the risks of copyright infringement by users of the platforms. These features are aligned with the copyright regimes, although their influence is limited since the constraints experienced by users can easily be overcome with the other tools available on their web browsers, operating systems and so on. Thus, on balance, the social media platforms encourage content-generative activities more than they constrain them.

I have additionally elaborated on how some of the features that constrain content-generative activities reflect copyright considerations, beyond limiting the opportunities for users to engage in content-generative activities. These are the features which: ensure the attribution of the authorship of content; allow for copyright holders to request the removal of content; and filter out content with direct matches to the content of copyright holders. While the first category of features safeguards the moral right of an author to be attributed for his or her authorship of a work, the same features create opportunities for the violation of another moral right (ie, the right of integrity to a work) – this dilutes the strength of such features in upholding copyright considerations. In contrast, the latter two categories of features distinctively reflect and reinforce copyright considerations beyond legislative prescriptions.

I observe that users are, to a large extent, 'nudged'[105] to engage in content-generative activities on social media platforms. However, both the availability of the notice and takedown mechanisms, as well as the employment of filtering technologies on platforms such as YouTube, are strong reminders of the potential application of copyright laws to the content-generative activities on social media.

In the next chapter I will discuss prior empirical studies that illuminate the perceptions and awareness users have of intellectual property in general, or of copyright laws more specifically. I will also draw on scenarios one, two and three – in Chapters Two, Three and Four respectively – to examine how the regulatory factors of copyright laws, the TOS and the technological services impact, *in toto*, on the content-generative behaviours of users across the five selected social media platforms. I will then analyse the findings from these studies, together with the arguments made in the earlier chapters.

Notes

1. I draw, to some extent, from Yeung's method of classifying various design-based technological instruments that regulate the behaviours of people within an environment. This method focuses on the modalities of design; see Karen Yeung, 'Towards an Understanding of Regulation by Design' in Roger Brownsword and Karen Yeung (eds), *Regulating Technologies* (Hart Publishing, 2008) 85–7. The ways in which the desired objectives are sought define this manner of classification proposed by Yeung, such as encouraging desired changes in behaviours, changing the impact of harm-generating behaviours and preventing the harm-generating behaviours altogether. I have decided to identify only two main categories of technological features (ie, those that encourage and constrain content-generative activities), given that the features on social media that can reduce the harmful impact caused by the content-generative activities of a user to a third party can also constrain content-generative activities. An example is the notice and takedown mechanism under the *DMCA* that facilitates the convenient removal of content reported to be harmful to a third party, which arguably constrains subsequent content-generative activities.
2. My focus is on the platform interfaces with which users interact when they generate content on social media. Given the confined focus of this book, the chapter is not concerned with technology in general that has an effect on user behaviours. Thus the functions (for example, the 'copy image' function) available to users on web browsers that make it easy for them to, among other things, modify and disseminate content originally created by others will be omitted from consideration. In the same vein, the chapter is not concerned with the features of applications on operating systems (for example, Android, Linux, iOS and Microsoft Windows) that can be used independently or in conjunction with these functions to generate content.
3. See Thaler, R. and Sunstein, C. 2008.
4. See image 1 in Appendix 1.
5. See image 2 in Appendix 1.
6. See image 3 in Appendix 1.
7. See image 4 in Appendix 1.
8. See, for example, Pinterest Blog, *Pin a Video!* (22 May 2013) <https://blog.pinterest.com/en/pin-video>.
9. See image 5 in Appendix 1.
10. See images 6 and 7 in Appendix 1.
11. See image 8 in Appendix 1. See also Joshua Cohen, *YouTube Gives Creators Updates and Tools to Help with Content ID* (18 March 2014) <http://www.tubefilter.com/2014/03/18/youtube-content-id-updates-tools>; Cynthia Boris, *YouTube calms angry vidders with new tweaks in Content ID process* (19 March 2014) <http://www.marketingpilgrim.com/2014/03/youtube-calms-angry-vidders-with-new-tweaks-in-content-id-process.html>.
12. See image 9 in Appendix 1.
13. See image 10 in Appendix 1.
14. See image 11 in Appendix 1.
15. See image 12 in Appendix 1.
16. See image 13 in Appendix 1.
17. See image 14 in Appendix 1.
18. Gimp, *GNU Image Manipulation Program* <http://www.gimp.org/>.
19. Photoshop, *Photoshop.com* <http://www.photoshop.com/>.
20. See images 15, 16 and 17 in Appendix 1.
21. See image 18 in Appendix 1. Social plug-ins (ie, tools used so that experiences on YouTube, for instance, can be shared on Facebook) are used. Whether the user uses the Facebook, Pinterest or Twitter social plug-in, he or she will be prompted to write something at the same time.
22. This can be done using external tools. See, for example, ClipConverter.cc, *Free Online Media Recorder* <http://www.clipconverter.cc>.
23. See image 19 in Appendix 1.
24. See image 20 in Appendix 1.
25. See, for example, Adam Hyde et al, 'What is Collaboration Anyway?' in Michael Mandiberg (ed.), *The Social Media Reader* (New York University Press, 2008) 53, 54.
26. See image 21 in Appendix 1.

27. There are no elaborate content editing tools available, beyond tools that are used to modify existing articles.
28. The platform is, after all, an online encyclopedia intended to provide information on various topics to the public. It is not meant to provide as much interaction among users as other social media platforms do.
29. See image 22 in Appendix 1.
30. See image 23 in Appendix 1.
31. These are the Facebook users who are part of a user's defined network of 'friends' on Facebook.
32. See image 24 in Appendix 1.
33. See Pinterest, *Pinterest basic: All about boards* <https://help.pinterest.com/en/articles/all-about-boards?qa=3#Web>.
34. See image 25 in Appendix 1.
35. Public video clips are those that are made publicly available to all; private video clips can only be seen by the people a user selects – they do not show on search results and are invisible to other users; and unlisted video clips are those that can be seen by people to whom the relevant links are sent: again, they do not show on search results. See YouTube, *Video privacy settings* <https://support.google.com/youtube/answer/157177?hl=en>.
36. For example, when a YouTube video clip is shared on Facebook, the constituent members of the audience will depend on a user's privacy setting on Facebook.
37. See image 26 in Appendix 1.
38. In respect of 're-tweeting', the privacy setting of the user who 're-tweets' is relevant. In respect of responding to another user's 'tweet', the privacy setting of the latter user is relevant instead. If a user's 'tweets' are protected, the 'tweets' are only visible to a user's approved 'followers'. On the other hand, if a user's 'tweets' are not protected, they are available to the public. See Twitter, *Help Center: About public and protected Tweets* <https://support.twitter.com/articles/14016#>.
39. See image 27 in Appendix 1.
40. This original generator refers to the user who first shares the content on the relevant social media platform, whether or not he or she is the original creator of the relevant content.
41. See image 28 in Appendix 1.
42. See images 29 and 30 in Appendix 1.
43. See image 31 in Appendix 1.
44. See image 32 in Appendix 1.
45. Wikipedia, *Help: File Page* <http://en.wikipedia.org/wiki/Help:File_page>.
46. See images 33, 34 and 35 in Appendix 1. The word limit is 140 for a 'tweet', a 're-tweet' and a response to a 'tweet'.
47. These requirements are, among other things, that the subject must be considered 'worthy of notice' and that it is written with reference to reliable published sources. See Wikipedia, *Wikipedia: Your first article* <https://en.wikipedia.org/wiki/Wikipedia:Your_first_article>.
48. Wikipedia, *Wikipedia: Basic copyright issues* <http://en.wikipedia.org/wiki/Wikipedia:Basic_copyright_issues>.
49. Content may be deemed harmful for many reasons, including that it is offensive or that its availability on the relevant platform is an infringement of another's intellectual property rights.
50. See images 36, 37, 38, 39 and 40 in Appendix 1. The options for reporting an image are as follows: 'It's annoying or not interesting'; 'I'm in this photo and I don't like it'; 'I think it shouldn't be on Facebook'; and 'It's spam'. If the user selects 'I think it shouldn't be on Facebook', he or she gets directed again to another, longer list of options. The options include, inter alia, the following: 'This is nudity and pornography'; 'This humiliates me or someone I know'; and 'Something else'. If the user selects 'Something else', he or she gets asked to choose again from yet another list of options. One of the options on this list reads 'I think it's an unauthorized use of my intellectual property'. The options are similar in respect of reporting a post.
51. *DMCA* § 512.
52. Alternatively, such party can also submit a notice of copyright infringement by post to Facebook's designated agent. See Facebook, *Help Center: What is the contact information for your Digital Millennium Copyright Act designated agent?* <https://www.facebook.com/help/www/190268144407210>.
53. See images 41 and 42 in Appendix 1. The other options presented are as follows: 'I don't want to see this'; 'This is spam'; and 'This Pin isn't useful'.

54. See image 43 in Appendix 1. See also Pinterest, *Copyright Infringement Notification* <http://www.pinterest.com/about/copyright/dmca-pin/>.
55. See images 44 and 45 in Appendix 1. The other options presented are as follows: 'Sexual content'; 'Hateful or abusive content'; 'Harmful dangerous acts'; 'Child abuse'; 'Spam or misleading'; and 'Captions issue'. If the user proceeds on the basis that the video clip infringes his or her rights, there is a second drop-down menu from which three other options are presented. The three options are as follows: 'Infringes my copyright'; 'Invades my privacy'; and 'Other legal claim'.
56. YouTube, *Copyright Infringement Notification* <https://www.youtube.com/copyright_complaint_form>. See also YouTube, *Submit a copyright takedown notice* <https://support.google.com/youtube/answer/2807622/>. Alternatively the user, or any party for that matter, can choose to notify YouTube of copyright infringement via email, fax or post instead.
57. See images 46 and 47 in Appendix 1. The options are as follows: 'Unwanted commercial content or spam'; 'Pornography or sexually explicit material'; 'Hate speech or graphic violence'; and 'Harassment or bullying'. Here, unlike the case with a video clip, the user is not given the option to report a comment for copyright infringement. This could be because YouTube anticipates fewer instances where comments are copyright infringing than it does with video clips on the same platform. The user can, however, still choose to visit YouTube's web page that incorporates its copyright policy, and locate the online form to report copyright infringement. See YouTube Copyright Policy.
58. See images 48, 49, 50, 51 and 52 in Appendix 1. The other options presented are as follows: 'I am not interested in this Tweet'; and 'It's spam'. If the user proceeds on the basis that the content is abusive and harmful, he or she is directed to another list of options which includes the following: 'Includes private information'; 'Involves targeted harassment'; 'Threatening violence or physical harm'; and 'This person might be contemplating suicide or self-harm'.
59. Twitter, *Report copyright infringement* <https://support.twitter.com/forms/dmca>.
60. Wikipedia, *Wikipedia: Content Removal* <https://en.wikipedia.org/wiki/Wikipedia:Content_removal>.
61. Wikipedia, *Wikipedia: Contributor copyright violations* <http://en.wikipedia.org/wiki/Wikipedia:Contributor_copyright_investigations>.
62. Wikipedia Terms 2014, cl 8.
63. Wikipedia Terms 2014, cl 8.
64. YouTube Help.
65. As of now Facebook, Pinterest, Twitter and Wikipedia do not use a similar system to detect potential instances of copyright infringement by pre-emptive filtering. This could change in the near future.
66. The technological features constitute part of the architecture of the social media sites surveyed. Lessig notes that the constraints of architecture are self-executing, unlike the other modalities of regulation. See Lessig, L. 2006, 342.
67. This is consistent with Yeung's description of the modality-based taxonomy in Part I of this chapter – in particular, her description of the first category comprising design instruments that encourage desired changes in behaviours. See Yeung, K. 2008, 85.
68. See image 53 of Appendix 1.
69. See image 54 of Appendix 1.
70. See image 55 of Appendix 1.
71. Wikipedia, *Help: Editing* <https://en.wikipedia.org/wiki/Help:Editing>.
72. YouTube Help, *YouTube Video Editor* <https://support.google.com/youtube/answer/183851?hl=en>.
73. A similar assumption is made in Part II of Chapter Three, sub-section J.
74. In this respect I find that Zittrain's theory of generativity is useful in supplementing my understanding of how the technological features encourage users' content-generative behaviours. The term 'generativity' has been defined by him to denote a technology's capacity to produce spontaneous changes driven by mass uncoordinated audiences, with reference to four specific criteria: leverage across a range of difficult tasks through making them more achievable; adaptability to different tasks through offering additional kinds of uses; ease of mastery; and accessibility. See Jonathan Zittrain, 'The Generative Internet' (2006) 119 *Harvard Law Review* 1974, 1980–2.

75. The extent of 'generativity' varies across the platforms. All things considered, the technological features of YouTube are argued to be more generative than those of the other platforms. This is because the technological features on YouTube provide more *leverage*, are more *adaptable* and more *accessible* to a user than is the case with the other four platforms. For instance, the video editing tool and the automatic generator of transcripts on YouTube allow a user to create and modify content conveniently and with minimal effort on the YouTube platform. On the other hand, in respect of Facebook, Pinterest, Twitter and Wikipedia, with the general exception of text, images and video clips uploaded often have to be created and modified using external tools.
76. See William W. Gaver, 'Technology Affordances' (1991), *CHI'91 Conference Proceedings* 79, where the notion of 'affordances' was explored as a way of looking at the strengths and weaknesses of technologies with respect to the possibilities they might offer to the people who use them. The term 'affordance' was first introduced by James J. Gibson, 'The Theory of Affordances' in Robert Shaw and John Bransford (eds), *Perceiving, Acting and Knowing* (John Wiley & Sons, 1977) 127.
77. The term 'generativity' in the Zittrain sense and the term 'generative' to describe behaviours and activities are distinct from one another. In the context of this book, it is the generativity of social media platforms that encourages users to engage in content-generative activities.
78. This echoes the sentiment that generativity is also vulnerability, in the sense that content in a generative environment is more vulnerable to copyright infringement. See Zittrain, J. 2006, 1995.
79. This identification is limited, given that the actual identity of the author of content is not usually apparent from an identification through his or her username and further investigation is required. Also, on the Pinterest platform, although the preceding user cannot be identified from an image a user 'pins' from another user's pin-board, the identification of the original generator remains possible as the source website is indicated along with the 'pin'. See Part I of this chapter, sub-section B1.
80. See, for example, *The Guardian* 2015; D'Orazio 2015.
81. On the moral rights that authors have which allow them to control the treatment and presentation of their works, see Part I of Chapter Two, sub-section F.
82. Part I, sub-section B1.
83. This includes: the 'share' option on Facebook; the 'pin' option on Pinterest (where the source website is indicated and the original generator can be identified); the 'share', 'email' and 'embed' options on YouTube; the 're-tweet' option on Twitter; and the automatically generated file page on Wikipedia.
84. See *VARA*, § 106A(a)(3)(A); *UK Copyright Act*, ss 80(1) and 80(2); *Australian Copyright Act*, ss 195AI, 195AJ-AL.
85. See Bruns, A. and Bahnisch, M. 2009.
86. Part I of this chapter, sub-section B3.
87. *DMCA*, § 512(c)(1).
88. *DMCA*, §§ 512(g)(2) and (g)(3). For example, out of a total of 16,648 *DMCA* takedown notices issued over six months from 1 July to 31 December 2014, a total of only 13 counter-notices were issued on the Twitter platform. See Twitter, *Copyright Notices: DMCA takedown notices (July 1 – December 31, 2014)* <https://transparency.twitter.com/copyright-notices/2014/jul-dec>.
89. The user may wish to avoid copyright litigation, since the next logical step a copyright holder can choose to take (in response to a counter-notice received) is to file a copyright action; see *DMCA*, § 512 (c)(1). Another conceivable reason for this passivity could be the user's lack of understanding of copyright laws that will allow him or her to defend the relevant use in a counter-notice confidently.
90. *UK Copyright Act*, s 97A.
91. *Australian Copyright Act*, ss 116AE, 116AF and 116AH. It is not clear if a social media platform falls under the definition of a 'carriage service provider' in the *Telecommunications Act 1997* (Cth) s 87.
92. Part I of this chapter, sub-section B4.
93. See T.J. McIntyre and Colin Scott, 'Internet Filtering' in Roger Brownsword and Karen Yeung (eds), *Regulating Technologies* (Hart Publishing, 2008) 109, 112.
94. McIntyre, T.J. and Scott, C. 2008, 115.
95. See James Grimmelmann, 'Regulation by Software' (2005) 114 *Yale Law Journal* 1719, 1732, for a discussion on the application by software of rules, rather than standards.

96. McIntyre, T.J. and Scott, C. 2008, 116.
97. YouTube Help, *Dispute a Content ID claim* <https://support.google.com/youtube/answer/2797454/>.
98. With respect to the Content Id system, the copyright holder is given 30 instead of 10 days to respond to a notice disputing his or her Content Id claim. See *DMCA*, § 512(g)(2).
99. For a discussion on self-help systems see generally Kenneth W. Dam, 'Self-Help in the Digital Jungle' (June 1999) 28(2) *Journal of Legal Studies* 1.
100. *Lawrence Lessig v Liberation Music Pty Ltd*, Case 1:13-cv-12028-NMG (USDC Mass, 22 August 2013).
101. *Lawrence Lessig v Liberation Music Pty Ltd*, Case 1:13-cv-12028-NMG (USDC Mass, 22 August 2013). See also Corinne Hui Yun Tan, 'Lawrence Lessig v Liberation Music Pty Ltd: YouTube's Hands (or Bots) in the Overzealous Enforcement of Copyright' (2014) 36(6) *European Intellectual Property Review* 347; Electronic Frontier Foundation, *Lawrence Lessig Strikes Back Against Bogus Copyright Takedown* <https://www.eff.org/press/releases/lawrence-lessig-strikes-back-against-bogus-copyright-takedown>; PCWorld, *Creative Commons co-founder wages 'fair use' war over YouTube takedown notice* <http://www.pcworld.com/article/2047320/copyright-guru-claims-fair-use-to-fight-youtube-takedown-notice.html>.
102. See, for example, Electronic Frontier Foundation, *Lawrence Lessig settles fair use lawsuit over Phoenix music snippets* <https://www.eff.org/press/releases/lawrence-lessig-settles-fair-use-lawsuit-over-phoenix-music-snippets>; Michaela Fox, *Australian music label Liberation to pay damages to Harvard professor Lawrence Lessig in copyright battle* (28 February 2014) <http://www.smh.com.au/digital-life/digital-life-news/australian-music-label-liberation-to-pay-damages-to-harvard-professor-lawrence-lessig-in-copyright-battle-20140228-33pnj.html>.
103. This will be the case if copyright holders largely elect to block access to the content, among the other choices given.
104. See Zittrain, J. 2006. See also David G. Post, 'The Theory of Generativity' (2010) 78(6) *Fordham Law Review* 101, 106. Post comments that 'Generativity has been said to be both the good *and* the bad, at war with itself, bearing within itself the seeds of its own destruction'.
105. See Thaler, R. and Sunstein, C. 2008.

Chapter Five
How the terms of service and technological features affect copyright's regulation of content-generative behaviours

At the beginning of this chapter I consider earlier empirical studies conducted on the perceptions and awareness users have of intellectual property in general, or of copyright laws more specifically. This enables me to analyse the findings from these studies along with the arguments made in the earlier chapters of this book from three angles. Firstly, I discuss how users relate to copyright laws and how this affects their awareness of such laws. Secondly, I examine how the TOS (ie, terms of service) affect users' awareness of copyright laws. Thirdly, I consider the influence of the technological features on users' perceptions of copyright laws. I also refer to the earlier discussions on the relationship between each of the TOS and the technological features vis-à-vis the copyright regime.

I then bring together the conclusions arrived at under scenarios one,[1] two[2] and three[3] in the earlier chapters, in respect of the application of copyright laws, the TOS and the technological features respectively. The purpose of this is to evaluate the consistency of regulatory signals users receive from the following pairs of regulatory factors: the copyright regimes and the TOS; the copyright regimes and the technological features; and the TOS and the technological features.

I. Perceptions and awareness of copyright laws

I examine the following studies on the assumption that users are more likely to comply with copyright laws in generating content on social media when such laws are perceived to restrict what is illegitimate[4] and when users understand how these laws apply to regulate their content-generative activities. The studies are selected for the purpose of this book as they are of relatively recent vintage and their findings can illuminate the perceptions and awareness of copyright laws in users of social media platforms. These findings pertain to: the perceived irrelevance and poor understanding of copyright laws displayed by many users; the expectation for digital content to be free; and the greater impact of perceptions over awareness of copyright laws on users' compliance with copyright laws. The findings will be analysed together with the arguments made in the earlier chapters.

A. Prior studies

1. Perceived irrelevance and poor understanding of copyright laws

A study conducted on the perceptions and awareness of European users of intellectual property between December 2012 and August 2013 reveals that there is a gap between the subjective understanding which such users claim to have of intellectual property and the objective knowledge which they actually possess.[5] Under this study, 73 per cent of the EU citizens surveyed claimed to have a good understanding of the term 'intellectual property', although only 13 per cent of the respondents demonstrated a good knowledge of what it actually means.[6] Similarly, 85 per cent of those surveyed stated that they have a good understanding of the term 'copyright'.[7] However, their objective knowledge again painted a different picture. For example, when presented with the statement 'copyright allows all the creators to share freely everything they create', 49 per cent of the respondents stated that this statement is true and 12 per cent did not know.[8] Only 39 per cent of those surveyed answered that this statement is false.[9] Furthermore, the study found that 42 per cent of the respondents considered it acceptable to download copyright-protected content when it was for personal use.[10] In showing that users' objective levels of knowledge of intellectual property and its components is substantially lower than their declared understanding,[11] this study supports the observation made by the cartoonist and film-maker Nina Paley that people 'do not know that they do not know' how copyright laws work; they have only a vague idea that copyright laws protect their rights in their intellectual property.[12] The qualitative research carried out in the study, in addition to its quantitative research, also reflected that notions of intellectual property were perceived by many respondents to be irrelevant to them, and instead to affect mainly a small part of society, including large corporations, successful artists and lawyers.[13]

The study illuminates the poor understanding of copyright laws that users have.[14] It also reveals their perceptions of the acceptability of accessing digital copyright-protected content illegally for personal use, as well as the disconnection they experience with intellectual property in general. These findings are reflective of the awareness and perceptions of copyright laws that users have on social media when they engage in content-generative activities. The limitations of this study's applicability to this book are that the questions were posed to those surveyed to gauge their perceptions and understanding of *intellectual property in general*, including of patents and trademarks, rather than of copyright laws in particular. Moreover, while references were made in the study to the explosion of digital content and technology[15] – the circumstances that allow for the proliferation of social media platforms – the study was not specifically designed to gauge the awareness and perceptions of social media users to copyright laws.

2. Expectation that digital content is free

Another survey conducted in 2012 by the Pew Research Center[16] in the US gauged the views of arts organisations on the overall impact of technology on arts.[17] Of the arts organisations surveyed, 74 per cent agreed that the internet and related technologies have created an expectation among some audiences that all digital content should be free.[18] Notably, this survey draws on the views of right-holder arts organisations, rather than their audiences.

Similarly, a YouGov[19] report released in 2014[20] in the UK reveals the consensus held by its respondents that digital content should be free, or at least cheaper than the physical equivalent. This view is noted to be more prominent among children and young adults.[21] Of the children aged between 8 to 15 years old who were interviewed, 49 per cent strongly agreed that a person should be able to download or access content for free from the internet. Similarly, 49 per cent of the young adults between 16 to 24 years old who were interviewed held the view that online content should be free.[22] Cost concerns and the availability of content, as well as the convenience of accessing content, are identified as key motivators explaining why file-sharing continues to occur among children and young adults.[23] The group of children aged between 8 and 15 years old was found to have an above average propensity to agree that file-sharing websites are easy to use and that file-sharing has become 'a normal thing to do'.[24] Separately, while up to 16 per cent of the same group strongly agreed that it is ethically wrong to access content without the creator's permission, only 7 per cent of the interviewees agreed that file-sharing is a form of theft.[25]

Although the survey was conducted in relation to the use of file-sharing websites by children and young adults, the discovery of a consensus within this group that digital content should be free is relevant to this book. I argue that this general expectation that such content is free accounts, to some extent, for users' responses to copyright laws. I also argue that the convenience and ease of using the technological features available on social media platforms – just as is the case with file-sharing websites – encourage users to engage in content-generative activities on social media. Such users are more likely to see their content-generative activities as 'the normal thing to do' – in this sense conflating what they perceive to be 'normal' with what is actually legitimate.

Yet another survey conducted in 2014 by the Intellectual Property Office of Singapore[26] shows that the percentage of respondents surveyed who viewed downloading from unauthorised sources or unauthorised file-sharing as forms of theft has dropped since 2010.[27] This is in spite of the fact that most of the users surveyed were both aware that infringements of intellectual property rights could result in penalties under existing laws and agreed that it is important to protect the works of intellectual property creators.[28] The findings from this survey are relevant to the book insofar as they further exemplify how users generally expect to be able to use digital content available on the internet freely.

3. Greater impact of perceptions on compliance with copyright laws

Finally, a study conducted before 2009 to assess the factors that deter online copyright infringement – on a sample of university students in the US – reveals that consensus with copyright laws plays a more important role in deterring future file-sharing activities than an awareness of copyright laws.[29] 'Consensus with copyright laws' was defined under this study as the degree to which a user of a file-sharing service agrees that copyright laws on file-sharing are reasonable and updated, in the light of existing technologies. On the other hand, an 'awareness of copyright laws' was defined as the extent to which the same user is informed of copyright laws in relation to his or her file-sharing activities.[30]

The scope of the study here is confined to file-sharing activities, rather than broader content-generative activities on social media. Nonetheless, its finding is relevant to this book. In this respect I argue that the consensus with copyright laws referred to under this study contributes to users' perceptions of the relevance and legitimacy of copyright laws in regulating their content-generative activities. I argue further that such perceived legitimacy contributes to the effectiveness of copyright laws in securing compliance from social media users when they generate content.[31] This means that these users are more likely to comply with copyright laws when they perceive such laws to be reasonable in regulating their content-generative activities on social media.

B. Users' perceptions and awareness of copyright laws

In this sub-section I analyse the findings of the earlier studies highlighted above with the arguments made in Chapter Two, in relation to the regulation of users' content-generative behaviours by copyright laws. The purpose of this analysis is to understand better how users relate to copyright laws on social media. The effectiveness of copyright laws in regulating users' content-generative behaviours on social media depends on their ability to secure compliance from users, including deterring users from undertaking potentially copyright-infringing activities when they generate content.[32] With reference to the last study cited in sub-section (A), users' perceptions of legitimacy have a bigger impact in deterring behaviours not compliant with copyright laws than the awareness of copyright laws per se. In this respect, users' lack of consensus that copyright laws are reasonable and updated, as well as their expectations that digital content is free, could contribute to the perceived illegitimacy of copyright laws. Where copyright laws are perceived as illegitimate, their effectiveness in securing compliance from users will foreseeably be compromised.

At this juncture, I postulate that:

(i) Users' perceptions of the relevance and legitimacy of copyright laws, including whether they are reasonable and updated – as well as their expectations that digital content is free – are shaped by the technological features on social media platforms. In this respect, users are more likely to perceive copyright laws as reasonable and updated if such laws are aligned with the existing technologies.[33] I will consider how the technological features shape social media users' *perceptions* of copyright laws in sub-section (D).

(ii) In addition, users' *awareness* of how copyright laws can actually apply to their content-generative activities on social media will affect their compliance with such laws. I will consider this in the latter part of this sub-section.

(iii) Further, users' *awareness* of how copyright laws apply to their content-generative activities on social media platforms are affected to some extent by the understandings of copyright laws incorporated into the TOS of such platforms. I will consider this in sub-section (C).

Users' awareness of copyright laws (ie, an understanding of how they apply to their content-generative activities) has an impact on their compliance with copyright laws on social media. Copyright laws have been criticised for being counter-intuitive to ordinary people who are not copyright lawyers.[34] Many people do not believe that copyright laws can be applied to their activities and are hence of relevance to them.[35] Litman has suggested that this is because there is 'paucity', or inadequacy, of language under the copyright statutes in the US, the UK and Australia that relates back to the behaviours of individuals who are consuming rather than exploiting copyright-protected material.[36]

Moreover, particularly in relation to content-generative activities on social media, the focus against exploitation of copyright-protected content draws an artificial distinction between copyright holders and users. In modifying the content shared on social media to create new content, users may be inclined to assume that their conduct is lawful; once the content created by these users qualifies for copyright protection, such users – now copyright holders of the resulting new content – could be keen to enforce their copyrights against other users. As can be seen, users who actively engage in content-generative activities are also copyright holders of some content.

In addition, copyright laws comprise mainly complex rules. In this respect I find Black's characterisation of a rule useful. According to her, a rule's structure is made up of three main 'elements' or characteristics – precision, complexity and clarity.[37] The variation of these three 'elements' within the rules creates rules of three broad types – 'bright line' rules,[38] principles[39] and complex rules.[40] The level of complexity within detailed copyright rules framed in favour of copyright holders gives rise to uncertainties of interpretation[41] in their application to the content-generative activities they purport to regulate.

With reference to the discussion conducted on how copyright rules in the US, the UK and Australia apply to content-generative activities in Chapter Two,[42] ascertaining whether these activities are copyright infringing requires the issues of copyright subsistence and infringement set out below to be addressed:

(i) Whether the original content falls under the categories of content protected by copyright laws,[43] and how copyright laws' protection of expressions, not ideas,[44] apply, if at all, to determine which content is copyright protectable;
(ii) The satisfaction of the originality requirement,[45] as well as the applicability of the *de minimis* principle,[46] in relation to the content and its successive versions;[47]

(iii) The applicability of the human-centred authorship concept[48] to collaborative practices resulting in content, and further, to situations in which there is no human author;[49]

(iv) The satisfaction of the requirement of fixation,[50] recording[51] or reduction to material form,[52] as the case may be;

(v) The identification of the specific right that is infringed, whether of reproduction,[53] preparation of derivative works,[54] distribution,[55] performance and display[56] in the US (and their equivalent rights in the UK and in Australia);

(vi) The consideration as to whether moral rights of attribution and integrity,[57] as well as the copyright management provisions in the US (and their equivalent provisions in the UK and in Australia),[58] are breached;

(vii) Whether there is any bar to the copyright holders' claim for remedies, because of non-registration (in the US)[59] or because there were no reasonable grounds for copyright infringement by the defendant-users (ie, because there was no reason to believe that copyright subsisted in the content in the UK, *or* because such users had no reasonable grounds to suspect that their acts constituted infringement in Australia);[60] and

(viii) Whether defences including the fair use doctrine[61] or the fair dealing exceptions[62] apply, as the case may be, to excuse the uses of the relevant content.

The above issues have to be resolved with reference to the complex rules set out under the respective copyright statute. These complexities will prove challenging for courts, let alone regular social media users, to resolve. In addition, the application of copyright rules to content-generative activities and the corresponding outcomes are at times unpredictable, due to the uniqueness of each circumstance resulting in the generation of content on social media.

To compound the difficulties further, the copyright rules applicable to the content-generative activities of users based in different jurisdictions may vary, due to conflict of laws considerations. Scenario one has shown that the application of copyright rules in three jurisdictions – the US, the UK and Australia – to the content-generative activities of users can result in different outcomes being reached on the copyright liabilities of the respective users.[63] Moreover, even if the choice of governing law and jurisdiction made under the TOS in a copyright-related dispute is upheld, different laws may apply to questions of subsistence and infringement of copyright.[64]

In the absence of copyright rules that users can relate to, and the overall complexity of those rules,[65] I argue that the low levels of public awareness or understanding of copyright laws are amplified in social media users. It is therefore not surprising that a large majority of such users will not know how to apply the complex copyright rules to their content-generative activities, in order to ascertain whether they are acting in contravention of copyright laws.

C. Terms of service and users' awareness of copyright laws

In this sub-section I consider how the TOS of social media platforms can affect users' awareness of copyright laws. In doing so, I refer to the discussion of the relationship between the TOS and the copyright regimes in Chapter Three.[66] The purpose of this is to acquire a better understanding of how the TOS can influence, through affecting social media users' awareness of copyright laws, their compliance with those laws when they generate content.

In that chapter I have argued that while any alignment with the copyright regimes will reinforce the latter, any potential incompatibility with the copyright regimes compromises the effectiveness of copyright laws in regulating users' content-generative behaviours.[67] The TOS and the relevant copyright regime[68] are aligned to the extent that the *DMCA* notice and takedown mechanism is integrated into each of the copyright policies of the social media platforms studied.[69] In addition, such platforms reserve their rights to disable the accounts of users who have received more than one *DMCA* takedown notice.[70] Apart from limiting the monetary relief available from social media platforms arising in relation to potential secondary liability for the copyright infringement of their users under the safe harbour provisions,[71] these provisions in the TOS arguably remind users undertaking content-generative activities on the platforms to be mindful of complying with copyright laws. If this reminder is effective, the TOS exemplify how private ordering can promote users' compliance with copyright laws, through increasing their awareness of those laws.[72]

Notwithstanding the above, there are potential incompatibilities between the two regimes.[73] Pursuant to the ownership and licensing clauses of the TOS of the social media platforms studied, a user grants the relevant platform an unencumbered licence to use the content he or she owns, as well as another (typically more limited) licence to other users to use his or her content. In the case of the latter, the scope of permission granted varies under the TOS of the platforms surveyed. The grant of a licence by a user who generates content to the relevant social media platform and its users is necessary because of the advertiser-supported business models that many social media platforms, including Facebook, Pinterest, YouTube and Twitter, adopt. Reliance on advertising revenue would mean, as mentioned earlier,[74] that these platforms have an interest in attracting more users and accumulating more content, generated through their activities.

Further, the references made to the ownership of content by its users under the TOS may lead such users to assume that the content they generate is copyright protected and that they hold rights to restrict their use. However, the majority of such content on social media may not qualify for copyright protection in the first place, due to a failure to meet copyright subsistence requirements such as for originality[75] and fixation (or recording and reduction to material form).[76] Even if the content shared on social media meets the subsistence requirements and is hence copyright protected, its uses may be unrestricted. No further consent is to be sought, either because the elements of infringement are not made out or because the infringing uses fall under existing copyright exceptions such as fair use and fair dealing.

In other instances, where content is copyright protected, the licence granted under the relevant TOS may not cover the uses by third parties of such content, particularly when the intention to benefit these third parties is less clearly expressed. This is the case under the Facebook Statement and the Twitter Terms.[77] Because of these potential incompatibilities, I posit that the TOS, through their incorporation of ownership and licensing clauses, are responsible for fostering the following expectations in social media users:

(i) (In a 'copyright holder') The content a 'copyright holder' (also a user) generates on social media receives copyright protection.
(ii) (In a user) In the event that content is copyright protected, a user who modifies and/or disseminates another user's content is licensed to do so under the TOS.

The term 'copyright holder' in paragraph (i) above has a particular meaning in this context, and is intended to refer to users who believe that their content is accorded copyright protection even if this is not actually the case. 'Copyright holders' also include copyright holders of copyright-protected content who overreach their copyrights without considering the application of copyright exceptions. I further posit that the first expectation encourages 'copyright holders' to overreach by issuing copyright notices under the *DMCA* for alleged infringements of their rights. The threat of a copyright lawsuit in the form of a copyright notice could deter further legitimate uses of such content by other users.[78] The second expectation contradicts the first. On a plain reading of the TOS, a user of another's content may be led to believe that his or her use is contractually licensed, although the TOS may be too narrowly drafted to sanction such use.[79] Given that the provisions of these TOS could be incompatible with the copyright regime, they have the potential to encourage 'copyright holders' to overreach their rights under copyright laws, as they concurrently mislead users to think that their uses of copyright-protected content are licensed.

The TOS regulate users' content-generative behaviours by way of rules, just as is the case with copyright laws. Also, the TOS fit the description of principles (ie, the second type of rules) identified by Black in sub-section (B).[80] While the TOS are concise, the outcomes reached pursuant to the application of the TOS are not certain. This is because the application of the TOS to copyright-related activities necessarily refers back to the detailed rules under copyright laws – in particular, the TOS examined incorporate copyright policies that are aligned with the *DMCA*. Therefore the application of the TOS is less straightforward than it appears.

An assessment by a user as to whether a copyright-related activity has breached the relevant TOS could arguably be affected by the understandings of copyright laws embodied in the TOS – these are the expectations outlined which the TOS foster in 'copyright holders' and users. Such expectations, which potentially lead 'copyright holders' to misunderstand the scope of copyright protection and users to assume that copyright laws will not apply to their content-generative activities, could have an adverse impact on users' awareness of, and henceforth compliance with, copyright laws.

D. Technological features and users' perceptions of copyright laws

In this sub-section I consider how the technological features of social media platforms shape users' perceptions of copyright laws. I will refer to the discussion of the relationship between the technological features and the copyright regimes in Chapter Four.[81] This is done to acquire a better understanding of how the technological features both influence the content-generative behaviours of users and, at the same time, shape users' perceptions of copyright laws.

In that chapter I argued that the technological features which encourage the creation, modification and dissemination of content contribute to the 'generativity'[82] of the social media platforms examined and can be incompatible with the copyright regimes. This is because these features increase the possibilities for copyright infringement on social media.[83] I also argued that the technological features which constrain content-generative activities are aligned with the copyright regimes, as they reduce the risks of copyright infringement by social media users. In addition, I elaborated on how some of these features reflect copyright considerations, as set out below:

(i) The features that limit the modification of content when such content is shared, so that the original generator (ie, the user who first shares the content on the relevant social media platform, whether or not he or she is the original author) of the content and the source of the content are more likely to be attributed;[84]
(ii) The *DMCA*-compliant online forms available on the Facebook, Pinterest, YouTube and Twitter platforms that provide convenience to copyright holders who wish to initiate the *DMCA* notice and takedown mechanism in respect of their content shared on these platforms, as well as other self-help and community options offered on the Facebook and Wikipedia platforms, through which copyright holders can request the removal of content;[85] and
(iii) The Content Id system employed by YouTube that detects matches in content shared on YouTube and automatically implements the policy chosen by the relevant copyright holder (ie, to mute the audio, block the content, monetise the use of the content or to track viewership statistics).[86]

The technological features limiting the modification of content ensure that a consistent approach in terms of attribution is applied. This is regardless of where the generator of content is based, the copyright protect-ability of such content *or* the different scopes of application of moral rights in the US, the UK and Australia.[87] On the other hand, the same features permit the modification of the content that could occur at the expense of the right of integrity a copyright holder has to his or her content. This happens when a user modifies the content to the extent that it is prejudicial to the reputation of the copyright holder. Whether the technological features available to a user are employed in a way that respects or infringes the moral rights of others ultimately depends on the choice the user makes when he or she generates content.[88]

At the same time, the ease with which content can be removed pursuant to the use of the notice and takedown mechanisms made available to copyright holders, as well as the Content Id system on YouTube, can result in the unjustified removal of a large volume of non-copyright infringing content.[89] Given the convenience of using these technological features, such features make it easy for 'copyright holders' to request content to be removed – whether under the *DMCA* or otherwise – while concurrently allowing them to make claims that go beyond their proper entitlements. In this respect it has been suggested that users receiving erroneous notices requesting the removal of content, or of content matches under a filtering system (such as the Content Id system on YouTube), are inclined towards avoiding the risk of copyright litigation.[90] As such, these users are less likely to respond with counter-notices.[91]

I argue further that the encouragement of content-generative behaviours by the technological features identified, combined with the overall 'generativity' of social media platforms,[92] reinforce the expectation of users that digital content is free. This is particularly so as the technological features make it convenient, easy and 'normal' for users to engage in content-generative activities. In line with the findings from the YouGov report on file-sharing services discussed above,[93] the availability of technological features on social media may have the effect of fostering the expectation in users that the digital content available on social media is free. It is conceivable that many users could be inclined to assume that the content-generative activities they are 'nudged'[94] to undertake are legitimate and will not attract liabilities under copyright laws.

Therefore there is a disjunction between what 'copyright holders' can do to restrict use of their content and what users expect. The expectations of users may vary from the actual practices of 'copyright holders' on social media. I argue that this disjunction has an adverse impact on users' perceptions of, and hence compliance with, copyright laws. The gap between users' expectations and the practices of 'copyright holders' makes it likely that social media users will perceive copyright laws as unreasonable, outdated and irrelevant, in relation to their content-generative activities.

Although the technological features do not consist of express rules, unlike copyright laws and the TOS,[95] their impact on users' content-generative behaviours is akin to the influence of bright-line rules.[96] Because of the self-executing nature of the technological features surveyed in this book (ie, these features either enable or constrain specific activities), there is more certainty in the outcomes reached via their usage. On balance, the technological features on social media platforms encourage content-generative activities more than they constrain them.[97]

Notwithstanding this, the features 'copyright holders' can use to request the removal of content or to filter out content (for instance, with the Content Id system on YouTube) could result in the obliteration of subsequent generative possibilities in relation to content unjustifiably removed. Such features can operate over-inclusively,[98] as they enforce copyright rules in a bright-line manner and may not take into account the complex rules that copyright laws comprise. For example, the Content Id system notifies the 'copyright holder' of content matches, upon which he or she can choose to block other users' access to the relevant contact. This can happen regardless of whether the use constitutes a fair use in the US.

Overall, the technological features arguably have a significant impact on users' compliance with copyright laws when they generate content, through their shaping of users' perceptions of copyright laws. This is supported by the finding discussed earlier: that users' consensus with copyright laws (ie, that they are reasonable and updated) plays a more important role than their awareness of copyright laws in deterring them from undertaking copyright-infringing activities.[99]

II. Scenario four: regulation by copyright laws, the terms of service and technological features

The premise of the inquiry in this section is to compare copyright laws with other regulatory factors on social media. Here I recall how copyright laws and the TOS could apply to the activities of Jane and the other users in the case study. I also recall how the technological features could influence these activities. I do so to illustrate how social media users can be pulled in different directions by these regulatory factors. For this purpose, under scenario four, the consistency of the regulatory signals given by each of copyright laws, the TOS and the technological features to users, in relation to the specific content-generative activity, will be evaluated in a systematic way. The extent to which the positions reached are the same will be assessed through applying the following pairs of factors: firstly, the copyright laws and the TOS; secondly, the copyright laws and the technological features; and thirdly, the TOS and the technological features. These activities will be considered in the same order as under the respective scenarios in Chapters Two, Three and Four. The extent of consistency between any pair of factors examined – in relation to each activity – will be represented using 'Harvey Balls'[100] in tables following the discussions. Where there is consistency between the pair of factors examined, a completely shaded 'Harvey Ball' is used to represent this; where there is inconsistency between the pair of factors examined, an unshaded 'Harvey Ball' is used instead. This allows me to consider the extent to which copyright laws remain an effective regulator of content-generative behaviours, and can hence secure compliance from social media users such as Jane.

A. Jane's use of the music video clip on YouTube as her morning alarm

The earlier discussion suggested that Jane's use has infringed copyright laws in the UK and in Australia, but not in the US.[101] Further, her use is licensed under the YouTube Terms.[102] Where there is copyright infringement (ie, under the *UK Copyright Act* and the *Australian Copyright Act*) and yet Jane has not acted in breach of the relevant TOS, the copyright regimes and the TOS are inconsistent. Therefore unshaded circles are used to represent these inconsistencies between the respective copyright regimes and the TOS. With respect to the copyright regime in the US, as against the TOS, a shaded circle is used to represent the consistency.

Although the YouTube platform allows Jane to download the video clip, she needs to use an external application on her mobile device to play the video clip as her alarm.[103] Where there is copyright infringement and Jane's use is not enabled by the relevant platform, the copyright regimes and the technological features are consistent. Here shaded circles represent these consistencies with respect to each of the *UK Copyright Act* and the *Australian Copyright Act*, and to the technological features. On the other hand an unshaded circle represents the inconsistency between the copyright regime in the US, as against the technological features.

The TOS and the technological features are inconsistent. Jane's use, although licensed under the YouTube Terms, is not enabled solely by YouTube's technological features. An unshaded circle represents this inconsistency.

Similar representations for the consistencies and inconsistencies of the regulatory signals given by each of copyright laws, the TOS and the technological features will be adopted in respect of the other content-generative activities set out below.

Table 5.1 Consistency table 1

Regulatory factors		**Consistency**
Copyright: TOS	US	●
	UK	○
	Australia	○
Copyright: Technological features	US	○
	UK	●
	Australia	●
TOS: Technological features		○

B. Jane's 'pinning' of the YouTube music video clip on her pin-board titled 'My Favourite Things' on Pinterest

The earlier discussion indicated that Jane's use has infringed copyright laws in the US, the UK and Australia.[104] Further, her use is licensed under the YouTube Terms.[105] Because there is copyright infringement in all three jurisdictions, although there is no breach of the relevant TOS, the copyright regimes are inconsistent with the TOS in all three instances.

The 'pin' option on Pinterest has enabled Jane to share the video clip with other users on this platform. Moreover, YouTube provides social plug-ins that enable Jane's sharing of the video clip directly on other platforms, including Pinterest.[106] Where there is copyright infringement and yet Jane's use is enabled on the relevant platforms, the copyright regimes and the technological features are inconsistent. There are hence inconsistencies across all three jurisdictions.

The TOS and the technological features are consistent. Jane's use, licensed under the YouTube Terms, is also enabled by the technological features on Pinterest and YouTube.

Table 5.2 Consistency table 2

Regulatory factors		Consistency
Copyright: TOS	US	○
	UK	○
	Australia	○
Copyright: Technological features	US	○
	UK	○
	Australia	○
TOS: Technological features		●

C. Jane's use of Evangeline's earlier commentary on Facebook to create her own commentary

The earlier discussion suggested that Jane's use has infringed copyright laws in the UK and in Australia, but not in the US.[107] Further, her use is likely to be licensed under the Facebook Statement.[108] Where there is copyright infringement (ie, under the *UK Copyright Act* and the *Australian Copyright Act*) and yet Jane has not breached the relevant TOS, the respective copyright regimes and the TOS are inconsistent. However, the copyright regime in the US is consistent with the TOS.

Jane has to use external tools, such as the 'copy and paste' function on her operating system, before she can weave her comments into

Evangeline's commentary and share the new commentary using the function on Facebook to post the 'status update'.[109] Where there is copyright infringement and Jane's use requires external tools on the relevant platform, the copyright regimes and the technological features are consistent. While the UK and Australian copyright regimes are hence consistent with the technological features, the US copyright regime is inconsistent.

The TOS and the technological features are inconsistent. Jane's use, although licensed under the Facebook Statement, is not one enabled solely by the technological features on Facebook.

Table 5.3 Consistency table 3

Regulatory factors		Consistency
Copyright: TOS	US	●
	UK	○
	Australia	○
Copyright: Technological features	US	○
	UK	●
	Australia	●
TOS: Technological features		○

D. Jane's use of multiple photographs of newborn babies available on the pin-boards of other Pinterest users to create a collage to share on Pinterest

Based on the earlier discussion, Jane's use has infringed copyright laws in Australia, but not in the US and the UK.[110] Further, her use is licensed under the Pinterest Terms.[111] Where there is copyright infringement (ie, under the *Australian Copyright Act*) and yet Jane has not acted in breach of the relevant TOS, the copyright regime and the TOS are inconsistent. However, each of the copyright regimes in the US and the UK is consistent with the TOS.

Jane has to use external tools, such as the 'save image as' function on her web browser, as well as image editing tools, before she can create and share her collage on Pinterest.[112] Where there is copyright infringement and Jane's use requires external tools on the relevant platform, the copyright regime and the technological features are consistent. While the Australian copyright regime is hence consistent with the technological features, the US and the UK copyright regimes are inconsistent.

The TOS and the technological features are inconsistent. Jane's use is licensed under the Pinterest Terms, but is not enabled solely by the technological features on Pinterest.

Table 5.4 Consistency table 4

Regulatory factors		Consistency
Copyright: TOS	US	•
	UK	•
	Australia	○
Copyright: Technological features	US	○
	UK	○
	Australia	•
TOS: Technological features		○

E. Jane's simultaneous sharing of the collage on Facebook and Twitter

For the same reasons as under sub-section (D), Jane's use has infringed copyright laws in Australia, but not in the US and the UK.[113] Further, her use is licensed under each of the Pinterest Terms, the Facebook Statement and the Twitter Terms.[114] Where there is copyright infringement (ie, under the *Australian Copyright Act*) and yet Jane has not acted in breach of the relevant TOS, the copyright regime and the TOS are inconsistent. However, each of the copyright regimes in the US and the UK is consistent with the TOS.

Jane is enabled by the social plug-ins on the Pinterest platform to share a 'pin' directly on Facebook and Twitter.[115] Where there is copyright infringement and Jane's use is enabled on the relevant platform, the copyright regime and the technological features are inconsistent. While the Australian copyright regime is hence inconsistent with the technological features, the US and the UK copyright regimes are consistent.

The TOS and the technological features are consistent. Jane's use, licensed under each of the relevant TOS, is also enabled solely by the technological features on Pinterest.

Table 5.5 Consistency table 5

Regulatory factors		Consistency
Copyright: TOS	US	•
	UK	•
	Australia	○
Copyright: Technological features	US	•
	UK	•
	Australia	○
TOS: Technological features		•

F. Jane's use of the same collage in her blog post on WordPress

For the same reasons as under sub-section (D), Jane's use has infringed copyright laws in Australia, but not in the US and the UK.[116] Further, her use is not licensed under the Pinterest Terms and WordPress's TOS.[117] Where there is copyright infringement (ie, under the *Australian Copyright Act*) and Jane has breached the relevant TOS, the copyright regime and the TOS are consistent. However, each of the copyright regimes in the US and the UK is inconsistent with the TOS.

Jane's use (ie, the attaching of the collage to her blog post) is enabled by the technological features on WordPress.[118] Where there is copyright infringement and yet Jane's use is enabled on the relevant platform, the copyright regime and the technological features are inconsistent. While the Australian copyright regime is hence inconsistent with the technological features, the US and the UK copyright regimes are consistent.

The TOS and the technological features are inconsistent. Although Jane's use is not licensed under the Pinterest Terms and WordPress's TOS, it is enabled solely by the technological features on WordPress.

Table 5.6 Consistency table 6

Regulatory factors		**Consistency**
Copyright: TOS	US	○
	UK	○
	Australia	●
Copyright: Technological features	US	●
	UK	●
	Australia	○
TOS: Technological features		○

G. Zee's contribution to Wikipedia on 'income inequality' using what Jane has written

Based on the earlier discussion, Zee's use has infringed copyright laws in the UK and in Australia, but not in the US.[119] Further, his use is likely to be licensed under the Facebook Statement and the Wikipedia Terms.[120] Where there is copyright infringement (ie, under the *UK Copyright Act* and the *Australian Copyright Act*) and yet Zee has not breached the relevant TOS, the respective copyright regime and the TOS are inconsistent. However, the copyright regime in the US is consistent with the TOS.

Zee's contribution of content is enabled by the technological features on Wikipedia.[121] Where there is copyright infringement and yet Zee's use is enabled on the relevant platform, the copyright regime and the technological features are inconsistent. While the UK and Australian copyright regimes are hence inconsistent with the technological features, the US copyright regime is consistent.

The TOS and the technological features are consistent. Zee's use, licensed under both the Facebook Statement and the Wikipedia Terms, is also enabled solely by the technological features on Wikipedia.

Table 5.7 Consistency table 7

Regulatory factors		Consistency
Copyright: TOS	US	●
	UK	○
	Australia	○
Copyright: Technological features	US	●
	UK	○
	Australia	○
TOS: Technological features		●

H. Jane's creation and sharing of a new video clip by way of 'vidding' on YouTube, and subsequently on Facebook

The earlier discussion indicated that Jane's use has infringed laws in the US and Australia, but not in the UK.[122] Further, her use is not licensed under the YouTube Terms and the Facebook Statement.[123] Where there is copyright infringement (ie, under the *US Copyright Act* and the *Australian Copyright Act*) and Jane has breached the relevant TOS, the copyright regimes and the TOS are consistent. However, the copyright regime in the UK is inconsistent with the TOS.

Jane's 'vidding' and sharing of the new video clip on YouTube and Facebook are enabled solely by the technological features on both platforms.[124] Where there is copyright infringement and the use is enabled on the relevant platform, the copyright regime and the technological features are inconsistent. While the US and Australian copyright regimes are hence inconsistent with the technological features, the UK copyright regime is consistent.

The TOS and the technological features are inconsistent. Jane's use, unlicensed under the YouTube Terms and the Facebook Statement, is enabled solely by the technological features on YouTube.

Table 5.8 Consistency table 8

Regulatory factors		Consistency
Copyright: TOS	US	•
	UK	○
	Australia	•
Copyright: Technological features	US	○
	UK	•
	Australia	○
TOS: Technological features		○

I. Cheryl's use of 'stills' from Jane's video clip as thumbnail images on her website

The earlier discussion suggested that Cheryl's use has infringed copyright laws in the UK and in Australia, but not in the US.[125] Further, her use is not licensed under the YouTube Terms and possibly not under the TOS of a standard website.[126] Where there is copyright infringement (ie, under the *UK Copyright Act* and the *Australian Copyright Act*) and Cheryl has breached the relevant TOS, the respective copyright regime and the TOS are consistent. However, the copyright regime in the US is inconsistent with the TOS.

Cheryl's use is not enabled solely by the technological features on both platforms.[127] Where there is copyright infringement and Cheryl's use is not enabled on the relevant platform, the copyright regime and the technological features are consistent. While the UK and Australian copyright regimes are hence consistent with the technological features, the US copyright regime is inconsistent.

The TOS and the technological features are consistent. Cheryl's use, unlicensed under the YouTube Terms (and probably also unlicensed under the TOS of a standard website), is not enabled by the technological features on YouTube or on such a website.

Table 5.9 Consistency table 9

Regulatory factors		Consistency
Copyright: TOS	US	○
	UK	•
	Australia	•
Copyright: Technological features	US	○
	UK	•
	Australia	•
TOS: Technological features		•

J. Other users' partial use of Jane's collage to create their own, then sharing the same on Pinterest, Facebook and Twitter

Based on the earlier discussion, these uses have infringed copyright laws in Australia, but not in the US and the UK.[128] Further, such uses are not licensed under each of the Pinterest Terms, the Facebook Statement and the Twitter Terms.[129] Where there is copyright infringement (ie, under the *Australian Copyright Act*) and these users have breached the relevant TOS, the copyright regime and the TOS are consistent. However, each of the copyright regimes in the US and the UK is inconsistent with the TOS.

The users have to use external tools, such as the 'save image as' function on their web browsers and other image editing tools, to download and modify Jane's collage to create versions of their own.[130] Where there is copyright infringement and such uses require external tools on the relevant platforms, the copyright regime and the technological features are consistent. While the Australian copyright regime is hence consistent with the technological features, the US and the UK copyright regimes are inconsistent.

The TOS and the technological features are consistent. The uses which are not licensed under the TOS of all three platforms are similarly not enabled by the technological features on the platforms.

Table 5.10 Consistency table 10

Regulatory factors		Consistency
Copyright: TOS	US	○
	UK	○
	Australia	●
Copyright: Technological features	US	○
	UK	○
	Australia	●
TOS: Technological features		●

K. Editor Jasper's use of Jane's collage on the cover page of his magazine

The earlier discussion suggested that Jasper's use has infringed copyright laws in the US, the UK and Australia.[131] Further, his use is not licensed under the Pinterest Terms, the Facebook Statement or the Twitter Terms, as the case may be.[132] Because there is copyright infringement in all three jurisdictions, where the relevant TOS are also breached, the copyright regime is consistent with the TOS in each of the three instances.

Jasper has to use external tools, such as the 'save image as' function on his web browser, if he downloaded the collage from the Pinterest and Twitter platforms. Even if Jasper downloaded the collage from the Facebook platform, he will have to rely on external tools to edit Jane's collage for use on his magazine cover.[133] Where there is copyright infringement and Jasper's use requires the adoption of external tools, the copyright regimes and the technological features are consistent. There are hence consistencies across all three jurisdictions.

The TOS and the technological features are consistent. Jasper's use, which is not permitted under the TOS of all three platforms, is also not enabled by their technological features.

Table 5.11 Consistency table 11

Regulatory factors		Consistency
Copyright: TOS	US	•
	UK	•
	Australia	•
Copyright: Technological features	US	•
	UK	•
	Australia	•
TOS: Technological features		•

L. Concluding observations

The following table, with reference to the tables above, summarises the number of instances – out of a total of eleven content-generative activities selected for consideration from the case study – where the regulatory signals given by each of copyright laws, the TOS and the technological features to users are assessed to be consistent, vis-à-vis the other regulatory factor concerned. While each shaded circle is counted as one instance of consistency, each unshaded circle is counted as one instance of inconsistency.

To explain further, in relation to the US copyright regime and the TOS, seven out of a total of eleven of the instances examined are consistent.[134] This figure is indicated in the relevant cell under the second main column below, as are the relevant figures in the respective rows.

Given that the consistency of copyright laws with each of the TOS and the technological features is considered across all three jurisdictions, the number of instances where the regulatory factors are consistent (ie, in relation to copyright laws vis-à-vis the TOS, and copyright laws vis-à-vis

Table 5.12 Summary of consistency tables

Regulatory factors		Consistency	Average consistency[i]
Copyright: TOS	US	7.0	5.3
	UK	4.0	
	Australia	5.0	
Copyright: Technological features	US	4.0	5.7
	UK	7.0	
	Australia	6.0	
TOS: Technological features		6.0	6.0

i. The actual figures are rounded up or down to one decimal place.

the technological features) has to be divided by the figure of three. This will ensure that the figure provided in the first two rows of the last main column is the equivalent of the figure provided in the last row (ie, where the pair of regulatory factors evaluated comprises the TOS and the technological features).

Each of the figures given in this last main column is given over a total of eleven content-generative activities. As such, the average number of instances where a pair of regulatory factors acts inconsistently can be easily calculated. For example, if there is an average of 5.3 instances where the factors act consistently (ie, in evaluating copyright laws and the TOS), there is a corresponding average of 5.7 instances (out of eleven) where these factors act inconsistently.

I observe that the regulatory factors in the three pairs are inconsistent in just slightly under half out of the total number of instances considered,[135] and argue that this exposes users to mixed signals regarding the activities that are legitimate on social media.

III. Regulation of content-generative behaviours by copyright laws

In this section I question whether copyright laws can effectively regulate content-generative behaviours of social media users by relating the earlier analyses to the observations made under scenario four. I note that:

(i) Because perceptions have a bigger impact on users' compliance with such laws than an awareness of copyright laws does, and *further*, as the technological features shape users' perceptions of copyright laws, these features could play a more important role either than copyright laws per se or the TOS in securing the compliance of users with these laws.[136] Such compliance is therefore achieved when users are unable to undertake potentially copyright-infringing activities on social media as the features are self-executing.

This is consistent with the general observation drawn from scenario four that the technological features are a significant contributor of mixed signals on social media platforms.[137] These signals confuse users regarding the activities that are legitimate on such platforms under copyright laws.

(ii) Users, including social media users, are inclined towards claiming to know more about copyright laws than they actually do. Their objective levels of awareness of copyright laws – in particular, how these laws apply to their specific activities – is typically low.[138]

In this respect Chapter Two has demonstrated,[139] through its discussion of the application of copyright subsistence and infringement rules and the challenges posed to the content-generative activities on social media, why it is not possible for regular social media users to have the level of understanding of copyright laws required to know how they apply to the activities such users undertake. Moreover, conflict of laws issues have to be resolved to ascertain which laws apply to questions of subsistence and infringement of copyright,[140] in a copyright-related dispute around content on social media. Further, scenario one[141] has shown that the application of the copyright laws of the three selected jurisdictions – the US, the UK and Australia – to the same content-generative activities under the case study can lead to differing conclusions. This book cannot determine with finality, even with reference to the relevant legislation and cases under scenario one, how the copyright subsistence and infringement issues will be resolved. In particular, where copyright infringement is found at first appearance on the facts given, there remains great uncertainty as to whether any exceptions to copyright laws apply.[142] The purpose of scenario one is instead to provide a general overview of the interaction between copyright laws and the generation of content in the social media context.

(iii) The TOS and the technological features foster the conflicting expectations in 'copyright holders' and users,[143] as discussed in Part II. The provisions of the TOS which are incompatible with the copyright regime have the potential to encourage 'copyright holders' to overreach their rights under copyright laws, as they concurrently mislead social media users to think that their uses of copyright-protected content are licensed. In this case, the expectation of the 'copyright holder' contradicts that of a user on social media. In respect of the technological features, the notice and takedown mechanisms and the Content Id system available to copyright holders facilitate 'copyright holders' in requesting the removal of content – and incidentally in permitting them to make claims that go beyond their legal entitlements. On the other hand, different technological features that make it easy for users to generate content serve to reinforce their expectation that digital content available on social media is free.[144] A user's expectation that content is free varies from the actual practices of a 'copyright holder' on social media. These expectations, whether fostered by the TOS, the technological features or in some other way, will be generally discussed as conflicting expectations.

This is consistent with the general observation drawn from scenario four that users are at the receiving end of mixed signals as to the content-generative activities that are legitimate on social media platforms under copyright laws.

In light of the above, copyright laws appear to play a limited role in regulating the content-generative activities of users and in securing their compliance. This is due to the environment of mixed signals and conflicting expectations in which users on social media platforms are immersed. Such a situation can have the effect of pulling users in different directions regarding whether they should engage in specific activities on these platforms. In this respect the technological features on social media platforms make a significant contribution to the mixed signals to which users are subject, and henceforth to influencing content-generative behaviours.

IV. Conclusion

In this chapter I have highlighted the findings from prior empirical studies that can illuminate the perceptions and awareness of copyright laws in users of social media platforms. I have analysed these findings together with the arguments made in Chapters Two, Three and Four. Pursuant to these analyses I have argued that the low levels of awareness of copyright laws in people generally are amplified in social media users. This is due to the combined effect of the inadequacy of copyright rules to which social media users can relate and the complex rules that copyright laws comprise – as well as the need to address the multiple issues set out in Chapter Two[145] to ascertain whether content-generative activities are indeed copyright infringing.

With scenario four, I have shown that the regulating factors of copyright laws, the TOS and the technological features apply inconsistently – in relation to slightly under half of the eleven content-generative activities considered from the case study. Users are exposed to mixed signals regarding the activities that are legitimate on social media platforms.

In relation to the TOS's effect on users' awareness of copyright laws, I have argued that the TOS foster conflicting expectations in 'copyright holders' and users. While 'copyright holders' expect that the content they generate on social media is copyright protected, users may expect that their content-generative activities are licensed under the TOS. The understandings of copyright laws that the TOS appear to embody – in particular as a result of the latter's potential compatibilities with the copyright regime set out in Chapter Three[146] – give rise to these expectations that contribute to users' poor awareness of copyright laws. Similarly, in relation to the influence of the technological features on users' perceptions of copyright laws, I have argued further that the technological features foster conflicting expectations in both 'copyright holders' and users. On the one hand, the availability of the notice and takedown mechanisms and filtering systems (such as the Content Id system on YouTube) facilitate 'copyright holders' in making their requests for content to be removed – whether under the *DMCA* or otherwise – and concurrently allow them to make claims that go beyond their proper entitlements under copyright laws. On the other hand, the encouragement of content-generative activities (ie, the creation, modification and dissemination of content) by the technological features identified in Chapter Four to be incompatible with the copyright regime,[147] as well as the overall 'generativity' of social media, reinforce the expectation of users that digital content is free and can be readily used.

With reference to the concept of 'nudging'[148] that I have adapted for the purpose of this book, many users appear to assume that the content-generative activities they are 'nudged' to undertake on social media platforms are legitimate and will not attract liabilities under copyright laws. These expectations of users vary from the actual practices of 'copyright holders'. Such conflicting expectations can contribute to users' negative perceptions of copyright laws – that copyright laws are illegitimate for being unreasonable, outdated and irrelevant. At the same time, the significant influence of the technological features on users' compliance with copyright laws when they generate content is reinforced by the fact that their impact is analogised to the application of bright-line rules, in contrast to the impact of the principles-based TOS (which also requires one to refer back to copyright laws) and the complex, rules-based copyright laws.

In view of the environment of mixed signals and conflicting expectations in which users on social media platforms are immersed, I question if it is unfair for users to be widely exposed to the risks of copyright infringement for the content-generative activities they undertake on these platforms. Further, given the significance of the technological features in influencing content-generative behaviours and their overall 'nudging' and encouragement of users to engage in the creation, modification and dissemination of content, the vulnerability of users to the risks of copyright infringement for the activities they engage in on social media needs to be given more consideration by legislators and policy makers. Users should not be expected to behave counter-intuitively (ie, against the direction of the 'nudges') on social media platforms to avoid the risks of copyright infringement altogether, while those platforms that wield great influence over their users' content-generative behaviours are afforded the shelter of safe harbour legislation.[149]

Notes

1. Part II of Chapter Two.
2. Part II of Chapter Three.
3. Part II of Chapter Four.
4. See Tom R. Tyler, *Why People Obey the Law* (Yale University Press, 1990) 61.
5. This study assesses EU citizens' perceptions of intellectual property, with the aim of extracting evidence that can be used to communicate the positive aspects of intellectual property to the public. In its quantitative stage, over 26,500 of EU citizens expressed their views through a questionnaire given on the telephone. The study was conducted in acknowledgement of European efforts to preserve the integrity and respect of intellectual property rights. Respondents of the study were asked to give true or false as an answer to seven statements about how intellectual property works. These statements were designed to assess a general understanding of the basic intellectual property concepts by members of the general public, and do not necessarily reflect specific legal provisions. See Office for Harmonization in the Internal Market, *The European Citizens and Intellectual Property: Perception, Awareness and Behaviour* (November 2013) <https://oami.europa.eu/tunnel-web/secure/webdav/guest/document_library/observatory/documents/IPContributionStudy/25-11-2013/european_public_opinion_study_web.pdf>.
6. Fifty-one per cent of the respondents displayed moderate knowledge and thirty-seven per cent of the respondents displayed poor knowledge. See Office for Harmonization in the Internal Market 2013.
7. This is a larger percentage of respondents than the percentages of respondents who claim to have a good understanding of the more general term 'intellectual property' and the term 'patent'.
8. Office for Harmonization in the Internal Market 2013.
9. Office for Harmonization in the Internal Market 2013.

10. A larger percentage of those surveyed aged between 15 and 24 years old (ie, 57 per cent) similarly considers it acceptable. Further, the reference to personal use in the survey is to be distinguished from making a personal copy of something a person legally acquires for private use – this will be introduced as a new s 28B to the *UK Copyright Act*. See Office for Harmonization in the Internal Market 2013; *UK Copyright Regulations 2014*, reg 3.
11. Office for Harmonization in the Internal Market 2013.
12. See Nina Paley's response to a question in Jessica Edmundson and Elizabeth Townsend Gard, 'Conversations with Renowned Professors and Practitioners on the Future of Copyright' (2011) 14 *Tulane Journal of Technology and Intellectual Property* 1, 58–9. Nina Paley states that artists are emotional about how copyright laws protect their intellectual property rights, although they have little understanding of how copyright laws actually work.
13. The qualitative research involved more than 100 hours of conversations with 250 EU citizens from nine countries. See Office for Harmonization in the Internal Market 2013.
14. The study also drew on earlier surveys conducted, one of which was a survey conducted through face-to-face interviews with 2,026 British consumers in 2009. Of the respondents surveyed, 73 per cent agreed that they were confused about copyright laws and can never be sure what is legal and illegal under current copyright laws. Sixteen per cent of the respondents neither agreed nor disagreed with the statement, and only ten per cent of those surveyed expressed their disagreement. For example, although format shifting is illegal under UK copyright legislation, only up to 26 per cent of the respondents thought so. See Consumer Focus, *Time to change the tune: Consumer research briefing on copyright* (February 2010) <http://www.consumerfocus.org.uk/assets/1/files/2010/02/Consumer-Focus-Time-to-change-the-tune1.pdf>. See also Office for Harmonization in the Internal Market 2013.
15. Office for Harmonization in the Internal Market 2013.
16. The Center is an independent not-for-profit research institute. See, for example, Pew Research Center, *About Pew Research Center* <http://www.pewresearch.org/about/>.
17. This survey was conducted to understand how arts organisations are using the internet, social media and other digital technologies to share content, communicate with patrons and manage their organisational objectives. See Pew Research Internet Project, *Arts Organizations and Digital Technologies: Section 6: Overall Impact of Technology on the Arts* <http://www.pewinternet.org/2013/01/04/section-6-overall-impact-of-technology-on-the-arts/>.
18. This expectation arises as geographical constraints previously encountered in accessing content are extinguished by technological advances. As such, content can now be shared online at a lower cost. See Pew Research Internet Project 2013.
19. YouGov is an international internet-based research firm. See, for example, Wikipedia, *YouGov* <https://en.wikipedia.org/wiki/YouGov>; YouGov UK, *About* <https://yougov.co.uk/about/about/>.
20. For this report, the survey drew on a sample of 1907 young adults aged 16 to 24 years old and 614 children aged 8 to 15 years old. These children and young adults were asked over 40 questions in relation to topics including their reasons for using file-sharing websites, their attitudes towards paying for digital content as well as piracy, and so on. See YouGov, *Digital content should be free say younger online users* <https://yougov.co.uk/news/2014/06/19/digital-content-should-be-free-say-younger-online-/>.
21. YouGov 2014.
22. Online services that are offered for free, including YouTube, Spotify, Blinkbox, etc, and that are supported by advertisements tend to be popular with the group of young adults of 16 to 24 years old interviewed. In the report cost was noted to be the major factor influencing children and young adults in their decision to continue to use file-sharing websites – 51 per cent of young adults and 44 per cent of children use file-sharing services to save money. See YouGov 2014.
23. YouGov 2014.
24. YouGov 2014.
25. YouGov 2014.
26. This is a statutory board under the Ministry of Law, Singapore. See, for example, Intellectual Property of Singapore, *What Do We Do?* <https://www.ipos.gov.sg/AboutUs/WhatDoWeDo.aspx>.
27. This study was conducted with the objective of measuring the awareness, attitudes and behavioural dispositions of users in Singapore towards intellectual property rights and related issues. The survey was conducted through face-to-face interviews with 1,002 Singapore

citizens and permanent residents. Of the respondents, 54.9 per cent viewed downloading from unauthorised sources as a form of theft in 2014 (as compared to 77.8 per cent of the respondents in 2010); and 49.2 per cent of the respondents viewed unauthorised file sharing as a form of theft in 2014 (as compared to 77.5 per cent of the respondents in 2010). See Intellectual Property Office of Singapore, *Annex A: IP Perception Survey Summary Report 2014* <https://www.ipos.gov.sg/Portals/0/Press%20Release/Annex%20A%20Perception%20Survey.pdf>.

28. In 2014, 81.7 per cent of interviewees were aware that the infringements of intellectual property rights could give rise to legal penalties, and 82.3 per cent of interviewees agreed that the works of intellectual property creators deserve to be protected. See Intellectual Property Office of Singapore 2014.
29. The 20 questions in the questionnaire the students were asked to complete asked them about their file-sharing activities and factors that deter them from engaging in such activities. Independent variables include perceived certainty of punishment, perceived stigma, awareness of and consensus with the laws; dependent variables include the frequency of current file-sharing activities and the likelihood of engaging in future file-sharing activities. See Xigen Li and Nico Nergadze, 'Deterrence Effect of Four Legal and Extralegal Factors on Online Copyright Infringement' (2009) *Journal of Computer-Mediated Communication* 307, 320.
30. Li, X. and Nergadze, N. 2009, 315.
31. See generally Tyler, T. R. 1990, 57.
32. The effectiveness of laws in regulating targeted behaviours to reach the desired outcomes depends on their ability to secure voluntary compliance from the regulated actors. This reference to laws includes criminal laws such as traffic laws, drug laws, gambling laws and alcohol laws. See Tyler, T. R. 1990, 57.
33. See Li, X. and Nergadze, N. 2009, 315.
34. See, for example, Jessica Silbey, *The Eureka Myth: Creators, Innovators, and Everyday Intellectual Property* (Stanford University Press, 2015) 282. Silbey highlights that practice norms and legal rules are misaligned, and further that an ongoing failure of the intellectual property rules to reflect the existing expectations of its subjects could lead to an undermining of the rule of law.
35. See also Litman, J. 2006, n 10, where an example given is that of copyright holders having the exclusive rights to authorise public performance of their works, and of bars and restaurants needing copyright licences to play the radio, television or recorded music. Many proprietors of small businesses, despite the affordability of the licences, continue to disbelieve the rules and hence do not comply with them. Such proprietors lose suits when they litigate to protect their rights to play the music. After many decades the refusal of these proprietors to acknowledge public performance as an exclusive right finally paid off when an expanded music performance exemption was codified under the *US Copyright Act*, § 110(5)(B). However, the provision has been challenged, in part successfully, by European collecting societies in the World Trade Organisation.
36. See Litman, J. 2006, 71, where Litman discusses the consequences of the 'paucity' of language addressing individual behaviours of consumers under the *US Copyright Act*. See also Ian Hargreaves, *Digital Opportunity: A Review of Intellectual Property and Growth* (May 2011) <https://www.gov.uk/government/uploads/system/uploads/attachment_data/file/32563/ipreview-finalreport.pdf>, where it is recommended that the impacts on consumers and other interests should be taken into account in the development of the intellectual property system (and balanced against the objectives of rights holders); ALRC 2013, which noted that Australian copyright law has traditionally been regarded as focusing on the protection of commercial activities designed to exploit material for profit and that reforms should be made to legalise common consumer practices.
37. Julia Black, 'Forms and Paradoxes of Principles-based Regulation' (2008) 3(4) *Capital Markets Law Journal* 425, 439.
38. A 'bright-line' rule sets out a single criterion – expressed as a quantitative measure – which needs to be satisfied for the rule to apply. Black, J. 2008, 439. See also Julia Black, Martyn Hopper and Christa Band, 'Making a Success of Principles-based Regulation' (May 2007) *Law and Financial Markets Review* 191, 194–5.
39. A principle expresses the aim of the rule, and is focused on the substantive objective. Black, J., Hopper, M. and Band, C. 2007, 194–5.

40. A complex rule is detailed and lists conditions that have to be met for the rule to apply. Black, J., Hopper, M. and Band, C. 2007, 194–5.
41. Black has argued that uncertainty arises from the interpretation of a rule, rather than its structure per se. See Black, J. 2008, 440.
42. Part I of Chapter Two.
43. See *US Copyright Act*, §§ 102 (a) and 103; *UK Copyright Act*, s 1(1); *Australian Copyright Act*, ss 32, 89–92.
44. Part I of Chapter Two, sub-section A.
45. See *US Copyright Act*, § 102(a); *UK Copyright Act*, s 1(1); *Australian Copyright Act*, ss 32(1) and 32(2).
46. Part I of Chapter Two, sub-section B.
47. See Ricketson, S. 2012.
48. See *US Copyright Act*, §§ 201(a) and 101; *UK Copyright Act*, ss 9(1) and 10(1); *Australian Copyright Act*, s 10. See also Part I of Chapter Two, sub-section C.
49. See Ricketson, S. 2012.
50. *US Copyright Act*, §§ 101 and 102.
51. *UK Copyright Act*, ss 3(1), 4, 5A and 5B. See also Part I of Chapter Two, sub-section D.
52. *Australian Copyright Act*, ss 10 and 22(1). See also Part I of Chapter Two, sub-section D.
53. See *US Copyright Act*, § 106(1); *UK Copyright Act*, s 16(1); *Australian Copyright Act*, ss 31(1)(a)(i) and 31(1)(b)(i). See also Part I of Chapter Two, sub-section E.
54. See *US Copyright Act*, § 106(2); *UK Copyright Act*, s 16(1); *Australian Copyright Act*, s 31(1)(a)(vi). See also Part I of Chapter Two, sub-section E.
55. See *US Copyright Act*, § 106 (3); *UK Copyright Act*, s 16(1); *Australian Copyright Act*, ss 31(1)(a)(ii) and 31(1)(b)(ii). See also Part I of Chapter Two, sub-section E.
56. See *US Copyright Act*, §§ 106(4)–(6); *UK Copyright Act*, s 16(1); *Australian Copyright Act*, ss 31(1)(a)(vi), 31(1)(a)(iv) and 31(1)(b)(iii). See also Part I of Chapter Two, sub-section E.
57. See *VARA*, § 106A; *UK Copyright Act*, ss 77, 80(1) and 80(2); *Australian Copyright Act*, Part IX, Divisions 2–4. See also Part I of Chapter Two, sub-section F.
58. See *DMCA*, § 1202(b)(1); *UK Copyright Act*, s 296ZG(1); *Australian Copyright Act*, s 116B. See also Part I of Chapter Two, sub-section F.
59. *US Copyright Act*, § 411.
60. See *UK Copyright Act*, s 97(1); *Australian Copyright Act*, s 115(3). See also Part I of Chapter Two, sub-section G.
61. *US Copyright Act*, § 107.
62. See *UK Copyright Act*, ss 29, 30 and 30A; *Australian Copyright Act*, ss 40, 41, 41A, 42, 103A, 103AA, 103B and 103C. See also Part I of Chapter Two, sub-section H.
63. See scenario one in Part II of Chapter Two, where the separate application of copyright laws of the three jurisdictions, to nine out of eleven of the content-generative activities under the case study, results in the arrival at contrasting positions on the copyright liabilities of the users concerned.
64. Part III of Chapter Three, sub-section B3.
65. These refer to the nature of copyright rules, the copyright subsistence and infringement issues to address and the challenges posed by conflict of laws issues.
66. Part III of Chapter Three.
67. Parts III and IV of Chapter Three.
68. The *US Copyright Act*. See also n 647.
69. Part III of Chapter Three, sub-section A.
70. See also Part I of Chapter III, sub-section B.
71. *DMCA*, § 512(c). See also Part III of Chapter Three, sub-section A.
72. It is noted, however, that a large number of users do not read or understand the implications of standard form contracts, such as the terms of use of social media platforms – in spite of their agreement to accept these terms before using the relevant services. See, for example, Natalie Helberger et al, 'Digital Content Contracts for Consumers' (2013) *Journal of Consumer Policy* 37, 50; Rory Cellan-Jones, *Social media told to simplify terms and conditions* (28 November 2014) <http://www.bbc.com/news/technology-30234789>.
73. Part III of Chapter Three, sub-section B.
74. Part I of the Introduction.
75. See *US Copyright Act*, § 102(a); *UK Copyright Act*, s 1(1); *Australian Copyright Act*, ss 32(1) and 32(2). See also Part I of Chapter Two, sub-section B.

76. See *US Copyright Act*, §101; *UK Copyright Act*, ss 3(1), 4, 5A and 5B; *Australian Copyright Act*, ss 10 and 22(1). See also Part I of Chapter Two, sub-section D.
77. Part III of Chapter Three, sub-section B2. See also Part I of Chapter Three, sub-section A.
78. See, for example, Jason Mazzone, *Copyfraud and Other Abuses of Intellectual Property Law* (Stanford University Press, 2011) 13.
79. Part III of Chapter Three, sub-section B2.
80. Black, J. 2008. See also Black, J., Hopper, M. and Band, C. 2007, 194–5.
81. Part III of Chapter Four.
82. Zittrain, J. 2006.
83. Part III of Chapter Four.
84. Part I of Chapter Four, sub-section B1.
85. Part I of Chapter Four, sub-section B3.
86. Part I of Chapter Four, sub-section B4.
87. Part III of Chapter Four, sub-section A.
88. In this sense, these technological features are neutral tools that users, in exercise of their autonomy, can decide to adopt for different purposes. This brings to mind the instrumental theory of technology, where technology is seen here as being neutral in its impact on human affairs. The emphasis here is on human autonomy and the decisions made by users to adopt technology. See, for example, Andrew Feenberg, *Between Reason and Experience: Essays in Technology and Modernity* (The MIT Press, 2010).
89. Part III of Chapter Four, sub-sections B and C.
90. See, for example, Mazzone, J. 2011.
91. Mazzone, J. 2011.
92. Parts I and III of Chapter Four.
93. YouGov 2014.
94. See Thaler, R. and Sunstein, C. 2008.
95. Sub-sections B and C.
96. This is the first type of rules referred to in Black, J. 2008. See also Black, J., Hopper, M. and Band, C. 2007.
97. Part III of Chapter Four.
98. Part III of Chapter Four, sub-sections B and C.
99. See Li, X. and Nergadze, N. 2009, 315. See also Part I, sub-section A3.
100. Wikipedia, *Harvey Balls* <https://en.wikipedia.org/wiki/Harvey_Balls>. 'Harvey Balls', or circles used to communicate qualitative information, including the degree to which a particular criterion is met, are appropriate for this purpose.
101. Part II of Chapter Two, sub-section A.
102. Part II of Chapter Three, sub-section A.
103. Part II of Chapter Four, sub-section A.
104. Part II of Chapter Two, sub-section B.
105. Part II of Chapter Three, sub-section B.
106. Part II of Chapter Four, sub-section B.
107. Part II of Chapter Two, sub-section C.
108. Part II of Chapter Three, sub-section C.
109. Part II of Chapter Four, sub-section C.
110. Part II of Chapter Two, sub-section D.
111. Part II of Chapter Three, sub-section D.
112. Part II of Chapter Four, sub-section D.
113. Part II of Chapter Two, sub-section E.
114. Part II of Chapter Three, sub-section E.
115. Part II of Chapter Four, sub-section E.
116. Part II of Chapter Two, sub-section F.
117. Part II of Chapter Three, sub-section F.
118. Part II of Chapter Four, sub-section F.
119. Part II of Chapter Two, sub-section G.
120. Part II of Chapter Three, sub-section G.
121. Part II of Chapter Four, sub-section G.
122. Part II of Chapter Two, sub-section H.
123. Part II of Chapter Three, sub-section H.
124. Part II of Chapter Four, sub-section H.

125. Part II of Chapter Two, sub-section I.
126. Part II of Chapter Three, sub-section I.
127. Part II of Chapter Four, sub-section I.
128. Part II of Chapter Two, sub-section J.
129. Part II of Chapter Three, sub-section J.
130. Part II of Chapter Four, sub-section J.
131. Part II of Chapter Two, sub-section K.
132. Part II of Chapter Three, sub-section K.
133. Part II of Chapter Four, sub-section K.
134. This means that there are a total of seven shaded circles counted from the tables above, in respect of the US copyright regime and the terms of use.
135. The average of the figures in the last column (ie, for average consistency) is 5.7. There will be a corresponding average of 5.3 instances (out of 11) where the factors act inconsistently.
136. See, for example, *William John Joseph Hoge v William M Schmalfeldt*, Civ No ELH-14-1683 (USDC Md, 1 July 2014) (*William Hoge*), where the plaintiff blog owner Mr Hoge filed a motion for a preliminary injunction against the defendant retired writer under the *US Copyright Act* and the *DMCA*, alleging that the defendant made infringing uses of his blog posts in books, as well as on internet websites and social media services such as Twitter. Although the judge did not grant the injunction, a point worth noting is that the plaintiff sought, among other things, an injunction against the defendant's use of image capturing in order to quote words presented in a text format as part of anything posted on the internet. The plaintiff's seeking of such an injunction brings to the fore his recognition of the importance of technological features – that a prohibition against using, or the lack of availability of certain technological features, can essentially constrain a person from interacting with the content of another person, and thus from undertaking potentially copyright infringing activities in relation to such content. See also *John Walmsley v Education Limited T/A Oise Cambridge* 2014 WL 2194626 (*Walmsley*), where the court awarded to the plaintiff photographer and author Mr Walmsley licence fees and damages for the breach of his moral rights, due to the defendant educational institution's use of his photographs on the defendant's blog. In delivering the judgement, the judge remarked that the employee of the defendant, Miss Roberts, 'found out how easy it is to copy images by the single click of a mouse, and these do get republished all over the internet, often without attribution'. The judge noted then that this problem of infringement 'can continue and escalate almost logarithmically' with people copying photographs on the internet, many of which are published in breach of the rights of the respective copyright holder. The judge recognised that existing technologies have a large part to play in enabling copyright-infringing activities.
137. There is an average of 5.3 instances in which the technological features act inconsistently with the copyright regimes and 5.0 instances (both out of 11) in which the technological features act inconsistently with the terms of service (TOS). See Part I, sub-section L.
138. See, for example, *North Jersey Media Group Inc v Jeanine Pirro and Fox News Network LLC*, Civ No 13 Civ 7153 (ER) (SDNY, 10 February 2015) (*North Jersey Media*), where the copyright owner (being New Jersey Media Group, the employer of the photojournalist Thomas Franklin) of a photograph taken on 11 September 2001 brought an infringement action against the television news network Fox News and its programme host Jeanine Pirro for juxtaposing the photograph in question with an iconic Second World War photograph and posting this combined image on a Facebook page created for a commentary programme hosted by Miss Pirro. The defendants contended that the sharing of the combined image was exempted under the fair use doctrine and applied for summary judgement. This was denied by the district court. Although the case was recently settled out of court under confidential terms, a point worth noting from the district court's judgment is that, in relation to the defendants' use of the combined image, a Fox News production assistant named Georeen Tanner was principally responsible for managing and posting content to Miss Pirro's Facebook page. Although Miss Tanner had no training in copyright laws, she acknowledged that she understood copyright generally to be 'something that is owned by someone else'. Miss Tanner did not seek legal advice from the Fox News legal department regarding the fair use of the combined images she found randomly using the Google search engine because she did not believe that she needed permission to use the images for the purpose of making a commentary in remembrance of the events of 11 September 2011. As can be seen, Miss

Tanner's actual understanding of how copyright laws are applied to the posting of the combined images in question fell short of her proclaimed general understanding of those laws. See also *Walmsley* 2014 WL 2194626, where the employee of the defendant, Miss Roberts, is an example of a user who has a low level of awareness of copyright laws, and of how these laws apply to her activities.

139. Parts I and III of Chapter Two.
140. Yu, P. K. 2001. See also Part III of Chapter Three, sub-section B3.
141. Part II of Chapter Two.
142. Part I of Chapter Two, sub-section H.
143. See, for example, *William Hoge,* Civ No ELH-14-1683 (USDC Md, 1 July 2014). A point worth noting is the defendant's argument that the plaintiff's blog entries were short and mostly contained information from other sources. The defendant argued that these entries were not creative and hence should not be protected under copyright laws. He further claimed not to have applied for copyright protection for his own works online as he 'rejects the whole idea of suing someone for using inconsequential snippets from another person's blog or Twitter account'. This appears to be reflective of the views of some social media users, who often assume that their content-generative activities will not attract liabilities under copyright laws. On the contrary, other users who are also the creators of content such as the plaintiff believe that their content is copyright protected and entitles them to exclusive rights.
144. See, for example, *Jeanine Pirro*, Civ No 13 Civ 7153 (ER) (SDNY, 10 February 2015), where Miss Tanner appeared to have expected to be able to use the images she extracted from the Google search engine freely.
145. Part I of Chapter Two.
146. Part III of Chapter Three, sub-section B.
147. Part I of Chapter Four, sub-section A.
148. See Thaler, R. and Sunstein, C. 2008.
149. *DMCA*, § 512(c).

Conclusion

In this book I have set out to provide an analysis as to how the content-generative behaviours of social media users are regulated from a copyright perspective. For this purpose I compare copyright laws with other regulatory factors such as the TOS (ie, terms of service) and the technological features on social media platforms. I have selected five social media platforms – namely Facebook, Pinterest, YouTube, Twitter and Wikipedia – for survey in the book. Each of these platforms falls under one of the four (out of six) categories of social media under Kaplan and Haenlein's classification system, being respectively social networking sites, content communities, blogs and collaborative projects.[1] These platforms serve as a good sample to survey how users' compliance with copyright laws can be influenced by the user policies and design choices of the platforms. In this respect, the case study detailing the content-generative activities of Jane Doe and other users on the selected social media platforms acts as an anchor for the discussions on how copyright laws, the TOS and the technological features of social media platforms regulate the content-generative behaviours of users.

I have considered the application of copyright laws to various uses on social media, and how this application is aligned with the TOS and the technological features of the selected social media platforms. In particular, I have examined the copyright laws of the US, the UK and Australia. I have argued that the effectiveness of copyright laws as a regulator of content-generative behaviours is compromised by the uncertainties in the application of copyright laws and variations between those laws in different jurisdictions, as well as by inconsistencies between the application of either of the regulatory factors or the copyright laws.

I recognise that it is important to expand our understanding of how social media platforms can alter – through their TOS and technological features – the effectiveness of the regulation of content-generative behaviours by copyright laws. This is especially so as internet users now spend more time on social media platforms than before.[2] Many users are also observed to engage regularly in behaviours that potentially fall within the scope of copyright infringement.[3] Despite the ubiquity of the use of social media platforms, there is a dearth of rigorous consideration given to how specific social media platforms affect the role laws, including copyright laws, play in securing compliance from their users. Moreover, social media platforms have their unique characteristics and business models that deserve separate analyses.

The conclusions drawn throughout this book highlight the need to address the vulnerability of social media users, widely exposed to the risks of copyright infringement in the content-generative activities that they are 'nudged'[4] to undertake on social media platforms. In particular, in Chapter Two, I demonstrated why it is not possible for any regular social media user to have the level of understanding of copyright laws required to assess the legitimacy of the content-generative activities he or she undertakes, through the application of copyright laws to these activities. In Chapter Three I noted that the TOS are aligned with the copyright regimes to some extent, and argued further that the TOS and the relevant copyright regime reinforce one another when they are in alignment. I also argued that three areas[5] give rise to potential incompatibilities between the TOS and the copyright regimes, and so compromise the effectiveness of copyright laws in regulating the content-generative behaviours of users.

In Chapter Four I argued that the 'generativity'[6] of social media platforms, in part due to their integration of technological features that encourage the creation, modification and dissemination of content, can increase the possibilities for copyright infringement on such platforms. These features can therefore be incompatible with the copyright regimes. On the other hand, I noted that the technological features that constrain content-generative activities limit the opportunities for users to interact with content and can reduce the risks of copyright infringement by users of the platforms. I argued further that although these features are aligned with the copyright regimes, their influence is limited since the constraints experienced by users can easily be overcome with external tools – on balance, the platforms encourage content-generative activities more than they constrain them. In addition, I elaborated on how some of the features that constrain content-generative activities reflect copyright considerations. Finally, in Chapter Five, I argued that users are exposed to mixed signals and conflicting expectations on social media platforms regarding the content-generative activities legitimate on these platforms.

I. Fairness from a user's perspective

A recurring theme throughout the chapters of this book has been the unequal positions of social media platforms and users relative to one another. In particular, while these platforms seek alignment with the copyright regime to secure the availability of the safe harbour provision for themselves,[7] users do not have the same privilege. I have argued that more attention needs to be paid to the vulnerability of users who are exposed to the risks of copyright infringement for the content-generative activities they undertake regularly on these platforms.[8] This is in view of the significance of the technological features in encouraging content-generative behaviours, as well as the environment of mixed signals and conflicting expectations in which users on social media platforms are immersed. Users are pulled in different directions by the examined regulatory factors on social media, with regard to the content-generative activities in which they engage. Further, I have argued that the conflicting expectations adversely shape users' perceptions and awareness of copyright laws in this environment, therefore compromising their effectiveness in securing compliance from users who generate content. These users may not take copyright laws seriously.[9]

Given that social media platforms wield great influence over the content-generative behaviours of their users, it is undesirable that users are widely exposed to the risks of copyright infringement for their everyday engagement in content-generative activities on these platforms. Together with the uncertainties users face in ascertaining how complex copyright rules (including exceptions to such rules) can apply to their content-generative activities on social media, these considerations give rise to the question of whether it is unfair for users to be exposed to the risks of copyright infringement for these activities. This is especially so since most of the social media platforms[10] are operated around advertiser-supported business models made viable by reason of the content generated by users of such platforms. Users receive the shorter end of the (copyright) stick: they face the risks of copyright infringement for the content-generative activities which they are 'nudged' to undertake, and which they believe to be legitimate on the platforms. The question as to whether this is unfair, and how it will be measured, are issues requiring further exploration outside the scope of the book.

II. Why regulating social media matters

This book contributes to the debate in the following ways. Firstly, the research conducted demonstrates the influence the selected five social media platforms could have over users' content-generative behaviours, by virtue of their TOS and technological features. In this respect the book is the first account using the approach it has adopted (ie, in comparing copyright laws with other regulatory factors on social media) to assess how specific social media platforms affect the ability of copyright laws to regulate content-generative behaviours effectively. Secondly, the question of unfairness to users that the book raises in view of its conclusions on the influence of social media can furnish an alternative angle for legislators and policy makers to consider when they reform existing copyright legislation. This will go beyond the usual reference made to balancing the rights of copyright holders and users. A distinction between these two groups is less meaningful on social media, where a copyright holder of any content on social media could also be a user of the content shared by others.

Therefore the specific course of copyright reform to which the book points may lie in expressly providing for the occurrence of content generation on social media as a factor to be considered,[11] *or* as a specific purpose exempt from copyright infringement (as the case may be), under the respective copyright statute.[12] In that event the provision has to be compliant with international obligations under the respective treaties to which the US, the UK and Australia are parties, including the three-step test.[13] In particular, relevant considerations will include the specificity of the provision and whether content-generative activities are seen to constitute a narrow category of cases,[14] as well as whether the content generated through these activities – leading to direct or indirect commercial benefits[15] for the authors of such content on social media – is seen to conflict with normal exploitations of the relevant copyright works.[16]

Copyright reform in this direction will benefit social media users more in jurisdictions such as Australia, in comparison with the US[17] and the UK. As scenario one has shown, seven out of eleven content-generative activities will not infringe the *US Copyright Act*, pursuant to the application of the fair use doctrine.[18] Thus, because of the availability of the doctrine in the US, users are arguably less exposed to the risks of copyright infringement than they are in Australia. Under the *UK Copyright Act*, five out of eleven content-generative activities are probably exempt as fair dealings, by virtue of the application of the new exception for the purpose of caricature, parody or pastiche.[19] In contrast, under the *Australian Copyright Act*, none of the content-generative activities is exempt as a fair dealing.[20]

If the adoption of existing solutions is preferred, jurisdictions such as Australia could consider providing an exception for fair use – this may reduce the exposure of social media users to the risks of copyright infringement.[21] Although the fair use exception in the US has been criticised for its open-ended nature, it has been applied by courts extensively over decades.[22] To this end, the Australian Law Reform Commission has recommended in its report on copyright reform that the fair use exception be introduced as an extension of Australia's existing fair dealing exceptions – as, among other things, the flexible fair use exception would be more responsive to technological changes.[23] This recommendation has been provisionally endorsed by the Productivity Commission.

If fair use is not enacted, an alternative will be to introduce a more specific exception to copyright infringement for UGC (ie, user-generated content) which allows a user to create new content using publicly available copyright works under specific conditions, as in Canada.[24] Although there are some uncertainties brought forth by its qualitative conditions (ie, whether it is *reasonable* in the circumstances to mention the source of a copyright work, and whether a user had *reasonable grounds* to believe that the existing copyright work, or copy of it, does not infringe copyright),[25] such an exception can have the effect of exempting more content-generative activities on social media from copyright infringement than is the case in its absence.[26] Notwithstanding its shortcomings, the exception can provide social media users with the greater peace of mind they need to engage in content-generative activities, unlike the fact-based analyses leading to uncertain applications in many fair dealing scenarios.[27]

In the UK, while no specific exception for UGC has been introduced, the status of UGC was considered in two recent reviews of copyright laws in the UK, both of which recommended the adoption in the UK of new fair dealing exceptions.[28] Following subsequent consultations, copyright law reforms were implemented in 2014, including the introduction of new fair dealing exceptions for the purposes of quotation, as well as for caricature, parody or pastiche.[29] As illustrated under scenario one, some content-generative activities are probably exempt from copyright infringement by virtue of the latter exception (ie, for caricature, parody or pastiche),[30] and in certain limited circumstances might also, or alternatively, benefit from the former (ie, for quotation).[31]

The UK reforms suggest that another alternative to fair use is to expand the fair dealing exception for the purpose of parody or satire in Australia[32] to include pastiche, as in the case of the UK.[33] Arguably, further consideration should also be given to designing an exception for the purpose of quotation which is along the lines of the limited form adopted in the UK.[34] Indeed, a quotation exception appears to be mandated under article 10 of the *Berne Convention*.[35] The introduction of an exception for the purpose of quotation has been explored in Australia.[36] Such an exception, I note, will only exempt social media uses in the limited circumstances that the conditions for its availability are satisfied. This may be difficult for the conditions which relate to the compatibility of the relevant use with fair practice,[37] and to the justification of the extent of the use by its purpose.[38]

While I have highlighted earlier that the condition of availability to the public is not likely to bar an exemption,[39] the last condition (ie, the need to attribute the source and the author)[40] might well in many instances. Nonetheless, my view is that these conditions, including that for attribution in a quotation exception, should remain, since they seemingly reflect fair practices and preferences. As mentioned earlier, social media users like to identify with the content they create.[41] Although I have outlined some approaches to copyright reform that can reduce the risks of copyright infringement to which social media users are exposed, the specific direction copyright reform (whether in Australia or in any other jurisdiction) should take and its implications on content-generative activities on social media fall beyond the scope of this book. Instead, this could be the subject of future research.

Yet another possible solution to address any potential unfairness of exposing social media users to copyright infringement for their content-generative activities is to acknowledge more explicitly the regulatory role of social media platforms. This provides a basis upon which one can call upon these platforms to play their part in ensuring the continuing relevance of laws such as copyright in regulating content-generative behaviours – and additionally in safeguarding users' rights in this digital space. In line with what Elkin-Koren has argued, granting online intermediaries that benefit from the distribution of copyright-protected content immunity from infringement under safe harbour provisions is no longer sufficient to ensure the free flow of information.[42] Because of the risks users face, including the risk of partial enforcement by the online intermediaries themselves,[43] online intermediaries should be subject to duties owed to users to honour the rights of users – among other things, to share and access content.[44]

The first step in this direction will be for social media platforms to take more care in ensuring that the regulatory factors that they design and with which users interact – such as the TOS and the technological features – convey a more consistent message to their users as to the activities that are legitimate on these platforms.[45] Given that such platforms are observed to have a huge influence over the content-generative behaviours of their users, any solution arrived at should see them shoulder a fairer burden of the risks resulting from the business models from which they have selected and benefited.[46] Social media platforms can continue working towards making their TOS more comprehensible for social media users. This may, however, be of limited effect, in view of the fact that many users do not read the TOS.[47] Among the five platforms studied in this book, YouTube makes the most resources on copyright laws available to its users.[48] These resources provide useful information to assist discerning users with navigating the risks of copyright infringement on the YouTube platform.[49]

Another way is to rely on the influence of the technological features as a regulatory factor, and to use these features to prompt users to consider specific copyright issues at suitable junctures when they create, modify or disseminate content on social media.[50] For instance, when a user downloads the video clips of other users on YouTube and creates a new video clip using snippets from each of the downloaded video clips with the video editing tool available to him or her, prompts could be given to the user along with his or her creation of the new video clip, ensuring that the user makes an informed decision when generating content. Beyond prompting users to take copyright issues into account, technological features can potentially be designed to eliminate user autonomy altogether, such that the decision to engage in content-generative activities which can infringe copyright laws no longer lies with the user in question.[51]

The copyright policies incorporating copyright laws such as the *DMCA* can thus be reinforced, in different ways, through the use of smart technologies embodied within the technological features available to users. Adopting such solutions reflects the understanding that users are vulnerable to influence from social media platforms. It also acknowledges that copyright laws may have to be backed by the technological features on these platforms in order to continue to be an effective regulator of the content-generative behaviours of social media users. The specific steps the platforms should take fall beyond the scope of this book, and again could be the subject of future research.

In this sense the book provides cause to reflect on the potential widespread illegality of the content-generative activities in which social media users engage with regularity. It also points to examining the underlying core policy behind the regulation of online intermediaries, such as social media platforms. Ideally the book will stimulate more critical reflections on how laws (including laws other than copyright) should develop to take into account the influence of social media platforms on user behaviours through reform that gives users more leeway for the activities in which they engage. This could give rise to interesting insights that will benefit law reformers and scholars interested in legal issues on social media; it will also appeal to a broader audience (including users of social media platforms) interested in the application of laws to their activities on these platforms. These reflections are crucial – not just to secure the survival of laws such as copyright, but also to ensure the continuing attraction of social media platforms as enabling avenues for creative play and free expression.

Notes

1. Kaplan, A. M. and Haenlein, M. 2010, 59.
2. See Nielsen 2012; Global Web Index 2015.
3. See, for example, Arewa, O. B. 2010; Tehranian, J. 2011.
4. See Thaler, R. and Sunstein, C. 2008.
5. These three areas relate to: the vesting of ownership under the TOS; the imposition of the TOS on third parties; as well as the choice of governing law and jurisdiction clauses. See Part III of Chapter Three, sub-section B.
6. See Zittrain, J. 2006.
7. *DMCA*, § 512(c).
8. For instance, through remixing, 'vidding', creating mash-ups, and so on.
9. In general we see a growing disrespect for copyright laws online (for example, through people who continue to 'steal' music online) to which Lessig refers. See Lawrence Lessig, *Remix* (The Penguin Press, 2008) 286.
10. This is with the exception of the Wikipedia project run by the Wikimedia Foundation.
11. For instance, under the *US Copyright Act*, § 107.
12. For instance, under the *UK Copyright Act*, ss 30 and 30A; *Australian Copyright Act*, ss 41 and 41A.
13. See *Berne Convention,* art 9(2); *TRIPS Agreement*, art 13; *WIPO Copyright Treaty*, art 10; *WIPO Performances and Phonograms Treaty*, art 16.
14. See Sam Ricketson, *WIPO Study on Limitations and Exceptions of Copyright and Related Rights in the Digital Environment* (5 April 2003) <http://www.wipo.int/edocs/mdocs/copyright/en/sccr_9/sccr_9_7.pdf>; Ricketson, S. and Ginsburg, J.C. 2005 [13.11]–[13.14].
15. See, for example, Mariam Awan, *The user-generated content exception: Moving away from a non-commercial requirement* (11 November 2015) <http://www.iposgoode.ca/wp-content/uploads/2015/11/Mariam-Awan-The-user-generated-content-exception.pdf>; Chik, W. 2011, 291 (what is considered to be normal exploitation will evolve or expand with rapid technological progress).
16. Under the three-step test (as set out in international instruments including the *Berne Convention*, the *TRIPS Agreement* and the *WIPO Internet Treaties*), exceptions to the rights of authors/copyright holders are restricted to certain special cases that do not conflict with normal exploitations of the works and unreasonably prejudice their legitimate interests.

17. Notwithstanding this, it has been acknowledged that there is a need to reduce the legal uncertainty which impedes the creation of remixes. See, for example, The Department of Commerce Internet Policy Task Force, *Copyright Policy, Creativity and Innovation in the Digital Economy* (July 2013) <http://www.uspto.gov/sites/default/files/news/publications/copyrightgreenpaper.pdf>.
18. Part II of Chapter Two.
19. *UK Copyright Act*, s 30A.
20. Although untested, the parody or satire defence in Australia appears to be narrower than the caricature, parody or pastiche defence in the UK. See *Australian Copyright Act*, ss 41A and 103AA.
21. This is particularly if the fair use defence can excuse common everyday practices, as illustrated by the application of copyright laws to the case study under scenario one.
22. See, for example, Chik, W. 2011, 290.
23. ALRC 2013.
24. One of these conditions is that the use of, or authorisation to disseminate, the new work or subject matter is for non-commercial purposes. See *Copyright Act*, RSC 1985, c C-42 (*Canadian Copyright Act*), s 29.21. On the other hand, the ALRC noted in its report on copyright reform that while *some* social uses (ie, non-private uses such as creating and sharing content on social media platforms) of copyright-protected content should be exempt as fair uses, social uses should not automatically be exempt under a specific exception aimed at fostering creativity. Instead, these uses are best considered on a case by case basis, applying the fair use exception and applying fairness principles, due to the wide spectrum of UGC.
25. *Canadian Copyright Act*, ss 29.21(1)(b) and 29.21(1)(c).
26. For example, with reference to the case study on the hypothetical user Jane, uses such as Jane's 'pinning' of the video clip on Pinterest may be exempted by such an exception, without the need to run through the fair dealing analyses under the *Canadian Copyright Act*, ss 29 (research, private study, education, parody or satire), 29.1 (criticism or review) and 29.2 (news reporting).
27. See Awan, M. 2015. Awan highlighted that a major shortcoming with the exception is that it conflates amateur creation with non-commercial use, although amateur content has indirect commercial benefits, in light of modern technological practices.
28. Andrew Gowers, *Gowers Review of Intellectual Property* (December 2006) <https://www.gov.uk/government/uploads/system/uploads/attachment_data/file/228849/0118404830.pdf>; Hargreaves, I. 2011.
29. *UK Copyright Regulations 2014*. See especially *UK Copyright Act*, ss 30 (newly amended) and 30A.
30. Cf *Australian Copyright Act*, ss 41A and 103AA, for the parody or satire defence in Australia. The defence does not exempt any use discussed under scenario one from Part II of Chapter Two.
31. *UK Copyright Act*, s 30(1ZA). See also Part I of Chapter Two, sub-section H.
32. *Australian Copyright Act*, ss 41A and 103AA.
33. *UK Copyright Act*, s 30A.
34. The *UK Copyright Act*, s 30(1ZA) mirrors the language in articles 10(1) and 10(3) of the *Berne Convention* to a considerable extent. Further, an exception for quotation should not be in conflict of the three-step test set out in international instruments such as the *Berne Convention*, the *TRIPS Agreement*, the *WIPO Internet Treaties*, and so on.
35. See Ricketson, S. and Ginsburg, J. C. 2005 [13.38]; Lionel Bently et al, *Letter to the Chairman of the Joint Committee on Statutory Instruments* (6 June 2014) <http://www.create.ac.uk/wp-content/uploads/2014/03/Scrutiny-Committee-Profs-letter-June2014.pdf>.
36. ALRC 2013. The ALRC noted, however, in its report that a quotation exception – such as the one under the (then) proposed UK model – incorporating the requirements under article 10 of the *Berne Convention*, would be narrower in some respects than the existing Australian fair dealing defence for the purpose of criticism or review (*Australian Copyright Act*, ss 41 and 103A).
37. See art 10(1) of the *Berne Convention*. Cf *UK Copyright Act*, ss 30(1ZA)(b) (referring instead to a *fair dealing*).
38. Cf *UK Copyright Act*, ss 30(1ZA)(c) (requiring similarly that the extent of quotation be no more than is required for the specific purpose).
39. Cf *UK Copyright Act*, ss 30(1ZA)(a) (requiring similarly that the work has been made available to the public). See also the discussion in Part I of Chapter Two, sub-section H.

40. See art 10(3) of the *Berne Convention*. Cf *UK Copyright Act*, ss 30(1ZA)(d) (requiring sufficient acknowledgement *unless this is impossible for reasons of practicality* or otherwise).
41. Part III of Chapter Four, sub-section A.
42. Niva Elkin-Koren, 'After Twenty Years: Revisiting Copyright Liability of Online Intermediaries' in Susy Frankel and Daniel Gervais (eds), *The Evolution and Equilibrium of Copyright in the Digital Age* (Cambridge University Press, 2014) 29, 48–9.
43. For instance, through the removal of content under the *DMCA* mechanism.
44. Elkin-Koren, N. 2014, 51.
45. See, for example, UGC Principles, *Principles for User Generated Content Services* <http://www.ugcprinciples.com/>. These principles are established jointly by leading copyright holders and UGC services (which can include social media platforms), including Viacom Inc. and MySpace. As an example, Principle 1 provides that UGC services should include in conspicuous places information that promotes respect for intellectual property rights and discourages users against copyright-infringing activities. Further, Principle 2 provides that during the uploading process UGC services should prominently remind users that they should not upload copyright-infringing content.
46. In this respect Austin has argued that online intermediaries whose business models are hampered by the risk of (copyright) liability have an interest, as much as copyright holders do, in negotiating durable solutions to address the concerns caused by their business models that aggregate infringing and non-infringing activities on a large scale – but that these solutions will prove elusive if one assumes that these online intermediaries (or firms) have no incentive to provide these solutions. See Graeme W. Austin, 'New Technologies and the Scale of Copyright Infringement' in Susy Frankel and Daniel Gervais (eds), *The Evolution and Equilibrium of Copyright in the Digital Age* (Cambridge University Press, 2014) 203, 220.
47. See Helberger, N. et al. 2013; Cellan-Jones 2014.
48. This is in line with Principle 1 of the UGC Principles.
49. YouTube, *What is fair use?* <https://www.youtube.com/yt/copyright/fair-use.html>.
50. This is in line with Principle 2 of the UGC Principles.
51. In the case of an ambient networked computing environment or automated environment. See, for example, Hildebrandt, M. 2008.

Bibliography

I. Articles/Books/Reports

A. Articles

Alcabes, Elisa, 'Unauthorised Photographs of Theatrical Works: Do They Infringe the Copyright?' (1987) 87 *Columbia Law Review* 1032

Aliprandi, Simone and Andrea Mangiatordi, 'Content Production and Perception of Copyright: An Analysis of Habits and Beliefs of Internet Users' (2013) 4(3) *European Journal of Law and Technology* 1

Ang, Steven, 'The Idea-Expression Dichotomy and Merger Doctrine in the Copyright Laws of the U.S. and the U.K.' (1994) 2(2) *International Journal of Law and Information Technology* 111

Arewa, Olufunmilayo B., 'YouTube, UGC, and Digital Music: Competing Business and Cultural Models in the Internet Age' (2010) 104(2) *Northwestern University Law Review* 431

Asay, Clarke D., 'Copyright's Technological Interdependencies' (2014) 18 *Stanford Technology Law Review* 189

Austin, Graeme W., 'Domestic Laws and Foreign Rights: Choice of Law in Transnational Copyright Infringement Litigation' (1999) 23 *Columbia-VLA Journal of Law & Arts* 1

Austin, Graeme W., 'Importing Kazaa-Exporting Grokster' (2006) 22 *Santa Clara Computer and High Tech Law Journal* 577

Austin, Graeme, 'The Two Faces of Fair Use' (2012) 25 *New Zealand Universities Law Review* 285

Baruah, Trisha Dowerah, 'Effectiveness of Social Media as a Tool of Communication and its Potential for Technology Enabled Connections: A Micro-level study' (May 2012) 2(5) *International Journal of Scientific and Research Publications* 1

Beebe, Barton, 'An Empirical Study of U.S. Copyright Fair Use Opinions, 1978–2005' (2008) 156 *University of Pennsylvania Law Review* 549

Bell, Andrew, 'The Future of Private International Law in Australia' (2012) *Australian International Law Journal* 11

Bently, Lionel, 'Copyright and the Death of the Author in Literature and Law' (1994) 5 *The Modern Law Review* 973

Biggs, Ella and Paul Kallenbach, 'Intellectual Property Rights and the Right to Freedom of Artistic Expression: Complementary or Contradictory?' (May 2014) *Australian Intellectual Property Bulletin* 86

Black, Julia, 'Constructing and Contesting Legitimacy and Accountability in Polycentric Regulatory Regimes' (2008) 2 *Regulation and Governance* 137

Black, Julia, 'Forms and Paradoxes of Principles-based Regulation' (2008) 3(4) *Capital Markets Law Journal* 425

Black, Julia, Martyn Hopper and Christa Band, 'Making a Success of Principles-based Regulation' (May 2007) *Law and Financial Markets Review* 191

Black, Julia and Robert Baldwin, 'Really Responsive Risk-based Regulation' (2010) 32(2) *Law and Policy* 181

Boddie II, Needham J., Thomas C. McThenia Jr., Fred B. Amos II and Douglas W. Kim, 'A Review of Copyright and the Internet' (1998) 20(2) *Campbell Law Review* 193

Bowrey, Kathy, 'The New Intellectual Property: Celebrity, Fans and the Properties of the Entertainment Franchise' (2011) 20(1) *Griffith Law Review* 188

Bowrey, Kathy and Michael Handler (eds), *Law and Creativity in the Age of the Entertainment Franchise* (Cambridge University Press, 2014)

boyd, danah, Scott Golder and Gilad Lotan, 'Tweet, Tweet, Retweet: Conversational Aspects of Retweeting on Twitter' (Paper presented at 43rd Hawaii International Conference on System Sciences, Kauai, 6 January 2010)

boyd, danah M. and Nicole B. Ellison, 'Social Network Sites: Definition, History and Scholarship' (2007) 13(1) *Journal of Computer-Mediated Communication* 11

Boyle, James, 'Foucault in Cyberspace: Surveillance, Sovereignty and Hardwired Censors' (1997) 66 *University of Cincinnati Law Review* 177

Braithwaite, John, 'The Essence of Responsive Regulation' (2011) 44 *University of British Columbia Law Review* 475

Brownsword, Roger, 'Code, Control and Choice: Why East is East and West is West' (2006) 25 *Legal Studies* 1

Chan-Olmsted, Sylvia M., Moonhee Cho and Sangwon Lee, 'User Perceptions of Social Media: A Comparative Study of Perceived Characteristics and User Profiles by Social Media' (October 2013) 3(4) *Online Journal of Communication and Media Technologies* 149

Chik, Warren, 'Paying it Forward: The Case for a Specific Statutory Limitation on Exclusive Rights for User-Generated Content under Copyright Law' (2011) 11 *The John Marshall Review of Intellectual Property Law* 240

Chiu, Aaron T., 'Irrationally Bound: Terms of Use Licences and the Breakdown of Consumer Rationality in the Market for Social Network Sites' (2012) 21 *Southern California Interdisciplinary Law Journal* 165

Cohen, Amy B., 'When Does a Work Infringe the Derivative Works Right of a Copyright Owner?' (1999) 17 *Cardozo Arts and Entertainment Law Journal* 623

Cohen, Julie E., *Configuring the Networked Self: Law, Code and the Play of Everyday Practice* (Yale University Press, 2012)

Collins, Craig and Heather Forrest, *Intellectual Property Law* (LexisNexis Butterworths, 2nd ed., 2014)

Cooley, Amanda Harmon, 'A Contractual Deterrence Strategy for User-Generated Copyright Infringement and Subsequent Service Provider Litigation' (2011) 64 *SMU Law Review* 691

Correa, Teresa, Amber Willard Hinsley and Homero Gil de Zuniga, 'Who Interacts on the Web?: The Intersection of Users' Personality and Social Media Use' (2010) 26(2) *Computers in Human Behaviour* 247

Daft, Richard L. and Robert H. Lengel, 'Organisational Information Requirements, Media Richness and Structural Design' (1986) 32(5) *Management Science* 554

Dam, Kenneth W., 'Self-Help in the Digital Jungle' (June 1999) 28(2) *Journal of Legal Studies* 1

Darrow, Jonathan J. and Gerald R. Ferrara, 'Social Networking Web Sites and DMCA: A Safe-Harbour from Copyright Infringement Liability or the Perfect Storm?' (Fall 2007) 6(1) *Northwestern Journal of Technology and Intellectual Property* 1

DeNardis, L. and W. M. Hackl, 'Internet Governance by Social Media Platforms' (2015) *Telecommunications Policy* 1

De Zwart, Melissa, 'For Fun rather than Profit: Playing around with Online Games' (2013) 18 *Media and Arts Law Review* 106

De Zwart, Melissa and Sal Humphreys, 'Playing in Contested Zones: Norms, Laws and Rules in MMOGs' (2012) 17(1) *Media and Arts Law Review* 1

Dickinson, Andrew, 'The Future of Private International Law in Australia' (2012) *Australian International Law Journal* 1

Dijck, Jose van, 'Facebook and the Engineering of Connectivity: A Multi-Layered Approach to Social Media Platforms' (2013) 19(2) *Convergence: The International Journal of Research into New Media Technologies* 141

Dinwoodie, Graeme B., 'Developing a Private International Intellectual Property Law: The Demise of Territoriality' (2009) 51 *William & Mary Law Review* 711

Dinwoodie, Graeme B., Rochelle Dreyfuss and Annette Kur, 'The Law Applicable to Secondary Liability in Intellectual Property Cases' (2010) 42 *New York University Journal of International Law and Politics* 201
Dolin, Melissa, 'Note: Joint Authorship and Collaborative Artwork Created through Social Media' (2011) 39(4) *American Intellectual Property Law Association Quarterly Journal* 535
Dorbeck-Jung, Barbel R., Mirjan J. Oude Vrielink, Jordy F. Gosselt, Joris J. van Hoof and Menno D.T. de Jong, 'Contested Hybridization of Regulation: Failure of the Dutch Regulatory System to Protect Minors from Harmful Media' (2010) 4(2) *Regulation and Governance* 154
Easterbrook, Frank H., 'Cyberspace and the Law of the Horse' (1996) *University of Chicago Legal Forum* 207
Edmundson, Jessica and Elizabeth Townsend Gard, 'Conversations with Renowned Professors and Practitioners on the Future of Copyright' (2011) 14 *Tulane Journal of Technology and Intellectual Property* 1
Edwards, L., B. Klein, D. Lee, G. Moss and F. Philip, 'Framing the Consumer, Copyright Regulation and the Public' (2013) 19(1) *Convergence: The International Journal of Research into New Media Technologies* 9
Elkin-Koren, Niva, 'Tailoring Copyright to Social Production' (2011) 12 *Theoretical Inquiries of Law* 309
Ellickson, Robert C., 'Law and Economics Discovers Social Norms' (1998) 27 *Journal of Legal Studies* 537
Erstad, Ola, 'The Agency of Content Creators: Implications for Personal Engagement and Media Industries' (2013) 20(2) *Javnost – The Public* 67
Fischman, Afori Orit, 'Flexible Remedies as a Means to Counteract Failures in Copyright Law' (2011) 29 *Cardozo Arts & Entertainment Law Journal* 2
Froomkin, A. Michael, 'ICANN 2.0: Meet the New Boss' (2003) 36 *Loyola of Los Angeles Law Review* 1087
Garnett, Richard, 'The Hague Choice of Court Convention: Magnum Opus or Much Ado about Nothing?' (2009) 5(1) *Journal of Private International Law* 161
Gaver, William W., 'Technology Affordances' (1991), *CHI'91 Conference Proceedings* 79
Gervais, Daniel, 'The Tangled Web of UGC: Making Copyright Sense of User-Generated Content' (2009) 11(4) *Vanderbilt Journal of Entertainment and Technology Law* 841
Gibson, James, 'Risk Aversion and Rights Accretion in Intellectual Property Law' (2007) 116 *The Yale Law Journal* 882
Ginsburg, Jane C., 'Moral Rights in the U.S.: Still in Need of a Guardian *Ad Litem*' (2012) 30 *Cardozo Arts & Entertainment Law Journal* 73
Ginsburg, Jane C., 'The Author's Place in the Future of Copyright' (2009) 153(2) *Proceedings of the American Philosophical Society* 147
Goldsmith, Jack, 'Against Cyberanarchy' (1998) 65 *University of Chicago Law Review* 1199
Gordon, Wendy, 'The Core of Copyright: Authors, Not Publishers' (2014) 52(2) *Houston Law Review* 613
Griffiths, Jonathan, 'Dematerialization, Pragmatism and the European Copyright Revolution' (2013) 33(4) *Oxford Journal of Legal Studies* 767
Grimmelmann, James, 'Regulation by Software' (2005) 114 *Yale Law Journal* 1719
Haas, Rebecca, 'Twitter: New Challenges to Copyright Law in the Internet Age' (2010) 10 *The John Marshall Review of Intellectual Property Law* 231
Helberger, Natalie, Loos M., Guibault L., Mak C. and Pessers L., 'Digital Content Contracts for Consumers' (2013) *Journal of Consumer Policy* 37
Hillman, Robert A. and Jeffrey J. Rachlinski, 'Standard Form Contracting in the Electronic Age' (2002) 77 *New York University Law Review* 429
Hogan, Bernie and Anabel Quan-Haase, 'Persistence and Change in Social Media' (2010) 30(5) *Bulletin of Science, Technology & Society* 309
Howard, Philip N., Aiden Duffy, Deen Freelon, Muzammil M. Hussain, Will Mari and Marwa Maziad, 'Opening Closed Regimes: What was the Role of Social Media during the Arab Spring?' (2011) 1 *Project on Information Technology and Political Islam* 1
Humphreys, Lee, 'Cellphones in Public: Social Interactions in a Wireless Era' (2005) 7(6) *New Media & Society* 810
Hunter, Dan and F. Gregory Lastowka, 'Amateur-to-Amateur' (2004–5) 46 *William & Mary Law Review* 951

Hutton, Graeme and Maggie Fosdick, 'The Globalization of Social Media – Consumer Relationships with Brands Evolve in the Digital Space' (December 2011) *Journal of Advertising Research* 564

Johnson, David R. and David Post, 'Law and Borders – The Rise of Law in Cyberspace' (1996) 48(5) *Stanford Law Review* 1367

Kapczynski, Amy, 'The Access to Knowledge Mobilization and the New Politics of Intellectual Property' (2008) 117 *The Yale Law Journal* 804

Kaplan, Andreas M. and Haenlein Michael, 'Users of the World, Unite! The Challenges and Opportunities of Social Media' (2010) 53(1) *Business Horizons* 59

Kietzmann, Jan H. Kristopher Hermkens, Ian P. McCarthy and Bruno S. Silvestre, 'Social Media? Get Serious! Understanding the Functional Building Blocks of Social Media' (2011) 54 *Business Horizons* 241

Klein, Hans, 'ICANN and Internet Governance: Leveraging Technical Coordination to Realize Global Public Policy' (2002) 18(3) *Information Society* 193

Konieczny, Piotr, 'Governance, Organisation and Democracy on the Internet: The Iron Law and the Evolution of Wikipedia' (2009) 24(1) *Sociological Forum* 162

Landes, William M. and Richard A. Posner, 'An Economic Analysis of Copyright Law' (1989) 18 *Journal of Legal Studies* 325

Lessig, Lawrence, 'The Law of the Horse: What Cyberlaw Might Teach' (1999) 113 *Harvard Law Review* 501

Leval, Pierre, 'Toward a Fair Use Standard' (1990) 103 *Harvard Law Review* 1111

Li, Xigen and Nico Nergadze, 'Deterrence Effect of Four Legal and Extralegal Factors on Online Copyright Infringement' (2009) *Journal of Computer-Mediated Communication* 307

Lin, Julia Ying-Chao, Angelina Nhat Hanh Le Shadab Khalil and Julian Ming-Sung Cheng, 'Social Media Usage and Work Values: The Example of Facebook in Taiwan' (2012) 40(2) *Social Media and Personality* 195

Litman, Jessica, 'Lawful Personal Use' (2007) 85 *Texas Law Review* 1871

Liu, Joseph P., 'Copyright Law's Theory of the Consumer' (2003) 44 *Boston College Law Review* 397

Llewellyn, Joseph Gibbons, 'Visual Artists Rights Act and the Protection of Digital Works of Photographic Art' (2010) 11(3) *North Carolina Journal of Law and Technology* 531

Lucchi, Nicola, 'Internet Content Governance and Human Rights' (2014) 16(4) *Vanderbilt Journal of Entertainment and Technology Law* 809

MacPherson, Daniel, 'Case Note: The Implications of Roadshow v iiNet for Authorisation Liability in Copyright Law?' (2013) 35 *Sydney Law Review* 467

Mangold, W. G. and D. J. Faulds, 'Social Media: The New Hybrid Element of the Promotion Mix' (2009) 52 *Business Horizons* 357

Marlin-Bennett, Renee and E. Nicole Thornton, 'Governance within Social Media Websites: Ruling New Frontiers' (2012) 36 *Telecommunications Policy* 493

Mateus, Alexandre M., 'Copyright Violation on the Internet: Extent and Approaches to Detection and Deterrence' (2011) *Dissertations, Paper 50*

Matulionyte, Rita, 'IP and Applicable Law in Recent International Proposals: Report for the International Law Association' (2012) 3(2) *Journal of Intellectual Property, Information Technology and Electronic Commerce Law* 263

Mayer-Schonberger, Viktor, 'The Shape of Governance: Analyzing the World of Internet Regulation' (2002–3) 43 *Virginia Journal of International Law* 605

McComish, James, 'Pleading and Proving Foreign Law in Australia' (2007) 31(2) *Melbourne University Law Review* 401

Moses, Lyria Bennett, 'Creating Parallels in the Regulation of Content: Moving from Offline to Online' (2010) 33(2) *University of New South Wales Law Journal* 581

Murray, Andrew and Colin Scott, 'Controlling the New Media: Hybrid Responses to New Forms of Power' (2002) 65(4) *The Modern Law Review* 491

Narayan, Bhuva, 'From Everyday Information Behaviours to Clickable Solidarity in a Place called Social Media' (2013) 5(3) *Cosmopolitan Civil Societies Journal* 32

Nathenson, Ira Steven, 'Best Practices for the Law of the Horse: Teaching Cyberlaw and Illuminating Law Through Online Simulations' (2012) 28 *Santa Clara Computer & High Technology Law Journal* 657

Nimmer, Raymond T. 'Information Wars and Challenges of Content Protection in Digital Contexts' (2010–11) 13 *Vanderbilt Journal of Entertainment and Technology Law* 826

Ochoa, Tyler T., 'Copyright, Derivative Works and Fixation: Is Galoob a Mirage, or Does the Form (GEN) of the Alleged Derivative Work Matter?' (2003–4) 20 *Santa Clara Computer & High Technology Law Journal* 991
O'Reilly, Tim, 'What is Web 2.0: Design Patterns and Business Models for the Next Generation of Software' (2007) 65 *Commerce and Strategies* 17
Peha, Jon M. and Alexandre M. Mateus, 'Policy Implications of Technology for Detecting P2P and Copyright Violations' (Jan 2014) 38(1) *Telecommunications Policy* 66
Perzanowski, Aaron, 'Fixing RAM Copies' (2010) 104 *Northwestern University Law Review* 1067
Pessach, Guy, 'Deconstructing Disintermediation: A Skeptical Copyright Perspective' (2013) 31 *Cardozo Arts and Entertainment Law Journal* 833
Quiggin, John and Dan Hunter, 'Money Ruins Everything' (2008) 30 *Hastings Commerce and Entertainment Law Journal* 203
Radin, Magaret Jane and R. Polk Wagner, 'The Myth of Private Ordering: Rediscovering Legal Realism in Cyberspace' (1998) 73 *Chicago-Kent Law Review* 1295
Reidenberg, Joel, 'Lex Informatica: The Formulation of Information Policy Rules through Technology' (1998) 76 *Texas Law Review* 553
Reuveni, Erez, 'Authorship in the Age of the Conducer' (2007) 54 *Journal of the Copyright Society of the U.S.A.* 1801
Richardson, Megan, 'Copyright in Trademarks? On Understanding Trade Mark Dilution' [2000] *Intellectual Property Quarterly* 66
Ricketson, Sam, 'Reflections on Authorship and the Meaning of a "Work" in Australian and Singapore Copyright Law' (2012) 24 *Singapore Academy of Law Journal* 792
Rojanakul, Kittichote and Hu Liang, 'Initiatives and Challenges in Countering Inappropriate Internet Use' (2009) *Proceedings of International Conference on Computer Technology and Development* 516
Rustad, Michael L. and Maria Vittoria Onufrio, 'Reconceptualising Consumer Terms of Use for a Globalized Knowledge Economy' (2011–12) 14(4) *University of Pennsylvania Journal of Business Law* 1085
Sag, Matthew, 'Predicting Fair Use' (2012) 73(1) *Ohio State Law Journal* 47
Salbu, Steven R., 'Who Should Govern the Internet?: Monitoring and Supporting a New Frontier' (1998) 11 *Harvard Journal of Law & Technology* 429
Sommer, Joseph H., 'Cyberlaw' (2000) 15 *Berkeley Technology Law Journal* 1145
Suzor, Nicolas, 'Free-riding, Cooperation and "Peaceful Revolutions" in Copyright' (2014) 28(1) *Harvard Journal of Law and Technology* 138
Suzor, Nicolas, 'Where the Bloody Hell does Parody Fit in Australian Copyright Law?' (2008) 13 *Media and Arts Law Review* 218
Tan, Corinne Hui Yun 'Lawrence Lessig v Liberation Music Pty Ltd: YouTube's Hands (or Bots) in the Overzealous Enforcement of Copyright' (2014) 36(6) *European Intellectual Property Review* 347
Tan, Corinne Hui Yun, 'Technological Nudges and Copyright on Social Media Sites' (2015) 1 *Intellectual Property Quarterly* 62
Tan, Corinne Hui Yun, 'Terms of Service on Social Media Sites' (2014) 19 *Media and Arts Law Review* 195
Tan, David, 'The Lost Language of the First Amendment in Copyright Fair Use: Leval's "Transformative Use" Doctrine Twenty-Five Years On' (2016) 26 *Fordham Intellectual Property, Media & Entertainment Law Journal* 311
Tan, David, 'The Transformative Use Doctrine and Fair Dealing in Singapore' (2012) 24 *Singapore Academy of Law Journal* 832
Tan, Tee Jim, 'New Law for Compilations and Databases in Singapore' (2012) 24 *Singapore Academy of Law Journal* 745
Tehranian, John, 'Towards a Critical IP Theory: Copyright, Consecration & Control' (2012) *Brigham Young University Law Review* 1237
Townsend Gard, Eizabeth, and Bri Whetstone, 'Copyright and Social Media: A Preliminary Case Study of Pinterest' (2012) 31 *Mississippi College Law Review* 249
Vaidhyanathan, Said, 'Afterword: Critical Information Studies' (2006) 29 (2–3) *Cultural Studies* 292
Wallace, Christine 'Overlapping Interest in Derivative Works and Compilations' (1984) 35 *Case Western Reserve Law Review* 103

Wauters, Ellen, Eva Lievens and Peggy Valcke, 'Towards a Better Protection of Social Media Users: A Legal Perspective on the Terms of Use of Social Networking Sites' (2014) *International Journal of Law and Information Technology* 1
Werbin, Kenneth C., 'The Social Media Contract: On the Paradoxes of Digital Property in This Digital Land' (2012) 46(2) *Journal of Canadian Studies* 245
White, Elizabeth, 'The Berne Convention's Flexible Fixation Requirement: A Problematic Provision for User-Generated Content' (2012–13) 13(2) *Chicago Journal of International Law* 685
Winner, Langdon, 'Do Artifacts have Politics?' (Winter 1980) 109(1) *Daedalus* 121
Wong, Wilson, and Eric Welch, 'Does E-government Promote Accountability? A Comparative Analysis of Website Openness and Government Accountability' (2004) 17(2) *Governance – An International Journal of Policy and Administration* 275
Wu, Tim, 'Tolerated Use' (2007–8) 31 *Columbia Journal of Law & Arts* 617
Zittrain, Jonathan, 'The Generative Internet' (2006) 119 *Harvard Law Review* 1974

B. Books

Adeney, Elizabeth, *The Moral Rights of Authors and Performers: An International and Comparative Analysis* (Oxford University Press, 2006)
Akdeniz, Yaman, Clive Walker and David Wall, *The Internet, Law and Society* (Pearson Education Limited, 2000)
Ballam, Damian, and Chris Fullwood, 'Fluidity of Personal Boundaries in Online Social Media: Implications for Netiquette' in Martin Anderson (ed.), *Contemporary Ergonomics and Human Factors: Annual Conference of the Institute of Ergonomics and Human Factors* (Taylor & Francis, 2010) 391
Barthes, Roland, 'The Death of the Author' in Stephen Heath (trans), *Image, Music, Text* (Hill and Wang, 1977) 142
Bartoletti, Massimo, Emilio Tuosto and Roberto Zunino, 'On the Realizability of Contracts in Dishonest Systems' in Marjan Sirjani (ed.), *Coordination Models and Languages* (Springer Berlin Heidelberg, 2012) 245
Benjamin, James, 'Tweets, Blogs and the Ethics of 21st-Century Communication Technology' in Hana S. Noor Al-Deen and Hohn Allen Hendricks (eds), *Social Media: Usage and Impact* (Lexington, 2011) 271
Benkler, Yochai, 'Sharing Nicely' in Michael Mandiberg (ed.), *The Social Media Reader* (New York University Press, 2008) 17
Benkler, Yochai, *The Wealth of Networks: How Social Production Transforms Markets and Freedom* (Yale University Press, 2007)
Bently, Lionel and Brad Sherman, *Intellectual Property Law* (Oxford University Press, 3rd ed., 2009)
Briggs, Asa and Peter Burke, *A Social History of the Media* (Polity Press, 3rd ed., 2009)
Black, Julia, *Rules and Regulators* (Oxford University Press, 1997)
Black, Julia, 'The Rise, Fall and Fate of Principles-based Regulation' in Kern Alexander and Niamh Moloney (eds), *Law Reform and Financial Markets* (Edward Elgar Publishing, Cheltenham, UK, 2011) 3
Brown, Lesley (ed.), *The New Shorter Oxford English Dictionary* (Clarendon Press, 1993)
Brownsword, Roger, 'So What Does the World Need Now?' in Roger Brownsword and Karen Yeung (eds), *Regulating Technologies* (Hart Publishing, 2008) 23
Brownsword, Roger, and Karen Yeung (eds), *Regulating Technologies* (Hart Publishing, 2008)
Brownsword, Roger, and Karen Yeung, 'Tools, Targets and Thematics' in Roger Brownsword and Karen Yeung (eds), *Regulating Technologies* (Hart Publishing, 2008) 3
Burgess, Jean, 'YouTube and the Formalization of Amateur Media' in Dan Hunter, Ramon Lobato, Megan Richardson and Julian Thomas (eds), *Amateur Media: Social, Cultural and Legal Perspectives* (Routledge, 2013) 51
Bygrave, Lee A., *Internet Governance by Contract* (Oxford University Press, 2015)
Bygrave, Lee A. and Jon Bing (eds), *Internet Governance: Infrastructure and Institutions* (Oxford University Press, 2009) 48
Campbell, David (ed.), *The Relational Theory of Contract: Selected Works of Ian MacNeil* (Sweet & Maxwell, 2001)
Cornish, William, David Llewelyn and Tanya Aplin, *Intellectual Property: Patents, Copyrights, Trademarks and Allied Rights* (Sweet & Maxwell, 7th ed., 2010)

DeNardis, Laura, *Protocol Politics: The Globalization of Internet Governance* (The MIT Press, 2009)
DeNardis, Laura, *The Global War for Internet Governance* (Yale University Press, 2014)
Dutton, William (ed.), *Oxford Handbook of Internet Studies* (Oxford University Press, 2013)
Elkin-Koren, Niva, 'After Twenty Years: Revisiting Copyright Liability of Online Intermediaries' in Susy Frankel and Daniel Gervais (eds), *The Evolution and Equilibrium of Copyright in the Digital Age* (Cambridge University Press, 2014) 29
Ellickson, Robert C., *Order without law: How neighbours Settle Disputes* (Harvard University Press, 1994)
Ellickson, Robert C., *The Household: Informal Order around the Hearth* (Princeton University Press, 2008)
Fawcett, James J. and Paul Torremans, *Intellectual Property and Private International Law* (Oxford University Press, 2nd ed., 2011)
Feenberg, Andrew, *Between Reason and Experience: Essays in Technology and Modernity* (The MIT Press, 2010)
Feenberg, Andrew, *Critical Theory of Technology* (Oxford University Press, 1991)
Feenberg, Andrew, *Transforming Technology: A Critical Theory Revisited* (Oxford University Press, 2002)
Fentiman, Richard, *Foreign Law in English Courts* (Oxford University Press, 1998)
Fenwick, Trevor, 'Why Copyright Remains Important: A Perspective from a Data Publisher' in Trevor Fenwick and Ian Locks (eds), *Copyright in the Digital Age: Industry Issues and Impacts* (Wildy, Simmons & Hill Publishing on behalf of The Stationers Company and individual contributors, 2010) 53
Fenwick, Trevor and Ian Locks (eds), *Copyright in the Digital Age: Industry Issues and Impacts* (Wildy, Simmons & Hill Publishing on behalf of The Stationers Company and individual contributors, 2010)
Foucault, Michel, 'What is an Author?' in James D. Faubion (ed., translated by Josue V. Harari) in *Aesthetics, Method and Epistemology* (The New Press, 1994) 205
Frankel, Susy and Daniel Gervais (eds), *The Evolution and Equilibrium of Copyright in the Digital Age* (Cambridge University Press, 2014)
Friedman, Thomas, *The World is Flat: A Brief History of the Twenty-First Century* (Farrar, Strous and Giroux, 2005)
Garnett, Kevin, Gillian Davies and Gwilym Harbottle, *Copinger and Skone James on Copyright* (Thomson Reuters, 16th ed., 2011)
Gibson, James J., 'The Theory of Affordances' in Robert Shaw and John Bransford (eds), *Perceiving, Acting and Knowing* (John Wiley & Sons, 1977) 127
Ginsburg, Jane C., 'Exceptional Authorship: The Role of Copyright Exceptions in Promoting Creativity' in Susy Frankel and Daniel Gervais (eds), *The Evolution and Equilibrium of Copyright in the Digital Age* (Cambridge University Press, 2014) 15
Goffman, Erving, *The Presentation of Self in Everyday Life* (Doubleday Anchor Books, 1959)
Goldsmith, Jack and Tim Wu, *Who Controls the Internet? Illusions of a Borderless World* (Oxford University Press, 2006)
Goldstein, Paul and Bernt Hugenholtz, *International Copyright: Principles, Law and Practice* (Oxford University Press, 3rd ed., 2013)
Griffiths, Jonathan, 'Fair Dealing after Deckmyn: the United Kingdom's Defence for Caricature, Parody or Pastiche' in Megan Richardson and Sam Ricketson (eds), *Research Handbook on Intellectual Property in Media and Entertainment* (Edward Elgar, 2017) 64
Halpern, Sheldon W., Craig Allen Nard and Kenneth L. Port., *Fundamentals of United States Intellectual Property Law: Copyright, Patent and Trademark* (Kluwer Law International, 4th ed., 2012)
Helfer, Laurence and Graeme Austin, *Human Rights and Intellectual Property: Mapping the Global Interface* (Cambridge University Press, New York, 2011)
Hetcher, Steven, 'Amateur Creative Digital Content and Proportional Commerce' in Dan Hunter, Ramon Lobato, Megan Richardson and Julian Thomas (eds), *Amateur Media: Social, Cultural and Legal Perspectives* (Routledge, 2013) 35
Hetcher, Steven A., *Norms in a Wired World* (Cambridge University Press, 2004)
Hildebrandt, Mireille, 'A Vision of Ambient Law' in Roger Brownsword and Karen Yeung (eds), *Regulating Technologies* (Hart Publishing, 2008) 175

Hunter, Dan, *The Oxford Introductions to U.S. Law: Intellectual Property* (Oxford University Press, 2012)
Hunter, Dan, Ramon Lobato, Megan Richardson and Julian Thomas, *Amateur Media: Social, Cultural and Legal Perspectives* (Routledge, 2013)
Hyde, Adam, Mike Linksvayer, Kanarinka, Michael Mandiberg, Marta Peirano, Sissu Tarka, Astra Taylor, Alan Toner and Mushon Zer-Aviv, 'What is Collaboration Anyway?' in Michael Mandiberg (ed.), *The Social Media Reader* (New York University Press, 2008) 53
Juden, Simon, 'Happy Birthday to Copyright' in Trevor Fenwick and Ian Locks (eds), *Copyright in the Digital Age: Industry Issues and Impacts* (Wildy, Simmons & Hill Publishing on behalf of The Stationers Company and individual contributors, 2010) 95
Kirby, Michael, 'New Frontier: Regulating Technology by Law and Code' in Roger Brownsword and Karen Yeung (eds), *Regulating Technologies* (Hart Publishing, 2008) 367
Kohl, Uta, *Jurisdiction and the Internet: Regulatory Competence over Online Activity* (Cambridge University Press, 2007)
Koops, Bert-Jaap, 'Criteria for Normative Technology: The Acceptability of "Code as Law" in Light of Democratic and Constitutional Values' in Roger Brownsword and Karen Yeung (eds), *Regulating Technologies* (Hart Publishing, 2008) 157
Lahore, James, *Intellectual Property in Australia: Copyright* (Butterworths, 1977)
Lastowka, Greg, 'Minecraft as Web 2.0' in Dan Hunter, Ramon Lobato, Megan Richardson and Julian Thomas (eds), *Amateur Media: Social, Cultural and Legal Perspectives* (Routledge, 2013) 153
Lobato, Ramon, Julian Thomas and Dan Hunter, 'Histories of User-generated content: Between Formal and Informal Media Economies' in Dan Hunter, Ramon Lobato, Megan Richardson and Julian Thomas (eds), *Amateur Media: Social, Cultural and Legal Perspectives* (Routledge, 2013) 3
Lessig, Lawrence, *Code Version 2.0* (Basic Books, 2nd ed., 2006)
Lessig, Lawrence, *Code and Other Laws of Cyberspace* (Basic Books, 1999)
Lessig, Lawrence, *Free Culture* (The Penguin Press, 2004)
Lessig, Lawrence, *Remix* (The Penguin Press, 2008)
Lessig, Lawrence, 'Remix' in Michael Mandiberg (ed.), *The Social Media Reader* (New York University Press, 2008) 155
Litman, Jessica, *Digital Copyright* (Prometheus Books, 2006)
Mandiberg, Michael (ed.), *The Social Media Reader* (New York University Press, 2008)
Matulionyte, Rita, *Law Applicable to Copyright: A Comparison of the ALI and CLIP Proposals* (Edward Elgar Publishing, 2011)
Mazzone, Jason, *Copyfraud and Other Abuses of Intellectual Property Law* (Stanford University Press, 2011)
McDonagh, Luke, 'Copyright, Contract and Consequences' in M. Shemtov and I. Walden (eds), *Free and Open Source Software: Policy, Law and Practice* (Oxford University Press, 2013)
McIntyre, T. J. and Colin Scott, 'Internet Filtering' in Roger Brownsword and Karen Yeung (eds), *Regulating Technologies* (Hart Publishing, 2008) 109
McKeough, Jill, Andrew Stewart and Philip Griffith, *Intellectual Property in Australia* (Lexis Nexis, 3rd ed., 2004)
McLeod, Kembrew, *Freedom of Expression: Resistance and Repression in the Age of Intellectual Property* (University of Minnesota Press, 2007)
Mitchell, William, *City of Bits: Space, Place and the Infobahn* (The MIT Press, 1996)
Mjos, Ole J., *Music, Social Media and Global Mobility: MySpace, Facebook, YouTube* (Routledge, 2012)
Mueller, Milton L., *Networks and States: The Global Politics of Internet Governance* (The MIT Press, 2010)
Nygh, P. E. and M. Davies, *Conflict of Laws in Australia* (LexisNexis Butterworths, 7th ed., 2002)
Ochoa, Tyler, T., 'Copyright Duration: Theories and Practice' in Peter K. Yu (ed.), *Intellectual Property and Information Wealth: Copyright and Related Rights* (Green Publishing Group, 2007) 133
Okpaluba, Johnson, 'Digital Sampling and Music Industry Practices, Re-Spun' in Kathy Bowrey and Michael Handler (eds), *Law and Creativity in the Age of the Entertainment Franchise* (Cambridge University Press, 2014) 75
Postigo, Hector, *The Digital Rights Movement: The Role of Technology in Subverting Digital Copyright* (The MIT Press, 2012)

Rawls, John, *A Theory of Justice* (Oxford University Press, 1997)
Richardson, Megan and Jake Goldenfein, 'Competing Myths of Informal Economies' in Dan Hunter, Ramon Lobato, Megan Richardson and Julian Thomas (eds), *Amateur Media: Social, Cultural and Legal Perspectives* (Routledge, 2013) 18
Ricketson, Sam and Chris Cresswell, *The Law of Intellectual Property: Copyright, Designs and Confidential Information* (Thomson Reuters, 2015)
Ricketson, Sam, Megan Richardson and Mark Davison, *Intellectual Property: Cases, Materials and Commentary* (Lexis Nexis Butterworths, 5th ed., 2013)
Ricketson, Sam and Jane C. Ginsburg, *International Copyright and Neighbouring Rights: The Berne Convention and Beyond* (Oxford University Press, 2nd ed., 2005)
Rosen, Jay, 'The People Formerly Known as the Audience' in Michael Mandiberg (ed.), *The Social Media Reader* (New York University Press, 2008) 13
Rosen, Jeffrey and Benjamin Wittes (eds), *Constitution 3.0: Freedom and Technological Change* (The Brookings Institution, 2011)
Shapiro, Carl and Hal R. Varian, *Information Rules: A Strategic Guide to the Network Economy* (Harvard Business Press, 1999)
Sherman, Brad and Leanne Wiseman (eds), *Copyright and the Challenge of the New* (Law International, 2012)
Short, John, E. Williams and B. Christie, *Social Psychology of Telecommunications* (John Wiley & Sons Ltd, 1976)
Silbey, Jessica, *The Eureka Myth: Creators, Innovators, and Everyday Intellectual Property* (Stanford University Press, 2015)
Sinnreich, Aram, *The Piracy Crusade: How the Music Industry's War on Sharing Destroys Markets and Erodes Civil Liberties* (University of Massachusetts Press, 2013)
Solum, Lawrence, B., 'Models of Internet Governance' in Lee A. Bygrave and Jon Bing (eds), *Internet Governance: Infrastructure and Institutions* (Oxford University Press, 2009) 48
Sparrow, Andrew, *The Law of Virtual Worlds and Internet Social Networks* (Gower Publishing Limited, 2010)
Tapscott, Don and Anthony D. Williams, *Wikinomics: How Mass Collaboration Changes Everything* (Penguin Group, 2006)
Taylor, Kevin, 'Copyright in Practice: The Publisher Perspective' in Trevor Fenwick and Ian Locks (eds), *Copyright in the Digital Age: Industry Issues and Impacts* (Wildy, Simmons & Hill Publishing on behalf of The Stationers Company and individual contributors, 2010) 159
Tehranian, John, *Infringement Nation: Copyright 2.0 and You* (Oxford University Press, 2011)
Thaler, Richard H. and Cass R. Sunstein, *Nudge: Improving Decisions about Health, Wealth and Happiness* (Penguin Books, 2008)
Tyler, Tom R., *Why People Obey the Law* (Yale University Press, 1990)
Vaidhyanathan, Siva, 'Open Source as Culture / Culture as Open Source' in Michael Mandiberg (ed.), *The Social Media Reader* (New York University Press, 2008) 24
VerSteeg, Russ, 'Originality and Creativity in Copyright Law' in Peter K. Yu (ed.), *Intellectual Property and Information Wealth: Issues and Practices in the Digital Age* (Praeger Publishers, 2007) 1
Weatherall, Kimberlee, 'The Relationship between User-generated Content and Commerce' in Dan Hunter, Ramon Lobato, Megan Richardson and Julian Thomas (eds), *Amateur Media: Social, Cultural and Legal Perspectives* (Routledge, 2013) 59
Weiler, Paul C. and Gary Myers, *Entertainment, Media, and the Law: Text, Cases and Problems* (Thomson Reuters, 4th ed., 2011) 347
Wiseman, Leanne, and Brad Sherman, 'Facilitating Access to Information: Understanding the Role of Technology in Copyright Law' in Susy Frankel and Daniel Gervais (eds), *The Evolution and Equilibrium of Copyright in the Digital Age* (Cambridge University Press, 2014) 221
Worlock, David R, 'Other Men's Flowers' in Trevor Fenwick and Ian Locks (eds), *Copyright in the Digital Age: Industry Issues and Impacts* (Wildy, Simmons & Hill Publishing on behalf of The Stationers Company and individual contributors, 2010) 63
Wu, Tim, 'Is Filtering Censorship? The Second Free Speech Tradition' in Jeffrey Rosen and Benjamin Wittes (eds), *Constitution 3.0: Freedom and Technological Change* (The Brookings Institution, 2011) 83
Yeung, Karen, 'Towards an Understanding of Regulation by Design' in Roger Brownsword and Karen Yeung (eds), *Regulating Technologies* (Hart Publishing, 2008) 79

Yu, Peter K., 'Digital Piracy and the Copyright Response' in Indrajit Banerjee (ed.), *The Internet and Governance in Asia: A Critical Reader* (Asian Media Information and Communication Centre, 2007) 340
Zappavigna, Michele, *Discourse of Twitter and Social Media: How we Use Language to Create Affiliation on the Web* (Continuum International Publishing Group, 2012)
Zittrain, Jonathan, 'Perfect Enforcement on Tomorrow's Internet' in Roger Brownsword and Karen Yeung (eds), *Regulating Technologies* (Hart Publishing, 2008) 125

C. Reports

Copyright Law Revision Report No. 94 – 1476 (Mr Kastenmeier) (1976, House of Representatives)
Directorate for Public Governance and Territorial Development, 'OECD Reference Checklist for Regulatory Decision Making' (Report, Organisation for Economic Co-operation and Development, 1995)
Productivity Commission, Australian Government, *Productivity Commission Draft Report on Intellectual Property Arrangements* (April 2016)
The Copyright Law Review Committee, Commonwealth of Australia, *Report of the Committee Appointed by the Attorney-General of the Commonwealth to Consider what Alterations are Desirable in The Copyright Law of the Commonwealth* (1959)

D. Others

American Law Institute, *Intellectual Property: Principles Governing Jurisdiction, Choice of Law, and Judgments in Transnational Disputes* (2007)
American Law Institute, *Restatement (Second) of Conflict of Laws* (1998)

II. Cases

A. US cases

A&M Records v Napster, 239 F 3d 1004 (9th Cir, 2001)
Acuff-Rose Music Inc v Jostens Inc, 155 F 3d 140 (2nd Cir, 1998)
Agence France Presse v Morel, 10 Civ 02730 (USDC SDNY, 14 January 2013)
Agence France Presse v Morel, 10 Civ 02730 (USDC SDNY, 21 May 2013)
Agence France Presse v Morel, 10 Civ 02730 (USDC SDNY, 22 November 2013)
Agence France Presse v Morel, 10 Civ 02730 (USDC SDNY, 13 August 2014)
Alfred Bell & Co v Catalda Fine Arts Inc, 191 F 2d 99 (2nd Cir, 1951)
American Dental Association v Delta Dental Plans Association, 126 F 3d 977 (7th Cir, 1997)
American Express Travel Related Servs Co Inc v Assih, 893 NYS 2d 438 (Civ Ct, Richmond County, 2009)
Angel Fraley et al v Facebook Inc et al (ND Cal, No 11- CV-01726, 4 April 2011)
Assessment Technologies v Wiredata, 350 F 3d 640 (7th Cir, 2003)
Atari Inc v North American Philips Consumer Electronics Corp, 672 F 2d 607 (7th Cir, 1982)
Atari Games v Oman, 979 F 2d 242 (DC Cir, 1992)
Baker v Selden, 101 US 99 (1879)
Baltimore Orioles v Major League Baseball Players, 805 F 2d 663 (7th Cir, 1986)
Bill Graham Archives v Dorling Kindersley Ltd, 448 F 3d 605 (2nd Cir, 2006)
Blanch v Koons, 467 F 3d 244 (2nd Cir, 2006)
BMG Rights Management (US) LLC v Cox Communications Inc et al, 2015 WL 7756130 (ED Va, 1 December 2015)
Board of Managers of Soho International Arts Condominimum v City of New York, US Dist LEXIS 10221 (SDNY, 2003)
Bowers v Baystate Techs Inc, 320 F 3d 1317 (Fed Cir, 2003)

BUC International Corp v International Yacht Council Ltd, 489 F 3d 1129 (11th Cir, 2007)
Burr v Beers, 24 NY 178 (1861)
Campbell v Acuff-Rose Music Inc, 510 US 569 (1994)
Capitol Records Inc v MP3 Tunes LLC, 2014 WL 4851719 (USDC SDNY, 22 August 2011)
Cariou v Prince, 714 F 3d 694 (2nd Cir, 2013)
Carnival Cruise Lines Inc v Shute, 499 US 585 (1991)
Carter v Helmsley-Spear, 71 F 3d 77 (2nd Cir, 1995)
Castle Rock Entertainment Inc v Carol Publishing Group Inc, 150 F 3d 132 (2nd Cir, 1998)
CCC Information Services Inc v Maclean Hunter Market Reports Inc, 44 F 3d 61 (2nd Cir, 1994), *cert denied*, 116 S Ct 72 (1995)
Childress v Taylor, 945 F 2d 500 (2nd Cir, 1991)
Christopher Boffoli v Twitter Inc, Case 12-01534 (USDC Wash, 10 September 2012)
Chuck Blore & Don Richman Inc v 20/20 Advertising Inc, 674 F Supp 671 (D Minn, 1987)
Columbia Pictures Industries Inc v Redd Horne Inc, 749 F 2d 154 (3rd Cir, 1984)
Computer Associates International v Altai Inc, 982 F 2d 693 (2nd Cir, 1992)
Concrete Machinery Co Inc v Classic Lawn Ornaments Inc, 843 F 2d 600 (1st Cir, 1988)
Continental Casualty Co v Beardsley, 253 F. 2d 702 (2nd Cir), *cert denied* 358 US 816 (1958)
Country Kids 'N' City Slicks Inc v Sheen, 77 F 3d 1280 (10th Cir, 1996)
Davis v Blige, 505 F 3d 90 (2nd Cir, 2007), *cert denied*, 129 S. Ct. 117 (2008)
Dellar v Samuel Goldwyn Inc, 104 F 2d 661 (2nd Cir, 1939)
Donald Graham v Richard Prince et al, 15 Civ 10160 (USDC SDNY, 30 December 2015)
Eden Toys v Florelee Undergarment Co, 697 F 2d 27 (2nd Cir, 1982)
Equal Employment Opportunity Commission v Arabian American Oil Co, 499 US 244 (26 March 1991)
Eldred v Ashcroft, 537 US 186 (2003)
Ellison v Robertson, 357 F 3d 1072 (9th Cir, 2004)
Elsmere Music Inc v National Broadcasting Co, 623 F 2d 252 (2nd Cir, 1980)
Entertainment Research Group Inc v Genesis Creative Group Inc, 122 F 3d 1211 (9th Cir, 1997)
Erickson v Trinity Theatre Inc, 13 F 3d 1061 (7th Cir, 1994)
Ets-Hokin v Skyy Spirits Inc, 225 F 3d 1068 (9th Cir, 2000)
Feist Publications Inc v Rural Telephone Service Company, 499 US 340 (1991)
Gaiman v McFarlane, 360 F 3d 644 (7th Cir, 2004)
Gershwin Publishing Corp v Columbia Artists Management Inc, 443 F 2d 1159 (2nd Cir, 1971)
Golan v Holder, 132 S Ct 873 (2012)
Gracen v Bradford Exchange, 698 F 2d 300 (7th Cir, 1983)
Grosso v Miramax Film Corp, 383 F 3d 965 (9th Cir, 2004)
Harper & Row Publishers Inc v Nation Enterprises, 471 US 539 (1985)
Itar-Tass Russian News Agency v Russian Kurier Inc, 153 F 3d 82 (2nd Cir, 1998)
Jean v Bug Music Inc, 2002 WL 287786 (SDNY, 27 February 2002)
Kelly v Arriba Soft Corporation, 336 F 3d 811 (9th Cir, 2003)
Kiobel v Royal Dutch Petroleum, 133 S Ct 1695 (2013)
Kregos v Associated Press, 937 F 2d 700 (2nd Cir, 1991)
Kristen Pierson v Twitter Inc, Case 15-5669 (USDC CD Cal, 27 July 2015)
L Batlin & Son Inc v Synder, 536 F 2d 486 (2nd Cir, 1976)
Lawrence v Fox, 20 NY 268 (1859)
Lawrence Lessig v Liberation Music Pty Ltd, Case 1:13-cv-12028-NMG (USDC Mass, 22 August 2013)
Lenz v Universal Music Corporation, 572 F Supp 2d 1150 (USDC ND Cal, 20 August 2008)
Lewis Galoob Toys Inc v Nintendo of America Inc, 964 F 2d 965 (9th Cir, 1992)
Lone Ranger Television Inc v Program Radio Corp, 740 F 2d 718 (9th Cir, 1984)
Mattel Inc v Walking Mountain Productions, 353 F 3d 792 (9th Cir, 2003)
Mavrix Photographs LLC v Livejournal Inc, 2014 WL 6450094, SD Cal (19 September 2014)
Meshwerks Inc v Toyato Motor Sales USA Inc, 528 F 3d 1258 (10th Cir, 2008), *cert denied*, 129 S Ct 1006 (2009)
Metro-Goldwyn-Mayer-Studios Inc v Grokster Ltd, 380 F 3d 1154 (9th Cir, 2004)
Mirage Editions Inc v Albuquerque A.R.T. Company, 856 F 2d 1341 (9th Cir, 1988)
Mirandah Tan and Hassan Miah v John Doe, Civ No 14-cv-2663 (ALC) (USDC SDNY, filed 5 May 2014)
Morissey v Proctor & Gamble Co, 379 F 2d 675 (1st Cir, 1967)

Murphy v Millennium Radio Group LLC, 650 F 3d 295 (3rd Cir, 2011)
Murray Hill Publications Inc v Twentieth Century Fox, 361 F 3d 312 (6th Cir), *cert denied*, 543 US 959 (2004)
Mywebgrocer LLC v Hometown Info Inc, 375 F 3d 190 (2nd Cir, 2004)
Norma Ribbon & Trimming Inc v Little, 51 F 3d 45 (5th Cir, 1995)
North Jersey Media Group Inc v Jeanine Pirro and Fox News Network LLC, Civ No 13 Civ 7153 (ER) (SDNY, 10 February 2015)
Online Policy Group v Diebold Inc, 337 F Supp 2d 1195 (ND Cal, 2004)
Parker v Google Inc, 2007 WL 1989660 (3rd Cir, 10 July 2007)
Perfect 10 Inc v Amazon.com Inc, 508 F 3d 1146 (9th Cir, 2007)
ProCD Inc v Zeidenberg, 86 F 3d 1447 (7th Cir, 1996)
Raanan Katz v Irina Chevaldina, Civ No 3D12-3189 (District Court of Appeal of Florida, Third District, 5 February 2014)
Reyher v Children's Television Workshop, 533 F 2d 87 (2nd Cir), *cert denied*, 429 US 980, 97 S Ct 492 (1976)
Richlin v Metro-Goldwyn-Mayer Pictures Inc, 531 F3d 962 (9th Cir, 2008), *cert denied*, 129 S Ct 1002 (2009)
Ringgold v Black Entertainment Television Inc, 1996 WL 535547 (USDC SDNY, 19 September 1996)
Ross, Brovins & Oehmke PC v LexisNexis, 348 F Supp 2d 845 (ED Mich, 2004)
Sandoval v New Line Cinema Corp, 147 F 3d 215 (2nd Cir, 1998)
Schrock v Learning Curve International Inc, 586 F 3d 513 (7th Cir, 2009)
Shapiro Bernstein & Co v Jerry Vogel Music Co., 221 F 2d 569 (2nd Cir, 1955)
Sheldon v Metro-Goldwyn Pictures Corp, 106 F 2d 45 (2nd Cir, 1939)
Sid & Marty Krofft Television Prods v McDonald's Corp, 562 F 2d 1157 (9th Cir, 1977)
Silverstein v Penguin Putnam, 368 F 3d 77 (2nd Cir, 2004)
Suntrust Bank v Houghton Mifflin Co, 268 F 3d 1257 (11th Cir, 2001)
Telecom Technical Services Inc v Rolm Co, 388 F 3d 820 (11th Cir, 2004)
The Bremen v Zapata Offshore Co, 407 US 1 (1972)
The Bridgeman Art Library, Ltd v Corel Corporation, 36 F Supp 2d 191 (SDNY, 1999)
Ultra International Music Publishing, LLC and Ultra Records, LLC v Michelle Phan (USDC Cal, filed 16 July 2014)
Update Art Inc v Modiin Pub Ltd, 843 F 2d 67 (2nd Cir, 1988)
Viacom International Inc v YouTube Inc, 718 F Supp 2d 514 (SDNY, 2010)
Walker v Time-Life Films Inc, 784 F 2d 44 (2nd Cir), *cert denied*, 476 US 1159 (1986)
Warren Publishing Inc v Microdos Data Corp, 115 F 3d 1509 (11th Cir, 1997)
Well-Made Toy Manufacturing Corp v Goffa International Corp, 354 F 3d 112 (2nd Cir, 2003)
William John Joseph Hoge v William M Schmalfeldt, Civ No ELH-14-1683 (USDC Md, 1 July 2014)

B. UK cases

British South Africa Co v Companhia de Mocambique [1893] AC 602
CBS Songs Ltd v Amstrad Consumer Electronics Plc [1988] 1 AC 1013
Confetti Records (a firm) v Warner Music UK Ltd (trading as East West Records) [2003] EWJC 1274
Designers Guild Ltd v Russell Williams (Textiles) Ltd [2000] UKHL 58
Donoghue v Allied Newspapers Limited (1938) Ch 106
Ernest Turner Electrical Instruments Ltd v Performing Right Society Ltd [1943] Ch 167
Express Newspapers plc v News (UK) Ltd [1990] 1 WLR 1320
Exxon Corp. v. Exxon Insurance Consultants International Ltd [1982] Ch 119
Falcon v Famous Players Film Company [1926] 2 KB 474
Francis Day and Hunter v Twentieth Century Fox Film Corporation [1940] AC 112
Hawkes & Son (London) Ltd v Paramount Films Service Ltd [1934] 1 Ch 593
Hollinrake v Truswell (1894) 3 Ch D 420
Hubbard v Vosper [1972] 2 QB 84 at 94
Hyperion Records v Sawkins [2005] 1 WLR 3281
Interlego v Tyco [1989] AC 217

Jennings v Stephens [1936] Ch. 469
John Walmsley v Education Limited T/A Oise 2014 WL 2194626
Jones v London Borough of Tower Hamlets [2001] RPC (14) 379
Kenrick v Lawrence (1890) 25 QBD 99
Kirk v Fleming [1928–35] Mac CC 44
Ladbroke (Football) Ltd v William Hill (Football) Ltd [1964] 1 All ER 465
Lucasfilm v Ainsworth [2011] UKSC 39
Norowzian v Arks Ltd (No 2) [2000] FSR 363
Pasterfield v Denham [1999] FSR 168
Performing Right Society Ltd v Harlequin Record Shops Ltd [1979] 2 All ER 828
Spiliada Maritime Corporation v Consulex Ltd [1987] 1 AC 460
TCN Channel Nine Pty Ltd v Network Ten Pty Ltd (2002) 55 IPR 112
The Newspaper Licensing Agency and others v Meltwater Holding BV and others [2011] EWCA Civ 890
Tidy v Trustees of the Natural History Museum (1995) 39 IPR 501
Twentieth Century Fox Film Corporation v Newzbin Limited [2010] EWHC 608
University of London Press Ltd v University Tutorial Press Ltd [1916] 2 Ch 601
Walter v Lane [1900] AC 539

C. Australian cases

Aristocrat Technologies Australia Pty Ltd v DAP Services (Kempsey) Pty Ltd (in liq) (2007) 71 IPR 437
Australian Olympic Committee Inc v The Big Fights Inc (1999) 46 IPR 53
Autodesk Inc v Dyason (No 1) (1992) 173 CLR 330
Avel Pty Ltd v Multicoin Amusements Pty Ltd (1990) 171 CLR 88
CBD Records Australia Ltd v Gross (1989) 15 IPR 385 (Federal Court of Australia)
Copyright Owners Reproduction Society v EMI (Australia) Pty Ltd [1958] HCA 54
Data Access v Powerflex [1999] HCA 49
De Garis v Neville Jefress Pidler (1990) 37 FCR 99
Elwood Clothing Pty Ltd v Cotton On Clothing Pty Ltd [2008] FCAFC 197
EMI Songs Australia Pty Ltd v Larrikin Music Publishing Pty Ltd [2011] FCAFC 47
Fairfax Media Publications Pty Ltd v Reed International Books Australia Pty Ltd [2010] 88 IPR 11 (Federal Court of Australia)
Ice TV Pty Limited v Nine Network Australia Pty Ltd [2009] HCA 14
Neilson v Overseas Projects Corporation of Victoria Ltd [2005] HCA 54
Network Ten Pty Ltd v TCN Channel Nine Pty Ltd [2004] HCA 14
Puttick v Fletcher Challenge Forests Ltd [2006] VSC 370
Rank Film Production Ltd v Colin S Dodds (1983) 2 IPE 113
Roadshow Films v iiNet Limited [2012] 286 ALR 466
Seafolly Pty Ltd v Madden (No 2) [2013] FCA 46
State of Victoria v Pacific Technologies (Australia) Pty Ltd (No 2) [2009] FCA 737
Telstra Corporation v Australasian Performing Right Association (1997) 38 IPR 294
Telstra Corporation Ltd v Desktop Marketing Systems Pty Ltd [2002] FCAFC 112
Telstra Corporation Ltd v Phone Directories Company Pty Ltd (2010) 194 FCR 142
Telstra Corp Ltd v Royal & Sun Alliance Insurance Ltd (2003) 57 IPR 453
Trident General Insurance Co Ltd v McNiece Bros Pty Ltd [1988] 165 CLR 107
Universal Music Australia Pty Limited v Sharman License Holdings Limited [2005] FCA 1242
Victoria Park Racing and Recreation Grounds Co. Ltd v Taylor (1937) 58 CLR 479
Voth v Manildra Flour Mills Pty Ltd [1990] HCA 55
Zeccolo v Universal Studios Inc (1982) 46 ALR 189 (Full Federal Court of Australia)

D. Other cases

Gestevision Telecinco SA and another v YouTube LLC, Case 11 / 2014 (Madrid Court of Appeal (Civil Division), 14 January 2014)

Infopaq International A/S v Danske Dagblades Forening (Court of Justice of the European Union, C-5/08, 16 July 2009)
ITV Broadcasting Ltd And Others (Court of Justice of the European Union, C-607/11, 7 March 2013)
Johan Deckmyn and Vrijheidsfonds VZW v Helena Vandersteen and Others (Court of Justice of the European Union, C-201/13, 3 September 2014)
Nils Svensson et al v Retriever Sverige AB (Court of Justice of the European Union, C-466/12, 13 February 2014)
Tod's SpA v Heyraud SA, Case C-28/04, 2005 ECR I-05781

III. Legislation

A. US legislation

Berne Convention Implementation Act, 17 USC § 101 (1988)
Code of Federal Regulations, 37 CFR § 202.1 (1991)
Copyright Act, 17 USC (1976) §§ 101–810
Digital Millennium Copyright Act, 17 USC § 512 (1998)
United States Constitution, art I § 8, cl 8 (1787)
Visual Artists Rights Act, 17 USC § 106A (1990)

B. UK legislation

Contracts (Rights of Third Parties) Act 1999 (UK)
Copyright, Designs and Patents Act 1988 (UK) c 48
Statute of Anne 1709 (UK) c 19, as repealed by the *Copyright Act 1842*
The Copyright (Application to Other Countries) Order 1993 (UK) SI 1993/942
The Copyright and Rights in Performances (Personal Copies for Private Use) Regulations 2014 (UK) SI 2014/2361

C. Australian legislation

Copyright Act 1968 (Cth)
Copyright (International Protection) Regulations 1969 (Cth)
Insurance Contracts Act 1984 (Cth)
Property Law Act 1969 (WA)
Property Law Act 1974 (Qld)
Property Law Act 2000 (NT)
Telecommunications Act 1997 (Cth)

D. Other legislation

Copyright Act, RSC 1985, c C-42

IV. Treaties/Supranational materials

Agreement on Trade-Related Aspects of Intellectual Property Rights, signed 15 April 1994 (entered into force 1 January 1996)

Berne Convention for the Protection of Literary and Artistic Works, signed 9 September 1886 (entered into force 5 December 1886)

International Covenant on Economic, Social and Cultural Rights, 993 UNTS 3 (16 December 1966)

Regulation (EC) No 1215/2012 of 12 December 2012 on Jurisdiction and the Recognition and Enforcement of Judgments in Civil and Commercial Matters [20 December 2012] OJ L 351/1

Regulation (EC) No 593/2008 of 17 June 2008 on the law applicable to contractual obligations (Rome I) [4 July 2008] OJ L 177/6

Universal Copyright Convention, opened for signature 6 September 1952, UNTS No. 2937 (entered into force 16 September 1955)

Universal Declaration of Human Rights, GA Res 217A (III), UN GAOR, 3rd sess, 183rd plen mtg, UN Doc A/810 (10 December 1948)

WIPO Copyright Treaty, signed 20 December 1996 (entered into force 6 March 2002)

WIPO Performances and Phonograms Treaty, signed 20 December (1996) (entered into force 20 May 2002)

V. Others

Aufderheide, Patricia and Peter Jaszi, *Recut, Reframe, Recycle: Quoting Copyrighted Material in User-Generated Video (January 2008)* Center for Social Media, School of Communication, American University in Washington, D.C. <http://www.centerforsocialmedia.org/sites/default/files/CSM_Recut_Reframe_Recycle_report.pdf>

Australian Human Rights Commission, *What is the Universal Declaration of Human Rights?* <https://www.humanrights.gov.au/publications/what-universal-declaration-human-rights>

Australian Law Reform Commission, *Classification – Content Regulation and Convergent Media* (February 2012) <http://www.alrc.gov.au/sites/default/files/pdfs/publications/final_report_118_for_web.pdf>

Australian Law Reform Commission, *Copyright and the Digital Economy* (November 2013) <http://www.alrc.gov.au/sites/default/files/pdfs/publications/final_report_alrc_122_2nd_december_2013_.pdf>

Awan, Mariam, *The user-generated content exception: Moving away from a non-commercial requirement* (11 November 2015) <http://www.iposgoode.ca/wp-content/uploads/2015/11/Mariam-Awan-The-user-generated-content-exception.pdf>

Barlow, John Perry, *A Declaration of the Independence of Cyberspace* (8 February 1996) <https://projects.eff.org/~barlow/Declaration-Final.html>

Barlow, John Perry, *The Economy of Ideas* (March 1994) <http://archive.wired.com/wired/archive/2.03/economy.ideas.html>

Barnett, Katy, *Trident v McNiece twenty-five years on* (18 October 2013) <https://blogs.unimelb.edu.au/opinionsonhigh/2013/10/18/trident-v-mcniece-twenty-five-years-on/>

BBC, *YouTube star Michelle Phan sued over copyright breach* <http://www.bbc.com/news/technology-28418449>

Bently, Lionel, Tanya Aplin, Robert Burrell, Norma Dawson, Ronan Deazley, Estelle Derclaye, Graeme Diwoodie, Sir Robin Jacob, Martin Kretschmer, Hector MacQueen, Paul Torremans and Charlotte Waelde, *Letter to the Chairman of the Joint Committee on Satutory Instruments* (6 June 2014) <http://www.create.ac.uk/wp-content/uploads/2014/03/Scrutiny-Committee-Profs-letter-June2014.pdf>

Bloomberg Businessweek, *Facebook: The Making of 1 Billion Users* (4 October 2012) <http://www.businessweek.com/articles/2012-10-04/facebook-the-making-of-1-billion-users>

BookCrossing, *bookcrossing.com* <www.bookcrossing.com>

Boris, Cynthia, *YouTube calms angry vidders with new tweaks in Content ID process* (19 March 2014) <http://www.marketingpilgrim.com/2014/03/youtube-calms-angry-vidders-with-new-tweaks-in-content-id-process.html>

Bruns, Axel and Mark Bahnisch, *Social Media: Tools for User-Generated Content – Social Drivers behind Growing Consumer Participation in User-Led Content Generation* (March 2009) Volume 1 <http://www.smartservicescrc.com.au/files/files/Social_Media_State_of_the%20Art_March2009.pdf>

Cellan-Jones, Rory, *Social media told to simplify terms and conditions* (28 November 2014) <http://www.bbc.com/news/technology-30234789>

Chung, Andrew, *Fox News, publisher, settle copyright dispute over iconic 9/11 photo* (16 February 2016) <http://www.reuters.com/article/us-ip-fox-news-photo-idUSKCN0VP2HY>

ClipConverter.cc, *Free Online Media Recorder* <http://www.clipconverter.cc/>

Christie, Andrew F., *Private International Law Issues in Online Intellectual Property Infringement Disputes with Cross-Border Elements: An Analysis of National Approaches* (2015) <http://www.wipo.int/edocs/pubdocs/en/wipo_rep_rfip_2015_1.pdf>

Considered, *Can Technology Drive Behaviour Change?* <http://considered-creative.co.uk/can_tech_drive/>

Consumer Focus, *Time to change the tune: Consumer research briefing on copyright* (February 2010) <http://www.consumerfocus.org.uk/assets/1/files/2010/02/Consumer-Focus-Time-to-change-the-tune1.pdf>

Consumerist, *Facebook's New Terms of Service: "We can Do Anything We Want With Your Content. Forever."* <http://consumerist.com/2009/02/15/facebooks-new-terms-of-service-we-can-do-anything-we-want-with-your-content-forever/>

Council of Europe – Commissioner for Human Rights, *Social Media and Human Rights* (February 2012) <www.commissioner.coe.int>

Creative Commons, *Attribution-ShareAlike 3.0 Unported* <http://creativecommons.org/licenses/by-sa/3.0/>

Creative Commons, *Creative Commons* <http://creativecommons.org/>

D'Orazio, Dante, *Twitter is deleting stolen jokes on copyright grounds* (25 July 2015) <http://www.theverge.com/2015/7/25/9039127/twitter-deletes-stolen-joke-dmca-takedown>

Electronic Frontier Foundation, *Lawrence Lessig settles fair use lawsuit over Phoenix music snippets* <https://www.eff.org/press/releases/lawrence-lessig-settles-fair-use-lawsuit-over-phoenix-music-snippets>

Electronic Frontier Foundation, *Lawrence Lessig Strikes Back Against Bogus Copyright Takedown* <https://www.eff.org/press/releases/lawrence-lessig-strikes-back-against-bogus-copyright-takedown>

European Max Planck Group, *Principles on Conflict of Laws in Intellectual Property* (1 December 2011) <http://www.ip.mpg.de/fileadmin/ipmpg/content/clip/Final_Text_1_December_2011.pdf>

Facebook, *Community Standards* <https://www.facebook.com/communitystandards>

Facebook, *Data Policy* <https://www.facebook.com/privacy>

Facebook, *Facebook* <https//www.facebook.com>

Facebook, *Facebook HQ* <https://www.facebook.com/Facebook-HQ-166793820034304/>

Facebook, *Facebook Principles* <https://www.facebook.com/principles.php>

Facebook, *Facebook Reports First Quarter 2015 Results* (22 April 2015) <http://investor.fb.com/releasedetail.cfm?ReleaseID=908022>

Facebook, *Government Requests Report* <https://govtrequests.facebook.com/>

Facebook, *Help Center: About Copyright* <https://www.facebook.com/help/249141925204375>

Facebook, *Help Center: About Intellectual Property* <https://www.facebook.com/help/399224883474207>

Facebook, *Help Center: What is the contact information for your Digital Millennium Copyright Act designated agent?* <https://www.facebook.com/help/www/190268144407210>

Facebook, *Statement of Rights and Responsibilities* (30 January 2015) <https://www.facebook.com/terms>

Forbes, *Facebook NewsFeed Manipulation Prompts FTC Complaint, Investigation Possible* (4 July 2014) <http://www.forbes.com/sites/gregorymcneal/2014/07/04/facebook-faces-possible-ftc-investigation-for-manipulation- study/>

Forbes, *Kaskade and Michelle Phan: Burn the Copyright Law!* <http://www.forbes.com/sites/oliverherzfeld/2014/07/23/kaskade-and-michelle-phan-burn-the-copyright-law/>

Fox, Michaela, *Australian music label Liberation to pay damages to Harvard professor Lawrence Lessig in copyright battle* (28 February 2014) <http://www.smh.com.au/digital-life/digital-life-news/australian-music-label-liberation-to-pay-damages-to-harvard-professor-lawrence-lessig-in-copyright-battle-20140228-33pnj.html>

Gabbert, Elisa, *Find Your Old Tweets: How to See Your First (Worst?) Tweet* (10 October 2013) <http://www.wordstream.com/blog/ws/2013/10/10/how-to-find-your-old-tweets>

Gajanan, Mahita, *Controversial artist Richard Prince sued for copyright infringement* (5 January 2016) <http://www.theguardian.com/artanddesign/2016/jan/04/richard-prince-sued-copyright-infringement-rastafarian-instagram>

Gimp, *GNU Image Manipulation Program* <http://www.gimp.org/>

Ginsburg, Jane C., *Comments in response to the US Copyright Office's Notice soliciting further comments on the 'Right of Making Available' dated 15 July 2014* (3 September 2014) <http://copyright.gov/docs/making_available/comments/docket2014_2/reply/Ginsburg_Jane.pdf>

Global Web Index, *Daily time spent on social networks rises to 1.72 hours* (26 January 2015) <https://www.globalwebindex.net/blog/daily-time-spent-on-social-networks-rises-to-1-72-hours>

GNU Operating System, *GNU Free Documentation License* (3 November 2008) <http://www.gnu.org/copyleft/fdl.html>

Google, *Transparency Report* <https://www.google.com/transparencyreport/removals/copyright/>

Google Play, *Easy Alarm YouTube* <https://play.google.com/store/apps/details?id=com.cimleah.easyalarm&hl=en>

Gowers, Andrew, *Gowers Review of Intellectual Property* (December 2006) <https://www.gov.uk/government/uploads/system/uploads/attachment_data/file/228849/0118404830.pdf>

Grant, John, *The Robots Are Coming: Protecting Website Owners from Copyright Infringement Claims* (Fall 2008) <http://www.americanbar.org/newsletter/publications/law_trends_news_practice_area_e_newsletter_home/business_grant.html>

Hargreaves, Ian, *Digital Opportunity: A Review of Intellectual Property and Growth* (May 2011) <https://www.gov.uk/government/uploads/system/uploads/attachment_data/file/32563/ipreview-finalreport.pdf>

Hickey, Matt, *Twitter likely expanding 140-character tweet limit with new product* (29 September 2015) <http://www.forbes.com/sites/matthickey/2015/09/29/twitter-likely-expanding-140-character-tweet-limit-with-new-product/>

Huang, Tai-Jan, *Copyright Consciousness and Intellectual Property Discourse: The Politics of Creative Commons* (May 2013) <https://archive.org/stream/CCCopyrightConsicouseness_201308/CC_Copyright%20Consicouseness#page/n3/mode/2up>

Intellectual Property Office, *Exceptions to Copyright: Guidance for Creators and Copyright Owners* (October 2014) <https://www.gov.uk/government/uploads/system/uploads/attachment_data/file/448274/Exceptions_to_copyright_-_Guidance_for_creators_and_copyright_owners.pdf>

Inside Facebook, *Facebook Announces First-Ever User Vote on Terms of Service Changes* <http://www.insidefacebook.com/2009/04/06/facebook-announces-first-ever-user-vote-on-terms-of-service-changes/>

Inside Facebook, *Facebook Reverts Terms of Service After Complaints* <http://www.insidefacebook.com/2009/02/18/facebook-reverts-terms-of-service-after-complaints/>

Intellectual Property Office of Singapore, *Annex A: IP Perception Survey Summary Report 2014* <https://www.ipos.gov.sg/Portals/0/Press%20Release/Annex%20A%20Perception%20Survey.pdf>

Intellectual Property of Singapore, *What Do We Do?* <https://www.ipos.gov.sg/AboutUs/WhatDoWeDo.aspx>

International Business Times, *Google Plus Becomes World's No. 2 Social Network after Facebook, Knocking off Twitter* (28 January 2013) <http://www.ibtimes.com/google-plus-becomes-worlds-no-2-social-network-after-facebook-knocking-twitter-1042956>

ITP.net, *Twitter tweaks terms to include advertising* <http://www.itp.net/573783-twitter-tweaks-terms-to-include-advertising#.Ujpvc3fhdS8>

Jones, Thomas, *Short Cuts* (17 July 2014) <http://www.lrb.co.uk/v36/n14/thomas-jones/short-cuts>

Kamen, Matt, *Twitter sued over photo copyright* (29 July 2015) <http://www.wired.co.uk/news/archive/2015-07/29/twitter-sued-over-photo-copyright>

Klie, Leonard, *YouTube Expands Video Transcription Option for All* (5 March 2010) <http://www.speechtechmag.com/Articles/News/News-Feature/YouTube-Expands-Video-Transcription-Option-for-All-61571.aspx>

Lievens, Eva, Peggy Valcke and Pieter Jan Valgaeren, *State of the art on regulatory trends in media* (December 2011) <https://lirias.kuleuven.be/bitstream/123456789/350852/1/EMSOC_ICRI_D+1+2+1_2011.pdf>

Macquarie Dictionary, *Pastiche* <https://www.macquariedictionary.com.au/features/word/search/?word=pastiche&search_word_type=Dictionary>

Mashable, *Pinterest Updates Privacy Policy, Terms of Service* <mashable.com/2012/03/24/pinterest-updates-privacy-policy-terms of service/>

Mashable, *YouTube Star Michelle Phan Fights Back Against Multimillion-Dollar Lawsuit* <http://mashable.com/2014/07/24/michelle-phan-lawsuit/>

Mayfield, Antony, *What is social media* (1 August 2008) <http://www.repromax.com/docs/113/854427515.pdf>

McFarlane, Greg, *How Facebook, Twitter, Social Media Make Money From You* (2 September 2014) <http://www.investopedia.com/stock-analysis/032114/how-facebook-twitter-social-media-make-money-you-twtr-lnkd-fb-goog.aspx>

McKenzie, Pamela J., Jacquelyn Burkell, Lola Wong, Caroline Whippey, Samuel E. Troscow and Michael McNally, 'User-generated online content 1: Overview, current state and context' (4 June 2012) 17(6) *First Monday* 1 <http://firstmonday.org/htbin/cgiwrap/bin/ojs/index.php/fm/article/view/3912/3266>

McKinsey Global Institute, *The social economy: Unlocking value and productivity through social technologies* (July 2012) <http://www.mckinsey.com/insights/high_tech_telecoms_internet/the_social_economy>

McNally, Michael B., Samuel E. Troscow, Lola Wong, Caroline Whippey, Jacquelyn Burkell and Pamela J. McKenzie, 'User-generated online content 2: Policy implications' (4 June 2012) 17(6) *First Monday* 1 <http://firstmonday.org/htbin/cgiwrap/bin/ojs/index.php/fm/article/viewArticle/3913/3267>

Mesch, Gustavo S., *The Internet and Youth Culture* <http://www.iasc-culture.org/THR/archives/YouthCulture/Mesch.pdf>

Nelson, Jack Wright, *The Hague Convention on Choice of Court Agreements: Return of the Litigators?* (30 April 2015) <http://www.youngicca-blog.com/the-hague-convention-on-choice-of-court-agreements-return-of-the-litigators/>

Nielsen, *Social Media Report 2012* (8 January 2013) <http://blog.nielsen.com/nielsenwire/social/2012/>

Norton Rose Fulbright's Social Media Team, *Agence France Presse v. Morel & The Scope of Twitter's Copyright License* <http://fulbrightsocialmediablog.com/2013/02/22/agence-france-presse-v-morel-the-scope-of-twitters-copyright-license/>

Office for Harmonization in the Internal Market, *The European Citizens and Intellectual Property: Perception, Awareness and Behaviour* (November 2013) https://oami.europa.eu/tunnel-web/secure/webdav/guest/document_library/observatory/documents/IPContributionStudy/25-11-2013/european_public_opinion_study_web.pdf>

Olmstead, Kenneth and Kristine Lu, *Digital News: Revenue – Fact Sheet* (29 April 2015) <http://www.journalism.org/2015/04/29/digital-news-revenue-fact-sheet/>

PC World, *Creative Commons co-founder wages 'fair use' war over YouTube takedown notice* <http://www.pcworld.com/article/2047320/copyright-guru-claims-fair-use-to-fight-youtube-takedown-notice.html>

PC World, *Facebook Privacy Change Sparks Federal Complaint* <http://www.pcworld.com/article/159703/facebook.html>

PC World, *Rewriting Facebook's Terms of Service* <http://www.pcworld.com/article/160358/facebook_new_tos.html>

Pew Research Center, *About Pew Research Center* <http://www.pewresearch.org/about/>

Pew Research Internet Project, *Arts Organizations and Digital Technologies: Section 6: Overall Impact of Technology on the Arts* <http://www.pewinternet.org/2013/01/04/section-6-overall-impact-of-technology-on-the-arts/>

Pew Research Internet Project, *Summary: 15 Theses About the Digital Future* (11 March 2014) <http://www.pewinternet.org/2014/03/11/digital-life-in-2025/>

Photoshop, *Photoshop.com* <http://www.photoshop.com/>

Pinterest, *Acceptable Use Policy* <https://about.pinterest.com/en/acceptable-use-policy>

Pinterest, *Copyright Infringement Notification* <http://www.pinterest.com/about/copyright/dmca-pin/>

Pinterest, *Copyright* <https://about.pinterest.com/en/copyright>

Pinterest, *Pinterest* <https://www.pinterest.com>

Pinterest, *Pinterest basic: Secret boards* <https://help.pinterest.com/en/articles/secret-boards#Web>
Pinterest, *Pinterest's Brand-New San Francisco Office* <https://www.pinterest.com/owenthomas/pinterest-s-brand-new-san-francisco-office/>
Pinterest, *Privacy Policy* <https://about.pinterest.com/en/privacy-policy>
Pinterest, *Transparency Report* <https://help.pinterest.com/en/articles/transparency-report>
Pinterest, *Terms of Service* <https://about.pinterest.com/en/terms-service>
Pinterest Blog, *Pin a Video!* (22 May 2013) <https://blog.pinterest.com/en/pin-video>
Pring, Cara, *216 Social Media and Internet Statistics* (September 2012) <http://thesocialskinny.com/216-social-media-and-internet-statistics-september-2012/≥
Quartz, *Pinterest, which just hit 100 million users, is growing much faster than expected* (17 September 2015) <http://qz.com/504823/pinterest-which-just-hit-100-million-users-is-growing-much-faster-than-expected/>
Reinberg, Consuelo, *Are Tweets Copyright Protected?* (July 2009) <http://www.wipo.int/wipo_magazine/en/2009/04/article_0005.html>
Reznik, Eugene, *How the photo community would reimagine copyright* (16 July 2015) <http://www.americanphotomag.com/how-photo-community-reimagines-copyright>
Rich, L. J., *How can social networks make money* (15 April 2011) <http://news.bbc.co.uk/2/hi/programmes/click_online/9457946.stm>
Ricketson, Sam, *WIPO Study on Limitations and Exceptions of Copyright and Related Rights in the Digital Environment* (5 April 2003) <http://www.wipo.int/edocs/mdocs/copyright/en/sccr_9/sccr_9_7.pdf>
Sawers, Paul, *Everything's Social: A Day in the Life of Jack, a Social Media Geek* (23 May 2011) <http://thenextweb.com/socialmedia/2011/05/23/everythings-social-a-day-in-the-life-of-jack-a-social-media-geek/>
Shrimsley, Robert, *Facebook: why we're all lab rats now* (4 July 2014) <http://www.ft.com/cms/s/2/81196950-023c-11e4-ab5b00144feab7de.html#axzz37quSJedp>
Social Media News, *Social Media Statistics Australia – September 2013* (1 October 2013) <http://www.socialmedianews.com.au/social-media-statistics-australia-september-2013/>
The Department of Commerce Internet Policy Task Force, *Copyright Policy, Creativity and Innovation in the Digital Economy* (July 2013) <http://www.uspto.gov/sites/default/files/news/publications/copyrightgreenpaper.pdf>
The Guardian, *Twitter removes lifted jokes over copyright infringement claims* (27 July 2015) <http://www.theguardian.com/technology/2015/jul/27/twitter-removes-lifted-jokes-copyright-infringment-claims>
The Market Oracle, *How do social media companies like Facebook and Twitter make money* (11 October 2013) <http://www.marketoracle.co.uk/Article42647.html>
The New York Times, *Facebook Withdraws Changes in Data Use* <http://www.nytimes.com/2009/02/19/technology/internet/19facebook.html?_r=0>
The Shannon Company, *Top 15 Social Media Sites in Australia* (10 June 2013) <http://theshannoncompany.com.au/blog/?p=1321>
The Social Media Guys, *The Complete Guide to Social Media* (8 November 2010) <http://www.thesocialmediaguys.co.uk/wp-content/uploads/downloads/2011/03/CompleteGuidetoSocialMedia.pdf>
The Window Seat, *Dear Pinterest, Thanks for changing your terms* <http://www.knoed.com/thewindowseat/dear-pinterest-thanks-for-changing-your terms/>
Tribar Opinion Committee, *Supplemental Report: Opinions on Chosen-Law Provisions under the Restatement of Conflict of Laws* <http://www.americanbar.org/content/dam/aba/publications/business_lawyer/2013/68_4/report-chosen-law-provisions-201308.authcheckdam.pdf>
Troscow, Samuel E., Jacquelyn Burkell, Nick Dyer-Witheford, Pamela McKenzie, Michael B. McNally, Caroline Whippey and Lola Wong, *Mobilizing User-Generated Content for Canada's Advantage (1 December 2010)* Faculty of Information and Media Studies at the University of Western Ontario <ir.lib.uwo.ca/fimspub/21/>
Twitch, *Twitch* <http://www.twitch.tv/>
Twitter, *Agence France-Presse @AFP* <https://twitter.com/AFP>
Twitter, *Company* <https://about.twitter.com/company>
Twitter, *Copyright Notices: DMCA takedown notices (July 1 – December 31, 2014)* <https://transparency.twitter.com/copyright-notices/2014/jul-dec>

Twitter, *Coming soon: express even more in 140 characters* (24 May 2016) <https://blog.twitter.com/express-even-more-in-140-characters>.
Twitter, *Help Center: About public and protected Tweets* <https://support.twitter.com/articles/14016#>
Twitter, *Help Center: Copyright policy* <https://support.twitter.com/articles/15795#>
Twitter, *Help Center: I'm missing Tweets* <https://support.twitter.com/articles/277671#>
Twitter, *Help Center: New user FAQs* <https://support.twitter.com/articles/13920#>
Twitter, *Help Center: Posting a Tweet* <http://support.twitter.com/articles/15367-posting-a-tweet>
Twitter, *Privacy Policy* (27 January 2016) <https://twitter.com/privacy>
Twitter, *Report copyright infringement* <https://support.twitter.com/forms/dmca>
Twitter, *Terms of Service* (27 January 2016) <https://twitter.com/tos>
Twitter, *The Twitter Rules* <http://support.twitter.com/articles/18311#>
Twitter, *Transparency Report: Copyright Notices* <https://transparency.twitter.com/copyright-notices/2013/jul-dec>
Twitter, *Transparency Report: Copyright Notices* <https://transparency.twitter.com/copyright-notices/2015/jul-dec>
Twitter, *Tweets in broadcast* <https://about.twitter.com/company/broadcast#>
Twitter, *Twitter* <https://www.twitter.com>
Twitter Blogs, *Twitter's New Terms of Service* <https://blog.twitter.com/2009/twitters-new-terms-service>
UGC Principles, *Principles for User Generated Content Services* <http://www.ugcprinciples.com/>
United States Copyright Office, *eCO Registration System* <http://copyright.gov/eco/>
United States Copyright Office, *The Making Available Right in the United States* (February 2016) <http://copyright.gov/docs/making_available/making-available-right.pdf>
University of Oxford IT Services, *Podcasting* <https://www.oucs.ox.ac.uk/podcasts/index.xml?ID=whatis>
Valentine, Colton, *Richard Prince Sold Strangers' Instagram Photos for $90k – And It's Probably Legal* <http://www.huffingtonpost.com/2015/06/30/richard-prince-appropriation-art_n_7674786.html>
Vernon, A, *Open source brings new meaning to user-generated content* (17 June 2010) <http://www.networkworld.com/community/blog/open-source-brings-new-meaning-user-generated>
Wagner, Kurt, and Jason Del Ray, *Twitter plans to go beyond its 140-character limit* (29 September 2015) <http://recode.net/2015/09/29/twitter-plans-to-go-beyond-its-140-character-limit/>
Wikimedia Foundation, *Contact us* <https://wikimediafoundation.org/wiki/Contact_us>
Wikimedia Foundation, *Copyright problems* <https://meta.wikimedia.org/wiki/Copyright_problems>
Wikimedia Foundation, *Privacy Policy* (6 June 2014) <https://wikimediafoundation.org/wiki/Privacy_policy>
Wikimedia Foundation, *Resolution: Licensing Policy* <https://wikimediafoundation.org/wiki/Resolution:Licensing_policy>
Wikimedia Foundation, *Terms of Use* (16 June 2014) <https://wikimediafoundation.org/wiki/Terms_of_Use>
Wikimedia Foundation, *Transparency Report – Requests for Content Alteration & Takedown* <https://transparency.wikimedia.org/content.html>
Wikimedia Foundation, *Commons: Licensing* <https://commons.wikimedia.org/wiki/Commons:Licensing>
Wikimedia Foundation, *WikimediaAnnounce-L: Announcements and Reports of the Wikimedia Movement* <https://lists.wikimedia.org/mailman/listinfo/wikimediaannounce-l>
Wikipedia, *Blog* <https://en.wikipedia.org/wiki/Blog>
Wikipedia, *Copyright Alert System* <https://en.wikipedia.org/wiki/Copyright_Alert_System>
Wikipedia, *Copyright Violations* <https://en.wikipedia.org/wiki/Wikipedia:Copyright_violations>
Wikipedia, *Criticism of Facebook* <https://en.wikipedia.org/wiki/Criticism_of_Facebook>
Wikipedia, *File: Copyright Tags* <https://en.wikipedia.org/wiki/Wikipedia:Image_copyright_tags>
Wikipedia, *Harvey Balls* <https://en.wikipedia.org/wiki/Harvey_Balls>
Wikipedia, *Help: Books* <https://en.wikipedia.org/wiki/Help:Books>
Wikipedia, *Help: Editing* <https://en.wikipedia.org/wiki/Help:Editing>

Wikipedia, *Help: File Page* <https://en.wikipedia.org/wiki/Help:File_page>
Wikipedia, *List of Social Networking Websites* <https://en.wikipedia.org/wiki/List_of_social_networking_websites>
Wikipedia, *Manage your book* <https://en.wikipedia.org/wiki/Special:Book>
Wikipedia, *Norm (social)* <https://en.wikipedia.org/wiki/Norm_(social)#cite_note-marshall-1>
Wikipedia, *Pinterest* <https://en.wikipedia.org/wiki/Pinterest>
Wikipedia, *Podcast* <https://en.wikipedia.org/wiki/Podcast>
Wikipedia, *Social bookmarking* <https://en.wikipedia.org/wiki/Social_bookmarking>
Wikipedia, *Social media* <https://en.wikipedia.org/wiki/Social_media>
Wikipedia, *Twitter* <https://en.wikipedia.org/wiki/Twitter>
Wikipedia, *Vidding* <https://en.wikipedia.org/wiki/Vidding>
Wikipedia, *Virtual world* <https://en.wikipedia.org/wiki/Virtual_world>
Wikipedia, *Wikipedia* <https://www.wikipedia.org/>
Wikipedia, *Wikipedia: Basic copyright issues* <https://en.wikipedia.org/wiki/Wikipedia:Basic_copyright_issues>
Wikipedia, *Wikipedia: Content Removal* <https://en.wikipedia.org/wiki/Wikipedia:Content_removal>
Wikipedia, *Wikipedia: Contributor copyright violations* <https://en.wikipedia.org/wiki/Wikipedia:Contributor_copyright_investigations>
Wikipedia, *Wikipedia: Copyright Violations* <https://en.wikipedia.org/wiki/Wikipedia:Copyright_violations>
Wikipedia, *Wikipedia: Dispute Resolution* <https://en.wikipedia.org/wiki/Wikipedia:Dispute_resolution>
Wikipedia, *Wikis* <en.wikipedia.org/wiki/Wiki>
Wikipedia, *Wikipedia: Your first article* <https://en.wikipedia.org/wiki/Wikipedia:Your_first_article>
Wikipedia, *YouGov* <https://en.wikipedia.org/wiki/YouGov>
Wikipedia, *YouTube* <https://en.wikipedia.org/wiki/YouTube>
WordPress, *Terms of Service* <en.wordpress.com/tos/>
World Intellectual Property Organisation (WIPO), *WIPO-Administered Treaties: Contracting Parties – Berne Convention* <http://www.wipo.int/treaties/en/ShowResults.jsp?treaty_id=15>
Wunsch-Vincent, Sascha and Graham Vickery, *Participative Web: User-Created Content* (12 April 2007) <http://www.oecd.org/sti/38393115.pdf>
YouGov UK, *About* <https://yougov.co.uk/about/about/>
YouGov, *Digital content should be free say younger online users* <https://yougov.co.uk/news/2014/06/19/digital-content-should-be-free-say-younger-online-/>
YouGovReports, *The Future of Digital Consumption 2014* <http://reports.yougov.com/sectors/media/media-uk/future-digital-consumption-2014/>
YouTube, *Community Guidelines* <https:// www.youtube.com/t/policyandsafety/community_guidelines.html>
YouTube, *Copyright Infringement Notification* <https://www.youtube.com/copyright_complaint_form>
YouTube, *Copyright on YouTube* <https://www.youtube.com/yt/copyright>
YouTube, *Keep your YouTube account in good standing* <https://support.google.com/youtube/answer/2797387>
YouTube, *Privacy Guidelines* <http://www.youtube.com/static? template=privacy_guidelines>
YouTube, *Submit a copyright takedown notice* <https://support.google.com/youtube/answer/2807622/>
YouTube, *Terms of Service* (9 June 2010) <https://www.youtube.com/static?template=terms>
YouTube, *Video privacy settings* <https://support.google.com/youtube/answer/157177?hl=en>
YouTube, *YouTube* <https://www.youtube.com>
YouTube, *What is fair use?* <https://www.youtube.com/yt/copyright/fair-use.html>
YouTube Help, *Dispute a Content ID claim* <https://support.google.com/youtube/answer/2797454/>
YouTube Help, *How Content ID works* <https://support.google.com/youtube/answer/2797370>

YouTube Help, *YouTube Video Editor* <https://support.google.com/youtube/answer/183851?hl=en>

Yu, Peter K., 'Conflict of Laws Issues in International Copyright Cases' (originally) on GigaLaw.com (2001) < http://www.peteryu.com/gigalaw0401.pdf>

ZDNet, *Facebook remains top social network, Google+, YouTube battle for second* (14 May 2013) <http://www.zdnet.com/facebook-remains-top-social-network-google-youtube-battle-for-second-7000015303/>

Appendix 1
Screenshots of the technological features

I. Technological features

A. Technological features that encourage content-generative activities

1. Creation

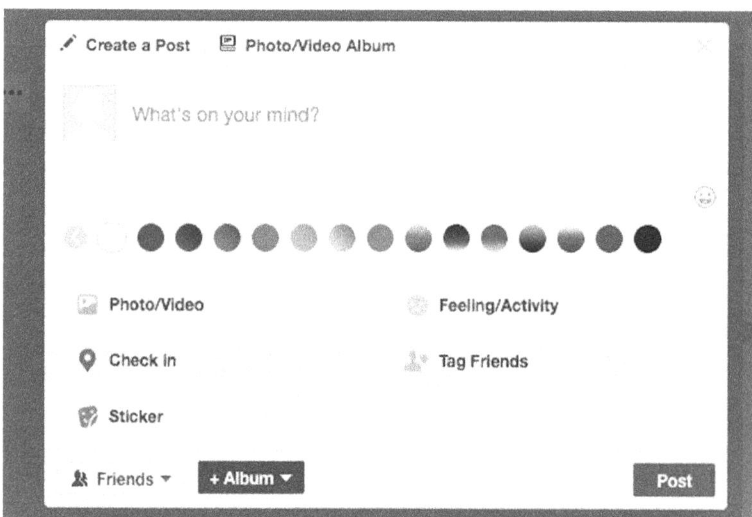

Image 1 Facebook

Image 2 Facebook

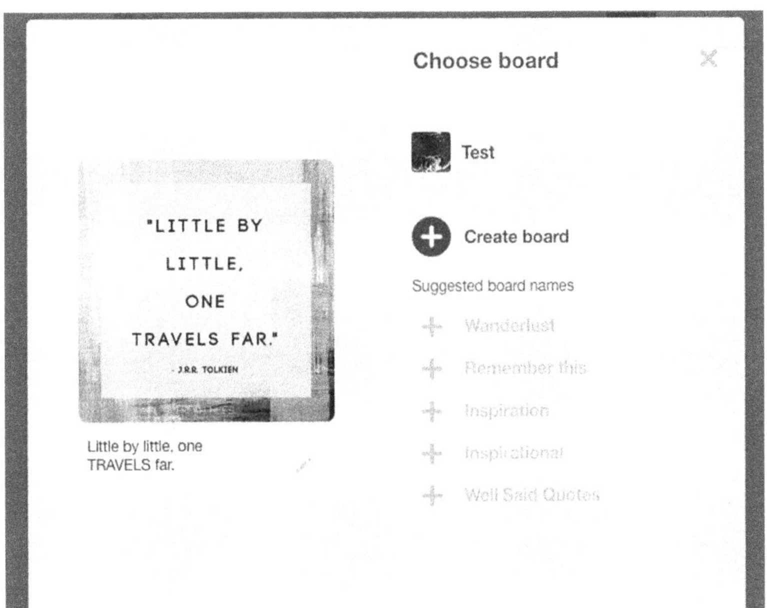

Image 3 Pinterest

Image 4 Pinterest

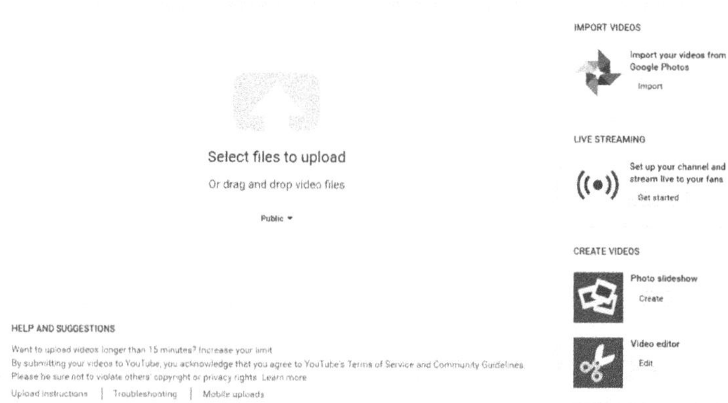

Image 5 YouTube

Image 6 YouTube

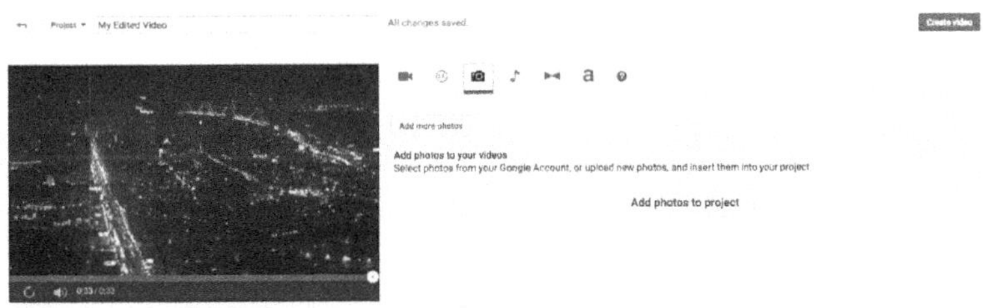

Image 7 YouTube

Image 8 YouTube

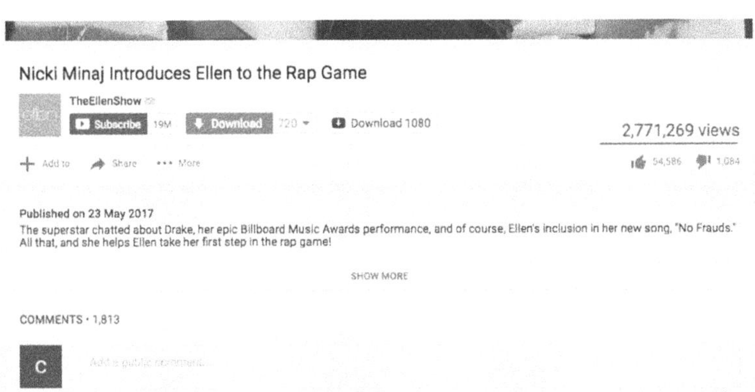

Image 9 YouTube

Image 10 Twitter

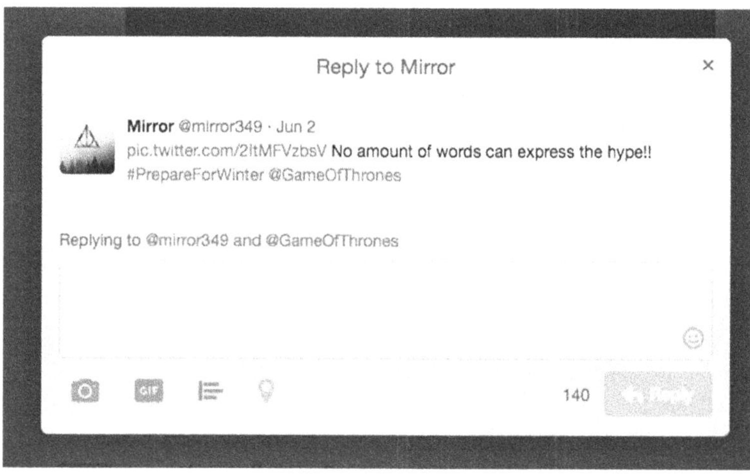

Image 11 Twitter

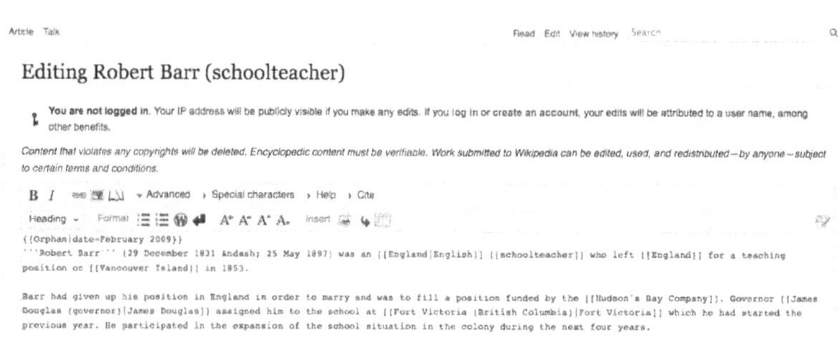

Image 12 Wikipedia

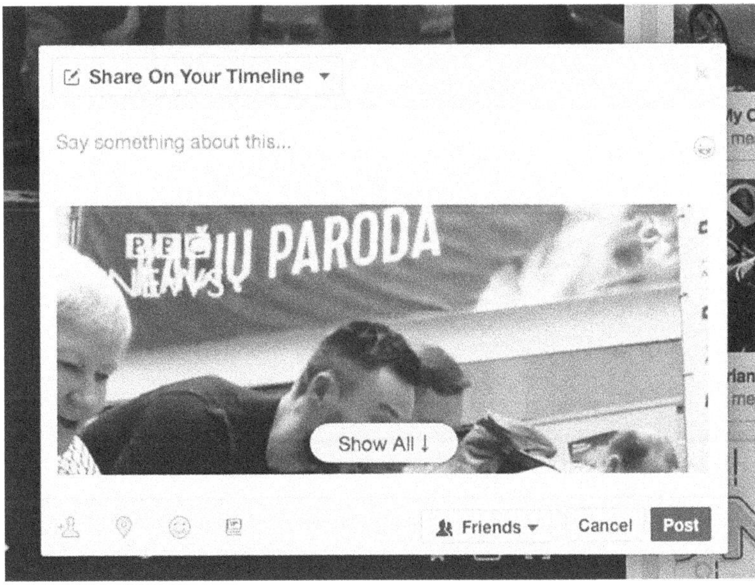

Image 13 Facebook

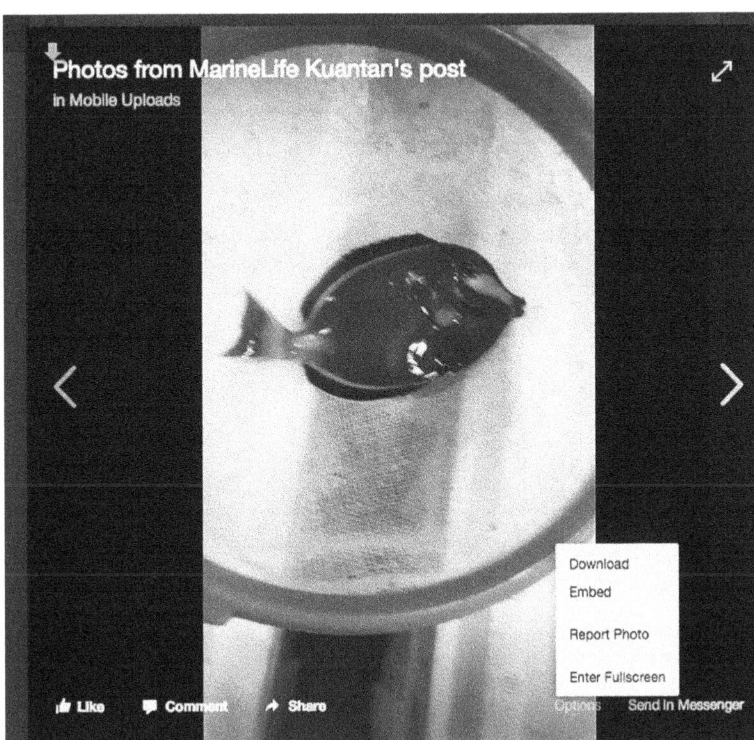

Image 14 Facebook

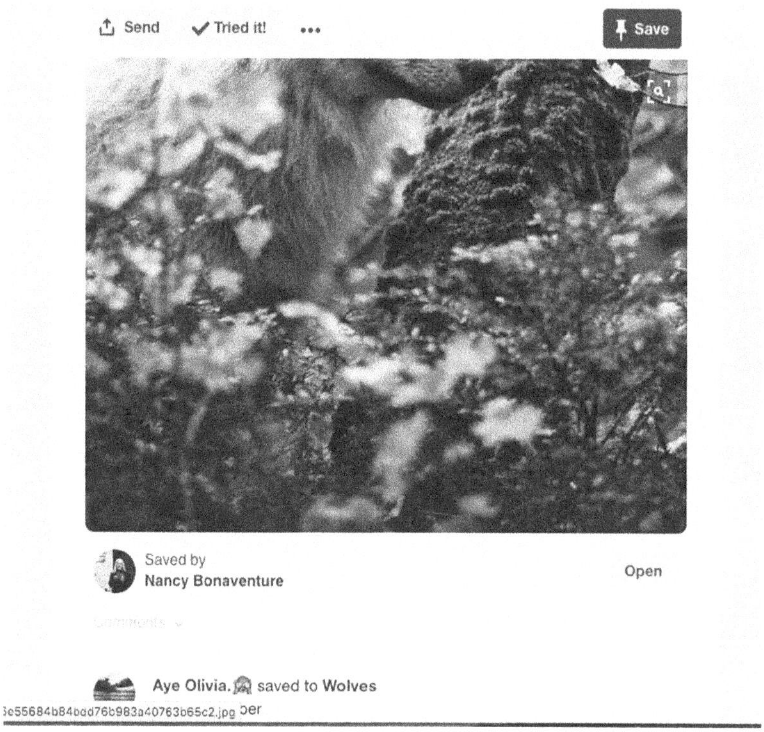

Image 15 Pinterest

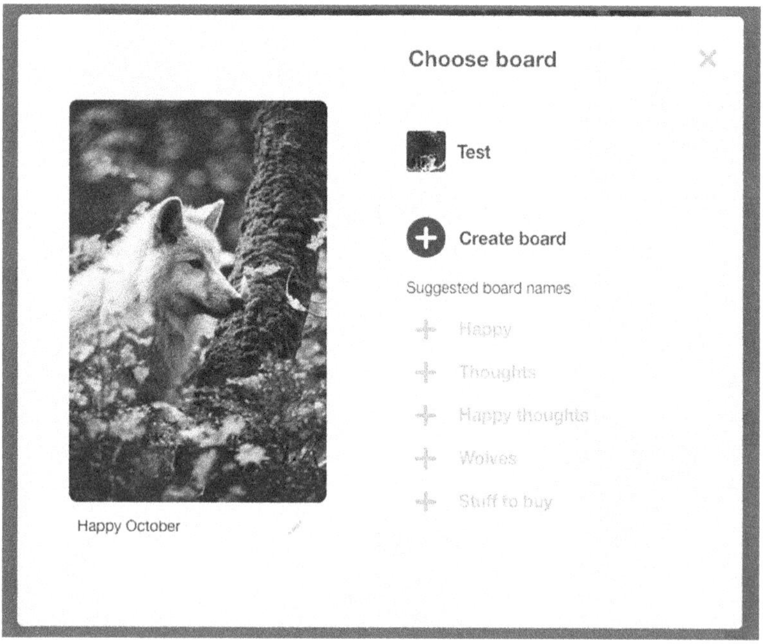

Image 16 Pinterest

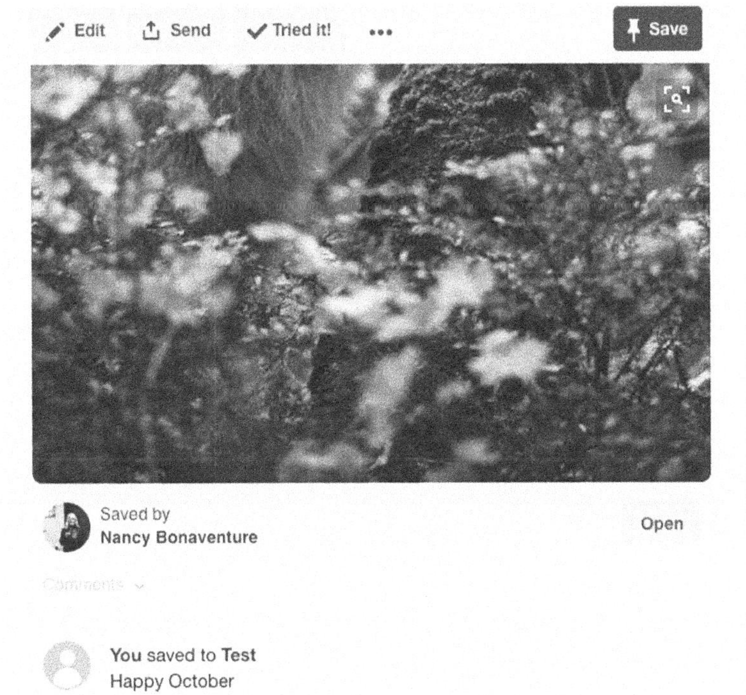

Image 17 Pinterest

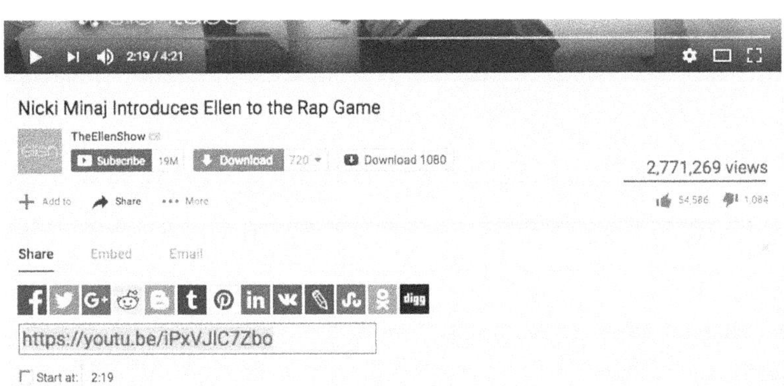

Image 18 YouTube

Image 19 Twitter

Image 20 Twitter

Image 21 Wikipedia

3. Dissemination

Image 22 Facebook

Image 23 Facebook

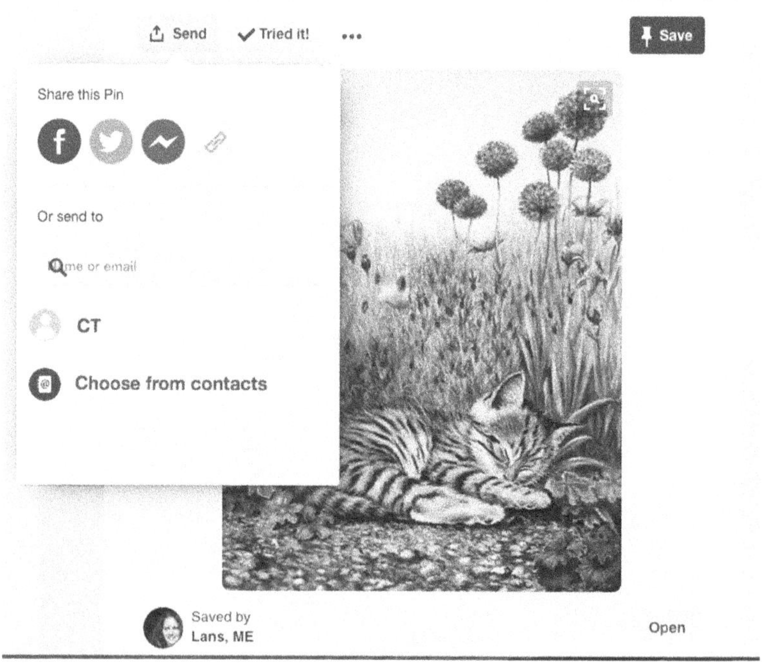

Image 24 Pinterest

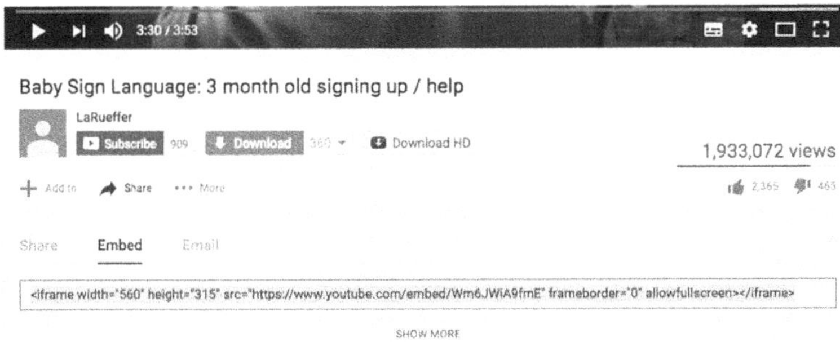

Image 25 YouTube

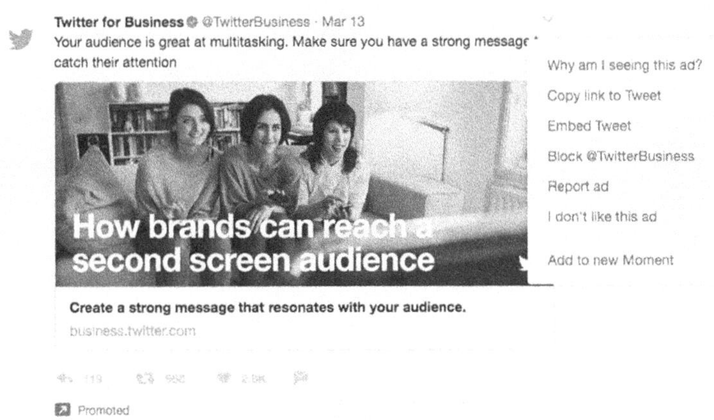

Image 26 Twitter

Image 27 Wikipedia

B. Technological features that constrain content-generative activities

1. Limiting the modification of content

Image 28 Facebook

Image 29 Pinterest

Image 30 Pinterest

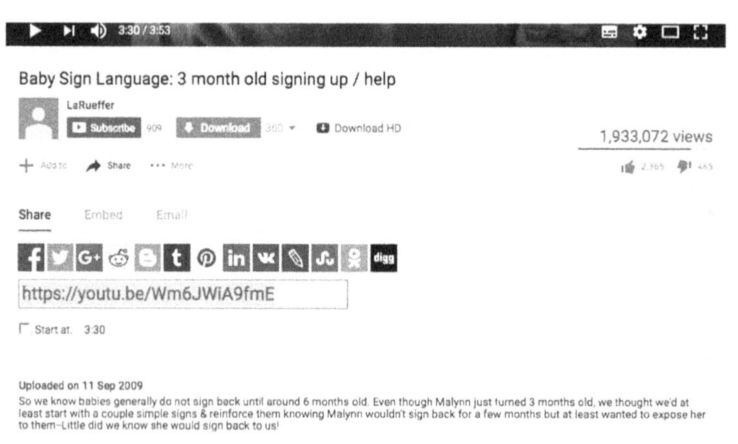

Image 31 YouTube

Image 32 Twitter

2. Limiting the opportunities to engage in further content-generative activities

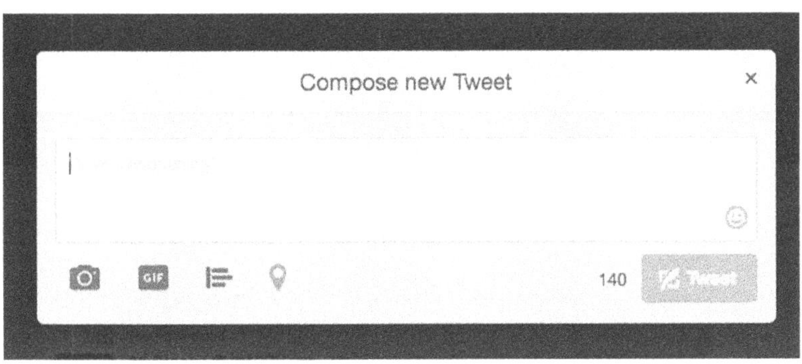

Image 33 Twitter

Image 34 Twitter

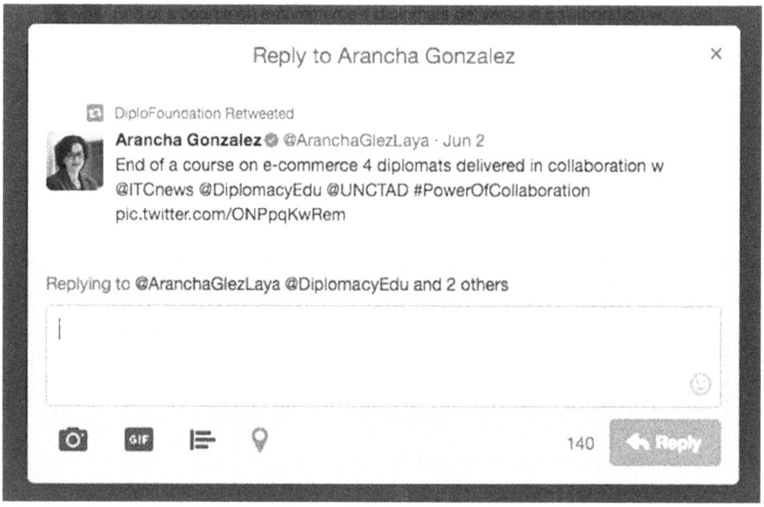

Image 35 Twitter

3. Allowing for requests to remove content

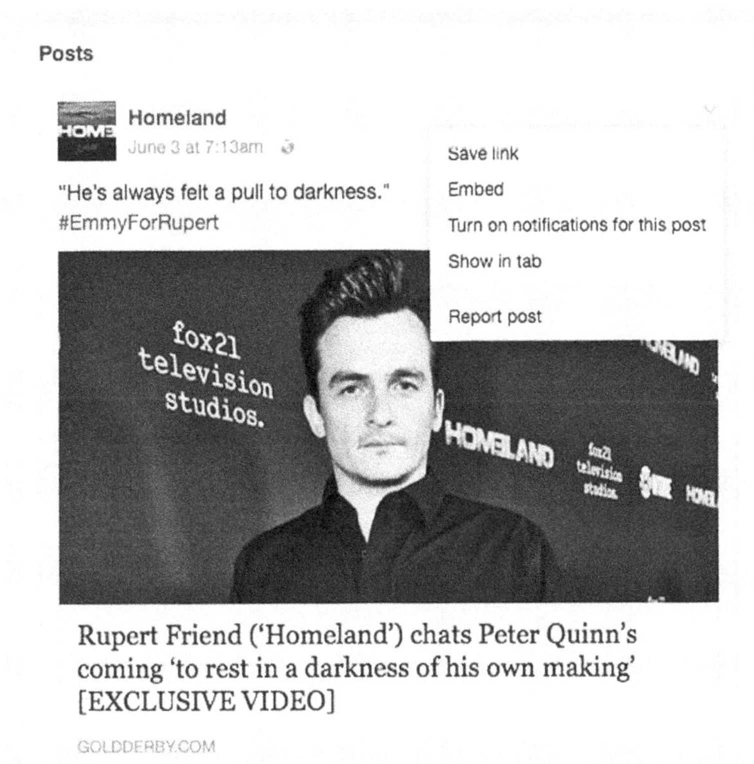

Image 36 Facebook

Image 37 Facebook

Image 38 Facebook

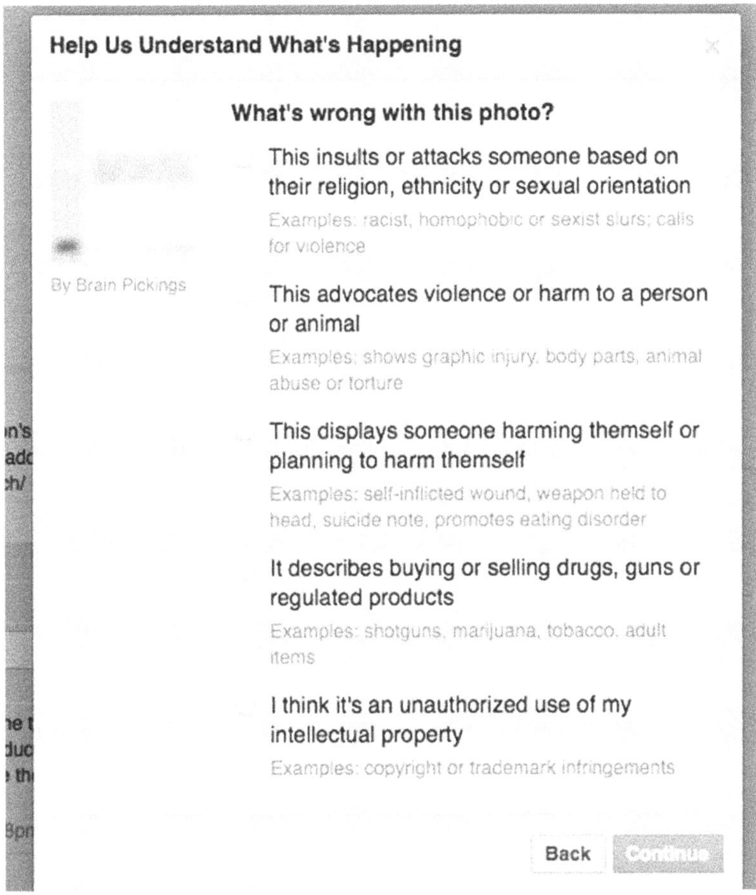

Image 39 Facebook

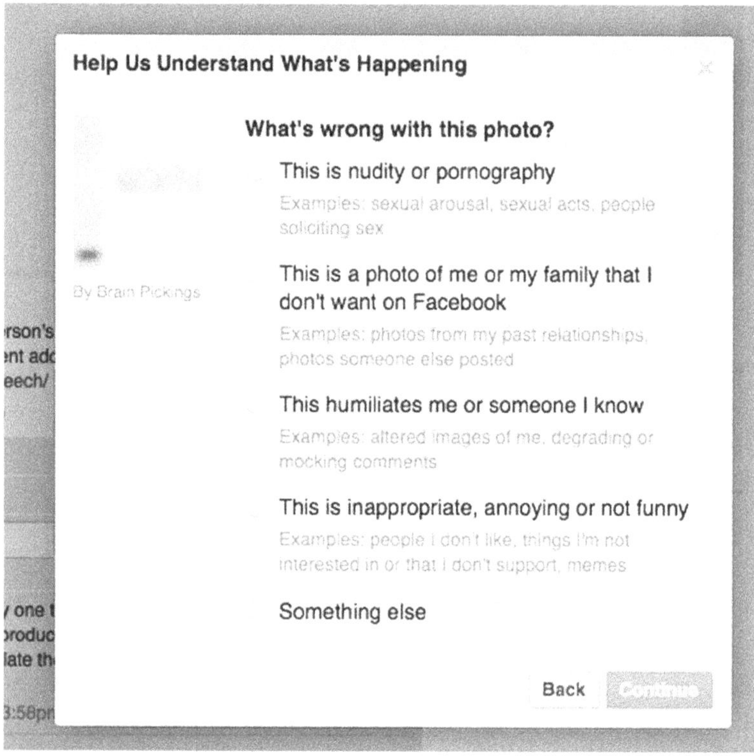

Image 40 Facebook

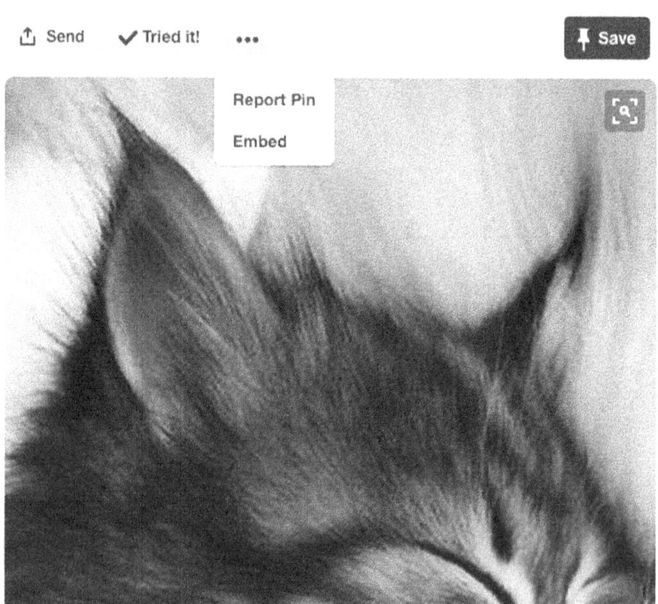

Image 41 Pinterest

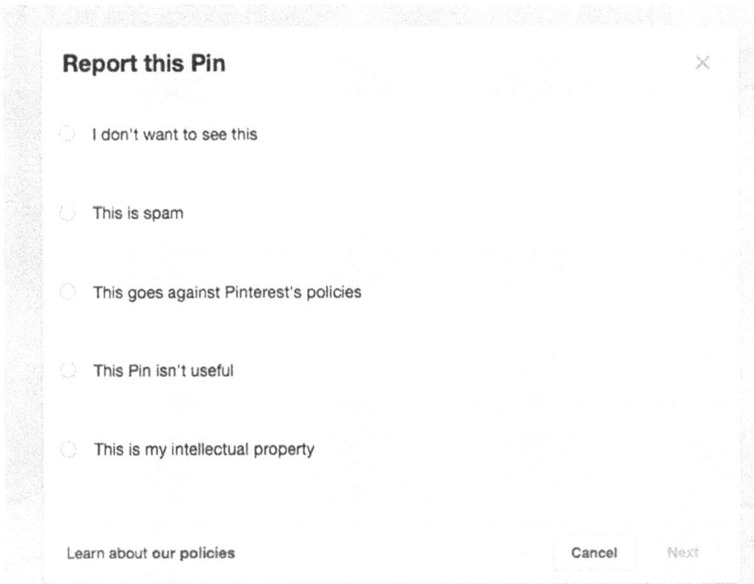

Image 42 Pinterest

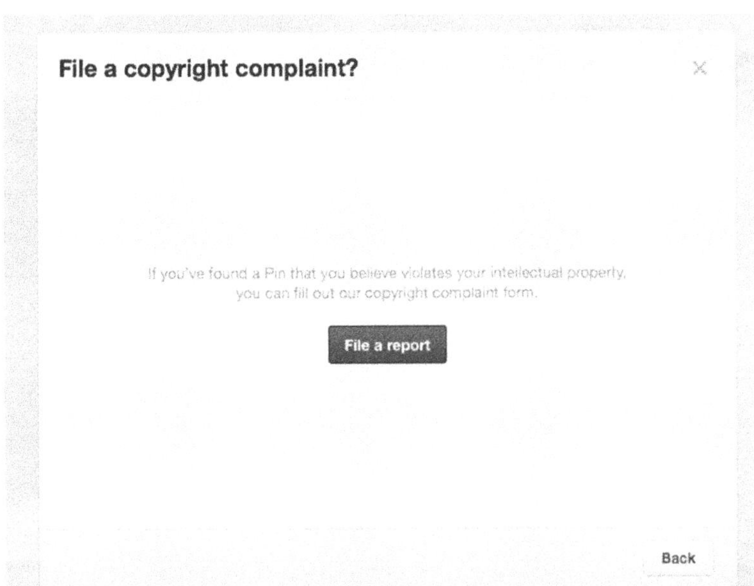

Image 43 Pinterest

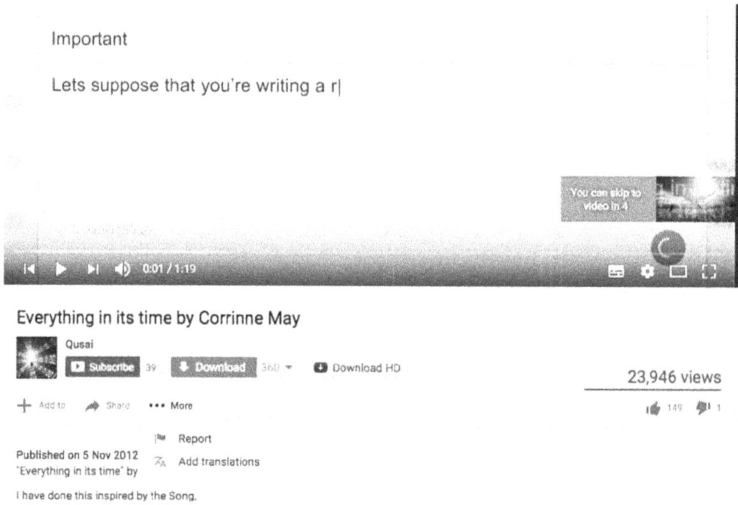

Image 44 YouTube

Image 45 YouTube

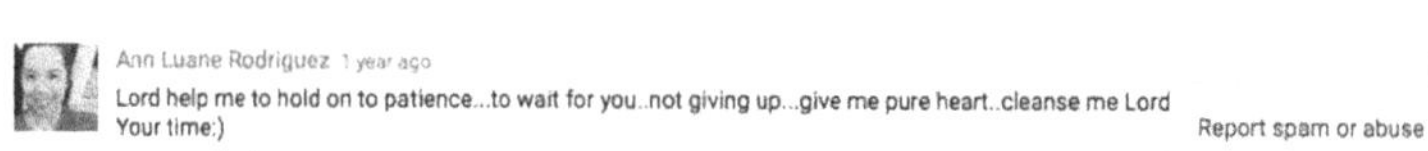

Image 46 YouTube

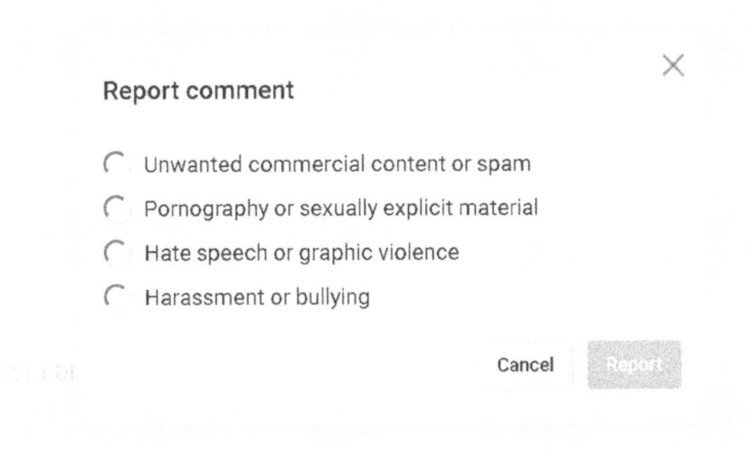

Image 47 YouTube

Image 48 Twitter

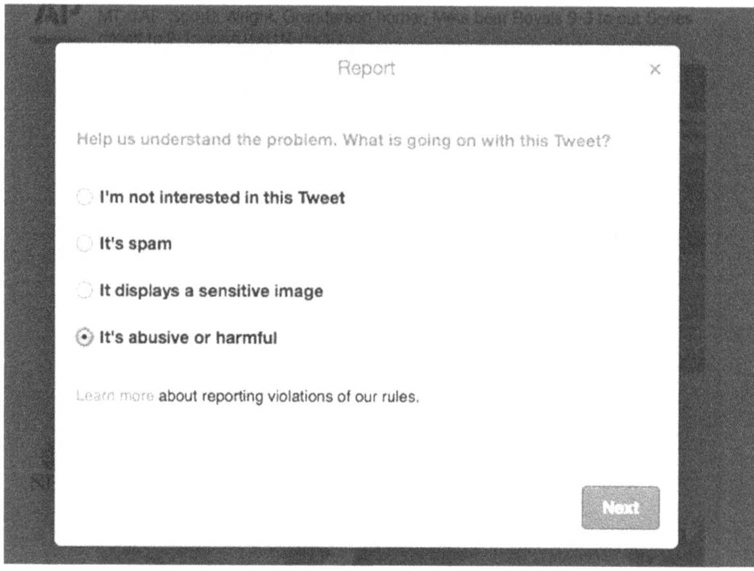

Image 49 Twitter

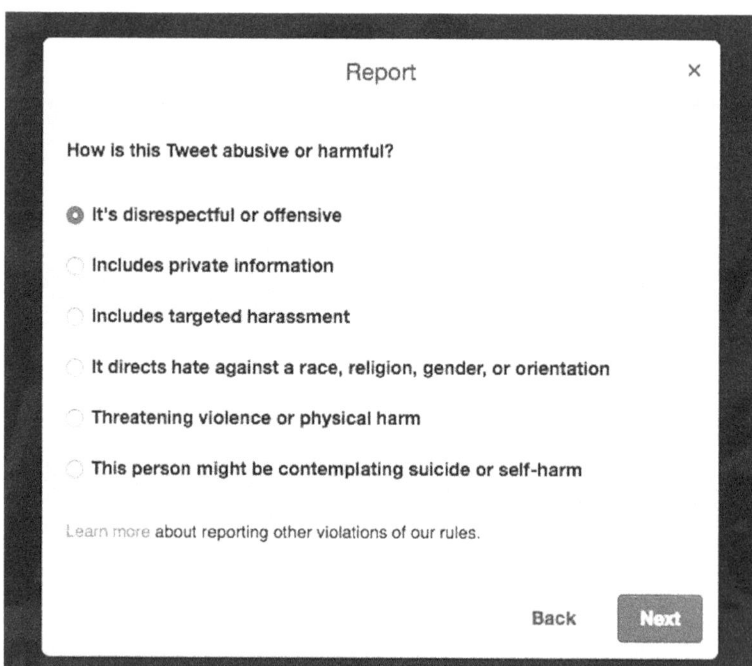

Image 50 Twitter

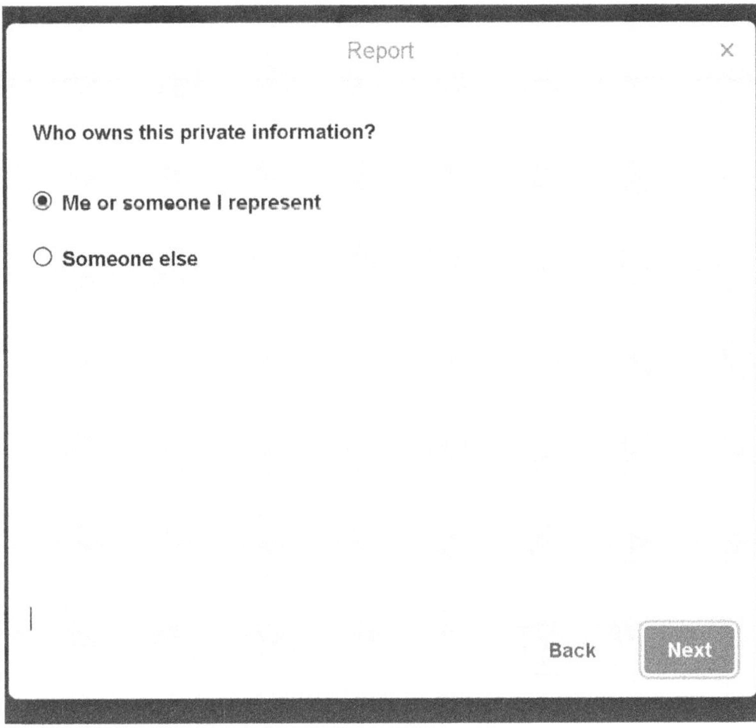

Image 51 Twitter

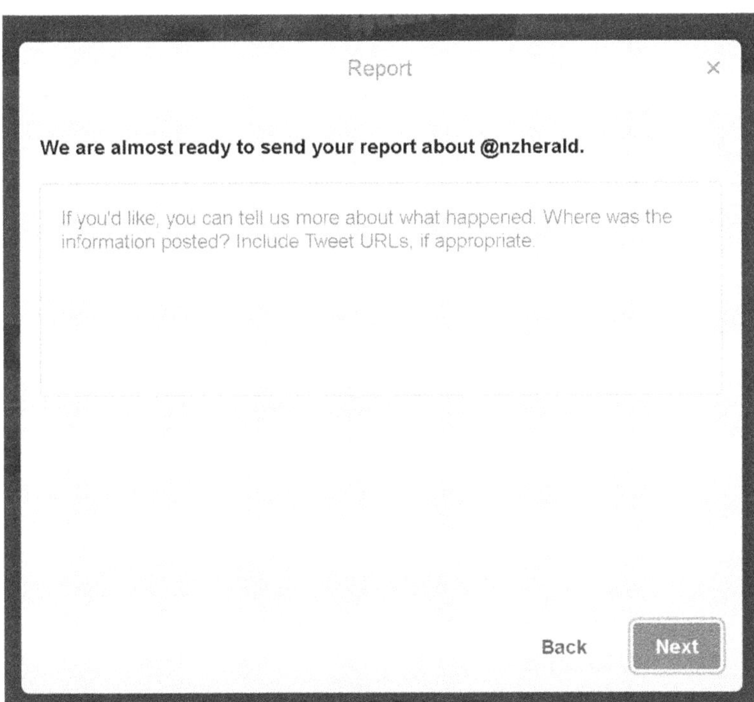

Image 52 Twitter

II. Scenario three: the influence of the technological features

A. Jane's use of the music video clip on YouTube as her morning alarm

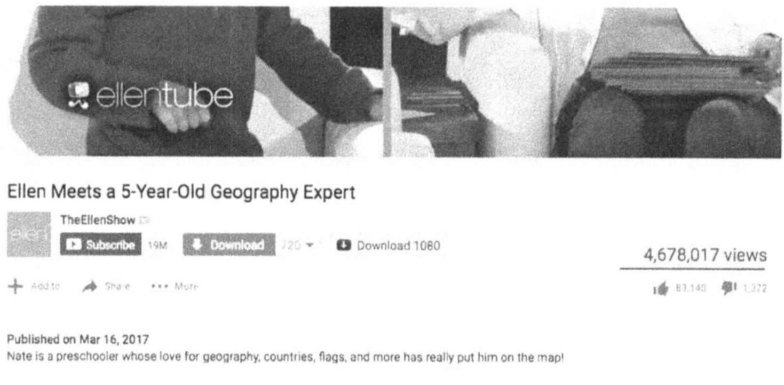

Image 53 YouTube

F. Jane's use of the same collage in her blog post on WordPress

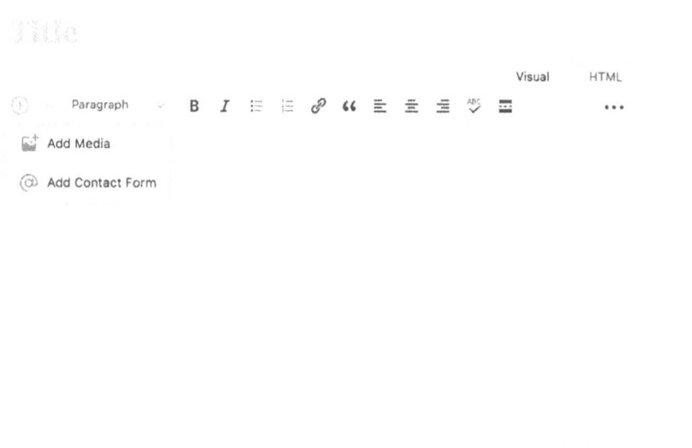

Image 54 WordPress

G. Zee's contribution to Wikipedia on 'income inequality' using what Jane has written

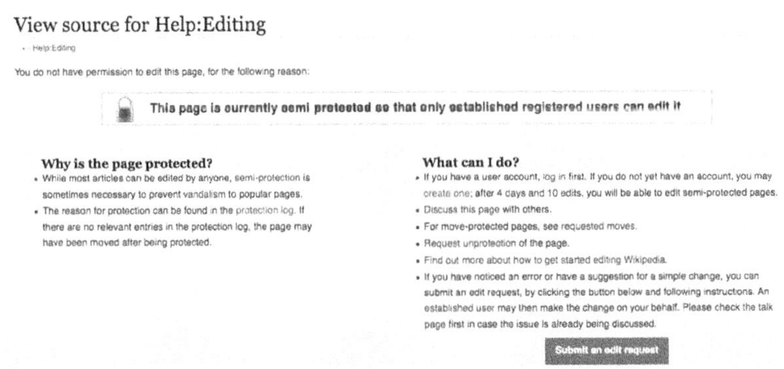

Image 55 Wikipedia

Note: Screenshots taken on the Facebook, Pinterest, YouTube, Twitter and Wikipedia platforms respectively, as of 7 June 2017.

Index

Page numbers in bold indicate tables and appendix

Lightning Source UK Ltd.
Milton Keynes UK
UKHW021907270319
340021UK00002B/48/P

9 781787 351721